Memories

Memories
1898-1939

C. M. Bowra

HARVARD UNIVERSITY PRESS
Cambridge, Massachusetts
1967

© 1966 by C. M. Bowra
Library of Congress Catalog Card Number: 67-27994
Printed in Great Britain

To John Sparrow

Contents

Illustrations

Preface

As the title indicates, this book is not a formal autobiography, but a record of events and personalities which have over the years imprinted themselves on my memory. I have begun as early as possible, and I have stopped in 1939, though occasionally I have passed beyond it to conclude an uncompleted theme. Though I have followed a roughly chronological scheme, I have arranged my subjects less in sequence than in homogeneous groups, but I trust that this has not obscured the passage of time or the difference between one period and another. I have never kept a diary, but I have preserved letters and at intervals written short records of events or conversations which seemed to be of interest. For the rest I have relied upon my memory, though I am well aware how risky this is and what tricks memory may play in enlarging or transforming what has happened. To counter this, I have tried, whenever possible, to find external confirmation for what I have written, but it has seldom been available. I am deeply indebted to those who have helped me – to Mr John Sparrow and Mr A.F. Thompson for reading large parts of my typescript and making many helpful suggestions; to Lord Boothby, Mr Siegfried Sassoon, Mr Cyril Connolly, Mr John Betjeman, Mr Evelyn Waugh, Sir Isaiah Berlin, and Baroness Wangenheim for comments on what I have written about them; to the Earl of Birkenhead for performing the same service for his father and for allowing me to print a letter by him; to Mrs Sybil Harton for a similar permission for her husband; to Miss Anne Yeats and Mr M.B. Yeats for permission to print an unpublished poem and two unpublished letters by their father, the late W.B. Yeats; to Dr G. Katkov, Sir Kenneth Clark, the Hon Mrs Betjeman, Professor P.A.S.Hadley, Mr A.N.Bryan-Brown, Lord Annan, and Mr R.S.Dawson for kindly answering questions; and to my sister, Mrs Wales, for help in collecting photographs.

April 1966   C.M.B.

1

Beginnings

I was born in the Chinese city of Kiukiang, which lies on the river Yangtse some thousand miles from its mouth, and the time was 3 p.m. on Good Friday, 8 April, 1898. Family tradition preserves little information about my earliest years, except that I had chicken-pox when I was five days old, and no doubt this explains why I have never had it again, even at school when it would have been highly welcome. It seems too that even at a very early age I was a greedy child. Once when I howled for my food half an hour before the right time, my Chinese amah wanted to give it me, but my mother pointed to the clock and refused, at which the amah said in her beautiful pidgin English, 'Maskee mississy clock, he no savvy. Baby clock, he inside tummy, he savvy'. But of Kiukiang I myself remember nothing; for soon after my birth my father, Cecil Arthur Verner Bowra, who was in the Chinese Customs Service, was transferred to Newchwang in Manchuria, which had just been opened to international trade. The foreign settlement, in which our house was situated, lay alongside the Bund, the long, open, wide space between the great estuary, which provided the harbour, and the rich, flat country inland. Here in 1900 I had my first experience of war, but of it too I remember nothing. Though the Boxer Rebellion is famous chiefly for the siege of the Legations in Peking, it raged with equal savagery and usually with more success in many other parts of

China, and the 'red barbarians' of Newchwang were marked for destruction. My mother, with my elder brother Edward and myself, was packed off in a small steamer to Japan, while my father, who had been warned from Peking of what was coming, organized the defence of the small foreign settlement at Newchwang. This appealed to him greatly. He liked excitement and adventure and was inspired by them to vigorous action. He turned our garden wall into his front line and strengthened it with large slabs of stone which had been meant for the Bund. He spread rumours among the Chinese that a Russian force was on its way, and he and his small company kept off the Boxers with rifles and sporting-guns. Rather to his surprise the Russians arrived, and the Boxers suddenly dispersed. My father, who was just over thirty, was awarded the China Expeditionary Medal, and though he was later to collect a fine array of decorations, this was the one that he prized most, perhaps because it was the only sign of recognition that he ever got from the British Government. My mother returned with her two children from Japan, and from some two years afterwards my first memories start.

The Russians, despite many protestations to the contrary, intended to stay, and Newchwang began to attract notice. They had troops on land and gunboats in the river, which were soon followed by British gunboats, notably smarter and more up to date. The ships lay alongside the Bund at a very short distance from our house, which was a roomy and comfortable bungalow. We had a host of Chinese servants, of whom the most important in my eyes were a tall, thin gate-keeper and a fat No. 1 Boy. While I learned English from my parents, I learned Chinese from the servants. My knowledge must have been very limited, and that may explain why it very soon deserted me. I have never learned it again, but when I hear it spoken, I know what it is, and it does not sound like a monkey-language but has fully articulated and recognizable sounds, of which to my grief I do not understand a word. The Chinese had the utmost contempt for the Russians, whom they regarded, not as 'foreign devils' like ourselves, but simply as barbarians. For this they had some reason.

The Russians not only got drunk far more often and far more gloriously than any Chinese, but suffered from sudden fits of panic, when, for no clear reason, they would round up a number of Chinese and shoot them. The hard-headed Chinese saw an opportunity even in this. The widows, real or self-appointed, of the victims would come weeping to the Russian officers, who would be deeply touched, burst into tears of sympathy, and give them handfuls of roubles. From this a technique was developed, and if any shooting was in the offing, the Chinese grandmothers, who ruled their households, would see that the family ne'er-do-wells were the first to face the firing-squad and that handsome compensation was paid for them. In the intervals much quiet teasing went on. Our Chinese servants would persuade me to go up to a Russian sentry and say innocently, 'Who are you?', and when he replied in Russian 'Soldat', meaning 'Soldier', I would counter in Chinese with 'Tsang ta-tzu', meaning 'Dirty Tartar'.

Life at Newchwang was particularly agreeable for children. The settlement was small, and children were few. Distinctions of language did not matter since we talked our own nursery Chinese to one another. Parties were frequent, and there was an admirable custom that at them the children received large presents. The Russians not only outnumbered all other Europeans and Americans but, having little to do and being faced by hideous boredom, applied on a large scale their genius for making life pleasant, especially for children. On the slightest hint their naval officers, to the shocked horror of their British rivals, would turn on search-lights or even fire guns, presumably with blank ammunition, though of that one could not be certain. The Russians outbid everyone in the splendour of their parties and the extravagance of their gifts, which ranged from real swords and gigantic boxes of chocolates to toy railways that covered the nursery floor. Their sense of style took many imaginative forms, as once, when my father and mother were coming back at night from the railway station to our house, they found themselves accompanied by a party of Cossacks on horseback with flaming torches. Later I learned that though the Russians paid us these handsome courtesies,

3

my father had a very tricky time with them. One of their chief aims was to oust him from his post, since they thought that both as an Englishman and as a servant of the Chinese Government, he was bound to oppose their policy of annexing Manchuria. Nor were they wrong. His first duty was to China, and though sometimes he found it difficult to distinguish between this and his duty to Great Britain, he was from both angles opposed to the extension of Russian power at the expense of China. He was strongly supported by his remote but omnipresent chief, Sir Robert Hart, who was the most powerful foreigner in China and determined to hamper the Russians in their imperial ambitions. Though my father liked the Russians and was on good terms with their commander-in-chief, Alexeyev, he was shocked by their incompetence, their unreliability, and their corruption. He could not bear to see a Russian postman drunkenly scattering letters on the snow at New Year, nor could he dream of offering the bribes which the Russians regarded as indispensable to any services rendered. Nor did he share their taste for vodka, but when he dined with them he took his Boy with him who had a vodka bottle full of water, which my father drank freely, thus unsportingly earning much admiration for the strength of his head. His intimate acquaintance with the Russians at this time formed in his mind a notion of them which he kept for years, and even at the end of his life, when he knew that they had undoubtedly changed some of their habits, he found it very hard to believe and never ceased to be amazed at it.

My memories of these first years are almost all of unclouded happiness, and only one painful incident has stuck in my mind. I was not going to sleep as I should, and a new amah tried to frighten me into silence by saying that there was a tiger under my bed. I burst into hysterical screams, and my mother came and, quite against her wont, was furious with the amah. The poor woman was probably trying to do her little bit of private magic, and meant no harm, but the moment of terror which she caused me used to recur for years through my childhood. The Chinese were extremely kind to children but expected them to behave properly, and in their view I was not doing so. Against this one episode I can set a glow of happiness in which I could do what I liked and was encouraged in it. Of course I was 'spoiled', but it was well worth it, and I have nothing but gratitude to those who did it. Though I was to visit China twice again before I was twenty, these first events sunk deeply into me and left a lasting mark. I still have a special affection for large rivers and wide, open plains like those of Manchuria. Certain sights and smells remain so faithfully with me that, when I encounter them, I am carried straight back to Newchwang, while the thought of a Chinese junk with its spreading sails and its gaily painted eye on the prow fills me with a luxurious homesickness.

In April 1903 my father, who had not been in England since 1896, was granted long leave, and we came home slowly by way of Japan and the United States. New impressions came in rapid sequence – the paper windows in Japan, through which I put my fingers and was rightly chidden; chopsticks, with which I was as clumsy then as I am now; the excitements of a real liner in which I often got lost, as I still am in dreams; the Pacific with its flying-fish and, once, a whale spouting water; a drive along the shore of a bright blue sea at Honolulu through an avenue of palm-trees; Hawaians looking very different from Chinese and wearing far fewer clothes; San Francisco before the earthquake of 1906, with its streets rising up from the water into the sky and its seals sunning themselves on rocks in the sea; a picnic in Oregon in a forest where trees were being felled and floated down a river, when a snake appeared from under a log and was smartly killed; the excitement of an upper berth in a sleeping-car; a visit to Washington's house at Mount Vernon and much annoyance at not being allowed into the actual rooms, which were shut off by grilles; the overhead railway in New York and the Flat Iron Building, which was then one of the wonders of the world; a garden-party for old soldiers of the Civil War, one of whom gave me a rose. We crossed the Atlantic in the *St Paul*, which was thought enormous with its 10,000 tons, and as we came near to Southampton, there was a thick fog from which the Needles emerged in much better shape than they are today. On arriving at Waterloo Station we were met by a party of relations, and in a sudden panic

I tried to hide under the seat of the railway-carriage, and though I was safely extracted, I did not make a favourable first impression on my assembled aunts.

My father had a strong sense of family, but it did not extend to wishing to see much of it. His idea of England was to live in the country and enjoy its more tranquil relaxations. As my Aunt Ethel complained, 'No sooner does he come to England than he buries himself in the depth of the country'. In this case it meant that he took a house at Knockholt in Kent, which would by modern standards be almost suburban, but was then reasonably remote, since it was six miles from the station, and the station itself was on the old London, Chatham, and Dover line, renowned neither for the punctuality, nor for the cleanliness of its trains. Our house stood outside the village and had plenty of open space round it. Knockholt was short of children, and Edward and I were quite happy to invent our own amusements. In this we were helped by the gardener and handyman, Alfred Chilton, who looked after the pony and made me a toy shield and a toy sword for imaginary adventures. The country was still unspoiled, and we often went for expeditions in a pony-cart, which my mother drove, but unfortunately that part of Kent consists largely of hills and much of the time was spent walking either up or down them 'to save the pony', and I developed an aversion to walking up hills which I have never overcome. In 1904 my mother had another child, my sister Norah, and this meant that she was less free to be with us than she had been. She used however to read aloud about little Black Sambo and little Detchy Head, and especially from *Just So Stories*, and made us dissolve into giggles at the 'great grey-green, greasy Limpopo' and 'have you forgotten the suspenders?' Neither my father nor my mother was much interested in the local people, and though they were for a time taken up by some rich stockbrokers because they knew about the Russo-Japanese War which had just broken out, they were not flattered and preferred their own company. Edward and I had reached the age when lessons were urgent, and we were taught by a gifted and delightful young woman who lived with her family not far down the road. She was called Ella Dell, and we both loved her. Nor could she have been more skilful with us. I had somehow learned to read before she took charge, but she encouraged me in it and sought out the right books to keep me happy. She was to be a steadfast and generous friend for many years, and my parents liked her as much as Edward and I did, while she was enchanted by my father's talk about the Great Powers and Spheres of Influence and what a Japanese victory in eastern Asia would mean. Our placid round of country life was broken by occasional visits to London for amusements. In the winter of 1904 we saw *Peter Pan* in its first season, and though I was fascinated by all the flying, I thought nothing of Peter or Wendy and a lot of Captain Hook and the crocodile. On another occasion we went to the London Hippodrome where the programme ended with an enthralling attack by Red Indians on a stockade with tomahawks, arrows and burning torches. Unfortunately Edward and my cousin Geoffrey burst into tears of agony, and my mother thought it prudent to take us all out before it got worse. I was deeply disappointed.

In February 1905 my father and mother went back to China, taking with them my baby sister, while Edward and I were left behind to be educated. This was the correct procedure for English families living in the Far East, as it had long been for those in India, and it was regarded as inevitable. There was indeed quite a good English school, run by missionaries, at Chefoo in China, but my parents would never have dreamed of sending their children there, partly from fear that we might pick up undesirable knowledge from the Chinese in our spare time, but more from a deep anxiety that we might be alienated from England, to which in their long absences from it they felt themselves more and more to belong. My mother felt the wrench deeply and must have found it hard to control herself when she said good-bye to us. Like many parents in her situation at this time she feared at the back of her mind that we might be treated like Punch in Kipling's all too true story *Baa, Baa, Black Sheep*. But on this score she need not have had the slightest worry. We were left with my father's mother, who had nothing at all in common with the ghoulish 'Antirosa'. Since at this point she began to take a leading part in our lives, something must be said about her background and the Bowras in general.

The Bowras were a middle-class family, who came from the Kent and Sussex borders in the region of Tunbridge Wells. The name, originally spelt Bowrer, had been changed to its present misleading form by a crank in the seventeenth century. In that century they had produced a well-known smuggler and in the eighteenth a fellow of Pembroke College, Cambridge who wrote an ode to celebrate the coronation of George II. Otherwise they had their ups and downs, without being distinguished or interesting. From this rather dull stock my grandfather, Edward Charles Bowra, was surprisingly born. A man of untiring energy and unusual intelligence, he was a romantic Victorian with a taste for adventure. In 1860 he fought under Garibaldi, and when this came to an end, he joined the new Chinese Customs Service. He was in Shanghai when Gordon was fighting the Taipings, and himself took part in more than one battle. He was also an excellent scholar, who mastered Chinese rapidly, and made contributions to Chinese history. In 1866 the Chinese decided to send a Manchu noble, Pin Chun, to Europe, and my grandfather accompanied him. Receptions were given for them in Paris, and in England they were received by Lord Clarendon, given a garden-party by Mr Gladstone, invited to a state ball at Buckingham Palace, and presented to Queen Victoria at Windsor. They also visited other European capitals and had similar treatment. Pin Chun found it all extremely boring and composed on it a long poem said to be remarkable more for its technique than its contents. My grandfather went back to China, where he made a name for himself by his adaptation of Canton to the new agreements about foreign trade. In 1872 he was seconded to collect suitable objects for the Chinese section of the exhibition to be held at Vienna in the next year. This he did with uncommon success, and was sent with a party to Vienna, where he was presented to the Emperor Francis Joseph. He loved outdoor activities, and it was these that killed him. In swinging himself round an upright pole in a horizontal position he did irreparable damage to his heart, and on 15 October 1874 he suddenly died at East Grinstead. His children were told

summarily by the Chinese amah, 'Papa he makee die.' My grandmother was left in an appalling situation. She was just over thirty,
and with very little money she had to bring up four small children.
In China and elsewhere my grandfather had not only run the
household but accustomed her to a high level of living which she
took for granted. They had saved almost nothing, and the prospects were bleak and bitter. So long as her husband was alive,
she had not revealed her remarkable character, but now with an
indomitable spirit she rose heroically to the occasion, and in this
showed some qualities inherited from her unusual ancestry.

Her father, Samuel Woodward, had been in the service of the
East India Company and was a natural son of the Marquess Corn-
wallis, Governor-General of India. He looked after the boy, had
him well educated, and got him a job. He in his turn married a
young woman called Margaret Delahunt, whose father, an Irish
Protestant from Co Tipperary, had taken part in the rebellion of
1798 and, when it failed, avoided execution by leaving the country
for South Africa. My grandmother was an only child, but she
knew little of her parents, for they both died in India when she
was a small girl. She was then sent home, crossing from Suez to
Port Said on a camel. She was brought up at Knockholt by some
maiden ladies called Martyr, and married my grandfather before
she was twenty. As a young woman she was strikingly handsome,
and even in old age kept a splendid bearing and style. Robert
Hart, who had liked and admired my grandfather, helped her
with the education of her two boys, and promised to keep a place
for my father when he grew up. By extreme economy and rigid
control she managed to bring up her children and in due course
to send them into the world. At first she lived in a small house in
West Kensington, and my father's memories of his childhood
were of austerity and hardship, but he may perhaps have exaggerated these in retrospect since he grew up to be a strong man and
had a good education at St Paul's School. A few years after the
death of her first husband my grandmother married George
Mackie, a clergyman in the Church of England, who had, what
was rare in those days, taken a degree in science at London
University and had been for a short time a schoolmaster at

Christ's Hospital. They moved to Putney, and to them Edward and I were entrusted in 1905.

The household also contained Aunt Mabel, a tall, handsome, lively young woman, who had been stopped by my grandmother from marrying the man whom she loved because he was thought to be socially unsuitable. She had recently been sent off to stay with my Uncle Edward in Brazil in the tacit hope that she would pick up a husband. This she had failed to do, and she was now in the painful position of an unmarried daughter living at home. To her at first fell the chief part in looking after Edward and me, and to it she gave herself heart and soul. Until she eventually got married in 1908, she was really a second mother and expended on us all the affection that she longed to give to someone. She had much gaiety and humour and a delicious laugh. She never failed in ideas of what we might like and took us sightseeing to all manner of fascinating places and showed us such thrilling objects as the brass tiger in which Tippoo Sahib tortured his victims, or the pagoda in Kew Gardens, or the stone dinosaurs at the Crystal Palace. Nor was the theatre forbidden. My grandmother seldom went, and when she did, it was a great occasion in which we travelled both ways in a four-wheeler driven by a much trusted cabman called Gannon, but Aunt Mabel would take us less luxuriously by bus to see Lewis Waller in *Henry V* or F. R. Benson in *The Merchant of Venice*, or in the Christmas holidays to the wonderful conjuring performances of Maskelyne and Devant, which we tried to explain but never could.

My step-grandfather, George Mackie, was a man of unbounded sweetness and gentleness. My father thought him rather a come-down after his own gallant and romantic father, but from the moment I first saw him I formed a lasting trust and affection for him. I never heard him say a harsh word to anyone, and in this he differed from the Bowras, whose critical sense of humour was on the sharp side and often turned into stern reprobation. He let his wife run everything and, being entirely without ambition, never sought to get a better post or complained about his lot. His absorbing hobby was photography. He photographed every-one with relentless optimism, and though the results were universally derided, he argued that 'the camera cannot lie', and that was that. However true this may have been at first, it was not true when he began to touch up his photographs with colours and to defy any resemblance to the original subjects. The bathroom was full of plastic trays in which he developed negatives, and the windows were obstructed by wooden frames in which prints were made. His only extravagance was with cameras, with which he liked to experiment, though to us the results always seemed equally deplorable. He was chaplain to an infirmary in the Fulham Road, where he went on four days a week, as well as on Sundays. The place was dark and gloomy, and the inmates mostly old women who talked about their grievances and illnesses. He entered into their troubles with a natural sympathy and cheered them by his easy jokes. He took everything with a happy resignation and had a quiet sense of comedy in dealing with the most common-place things. I found him wonderfully agreeable. He treated me as an equal and always did his best to satisfy my insistent demand, 'Grandfather, do say something funny.' He was entirely single-minded in his religion, and despite his scientific training was not troubled by the doubts which irked my father. He seldom talked about it, but in his heart of hearts he needed something to keep him secure, and found it in God. He was quite unperturbed by any crisis and yet managed to comfort everyone round him by his warmth and tolerance.

My grandmother held the household together. She was never dictatorial and never showed signs of irritation or temper, but there was no doubt that she was in command. She would some-times talk with regret of the golden past in China or in Vienna, and she was proud of the few beautiful things which she had treasured from it. She did not mix easily with the neighbours at Putney, perhaps because she rather looked down on them, but more because she had very little in common with them, and years of struggle and abnegation had taught her not to give herself away to others. She had a few old friends from earlier days, who would come to see her, and then she would open out and regain some of the gaiety which she had had as a young woman. Once her sons were well placed in jobs and her daughters married, she was better off, and life in her house was comfortable in a simple, solid way. Edward and I had a large room on the second floor, where we could do what we liked and were quite free from interference. With advancing years she became less formidable and more forthcoming, and to Edward and myself she showed openly an affection which she had felt for her children but never made clear to them. She had a truly Victorian dignity, was well dressed in black or on festal occasions in mauve, and had a magnificent head of white hair with which she took much trouble. Though at times she retired to bed with various ailments, they were never serious, and in her last years she was remarkably strong and capable. Though at times she rightly reproved me for my faults, she did so with an unusual calm and inflicted no punishments, with the result that I could not but be impressed and bore no resentment. She treated her husband as a gentle child who must be humoured and allowed to do what he liked, and often referred to him as 'that foolish old man'. They were entirely happy together, though I doubt if they were at all intimate except at rare moments of family crisis.

On the other side of London, at Blackheath, lived my maternal grandmother, who had lost her husband just before my mother's marriage to my father in January 1896. She too had once known affluence and was now living on restricted means. Her husband, Valentine Locke Lovibond, had been a successful brewer and kept a large house with a big garden and a swimming bath in Fulham. His four daughters were taken daily to school in a carriage, and he himself was a happy, ironical, affectionate man. He was a collateral descendant of John Locke but preferred to claim that he was descended from the last Englishman to be hanged for forgery. He died in his early forties, and my grandmother, who was a keen feminist and advocate of women's rights, thought that she could manage the business by herself. The result was that she fell into the hands of crooks, and within a few months not only had the business disappeared but she herself was prosecuted by shareholders. She was defended by the young Rufus Isaacs and acquitted, and many years later, when I met him and asked him about her, he said that she was perfectly innocent but extremely foolish. The crooks, as might be expected, got away with the money. Thenceforward she lived quietly with her second daughter, Beatrice, who was a doctor and our chief eccentric, but she abated none of her convictions and was very much a woman of the left. In the General Election of 1906 I remember how the Mackies, who were staunch Conservatives, spoke with ill-concealed dismay of her opinions and, without actually warning me against her, hinted that her views were not what any decent person would hold. Edward and I were dutifully sent over at intervals to visit her, usually under the protection of Aunt Mabel, and I found her rather formidable. She was short and stout and seemed never to leave her seat by the fire. Moreover, there was always a danger that Aunt Beatrice would take it into her head that we looked pale and needed a dose, which she would administer at once with ruthless determination. My grandmother had a brother called Frederick Fleay, whom we knew as 'Great-uncle Fred' and some-times met with her. He was a friendly old man with a beard, and it was not till later that I discovered that he was both distinguished and peculiar. After taking Holy Orders as a young man he relin-quished them in 1884 and became a serious scholar. He did solid work on Elizabethan drama and in later life turned to Egyptian and Assyrian studies. His domestic life was less successful. For years he kept an excellent cook, but then he married her, and she ceased to cook and was not a good wife. In the first years my grandmother had also her youngest daughter Florence living with her. She shared her mother's political convictions and had a post as Inspector of Factories. She was very intelligent and charming and arranged treats for Edward and me with a skill equalled only by Aunt Mabel. A little later I learned to know Grandma, as we called her, much better and to see how remarkable she was. She had lost not only most of her money, but her young son from diphtheria in boyhood, and this left a lasting scar. Like my other grandmother, she had her own kind of courage and never com-plained nostalgically about the wealthy past.

Edward and I went to a day-school called Willington in the Upper Richmond Road. The house has been destroyed, but the school still flourishes. It was then run by two Scottish ladies, the

Misses Hale, or rather Miss Hale and Miss Ada as everyone called them. Miss Hale taught scripture and English, and kept a firm control of affairs by a skilful manipulation of her pince-nez; Miss Ada taught Latin and Greek. The teaching was excellent. There were rewards but no punishments, and both ladies succeeded in making instruction a pleasure. In my last year I was given lessons once a week by Mr Cecil Botting, a master at St Paul's School, who had written textbooks with his High Master, Hillard, and inspired us with some awe. He carried a number of fountain-pens, each filled with a different coloured ink, and the colour emphasized the degree and character of our mistakes. He was said to have an extravagant wife and to be forced to earn additional money by taking such classes. If this was his reason, it abated in no way his meticulous attention to us. Life at Willington was not confined to lessons. Though there were no compulsory games, and such games as there were I did not take part in, in the winter a dancing-class was held weekly after tea in the big schoolroom, when we wore Eton suits, and Miss Bridgman, in what seemed to be evening-dress with a skilfully managed train, instructed us in the Waltz – she called it 'Valss' – the Two-step, the Polka, the Lancers, Sir Roger de Coverley, and even the Irish Jig. Edward and I made friends among our contemporaries and were asked to their houses, and my grandmother would ask them back to ours, usually for a dance in the Christmas holidays, when the drawing-room was converted into a ball-room and enormous care was given to a splendid supper, for which my grandmother herself made the more appetising dishes. In particular I remember a tall, thin boy, rather older than myself, called Basil Hart. He knew a lot of history, including information on new characters like Jugurtha and Belisarius; I swapped stamps and coins with him; and to my enthralled delight he introduced me to *The Three Musketeers*, but though he himself had read the sequels, which sounded marvellous, I was not able to get hold of them. I lost sight of him for many years until I found that he was the famous authority on military matters known to a large public as Captain Liddell Hart, and in 1965 I had the pleasure of meeting him again when he got an honorary D.Litt. at Oxford.

Church, as might be expected, played some part in our lives. My grandfather conducted short prayers before breakfast, and on Sundays we went both to Matins and to a children's service. On Sunday evenings we sometimes sang hymns, while my grandmother played, and at school Miss Hale taught us that science had proved the Bible to be right on such important matters as the Creation and the Flood, and pointed out how skilfully nature arranged that every pest should devour another pest and itself be devoured by a third. I did not mind going to church, but at times felt that I was not putting into it all that I should, and tried various kinds of devoutness, without success. A climax came when I was about eight. I had a kitten which I loved greatly. It disappeared and, having been told that, if I asked God for anything fervently enough, He would grant it, I passed some time in frenzied prayer, and the kitten returned next day, but it had been poisoned and died within a few hours. I felt that I had been tricked, and though I continued to conform and was for a time haunted by fears of Hell from Doré's illustrations to Dante's *Inferno*, of which my grandfather had a copy, I began to form a distrustful picture of the universe. The result was that I got bad marks for scripture, and this distressed my grandfather, who vaguely thought that he must be to blame and never held it against me in any way.

My grandmother had two friends who in very different ways illustrated the clerical life of the time. One was a handsome, white-haired American, called Cooper, who had fought on the Confederate side in the Civil War and lost everything. He had come afterwards to England, where in apostolic poverty he worked in the slums. He did not talk about religion, and I gathered that he was thought too fundamentalist to be sound, but he had the grand manners of the old South and treated my grandmother as a great lady. He wrote poems in free verse and read them aloud in a quiet even voice. He held himself very well and never spoke of the past. He was always scrupulously neat, and with his elaborate courtesy and scholarly speech he was quite unlike anyone else who visited us. In strong contrast with him stood a curate, who had been at Eton and Trinity, and was therefore made welcome. He played the piano, sang and even composed comic songs, and had travelled in various countries. In church he surprised but did not shock my grandparents by his melodramatic reading of lessons. In the middle of the account of Our Lord's trial, when Barabbas was mentioned, he stepped down from the lectern into the aisle and said in a loud voice, 'Now Barabbas was a robber', and then he went back and continued the lesson. He was very High Church, and that helped to endear him to my grandmother, who thought it rather dashing, and anyhow much better than being Low. There was a dark moment when he got married to a woman who was thought to have caught him and to be unworthy of him, and this meant that he had to discontinue his habit of taking good-looking schoolboys with him on his travels abroad. Soon afterwards he left Putney, and during the war I read that he had been found dead on a railway line.

In the summer holidays grandfather took a post as locum tenens in some country rectory and carried out the duties, which can never have been heavy, of the local incumbent, while we enjoyed ourselves in old-fashioned country life. We were sometimes joined by my Aunt Ethel and Uncle Ned and their two sons and daughter. The younger son, Geoffrey, was nine months older than myself and had an unusual talent for amusing himself and others. He was more severely brought up than Edward and I were, and once at the christening of a new cousin, when he and I were swinging in a hammock and one of the trees from which it hung broke, he was taken home at once and whipped, while I got off scot-free. He had a taste for pretty things, and was enchanted by the jewellery on show at the Franco-British Exhibition at the White City. He was a good athlete and sang very well, which endeared him to his mother, but his father, who had no control over his emotions, treated him with Victorian severity, and he never knew when he was going to be punished for some quite trivial offence. I liked him very much and shared many childish farces and fancies with him. On one occasion the large family party was joined by my Uncle Edward from Brazil, with his wife and four daughters. He sang comic songs after dinner to his own accompaniment and refused resolutely to go to church or to eat cold mutton for supper on Sundays. His songs, though never improper, were often mildly irreverent about such matters as Noah's Ark or the songs of the Angels in Heaven, but this did not in the least trouble my grandmother, who loved him most of her children and thought that everything he did was perfect. He was very kind to me and gave me books to read. Henty he thought stuffy, and he introduced me to Jules Verne, Fenimore Cooper, and Rider Haggard.

Life in Putney changed for the worse when my Aunt Mabel married in 1908 a man some years older than herself, and her place was taken by a 'lady-help'. She was a good enough soul, but not comparable in any way with Aunt Mabel. Neither Edward nor I liked her, and she must have felt sadly lonely and out of place, since my grandmother regarded her as rather inferior and did not take her into her confidence. She kept a photograph of a man with a full face and luxuriant moustache, to whom she was believed to be engaged and whom she could not yet marry because neither had enough money. Meanwhile Aunt Mabel went with her husband to Brazil, but returned to have her first and only child in Putney. It was a hot summer, and the whole affair was wrapped in such secrecy and silence that I could not make out what was happening or why we were not allowed to see her. Nor was the mystery dispelled when I was told that we had a new cousin, since I imagined that children somehow arrived intact from God. Aunt Mabel was properly concerned with her own affairs, and before long she moved to Clevedon in Somerset, where she had a large, comfortable house which was to provide us with much happiness in years to come.

In these years the memory of my father and mother inevitably grew fainter. At intervals wonderful parcels of Chinese toys or lacquer boxes or enamelled objects or clay figures would arrive, and every week Edward and I wrote dutifully about our doings. We knew that father was making a name for himself, but we did not quite understand what it was. In 1905 he had been appointed Inspector-General of the Korean Customs, but the Japanese, emboldened by their defeat of the Russians and eager to annex Korea, eased him out after a slight international incident from which even Hart could not save him. He was then transferred as Commissioner of Customs to Amoy in southern China, whence magnificent photographs used to come of his ponies winning in the local races, or of the fine junketings for the visit of the American Fleet. Once indeed he made his presence felt in a rather disturbing way. My grandfather had sent him a photograph of myself, which filled father with alarm. To him I seemed to have every physical defect. After secret conclaves between my grandmother and grandfather, I was let off morning-school and taken by my grandmother to a specialist in Harley Street. With some embarrassment she carried a specimen of my water in a medicine-bottle. The doctor said that there was nothing at all wrong with me, and due blame was ascribed to grandfather's photography and to my making a face when the picture was taken. Still the matter did not end there. My father was brooding on his sons' upbringing and matured a bold plan. In the spring of 1909 mother came home with my sister Norah and at once restored the intimate affection which had been broken for four years. We all stayed together in Somerset, and then Edward and I heard to our delight that we were to go with her to Mukden, where my father now was, when she returned in September.

We travelled via Siberia, and the journey took ten days. It started at Ostend, and we changed trains at Warsaw, Moscow, Irkutsk, Harbin, and Changchun. My mother and sister had one *coupé*, and Edward and I another, and we shared a washing-place. We had a glimpse of Berlin in the morning and did not think much of it, and later a fine view of Smolensk with its old defences. Our changes at Warsaw and Moscow were both at night; so we saw nothing of them. The real delight was Siberia, first the endless forests beginning to change colour with the autumn but still warm and sunny, then the journey round the southern shore of Lake Baikal with its huge mountains and rushing cataracts, and so into the great rolling country beyond it, like an immensely magnified Sussex, and the fertile plain of northern Manchuria with its square walled cities. Among the chief excitements were the vast rivers, the Irtish and the Yenisei, flowing from central Asia to the Arctic. The bridges across them seemed endless, and

at each crossing the train was invaded by soldiers with fixed
bayonets, who cast suspicious looks at everyone, as if we wished
to blow up the bridge and the train with it. The stops at stations
were many and various, and often offered some new spectacle,
like Kalmucks coming to sell sour milk, or lines of camels resting
while their owners tried to sell toys or food. Once there was a
painful episode. A French lady was travelling with a small girl
and a small boy, both of whom she spoiled terribly, and the boy
especially was not at all in hand. One day he could be found nowhere on the train, and the poor woman, searching frenziedly up
and down, was terrified that he had walked out of the door at
the back of the last carriage. When she was almost off her head
with despair, he was found hiding in the conductor's cupboard,
but instead of being spanked was covered with kisses. I was extremely distressed by the mother's grief and rather shocked by
her rapid forgiveness. No doubt I was wrong. The boy was
only playing, and there was not much wrong in that, but for the
first time I felt what it must feel like to lose someone deeply
loved.

Mukden was a walled Chinese city, with a miniature Forbidden
City in the centre, a Drum Tower and a Bell Tower in the main
thoroughfare, and typically Chinese streets, where the shops
advertised their wares with projecting painted signs; mules,
camels and Chinese carts jostled against each other; and appetizing
food was cooked out of doors. Almost the only buildings of more
than one storey were the new Japanese banks, built of red brick in
gross, Germanic designs. The Japanese were seeping in, but were
not yet too obvious or too uppish, and the way of life everywhere
was emphatically Chinese. Our house lay outside the walls, and
was a large, spreading Chinese building, which my father had
altered and enlarged. It was in a compound, with a formal gate
and a gate-keeper in a lodge, but as you entered you were faced
by an isolated small wall with a picture of a horrific dragon whose
job was to keep out devils. You walked round this and then on
three sides you saw the house, with its curving Chinese roof and
its carved woodwork. It had large sitting-rooms and extensive
back areas, where the servants lived and where my father kept his

horses and had erected an enormous swing for Edward and me. We had a very cold bedroom with hard beds and washed in a deep bath-tub of glazed green pottery, for which the servants brought hot water in kerosene tins.

The day began with the arrival of my father in a towel dressing-gown, and we did a round of physical exercises. He had in his twenties nearly died of typhoid fever in China, and this strengthened an already strong belief in the primary value of bodily fitness. So in the freezing room we performed the right contortions and were at least warmed by them. After breakfast came lessons in a warm room across the courtyard. These were conducted by the young daughter of a missionary from Ulster. Her name was Kathleen Fulton, and she must still have been in her 'teens. She had charm, humour and good looks, but also authority, as she followed a programme laid down by my father. Latin and Greek, so assiduously inculcated by the Misses Hale, were off, and in their place came history, in which a central place was taken by the English conquest of Ireland, and French, which was learned from a phrase-book containing a number of rare words, most of which I have never seen or heard since. Twice a week we went to learn German from the German Vice-Consul, Herr Witte. He was a short, pompous little man, with moustaches modelled on the Kaiser's, and he made a great to-do about methodology. We first learned the *deutsche Schrift*, which I soon forgot, and began the elements of grammar. We did not get very far, but when many years later I set out to teach myself German, I found that the foundations were well laid. Herr Witte was a notable patriot. From him I first heard the word *Kultur*, and he liked to explain how superior his country was in every way to all others. His clinching example was that German has more words in its vocabulary than any other language, and to prove this he pointed to the enormous volume of Muret-Sanders' lexicon, against which there was no appeal. He lived in the country in a Buddhist temple, which had a roof of yellow tiles, and he kept a tame deer, which he generously gave us. At the Chinese New Year devil-dances were conducted in his courtyard, and men with animal masks danced with interminable vigour, but I was disappointed that they did not live up to the wicked expectations which I had formed of them.

The Manchurian winter was long and fierce like the Russian. By November the earth was frozen, and out of doors we wore padded coats and fur caps with ear-flaps. Indoors we had Russian stoves in the main rooms, while servants had charcoal-burners which were liable to suffocate them if they fell asleep after drinking too much. The weather did not prevent us from spending a lot of time in the open, and this was part of my father's plan to toughen us after the enervating ease of Putney. Edward and I had China ponies, short, hard-mouthed little animals, full of wilfulness and character. The huge, flat countryside lay open in every direction since the millet-crop had been gathered, and we could go where we liked. There were almost no roads, and the cart-tracks were frozen hard. Trees were rare, except in small groups found in graveyards, where to cut them down would enrage the ghosts of the buried ancestors. Our favourite places, if time allowed, were the Tung-ling and the Pei-ling, the East Wood and the North Wood, which were substantial plantations of large and ancient trees, almost all of them laden with mistletoe. These were the burial places of the two first Manchu Emperors, Nurhachi and Huang Tai Chi, before their dynasty conquered China. The actual graves were miniature walled cities with a yellow-tiled mausoleum in the centre. Before it got too cold we used to go to one or the other of them for picnics on Sundays. My father, Edward, and I rode out, and my mother and Norah drove in an open carriage. We were preceded by servants in Chinese carts, who took with them a table and chairs, and a full apparatus for cooking a large hot lunch. On one occasion we rode out to visit the battlefield, where the Japanese had defeated the Russians in 1905. The front line of the Russians had been about a hundred miles long, and there were still many trenches intact, and we picked up relics such as bayonets and empty shell-cases. The battle had lasted for days and was a forecast of what was to happen in Europe when trench-warfare set in at the end of 1914. But to us then, though the trenches were only four years old, they seemed a relic of a bygone age. It was easy to imagine the battle, and my father explained what happened and why the Russians decided that they had been defeated. For years a large brass shell-case, picked up on the battlefield, served as an umbrella-stand in our hall.

Mukden was an important railway-junction, and many travellers in the Far East stopped there before embarking on the next stage of a journey. Here for his own purposes came in the winter of 1909 Lord Kitchener. He was an avid and not always very discerning collector of Chinese pottery, and in Peking the Regent, who acted for the child Emperor Hsuan Tung, had given him four pieces of peach-bloom porcelain. He was delighted with them but much chagrined later when dealers in London told him that they were modern copies and worth very little. He now came to Mukden to see what he could pick up. I had seen pictures of him in his South African War period and expected a splendid and handsome hero, and was appalled to see a huge, gross, purple-faced man, with blotchy eyes, who seemed to be bursting at every point from his field-marshal's uniform. My mother sat next to him at dinner with the British consul-general, and tried to open conversation by saying, 'I believe that your Excellency is interested in porcelain', to which he snapped back, 'Only Chinese', and after that she did not try again. In the morning my father took him to the Viceroy, who was a scholarly old mandarin with wonderful manners. Kitchener had a rescript from Peking saying that he could have two pieces of porcelain from the collection at Mukden which belonged to the Manchu emperors, and my father went round with him while he made his choice. He settled on two pairs, and when the Viceroy politely pointed out that the paper said 'two pieces', Kitchener answered, 'Two pairs is the same as two pieces', and the Viceroy, unwilling to offend the distinguished guest, said, 'It is as your Excellency pleases', and gave them to him. The next day my father asked the Viceroy what he thought of the great English general, and the Viceroy with the faintest twinkle of a smile, said, 'He was wonderful; he was just like the god of war.' The image was delightfully apt, since the Chinese god of war is usually depicted as a large swollen figure with a purple face.

Kitchener's visit was suddenly disturbed by the news that the veteran Japanese statesman Prince Ito had been murdered at

Harbin by a Korean patriot, who may well have had good reasons for his action, since Ito had played a leading part in the oppression of Korea by the Japanese. But Great Britain was still an ally of Japan, and the death of the man who had done more than anyone to modernize Japan could not pass unnoticed even at Mukden. So a memorial service was held in our drawing-room. It was conducted by the Anglican Bishop of North China, and Kitchener attended and behaved with becoming gravity. Just as the service was about to begin there was a clatter in the courtyard, and there appeared a palanquin carried by eight bearers and accompanied by a number of outriders on horseback. From this emerged the Viceroy who had come to do honour to a dead man whom he can have had no reason to love. He was placed in the front row, and though he had never before been to a Christian service, he behaved with absolute correctness at every point. Courtesy was so bred into his bones that even in these complex and alien rites he made no mistakes.

For Christmas and New Year we all went to Newchwang, which seemed much smaller than it used to be and lacked the enthralling glamour of the Russians, who had evacuated it after the war with Japan. But there were still endless parties with presents. There was a skating rink on which I learned with a chair to propel myself along and even to move precariously on my own resources. More exciting were the small hints of trouble among the grown-ups which reached us. Our host, Dr Daly, was an exuberant and amusing Irishman, and he had a deadly quarrel with a trader called Harry Bush. Bush was thought to have done too well too often by claiming insurance for warehouses which had been destroyed by fire and which he swore to be full of opium and therefore enormously valuable. Daly made sharp comments, and the small British colony was rent into factions. This was common enough in such outposts, but to me it was highly dramatic, especially when I saw Daly and Bush together and was much surprised that they maintained the usual appearances of politeness. At Newchwang I ate my first oyster. It was at Christmas dinner with an American couple called Carl, and the first course looked to me like a special kind of ice-cream, but on being tasted did not fulfil its promise, being in fact an oyster-cocktail. I am ashamed to say that I did not like it and was much relieved to be told that I need not eat it.

In February, after long discussions and correspondence, my father decided to take Edward and me home to school in England, while mother and Norah stayed in Mukden. He had made up his mind that it was time for us to go to boarding-school. As a keen Kentish man he thought of sending us to Tonbridge or King's School, Canterbury, but his choice was settled when he decided that Edward should go into the army. He had himself much admiration for the military life and had enjoyed his only taste of fighting in the Boxer Rebellion, and he thought, rightly, that Edward would make a good soldier. If he was to go into the army, he must go to Cheltenham College, which was then at the height of its fame for passing boys into the top places at the Royal Military Academy, Woolwich. If Edward went to Cheltenham, it followed that I should go there too, though even at this early date my father did not see me as likely to become a soldier. All was fixed that we should go to Cheltenham for the summer term of 1910.

We came home on a voyage which lasted six weeks. We travelled by train to Dairen through the battlefields of the Russo-Japanese War, then took a ship to Shanghai, where we took another ship, the *Lützow* of the Norddeutscher Lloyd. This German line was preferred to the French Messageries Maritimes, which was said to be dirty, the British P and O, which was said to be snobbish and stuffy, and the Japanese Nippon Yusen Kaisha, which was said to have indigestible food. It was a good choice. We were woken in the mornings and summoned to meals by a bugle, and exercise was provided in a room which had both an electric horse and an electric camel. I much preferred the camel, which called for considerable contortions but was easier than the immensely high-stepping horse. We called at a number of places, and each had its own striking personality. At Hong Kong the great mass of the island as it rose out of the sea was still free of buildings, and for the first time I saw ripe oranges on trees. At Singapore we visited the great mosque at Johore, and though I had seen a mosque at Mukden frequented by Muslim horse-dealers, it was a circular, three-tiered building with Chinese roofs and a crescent on the top, while this was a large, cool, cavernous and silent place. At Penang there were rich tropical gardens with waterfalls, at Colombo relics of Portuguese and Dutch occupation in walls and buildings, at Aden native boys diving for silver coins and always catching them, nor as yet had the sharks become so dangerous that the practice had to be forbidden. Our last port of call was Genoa, where we spent the day looking at palaces, which did not interest me, and at the nineteenth-century monuments in the Campo Santo, whose adroit realism stirred my amazed admiration. At Singapore came news that Sir Robert Hart, who had been Inspector-General of the Chinese Customs since 1863, had resigned his post. My father would have liked to succeed him and certainly had qualifications to do so, but his name was not on the short list which Hart sent to the Chinese authorities, and an old friend and near contemporary, Francis Aglen, was appointed. My father soon heard from him asking him to be Chief Secretary, which amounted to being second-in-command. My father accepted with gratitude. He saw that his services had been appreciated and that he would have a dignified and influential post in Peking. This meant that he could not stay long in England, and after placing Edward and me at Cheltenham he hurried back to China by way of Siberia.

2

Public School

Edward went straight to the senior school, and I went to the junior, which was for most purposes a separate institution. My first term in it seemed to last for an eternity, and I did not dare to think that it could ever come to an end. This was in no way the fault of the school authorities, who were perfectly considerate. We were well fed, well housed, and well taught. There was no bullying, and the headmaster, though rather remote and tongue-tied and given to scratching his ears and bald head with a nib and to spitting little pieces of chewed blotting paper, was perfectly just. If I was unhappy, it was my fault and the fault of my up-bringing. For a boy of twelve I had seen a lot of the world and moved too much among grown-ups. I was used to talking when I had something to say, and that was often. Nor had I the faintest inkling of the English convention that it was bad form to talk too much. I could ride a pony and skate after a fashion, but I had never played either cricket or football. I found myself flung among a lot of boys whose interests were not in the least like mine and whose upbringing had been in a single, severe mould, which made them regard deviations with suspicion. At first they looked on me with surprise, then decided that I was not one of them and left me alone. This was not in the least unkind, but I was not ready to live on my own resources, and I felt abandoned by God and man. My mother had told me that her father had run away from four schools, and I deeply sympathized with him, but I never thought of doing the same myself. I could not get away, and anyhow there was nowhere to go. My happiest hours were those which I spent in bed or in the college chapel, which we shared with the senior school, for then I could at least enjoy my own thoughts. This solitude was made more bitter by an unforeseen contingency. I had hitherto taken my lessons in my stride and rather fancied myself at them, but now, after a year away from Latin and Greek, I had no confidence in myself and began to think that I must be an idiot. The chief classical master, who was an old man and proud of his idiosyncrasies, had no pity for me as in my terrified uncertainty I mumbled and stumbled in trying to translate Sallust or a potted version of the *Medea*. He would throw up his hands and cry, 'What is the creature saying?', and that put an end to any audible efforts on my part. On the few occasions when general knowledge was required I could usually provide it, but it did me no good, since I was thought to be showing off. I so lost confidence in myself that I could not concentrate, was thought to be idle, and became so. Outside school hours cricket was the main activity. I was no good at it, and what with clumsiness, cowardice, astigmatism, and an inability to throw, I was the last to be chosen in any pick-up and relegated to be long stop. I did not see Edward except sometimes on Sunday afternoons when we were allowed to go for a walk together. The college lay on the outskirts of Cheltenham, and it was easy to get into the country. He had settled in much better than I had, and his company made me feel that I was still human.

The top event of the term was the death of Edward VII. It came quite unexpectedly and was made the most of in chapel, where, with tactful omissions, the dead king's virtues were extolled. But this welcome interlude did not last for long, and the leaden days followed with appalling slowness. At last, when the end was almost in sight, we did examinations. The masters expected nothing from me and said so, but, left to myself and free from being badgered and pushed around, I was seized by a demon, and my memory, which seemed to have given up work, came back into action with floods of information. I wrote as much as I could with a savage speed and in the result got much higher marks than anyone else in the form. This caused some consternation, as I had hitherto been very low in my weekly marks, and, what was worse, my report had already been written and more than hinted at my lack of capacity. It was hurriedly corrected with a few perfunctory remarks that I had done well in examinations, but this only served to suggest that my previous lack of effort was all the more discreditable. I, however, was delighted. It was clear that I was not after all an idiot, and though in the long run I suffered too long from the dangerous belief that I could always bring it off 'on the day', for the moment all was well. In the following holidays I learned to swim and that removed another item from my list of shortcomings.

After this shaky and uncomfortable start I worked out a way of life which was more congenial. A new master, who was thought 'common', because he showed much more zest and energy than his colleagues, interested me in Latin and Greek, and in the summer of 1911 I won a scholarship to the senior school. It was not a grand one, being worth £40 a year, but it was what my father wanted, and in due course I turned it into something better. But my real discovery, which was to last for the rest of my time at Cheltenham, was that schoolboys will forgive anything for a joke. I set out to amuse the other boys and by such simple devices as imitating the masters or inventing fantasies about their private lives I got myself accepted. I was asked to tell stories after dark in the dormitory and by drawing on what I had picked up in China did not find this difficult, though I did not always adhere strictly to the truth. I found football less intolerable than cricket and managed to get along at it. I even made a friend. His name was H. N. Crooke, and like me he was thought an oddity and not much liked. He was rich in witticisms and, being the son of an Indian Civil Servant, had a background not unlike mine. I went everywhere with him, and a sarcastic master compared us with 'a pair of turtle-doves or two young pigeons'. We did not mind, but did not think it funny. My friendship with him lasted for no more than a year, but not through any fault in either of us. When we moved to the senior school, we were in different houses and so not allowed to speak to each other, and later he was killed in France in the war. But between us we evolved a technique of survival in a society which would otherwise not have found us easy to digest.

My move from the junior to the senior school was made easy by Edward having settled in a house called 'Cheltondale' and being able to tell me what to do. As a scholar I was exempted from fagging, and though my first two years were passed in a gloomy work-room where I had a desk and a cupboard and nothing else, there were alleviations like cooking in the boot-room. My house-master, Tommy Hyett, was a shy, tongue-tied, conscientious bachelor who taught mathematics and, having been educated at Cheltenham Grammar School, was thought to be socially not quite right. He was devoted to his house in a strange inarticulate way and did his best to promote its successes. He watched all house-games and occasionally uttered a wry comment as when, if a kick had been foozled and we all politely said, 'Bad luck!', he, with more truth, said, 'Bad kick!'. On other occasions he could be more frightening, as when a boy swore in the scrum and was at once led off the field and beaten. At games we never won any cups except once at athletics, but even then he refused to allow the mild relaxation of a house-supper to celebrate it, since he was frightened that something appalling might happen if our iron taboos were for a moment relaxed. He was convinced that we were all far too close to mortal sin, but he comforted himself with the belief that he knew at any time of night or day what we were doing. He once boasted of this to my mother, who was deeply shocked, and anyhow it was far from true. His fears for our behaviour were not helped by his attempts to instruct us in the facts of life. Early in my time I was sent for, and Hyett read out, with painful embarrassment to himself and to me, a pamphlet about the love-life of flowers. In itself it was highly interesting, but it had nothing to do with anything that I knew about, and I was unable to see why he had read it. In winter we were locked up at 5 p.m. and in summer at 7 p.m. Our only free time was Sunday afternoon when we either went for walks in the country, or gorged ourselves on sausages and scrambled eggs. The house was managed by Hyett's housekeeper, Miss Brown. She was large, stately, imperious, and splendid, known alike as 'Braggers' and 'the Queen'. Hyett was terrified of her and never dared to act against her will. Under her rule the food was plentiful and good; the house was clean and reasonably warm; there was hot water in the shower-baths. On cold days soup was served after morning school, to the derisive jeers of boys in other houses, and on dark days she insisted that everyone must wear an overcoat. Later I got to know her well and to like and admire her. She was well educated, had excellent taste of a late Victorian kind, and put me on to books which I should otherwise not have read. She had an unrequited affection for poor Hyett and once said to me, 'There is nobody I admire so much as Mr Hyett.' They breakfasted together in decorous silence, and it is a testimony to their dignity that no boys ever hinted that their relations were anything but of the most Platonic kind.

I was on the Classical side, which was small and select in comparison with the large and highly efficient Military side, where boys were drilled into Woolwich and Sandhurst. I started in the Upper Fifth under a formidable master, H. V. Page, known as Puggy from his build and face and character. He had in his day played for England at Rugby football and for Gloucestershire at cricket and made a name for himself as one of the last cricketers to bowl underhand in first-class matches. He worked himself as hard as he worked us, and, being totally without self-control, was at the mercy of his moods, which ranged from an inspiring enthusiasm to fits of savagery. His chief subject was Greek and Latin grammar, and on this he drilled us partly by easily memorized jokes, which were both useful and funny, partly by explosions of phrenetic anger, when he would bang the desk with both fists and send the inkpots flying in the air as he shouted at some offending victim. To construe before him was always perilous, and there might come a terrible moment when he would cry out, 'Lordie, lordie, take the words, man!' and you knew that trouble lay ahead. If some offender was in his own house, he might take him at once into the next room and beat him. In his eyes intellectual failures were all moral failures, and while he made no allowance for stupidity or nervousness, he suspected wanton idleness at every turn and had no qualms about punishing it. I was not really frightened of him, and though he thought me rather a rabbit, he did not bully me, but reserved his more barbarous attentions for a body of boys at the back of the room, whom he called 'the pack' and subjected to a variety of insults and penalties. Yet he had a genuine love of Greek poetry, and though he seemed to treat the fighting before Troy as if it were a glorious football match, he would also treat a football match as if it were a fight before Troy. He read Homer with a fine resonant voice, almost breaking with emotion, and made even the dullest boys feel that here indeed was a heroic world.

At Cheltenham classical scholars spent at least three years in the Sixth Form, and this meant that most of our time was passed with two or three specialist masters. The most remarkable was a young man called Leonard Butler, who had taken first classes in classics and history at New College and now taught them with ebullient zest. He was round-headed and pink-faced, with a defiantly incongruous moustache. He wore a butterfly collar and a bow tie, which was thought rather dashing, and when he laughed, it was as if some spring inside him had got out of control. In classics he distilled into me a taste for writing Greek verses and, very much despite himself, a dislike for Cicero; in history he was more sensational and excited both admiration and opposition. He had travelled in the Balkans and talked with eloquent bias about political problems of which we knew nothing. From him we heard for the first time of the Berlin–Baghdad railway, the Sanjak of Novi Bazar, Italia irredenta, *Weltpolitik*, and the Young Turks. He would paint large notices which he set up in the form-room, proclaiming such lessons as de Vigny's, 'Le vrai dieu, le dieu fort, c'est le dieu des idées', or Napoleon's, 'Pas d'extraits. La jeunesse a le temps pour la forte et longue lecture.' He made us draw maps, and consoled us for the labour with rich teas. When he was agitated, his voice rose in a hissing falsetto, and even in ordinary speech he isolated his words from each other in a way which made them both more memorable and more absurd. His politics were of a kind quite unfamiliar to me. In the age of triumphant Liberalism, of Lloyd George's budget and the Parliament Act, he taught that Liberalism was out of date and that its place had been taken by Tory Democracy, on which, however, he was not very explicit.

Such views could be fitted into the traditions of Cheltenham. There were indeed two notable Cheltonians in Asquith's cabinet, John Morley and the Lord Chancellor, Lord Loreburn, but I do not remember that they were ever mentioned on public occasions at Cheltenham. On the other hand we heard much about another Cheltonian, Houston Stewart Chamberlain, whose portentous work, *Die Grundlagen des neunzehnten Jahrhunderts*, had recently been translated into English as *The Foundations of the Nineteenth Century* and won respectful applause in *The Cheltonian*. In it Chamberlain, with a combination of real learning and muddled thought, established the Aryan myth, and won the thanks of the Kaiser in the words, 'It was God who sent your book to the German people and you personally to me.' Chamberlain became a naturalized German in 1916 and was decorated with the Iron Cross. Later, after the Kaiser had failed him, he saw in Adolf Hitler the incarnation of his dreams for Germany. Butler's views were of this kind. He believed in power as an end in itself, and liked the exercise of force. He was not exactly pro-German, but he had an unlimited admiration for Bismarck and wished that English statesmen would resemble him. He was rather too extreme even for the well-conditioned boys of Cheltenham, at least on the Classical side, which prided itself on not going all the way with the Military. On the other hand he combined these Germanic views with High Church Anglicanism and intended to take Holy Orders, which would surely have cost him his moustache. He advised me to read Bishop Gore's Commentary on the Epistle to the Romans, but I did not relish the idea. I liked him very much but did not believe a word of what he said. The first stirrings of Liberalism were at work in me, and I felt that I knew from my father much more about *Weltpolitik* than Butler did. He was innocently unaware of his own limitations, and this led to a personal disaster. He intended to make schoolmastering his profession, and foolishly became a house-tutor in a tough house, where he was ingeniously and mercilessly ragged. Against the imaginative stratagems of schoolboys the champion of blood and power was helpless. The result was that he accepted in 1914 a fellowship at St John's College, Oxford, but went instead to the war. He came to visit me when he was still in England, and it was only after very great obstruction that Hyett, suspecting heaven knows what, allowed him to see me. He was fatally wounded in the battle of the Somme, and, as he lay dying in no-man's-land, was seen to be tearing up his maps.

Our other chief teacher was built on a very different plan. G. F. Exton was a 'pure' scholar of the old Cambridge school, and his gods were accuracy and taste. By accuracy he meant a command of Greek and Latin syntax, and by taste he meant an ability to write the languages with elegance. He had a red face as if it had just been scrubbed, and a harsh, rasping voice in which the deeper notes sounded as if he had over-exerted them in his youth. He was neat and meticulous in everything, in his slightly pompous walk, his dapper clothes, his handwriting, both English and Greek, his correction of our errors by a graduated system of signs intended to show the degree of their monstrosity. His manner suggested his assurance that he could never be wrong, and we measured him by his own standards. We called him the Beetle, and myth said that this was because he was made to be crushed, but on his retirement many years later he explained that the nickname was not 'Beetle' but 'Baetyl'. This was obscure, since he had little in common with a sacred meteorite, and anyhow we had never heard of baetyls. He was a very conscientious teacher, who prepared everything with extreme care and knew all the answers to all the questions. But though he was more than ready to correct, and still more to condemn, he did not encourage, but left us with the conviction that we could never hope to be any good. This attitude called for gentle reprisals. We used to get him to parody himself in his own brand of polysyllabic English, and we were delighted when he said, for instance, 'Who is the perpetrator of this puerile outrage?', or 'It ill becomes you to traduce the tenets of scholarship'. So too, when he let loose a sarcasm, we either applauded it or, on rarer occasions, said, 'Not worthy of you, sir.' He did not mind this or suspect that he was being ragged. His highest term of praise was 'fair', and he much preferred some more damning judgement such as 'marred by gross grammatical inaccuracies'. That the classics meant more to him than a mere discipline is more than likely, and he would quote them on appropriate occasions. Once indeed he said of a piece of Anacreon 'Pretty little piece', and we were left speechless, since the piece hardly conformed to the standards preached at Cheltenham College.

Above and behind Butler and Exton loomed the portentous figure of the Principal, as the headmaster of the college was still called. The Reverend Reginald Waterfield had been appointed at the age of thirty-three and was now in his middle forties, though of course we thought of him as ageless. He was a man of powerful physique, character, and personality. He got up at six every day and wrote all his letters in his own hand with no help from a secretary. Nothing seemed to abate his energy, and I cannot remember that he was ever ill or indisposed. As a young man he had been a vigorous player of games, and even now he could be seen in a spare hour riding a horse on the top of Leckhampton Hill. He taught classics and scripture and took endless pains with both, with the result that we never got near to the end of our set books by the end of term, having devoted many hours to discussing whether St Paul wrote to the north or the south Galatians, or who was the author of the Epistle to the Hebrews. Waterfield was not a good teacher. His rotund manner of exposition – he had once won a prize for reading – killed the reality of the subject. We translated everything into his voice and his turns of phrase, and this was particularly false in dealing with Greek poetry which he put into the sham medieval English of the nineties. Under his touch the swift ease of Homer became an amalgam of absurd archaisms which destroyed the poetry in a way that old Puggy Page never did. In chapel, too, though he took equal care with his sermons and even quoted poetry in them, he did not catch our imagination. When there was a real bust-up and he would address the whole school on its iniquities, he was undeniably formidable, but his speech was still a performance which did not quite carry conviction. The truth was revealed to me later when

my mother, who was staying with the Waterfields, remarked to
his enchanting wife how well the Principal played charades, and
Mrs Waterfield said, 'Oh, but he has been acting all his life.' The
acting was almost unconscious, and Waterfield believed what he
said, but behind him stood the formidable ghost of Dr Arnold,
whom he sought to embody, with oddly enough a few mannerisms of Mr Gladstone, for whom he had very little respect, but
whose rounded periods appealed to him. His sense of humour
would desert him in the pulpit or on the platform, and sometimes
his more ambitious flights of eloquence provoked ribald interpretations from his flock. When he announced in a sermon,
'Cheltenham College has always stood for three things, flying
high, going straight, and sticking together to the end', we not
only thought it absurd but read into it meanings which it was not
intended to convey.

In the holidays Edward and I were based, as in earlier years, on
the Mackies at Putney but also went to stay elsewhere with
friends or relations. In 1912 our parents came home and took a
house at Cookham Dean amid beech woods. The summer was
one of the wettest on record, and our hopes of agreeable outings
on the Thames were always frustrated by rain, but some compensation came from a motor-car. It was an open Darracq, driven
by a succession of evil-looking chauffeurs who seemed to encourage it to break down. One of the worst occasions was when
our parents visited us at Cheltenham for Speech Day and took us
for a drive in the Cotswolds, only to be stopped by some inscrutable disaster. We got home late by train, and my father was
so depressed that he spent the next morning in bed and put an end
to any anticipated festivities. He was as keen as ever that we should
pursue manly pastimes, and the winter holidays were made
hideous by having to run over ploughed fields with beagles in
pursuit of invisible hares. At this time we got a letter from Miss
Dell saying that her sister Ethel had written a book called *The
Way of an Eagle*, which had been refused by seven publishers but
had at last been taken by Fisher Unwin – would we read it? We
did and, amid some mockery of its excesses, greatly enjoyed it.
It was a triumphant best-seller, and Miss Ethel, who was the

gentlest and most self-effacing of women and had a genius for teaching dogs to do elaborate tricks, began to make a lot of money. She and Miss Dell set up house outside Guildford and shut themselves off from the world by building a massive brick wall round the domain. Edward and I were often asked to stay there, and the comforts were such as we had never known, including a glass of sherry and a piece of plum-cake in the middle of the morning. Miss Dell also generously took us to different places, such as the New Forest or the Devonshire sea-coast, in the holidays, and for a time under her influence I even attempted to play golf. I found in her a most sympathetic companion in the literary interests which were beginning to dominate my mind. I used to show her my first efforts, which were dismally feeble, and she made encouraging but perceptive comments on them.

This widening of my horizon meant that I found the restrictions at school much more irksome than when I had assumed them to be an inevitable part of our common lot. Not only were we locked up in the evenings and allowed very little time for ourselves, but we were forbidden to talk to boys in other houses except in our form-rooms, and even in our own house society was practically restricted to contemporaries. There was no art, no handicraft, no music, no acting, no dancing with the girls from the Ladies' College, and only very occasionally a lecture, preferably about travel or nature-study with coloured slides of sunsets, which always evoked loud applause. For most boys games provided some sort of interest, but my house was not good at them, and hopes of success came to nothing. Topics of conversation being few, most boys talked smut, of which in fact they knew very little, and on which they were boring and repetitive. The very few highbrows tried to create some variety for themselves, especially when in their third year they had studies which made all the difference for privacy and quiet.

I had two particular friends, Felix Brunner and Miles Plowden. Felix came ultimately of a Swiss family, and his grandfather had been a co-founder of Brunner, Mond and Co, from which the vast empire of ICI eventually grew. His father was a Liberal

MP, and from Felix, who knew about current events, I picked
up much that counterweighed the Nietzschean doctrines of
Leonard Butler. His family had a comfortable house in Kensington and another in Cheshire near Northwich. He asked me to
stay there in the holidays, and there I even took part in a small
play. This was my one and only excursion into acting, and though
I enjoyed the preparations for it, I never understood what the
play was about. There too I met his sister, who was rather older
than he was, and a very lively and gifted girl, Kitty Maugham,
the daughter of the famous lawyer who eventually became Lord
Chancellor. She was unusually attractive and had a number of
amusing turns, such as the 'orange-peel slip', which amazed and
delighted me. So far the only girls I had met were my cousins,
and though I liked them, Kitty opened my eyes to something
quite different. I was much too solemn with her and with Joyce
Brunner. I was at an age when one thought about the universe,
preferably in the gloomiest terms, and this was not an enlivening
subject for conversation at an agreeable house-party.

Miles Plowden came from a military family, but his parents
had separated, and he had to divide his time between them. He
had a sharp wit and took a low view of most of our schoolfellows.
Unlike Felix and myself, he knew a lot about music, and he and
I acquired a second-hand gramophone and tried to educate ourselves on it. I knew nothing at all about music and am not sure
that I learned very much. But at least it was a protest against the
emptiness of our lives. Felix, Miles and I discovered that by taking
walks outside the usual range we could get excellent teas with
boiled eggs at farm-houses in the country, and this we did on
Sunday afternoons in defiance of rules. We occasionally read
plays together and vastly enjoyed Wilde's comedies, which had
recently come out in a cheap edition. What Hyett would have
done if he had found us, I shudder to think. I much enjoyed the
company of these two friends and was little interested in anyone
else. They both disliked Cheltenham as much as I did. The trouble
was that we were bored. We were beginning to develop our own
tastes and found it difficult to do so since we were hemmed in by
restrictions on every side. The authorities were so eager to keep

us virtuous that they gave us very little opportunity to be ourselves.

This boredom with the usual routine was harmful to my work.
The classical side at Cheltenham, as at most public schools at the
time, was devised to win scholarships at Oxford and Cambridge,
and, considering how small it was, it did remarkably well. But
the means designed to reach this end had serious drawbacks. For
our last three years we specialized in classics and did almost
nothing else except some scripture, which amounted to classics
since it consisted of a study of St Paul in Greek, and a weekly
essay, which was necessary since it was demanded in the scholarship examinations. At sixteen or earlier we knocked off mathematics, which I liked and would gladly have pursued further, and
French, which I fiercely disliked because it was taught by a Swiss
who had no taste for literature and no intention that we should
ever speak French. This early specialization may have brought
some rewards but they were not worth the price paid for them.
One obvious result was that some of the cleverer boys got bored
with the classics, and each year spent on them brought diminish-
ing returns. This was the case with me. I was well aware that there
was much that I could like in Greek and Latin, but we never
seemed to get it. The careful plodding through a text was too
slow for my eager curiosity, and the concentration on purely
textual and linguistic points seemed designed to destroy any
interest in the literature. The result was that for my last two years
in the Upper Sixth I skimped my work to a minimum but managed to get through somehow. Waterfield complained in a report,
'I am afraid that his industry is not commensurate with his
ability', and Exton was shocked at my reading outside the classical
curriculum, which in his view was all that was needed for success
and salvation. I did in fact read a good deal for myself. I saw how
much enthralling literature awaited me and I was afraid that life
would be too short to get through it. So I spent my pocket-
money on cheap editions and not only read the obvious English
writers and the new poets, but found that despite my preposterous
French master I could manage Verlaine and Baudelaire without
much trouble. I even tried Dante in a bilingual edition, and

survivals from Herr Witte's instruction took me to Heine, but without marked success.

I had already embarked on this way of life when war broke out in August 1914. Edward and I were all set to go to France to learn French with a Protestant family near Bordeaux, and we had just arrived at my Aunt Mabel's large house at Clevedon, when it was clear that the French trip was off. For three breathless days we knew that we were in a crisis, and on Tuesday, 4 August, war was declared. I was now sixteen years old and capable of forming my own ideas on what happened. The whole world seemed to be delighted and to think that rapturous adventures lay ahead. My Uncle Ned assumed that everyone wished to fight and sent his own son Geoffrey, who was just seventeen, into the Middlesex Regiment as a Second Lieutenant. Edward was taking the examination for Woolwich in December, and that fitted him. But I did not share the enthusiasm or the hopes. To me the outbreak of war seemed a monstrous betrayal by Providence. I had been told for years that we were bound sooner or later to fight Germany, but I had refused to believe it, and now to my disgust and horror it was true. Though I thought that we were right to fight, I did not like the prospect of army life. I knew too much about intending officers to think that they would be very congenial, and I did not believe that the war would soon be over. On this point I had the inexorable authority of Kitchener on my side, and that convinced me. But I did not think that it would be at all pleasant, and when even Miss Dell wrote, 'I expect you are longing to get at the Germans', I found it hard to answer. A little later, when Rupert Brooke's famous war-sonnets were published and acclaimed as proof of a new heroic spirit in England, I felt nothing of the kind. I did not share his view of 'half-men', or of 'swimmers into cleanness leaping', and I knew that I was right. The casualty lists soon began to tell their story, and, since among them were many young men who had recently been at Cheltenham, I saw how small the chances of survival were and made up my mind that I was certain in due course to be killed. Once I had come to this conclusion I felt much better, since it meant that I could pursue my own line and read what I wished. Fortunately my father also foresaw a long war and opposed attempts to send me early into the army. His notion was that I must first get a scholarship at Oxford, and for this I would try in December 1915.

The war had a gloomy effect on school. It was treated as a crusade to which everything, especially everything at all pleasant, must be sacrificed. We were expected to go without our minor comforts 'because of the poor boys in the trenches', and this seemed to be an unnecessary anticipation of horrors to come. Waterfield demanded that prize-winners should give half the value of their awards to the Red Cross, and, deluding himself and others, inserted in our prizes a printed statement that we had requested this to be done. This was a blow, as I had begun to win quite a number of prizes, which were abundant and easy to win, and relied upon them to make a library. OTC parades became longer and more frequent, and we did too many field-exercises, of which the point was quite obscure but which meant that we spent hours advancing in short rushes and falling down in cow-pats and sheep-droppings. Exton in a patriotic moment had joined the OTC as a private and was much taken to task by a corporal in his form for slowness in his movements and for not holding himself erect. The one stalwart resister to war-time sacrifices was Miss Brown, who was not going to let *her* house starve and continued her generous housekeeping in defiance of prices and shortages. In school Exton, who was not able to serve because of some physical defect, redoubled his efforts to instil method and taste into us, but never realized that his pupils could not give their whole attention to him, since they felt that all too soon their lives might be finished. Waterfield preached powerful sermons on the Christian's duty to fight and argued that though Our Lord might not have wished to be a combatant soldier, he would at least have joined the RAMC. Such lectures as were given were about the war, and we listened dutifully to Hilaire Belloc on the 'Napoleonic lozenge', which was meant to explain the Marne but failed to do so. The only survival of the arts was a house-singing competition, which we won, partly through Miles Plowden's skilful handling of the judge. Hyett was delighted and for the moment felt that all was well. But his euphoria did not last long. Habituated to boredom though the boys were, the new demands were rather more than they could endure and, whereas hitherto their talk about sex had been mainly theoretical, it was now translated into action, and before long an explosion came with the scandal of several expulsions. While Waterfield showed himself at his most masterful as a grand inquisitor, Hyett was broken and sought consolation in more frequent attendance at college chapel.

In my pursuit of literature I could not but wonder what men and women of letters were like. I had hardly met any, but I formed imaginary pictures of them and thought that they must be fountains of wisdom and humanity. There were very few people to whom I could talk about books. My relations were not interested, except my Aunt Florence, who was far too busy with her recent marriage to a gifted potter called Will Moorcroft and with her own family cares. However, some of my Aunt Mabel's friends in London asked me to more or less grown-up parties. At one of these I saw an elderly, rather short and stout gentleman bobbing up and down with a large bald head. He spoke with much gravity and total concentration to a few people and seemed to be entranced by what they had to say. I asked who he was, and was told that he was the novelist Mr Henry James. My literary snobbery was instantly aroused. I had read *The Turn of the Screw*, *The Aspern Papers* and *The Princess Cassamassima*. I even possessed a copy of *The Soft Side*, which I had bought cheap in Cheltenham from a discerning bookseller, but did not understand. I knew that James was one of the greatest novelists of the age, not really from my own reading but from what I had heard about him. I was now introduced to him. With a wonderful courtesy he gave his whole attention to me and asked a very long question. Of the introductory part I remember nothing exact except that he was plainly asking, with every kind of consideration and a long row of adverbs, something which he feared that I might think impertinent, but the second part, which was much shorter, remains with me and consisted quite simply of the words, 'Are you still at school?' I replied that I was, and with that he seemed content, when he was carried off by our hostess to speak to someone else.

I got through the first year of the war by not thinking too

much about it. The slaughter at the Dardanelles and at Loos brought home its reality, and I saw nothing to change in my view of it. I never thought of avoiding my obligation to do military service and was never able to see how conscientious objectors could cut themselves off from their fellows. Moreover I was not nearly good enough a Christian to regard pacificism as a religious duty. I thought that I should have to fight just because there was nothing else to do, and if my friends could face it, so could I. In Butler's place we had a new master, G. M. Patterson, who had been bred at Trinity College, Oxford, in the doctrines of the Round Table group and shared their liberal imperialism. I much preferred this to Butler's doctrines, but felt that it had little to do with reality as we now knew it. He was an attractive, warm-hearted man who treated us as equals and to whom we could say what we liked, even about Waterfield and Exton. We did essays for him, and when I wrote on literary matters, he praised me, but once he made us write about the war, whether it would be settled in the west or the east, and I failed lamentably. This was a matter on which my brain refused to function. He was appalled and felt that I was a selfish aesthete. But I was not discouraged. This was the way I was built, and I saw nothing wrong in it. In the Michaelmas Term of 1915 my age-group was polished up for the Oxford scholarship examination. I knew that this was important, and read for it quite a lot of Greek and Latin, though not the texts which we did in school. Before it Exton said to me, 'I don't think your classics are bad enough to prevent you getting a scholarship on your general paper.' I put New College first on my list of preferences, but also entered for a group in the following week and put St John's first. After two days of this second round I was beginning to become anxious and walked out early from my afternoon paper to New College, where I found a notice saying that I had won the top scholarship. I went straight back to Cheltenham and gave the news quietly to Hyett, who for the first time in my acquaintance showed real pleasure and congratulated me on bringing honour to the house.

As I was still too young for the army, I passed another term at Cheltenham and wasted it entirely. I made no attempt to do the prescribed work, and since I was a College Prefect and head of my house, nothing could be done to me. Exton despaired of me, suspecting not without reason that my example had corrupted his most conscientious pupil, a modest and charming boy called Moore, who, having also won a scholarship at Oxford, gave up regular labour and got as his half-term report 'Optimi corruptio pessima', while I got 'Facilis descensus'. But in the middle of the term everything was changed by the arrival of my mother via Siberia from China. It was clear that Edward, who had been commissioned into the Royal Engineers, would soon be sent abroad, and she wished to see both her sons before it was too late. She came to Cheltenham and, after three days of high propriety and much embarrassment with Hyett, she was asked to stay by the Waterfields and was enchanted by Mrs Waterfield. She was indeed one of the sweetest and most winning women I have ever known. She was small and rather plump but still kept the freshness of a rosebud. She was absolutely natural and spontaneous, and since she overflowed with kindness, everyone loved her. Nothing depressed her or diminished her angelic vitality. At home with her Waterfield was much less formidable than in school, and I began to appreciate him at his proper worth. There was an engaging innocence in their badinage with one another. Once I boldly said that I did not like St Paul, and Mrs Waterfield said at once, 'There's nobody Reggie loves so much as St Paul', to which he countered, 'Except you, my dear'. She amused my mother very much when, talking about me, she said, 'Is your husband a clever man?' Fortunately my mother was able to see something of Edward, and in the following holidays we all went to stay with Aunt Mabel at Clevedon. Then an important letter came from my father. He thought, very rightly, that I should do no good if I went back to school for yet another term and that it would be much better to go to Peking with my mother and stay there until my call-up was near. I had doubts whether I should be allowed to leave the country but friends at the Foreign Office removed any possible obstacles, and all was fixed for a new adventure.

3

Peking and Petrograd

The journey overland to China in 1916 was much more difficult than in 1909. Instead of travelling easily through Belgium and Germany we had to do a long detour first by sea from Newcastle to Bergen and then by land to Oslo, Stockholm, the northern end of the Gulf of Bothnia and so through Finland to Petrograd, as St Petersburg was now patriotically called. The passage over the North Sea was not free from the danger of U-boats, but, though we had to keep our life-jackets at hand, we had no alarms. We spent some hours in both Oslo and Stockholm and arrived at Petrograd about midnight. We were the prey of a nasty anxiety. Owing to a fall of snow in Norway we arrived later than the hour at which the Siberian express, which went only once a week and was always fully booked, was due to start. Our first task was to ask about this, and to our astonished delight we found that the Russians, for no very clear reason, had postponed the departure till the next evening. We had then to find somewhere to spend the night. The Cook's agent was quite unable to deal with all the passengers who beset him, and we did not fancy a long drive in a droshky in search of non-existent accommodation. But here again we were saved. With us was a young woman, Miss Finch, who was going out to Peking to marry *The Times* correspondent there. She was met at the station by Robert Wilton, the correspondent in Petrograd, who at once took not only her but my

mother, another lady, and myself to stay at his flat. On the following evening we set off on our long trip. It lasted some ten days.
The train went slowly but was clean and punctual, and there were
no signs of that breakdown in the railway system which was
beginning to be visible elsewhere in Russia. Siberia was at its most
engaging with its massed wild flowers under the silver birches
and rowans. There were even more soldiers on the train than in
1909. My mother, who was often taken for my wife, still looked
very young and received many courtesies from Russian officers,
who spoke excellent English and were determined to say nothing
about the war.

In 1916 Peking differed very little from the great city founded
by Kublai Khan and vastly embellished and extended by the
Manchu emperors of the seventeenth and eighteenth centuries.
From the first moment I was overwhelmed by its splendour. I
had of course seen very little of Europe, and though I had visited
some of the more famous English cathedrals and castles, I had
never seen a place so consistently magnificent on so large a scale.
Compared with it Mukden was a mere village, and I had thought
Mukden fine beyond words. What first struck me in Peking was
its colour. The great mass of houses was drab enough in its grey
brick, but the whole centre of the city, with the Forbidden City
at its heart, relied on colour quite as much as design to catch the
eye. The buildings were mostly of wood painted red, but the
curving roofs were of yellow or green tiles, and their brightness
was enhanced by the white marble causeways and bridges which
joined them. Nor did the repeated reds and yellows give an
effect of harshness or monotony. The bright air tempered their
brilliance but kept the outlines sharp, and these were always
varied and surprising. The builders of the Imperial City and of the
Summer Palace took full advantage of every small variation in
the landscape, of water and contour, to stress the contrasts between one building and another. The bright colours were mod-
erated by the abundant trees and the lotus-flowers on the lakes.
The external application of colour is not common in Europe, and
even in Venice, where it is, the colours are much milder and more
various than in Peking. One could not wish Peking otherwise.

The lines and outlines were captivating, but the use of colour gave them a new appeal. For the first time I found myself asking how an effect was produced, how the three circular tiers of the Temple of Heaven gain in design by the decrease of size as they ascend and how the blue tiles of the roof look all the more blue because of the white marble foundation on which the building is set.

In trying to absorb the dazzling impression which Peking made on me I found my aesthetic responses reinforced by the presence of a living past. This was quite as exciting as the sheer splendour of the visible scene. In the Confucian temple was a set of stone drums inscribed with a poem on hunting which dates from about the eighth century BC. The mere fact that the drums had been there for so many centuries brought home the strange continuity of Chinese history. Outside Peking to the west was the old Summer Palace, which was looted and destroyed by Lord Elgin in 1860, but still had enough remains to show how it was devised by French Jesuits to be a Chinese Versailles. The present Summer Palace was built to take its place in the last decades of the nineteenth century at the order of the Empress Dowager, Tzu-hsi, who applied to it the money which should have been spent on a Chinese navy. Her whim meant the complete defeat of China by Japan in 1894 and all the disastrous humiliations that followed from the greedy European powers. But the palace survives, and, like the Forbidden City, mingles landscape and architecture into a single pattern. It is a lesson on how surprise and novelty can be secured within a frame of very strict conventions. Almost everything in it could have been built in the preceding thousand years, but every building has its own personality, from the Camel-back Bridge to the hexagonal, four-storeyed Tower of Buddha's Fragrance. Here Tzu-hsi liked to pass the summer months, and it is the reflection of her highly educated taste. Brutal and ruthless though she was, she was in her way an artist, and the Summer Palace is her translation into solid form of many palaces imagined in Chinese pictures. Once indeed she, of all people, was led a little astray by an attempt at modernity. The marble barge in one of the lakes is almost Italianate with its round arches and its marble inlay, and something worse with its stained glass. Was she perhaps trying to revive western elegances patronized by her ancestors Kang-shi and Chien-lung? In his early days in China my father had seen her going from the Winter Palace to the Summer Palace in her palanquin, while attendants scattered yellow sand before her. She was just visible, and my father saw her richly enamelled face with its large slanting mouth and its eager predatory eyes.

If in the Summer Palace the shade of Tzu-hsi seemed almost benevolent, the Winter Palace in Peking held more sinister memories of her. Here was the well into which the Pearl Concubine was thrown for talking too much when the Empress was in a hurry to leave the capital before the Expeditionary Force reached it to suppress the Boxers. Here too was the small island of Ing-ti, the Ocean Terrace, where she kept the Emperor Kwang-shu in captivity, except when she let him out for ceremonial occasions. It had style and beauty, but it was impossible to forget the well-intentioned young man who thought that he could pit himself against his merciless aunt and was so cruelly betrayed and humiliated. There were still foreigners in Peking who had seen him on state occasions seated on a throne lower than hers and playing no part in the ceremonies which she conducted. But even Tzu-hsi was forgotten as we looked at the spreading splendours of the Winter Palace, the halls and pavilions facing each other across marble courts, the glazed yellow tiles on the roofs, the red walls inlaid with porcelain dragons, the dramatically placed pagodas, the fountains and clocks and astronomical instruments designed by Jesuit fathers before they incurred the wrath of the Emperor Chien-lung and were expelled from China for involving him in theological controversy with the Pope. Somehow Christian missionaries seemed out of place in the palace of the Manchu emperors, but they had been in Peking long before the Manchus came. Nor was their presence any stranger than that of Marco Polo, with whom a bridge at Lukouchiao outside Peking was traditionally associated. Though my father thought that Christian missionaries did more harm than good in China by breaking up a traditional way of life and putting nothing very secure in its place, his sense of history led him to prevent the export to America of the famous Nestorian stone at Si-ngan Fu, which was erected in AD 781 and contains an abstract of Christian doctrine and records the arrival of a first missionary with sacred books and images in AD 635.

This sense of a living past became more immediate when, with a young American colleague of my father, L. K. Little, I visited the tombs of the Ming Emperors and the Great Wall. In general the Ming tombs resembled those of the Manchu rulers outside Mukden, but were larger and had the special advantage of a formal approach, known as the Spirit Path. This was flanked on either side by big stone statues of animals, which at first looked rather strange and abnormal. I had never looked seriously at any sculpture, and knew even the Elgin Marbles only from pictures, since the British Museum was out of action for the war. With my very artless ideas of what sculpture ought to be, I was puzzled. The elephants seemed to me more detached and less friendly than they were in the illustrations to Kipling's *Jungle Books*, and the camels were clearly not intended to be graceful. But when I examined them, I saw their point. They were like the camels tethered in large numbers outside the walls of Peking, and caught their ungainly postures and their supercilious, sneering looks. More than this, these Chinese images made no attempt to emphasize, as so much western art does, what animals have in common with men; they are shown just as they are, with their own peculiarities, in all their independence of us. The Great Wall made a much more immediate appeal. It was an extension *ad infinitum* of all the castle walls which I had ever seen or imagined, and it was all the more exciting because it was said, not very correctly, to have been built to keep off the Huns and to have succeeded in turning them back towards Europe. As it climbs over the tops of hills so far as the eye can see, it is indeed the boundary and bastion of an ancient world against barbarism. It dominates the landscape, and from it the caravans could be seen coming from Inner Mongolia. I understood why China had for so long been a separate universe, developing without reference to what happened outside. I had never seen so vast a view or felt how even quite large mountains can fit neatly into a landscape without dominating it.

The Great Wall rounded off my picture of China as something strangely unique and unrelated to anything that I had known elsewhere.

Life in Peking afforded comforts such as I had never known before and have never known since. We had a large house near the Legation Quarter. It was built in a European style adapted to Asian conditions, and had cool, spacious rooms. We kept some thirty servants, and though some of these were needed because there was no drainage and all removal of refuse had to be done by coolies, others were required by consideration of 'face'. The head-cook, whose Chinese title was 'great eating professor', had been trained at the French Legation and had two other cooks under him. He was a master of his art, equally good at English, French, and Chinese cookery, but he was much aided by the superb abundance of the Peking market which offered every kind of fish from the Gulf of Chihli, birds, like the wild bustard, caught in the western hills, vegetables grown with loving care in market-gardens, and a whole range of fruits from the most familiar to the most exotic. The English in China were aware of its huge culinary advantages and spoke with pitying contempt of their poor brothers in India who had to be content with a much smaller and less appetizing range of food. In addition to the house in Peking we had a cottage in the country near the race-course, where we went for week-ends, and another house by the sea at Peitaho, where we spent July and part of August in a secluded spot with hills behind and the croaking of frogs all night long from a marsh. Nor were we in the least unique. Most of the well-placed Europeans in Peking lived in similar luxury and took it almost for granted. The normal method of getting from one place to another was on horseback for men and in a carriage for women, and we were duly provided with both kinds. When we rode out, a groom came with us to look after the horses if we dismounted. It was easy enough to walk about Peking itself, but outside there were hardly any roads, and a horse solved all problems. The Europeans were a fantastically privileged class, living under their own laws and paying no taxes to the Chinese Government. All this had been secured by a series of aggressive actions by the powers against a defenceless and hopelessly incompetent China. Even then it seemed to me too comfortable to last, and I was not far wrong.

In 1916 China was to outward view very much what it had been in the nineteenth century. A central government at Peking still ruled the country through provincial governors, and the revolution of 1912 led by Sun Yat-sen had petered out and left Yuan Shi-kai in command as president of an allegedly united China. Yuan had in his time betrayed first the Emperor Kwang-shu, when he tried to institute reforms, then the last Manchu rulers, whom he persuaded to resign from power, and finally Sun Yat-sen, from whom he snatched such victories as the revolution had brought. But when I was in Peking in the spring of 1916, Yuan Shi-kai's time was almost at an end. In the previous winter he had tried to make himself emperor and, after a proper pretence of reluctance, had consented to make the traditional sacrifice at the Temple of Heaven. It is true that he did this in his own way, driving to the Temple in an armoured car and wearing a field-marshal's uniform until he got to the top of the stairs, where he changed it not for a yellow robe but for a purple robe embroidered with dragons. All seemed to have passed off safely, but then Yuan was threatened not only by a large number of Chinese, but by Japan and the western powers. He hung on for a few months, but by 17 March 1916 he saw that his cause was hopeless and that he must give up claims to the monarchy. He abolished his Empire by decree, declaring that he had only acted as he had because of popular demand. He had 'lost face' to an appalling degree and could not possibly stay in power. The current story was that he had decided to die, and, like other Chinese, was able to do so, though it took him some weeks. Others said that he had a stroke. Assailed by abuse from every quarter, including most of his old friends, he died on 6 June. With his death began the disunity of China which was to last until the triumph of Mao Tse-tung in 1949. The crisis was in full swing when I arrived in Peking and I heard all about it from my father, who was well informed through the Chinese officials with whom he worked and was quite certain that Yuan was finished.

In his short period of rule Yuan Shi-kai had appropriated

quarters for himself in the Imperial City and was thus the neighbour of the dethroned emperor, who still occupied a vast part of the Forbidden City in undiminished splendour, enjoying the enormous revenues of his august family and maintaining a full court ceremonial with all its traditional offices, although he was totally without power. This was part of the deal which Yuan had made with the Regent when he persuaded the Manchus to abdicate, and to everyone's surprise he kept his word. In this glittering world of make-believe the ex-emperor, now some ten years old, lived in isolation. He saw Yuan Shi-kai only once, and that was when the demand was made for abdication. Nor did any foreigners see the boy at this time. None the less he was a centre for intrigue, since many Manchus wished to put him back on the throne, and there were rumours that some of the European powers would have supported such a move if only because it might help to unite China. Actually there was nothing in this. The Manchus were hopelessly discredited, and my father and his friends had no good word to say for them. Yuan Shi-kai's death created a new situation, and at least called for a magnificent funeral in the Imperial City. My father and mother and I attended it and were placed on a marble platform with a splendid view of the whole affair. It was a strange mixture of old and new. The catafalque was large and imposing in the ancient manner; the many concubines of the dead man, who was thought to have been unduly uxorious, marched behind it literally tearing their faces; there was a band of Confucian priests playing on archaic instruments made of snake-skin and other weird materials, and immediately after them marched soldiers in lurid modern uniforms playing, not very skilfully, Chopin's *Funeral March*. At the end white doves were set free to show that the dead man's spirit had ascended into the sky. Nothing in Yuan Shi-kai's career became him so well as his funeral. Then at least he was treated as if he were an emperor, and his treacheries were for a moment unmentioned.

The funeral of Yuan Shi-kai was the last grand ceremonial occasion in the Imperial City, and though for the moment it seemed to maintain the splendours of the Manchu Emperors, it was clear that any government would be built on very feeble foundations. China had begun to change some six years earlier, but Yuan had frustrated the revolution and kept things in hand, not very ably or strongly, by his tyrannical methods. China was still more or less united and more or less orderly, but the bonds that held it were cracking. I was made keenly aware of this by a remarkable daily paper, *The Peking Gazette*, which was written in both Chinese and English and edited by a very able politician, Eugene Chen. He had some of the merciless sharpness which could be found at the same time in *The Nation* in England under H. W. Massingham, and he was entirely on the side of the revolutionaries. He harried Yuan to his death, and was hardly less savage with his successor, an unpredictable soldier called Li Yuan-hung. I read the paper with total absorption and realized for the first time what was to be said on the other side. It acted as a corrective to the well-informed and indeed liberal views which I heard from my father and two of his friends, G. E. Morrison and A. Konovalov, who were advisers to the Chinese Government. Their position was complex. All three were servants of the Chinese Government and genuinely sought to promote its best interests. They were well informed on its peculiar difficulties and sought remedies for them. My father's first task was to administer the Chinese Customs Service, which he did with conscientious efficiency, while higher political questions were the concern of the Inspector-General, Francis Aglen. Not only was my father in daily touch with Aglen, but for considerable periods, when Aglen was away, took his place. He thus knew the inner situation of China from a special, informative angle, since the revenue provided by the Customs was the main source of money on which any Chinese Government relied. Aglen, like Hart before him, wielded enormous power, and like him believed that this must be used for the good of China, but when it came to deciding what this meant in detail, the answer was not easy.

My father talked freely to me about these matters, and from him I learned much about the extraordinary position of China at this stage of the First World War. His ideal was of an independent, united China under a good government. Though he had no respect for the last Manchus and had regarded the Empress Dowager as a

1 Cecil Bowra, the author's father, at Newchwang in 1901

2 Ethel Bowra, the author's mother, about 1930

3 Cecil Bowra, the author's father, about 1930

4. The author in 1903

5. The author in 1918

6. The author in 1928

most deleterious woman, he had friends among the higher Chinese officials and appreciated their patriotism in almost impossible circumstances. He did not believe that China was ready for a democratic government and put no trust in Sun Yat-sen, whom he thought a woolly-minded idealist. Still less did he believe in the partition of China among the Great Powers. He distrusted the Russians, disliked the Germans, and thought the French arrogant and touchy. Though he was a deeply patriotic Englishman, he did not wish to add China to the already heavy load of the White Man's Burden and thought that he and his kind could be most useful by instilling standards of efficient and honest administration. Here he was up against the immemorial Chinese custom of 'squeeze'. Everyone who did anything took money for doing so, and this my father saw as the cause of deep corruption and disorder. He was absolutely rigid about it. Handsome presents would arrive from his official friends, no doubt in the anticipation of favours in return, but they were always sent back at once, often to my mother's regret, since they were chosen with an eye to her percipient taste. In 1916 my father knew that China's real enemy was not the European powers, who were busy slaughtering each other in Europe, but Japan, who in January 1915 had made the notorious Twenty-one Demands, which in effect claimed that China should be put under Japanese control. The Demands had been hushed up, but Yuan Shi-kai was unable to resist them, and news about them leaked out at most levels of society. My father regarded the Japanese as the Prussians of the East and was eager to do anything he could to protect China from them. In this he lacked support from the British Government, and it was a heavy blow to him, when the British Minister, Sir John Jordan, whom he much liked and respected, advised the Chinese to give in to Japan.

My father thought that if China held out, she would in the end be assisted by Great Britain against Japan, and this was what he advised. It was not an impracticable policy, and in the end it succeeded up to a point, for China got out of most of the Twenty-one Demands. His Chinese colleagues knew what my father was working for and were grateful. He was less certain about the internal government of China. Having himself trained a large number of Chinese in administrative duties, he knew that they were fully capable of them, but he knew also how ill-educated the mass of Chinese were, and how hard it might be to create a large governing class. He appreciated the strength of Chinese national pride and understood how savagely it had been wounded for seventy years by European greed and brutality, but he did not know how to channel it into constructive channels, nor did he see where its real force lay. He had a genuine compassion for the Chinese people, who were at the mercy of floods and famines, and his cure was good administration on modern lines. Where the administration was to come from was another matter. Soon enough the cracks widened and became more obvious, and China passed into a period of intermittent civil wars. They had not begun when I was in Peking, and what I saw was the false equipoise which suggested that China was still intact, while in fact powers of dissolution, both within and without, were busy at work. To my father and his friends the right thing was to meet each need as it came and to hope that nothing appalling would happen, and indeed in the ensuing years the Chinese Customs Service kept going, despite endless obstacles, and was the main source of public revenue.

My father talked and wrote Chinese, and I once heard him make a speech in it, which was well received for its neat play with traditional maxims in the Chinese manner. I met some of his Chinese friends with him and was much touched by their courtesy and kindness. Even when they spoke very little English, they managed to suggest how interested they were in me and how they hoped that I would work hard and please my father by becoming a good scholar. I remembered how I had idled at Cheltenham and felt a twinge of shame. My mother sometimes asked their wives to tea, and they came and chattered endlessly about children, how many they had or hoped to have. My mother talked enough Chinese to be able to get on with them at this rather primitive level, but found them curiously restricted in comparison with their highly educated husbands. In Peking there was no colour-bar between Europeans and Chinese as there was in the much more mercantile society of Shanghai, where the Europeans in the Foreign Settlement regarded the Chinese as a different class of beings, useful and perhaps gifted, but not to be known. There was no doubt who were the real masters. The foreigners in Peking enjoyed a state far grander than that of the British in India, and though there were many rich Chinese who lived with a fine elegance and even luxury, they did not display it so flagrantly. It was impossible not to contrast the life of an Englishman in Peking with the life which he would have led if he had stayed in England, and it was abundantly clear why so many had come to China to make a career. They made it, and a good deal more beside. I knew that the Chinese resented us, for sometimes when I was out riding with my father in the country, the children would rush after us, shouting 'Foreign devils!' and even in the Peking temples, which made a good income from visitors, some of the priests found it hard to be civil, believing that we worshipped devils. The angry passions which had burst out in the Boxer Rebellion were not dead, and even among educated Chinese it was more fear of Japan than love of Great Britain that made them polite to us.

In the evenings after tea my father would often take me for a walk on the city walls, which were wide enough to permit two carts at a time, and from which you could see the whole enormous city in its imperial splendour and humming life. He would talk freely to me, and in these talks I came for the first time to know him. As a boy, I had been rather frightened of him, since his ideas of what a healthy schoolboy should like did not coincide with mine, and he was always telling me how to do things that I did not wish to do. Now he talked to me as if I were one of his few friends, and I greatly enjoyed it. The hardships of his childhood had shaped his character in a very special way. His driving ambition was to do what his father would have done if he had lived, and he was inspired by the image which he had made of a father whom he lost when he was a very small boy. The image was somewhat larger than life, and my father passed over his father's improvidence and mercurial temperament. What he admired was his taste for action and the talent which he put into it. This meant that my father was unashamedly ambitious and thought it right to be so. He used to insist to me that it was important to know what you wished to do and then to make every effort to do it. He had himself overcome many obstacles and done well at an early age, but he had paid a price for it. In order to get on he had learned to curb much that was most natural and most open in him. He was at all times in entire control of himself. I never saw him lose his temper or even show impatience. He took rebuffs to his ambition with no outward sign of depression. He was always entirely considerate even to those whom he disapproved or disliked. Like most men who have made their own way, he accepted the existing scheme of things as the only possible one and was militantly conservative in his main views. But at times when the facts suggested something else, he was willing to accommodate himself to them. Even when he spoke of people or causes which he despised, and he was not afraid of speaking freely, he was not fierce or uncontrolled. He was a British patriot in the Victorian tradition, but he applied to China a devotion which he was able to combine with a devotion to his own country.

My father had in his youth been deeply influenced by Huxley's assaults on established religion, and he never reverted to the Christianity in which he had been brought up. He liked to expose its absurdities to me and to confirm my own doubts. But he kept to the highest degree the full code of Victorian morality. I never knew him do a mean or dishonest thing, and he was deeply shocked when others did. He was absolutely sure of his own values, and this was a great strength to him in dealing with a service which contained a large assortment of very different men. When I was in Peking, he had sent for a Commissioner of Customs, who was known to be a drunkard. My father had decided that he must be sacked, and nothing would alter his mind on the matter. The poor man came to Peking, tried to be and to look sober, and told his grievances at tedious length in the Peking Club. My father refused to accept his excuses and sacked him after a short talk. In this he was probably right, since the man was no longer fit for his job, but what was extraordinary was that my father saw nothing odd in it and carried the whole thing through without the slightest

qualm. This was all the stranger since he was naturally a compassionate man, who understood suffering and felt for it. But
when he was sure that he was right to be hard, he had no misgivings.

My father's Huxleyism chimed with his political views. He
saw life as a struggle for the survival of the fittest and combined
this with ideas which were current in his youth and later. He had
built up a kind of philosophy, in which he was by no means alone
and which laid primary stress on race and heredity. It is true that
he dismissed with contempt the Germans' belief that they were a
master-race, if only because in his view they were not true
Nordics but largely Slavs, whom he did not respect. He gave his
devotion to the Anglo-Saxons, and saw in them a conquering
people who had made their way through the centuries by war.
He believed that they alone were capable of good government,
and found all sorts of reasons to explain why they were better
than the Germans or the French or the Russians. This creed was
perhaps to be explained by his having been so long away from
his own country and passing most of his active life in China. He
needed some assurance to keep him going, and found it in this
questionable doctrine. Yet it did not prevent him from being
extremely understanding with the Chinese, though he missed in
them the British virtues of efficiency and honesty, or from being
in ordinary affairs unusually kind and thoughtful. Yet his unfailing self-control meant that he was very slow to give himself away
or to say all that he felt. He preferred to maintain an almost public
manner even with me, and to discuss matters with a total detachment. He was obviously a very able man, with a gift for getting
to the heart of a practical problem and coming to a clean decision
on it, but his ideas were less interesting than his individual
application of them.

He was in the last resort lonely. He got on very well with others,
but he had only two or three intimate friends, and they were men
whom he had known in his youth. Sometimes he would be
captivated by the charm of a young couple and show them all
kinds of courtesy, but then suddenly he would feel that he was
guilty of favouritism, which would never do, and no less suddenly

clamp down. They were surprised and distressed, but he was sure that he had acted rightly. His position isolated him in many ways, but he was more isolated by his stern determination not to betray his feelings. Yet, though I remained rather in awe of him and realized that I must maintain a certain distance from him, I greatly enjoyed his company. He was well read in history, not only of the Far East but of Europe. He foresaw the self-aggrandisement of Japan, and though one of his best friends was a German, he had seen too much of the Germans in China to believe that fundamentally they were a nice people. He insisted that they were neurotic and that their neuroses made them brutal. After all, when the Kaiser sent troops to China in 1900, he told them to behave like Huns, and my father knew that they did what they were told. His general ideas did not interfere with his acute judgement of actual issues. The first, deeply depressing bulletin about the Battle of Jutland reached us when we were all at a garden-party for the King's birthday at the British Legation. It sounded as if the British Navy had taken a heavy knock and the consequences might be serious, but my father dismissed all doubts by pointing out that the German Navy had gone back to harbour, and if that was not an admission of defeat, what was? His patriotism was tempered by common sense, and his observations on any issue were always worthy of attention.

I also got to know my mother much better, for while my father was at his office I accompanied her on various activities, or talked to her at home. When she was in England in 1912, she had been busy with her fourth child, my sister Francesca, and I had not seen as much of her as I should have liked, but now, having travelled out with her, I delighted in her company. She had married my father when she was nineteen, and they had remained in love with each other ever since. Neither of them was in the least attracted by anyone else, and they had an entirely happy relationship of confidence and candour. My father discussed with her matters which he would not dream of discussing with others, such as his own ambitions or his views on the men with whom he worked. She understood him completely and relied upon him for all major decisions. But she was not in the least like him. She had an excellent sense of humour, and was constantly tickled by odd moments of absurdity in people and events. She knew that his sense of humour was more limited than her own, and she liked him all the more for it, though she never made fun of him. She was not very interested in general ideas, or even in politics, except when they impinged on her family, and such views as she had she took from my father, with an occasional unexpected survival from her Liberal childhood, as when she felt keenly the pathos of the narrow upbringing given to Chinese women, or condemned the use of corporal punishment in our public schools. Unlike my father, who presented much the same personality to everyone, she had an uncommon gift for understanding people from the inside and seeing things from their point of view. This meant that she got on very well with foreigners, and it was perhaps typical that her three best women friends were a French woman, a Russian, and an Australian. Neither my father nor she was very social, and both preferred old friends to new and were happiest with a small group of people. She had excellent taste and an eye for all kinds of visible things, and it was always a delight to go shopping or sightseeing with her. She was a first-class needle-woman and made charming clothes for her daughters. If she had to choose between her husband and her children, she would have chosen her husband, and this was the choice she had to make when she left Edward and me at home in 1905. She knew that my father could not get on without her and would sink into melancholy. But she managed to look after both husband and children without showing any signs of wishing to manage them or order them about. Indeed both she and my father were remarkably sparing in criticism and left me to go my own way as I wished. If I wanted advice, they would give it, but they believed in leaving me to my own devices, and I appreciated their forbearance.

Peking gets hot in the summer, and we spent July and the first part of August at Peitaho on the sea. We bathed in the morning, slept after luncheon, and went for mild walks in the evening. There was a certain amount of coming and going with guests, but none of them stayed very long, and the chief note was of idyllic idleness. My sisters, now aged twelve and four, had friends of their own age and there were many children about the place. I had never fully known the sea before, and I formed a lasting taste for it in these golden conditions. While we were all enjoying ourselves, the war was going on in Europe, and my older contemporaries were being slaughtered on the Somme. I was painfully aware of this, and conscious that I was much better off than I ought to be. It never crossed my father's mind, any more than it crossed mine, that we could possibly lose the war. After all there was still the British Navy between us and the Germans. But neither of us really saw what a hideous price was being paid for infinitesimal results. The tiny advances hailed as victories were close to defeats, and the whole battle of the Somme was a gigantic failure. We vaguely trusted that it was wearing the Germans down, but even in his most optimistic moods my father did not think that the end of the war was in sight. As in other matters, his intelligent realism warned him against believing all that he was told.

In the not too distant future stood my call-up, and I had to be back in England for it. I came back, as I had gone out, by Siberia, and began with unfavourable omens at Mukden. I had spent the night there with my father's successor in the Customs, F. R. Brewett-Taylor, and the train left about 10 p.m. The Chinese servant, who was in charge of my luggage, took it not to the Japanese station, which was my starting-place, but to the Chinese station, which was some five miles away. I boarded my train, expecting my luggage to come, but there was no sign of it, and I started a journey of at least three weeks with nothing but the clothes I was wearing. This may have made me an anxious traveller ever since, especially where luggage is concerned, but in practice it worked out very nicely. With help from friends at Harbin I bought enough clothes for the journey and a light Japanese basket for them, and the result was that for the rest of the trip, on which porters were always lacking, I marched ahead gaily with my bundle while others had to lug their suitcases as best they could. The train-journey was much as before, but it was late summer and not spring. We stopped often at small stations, and I bought food at them, cold birds, pickled fish, and smoked sturgeon, to vary the international diet of the dining-car. When we stopped, everyone took exercise walking up and down the platforms, while the more adventurous went outside. At the sound of two bells we hurried on board and the train started at three bells. The leisureliness of the train had its dangers, and later I heard of a painful example. In the spring of 1917 two English ladies were doing the same journey from China home and started to pick flowers by the railway. They did not hear the two bells, and at the three bells ran for the train, but just failed to get on to it. No other train for passengers went that way for three years. My adventures were not up to this level. Left to my own devices I explored the very mixed set of passengers with some curiosity. I shared my coupé with a Chinese diplomat, who was going to Berlin by way of Stockholm. He was clean and quiet and spent most of the time not even sleeping but lying quietly on his berth and smoking scented cigarettes.

In the dining-car I sat with a Dutchman, a Swede, and a Norwegian. I suppose that they were in their thirties and forties, and all of them were in some kind of business. I knew nothing of business men and was not very good at talking to them, but they were friendly and at times interesting. The Dutchman had in the luggage-van a trunk full of liquor. Of this he was inordinately proud, since liquor was extremely scarce in Russia during the war and a bottle of spirits was worth its weight in roubles. He was generous with his treasure and cheered us after dinner with Green Chartreuse and Benedictine – thus improving the conversation and curing a feverish cold which I was developing. The Swede was quite different. He too had excellent manners, but was not friendly or forthcoming, and I soon found out why. He was, quite simply, pro-German and not only wished the Germans to win the war, but thought that they would. This was because, like many of his countrymen, he feared the Russians and could not hide his feelings about them. I had never met anyone on the other side, and I tried to find out what he thought. His answers were straightforward and, as I gathered later, conventional. He said, 'Look at the map,' and that meant that the Germans were winning. If he was pressed about some of the more horrible German atrocities, he shrugged his shoulders and dismissed the subject with 'A la guerre comme à la guerre,' and there was no more to be said. The Norwegian was less polished, but made a more powerful impact. He was extremely emotional and prone to burst into tears when he spoke about his wife and family. He liked the English and did not like the Swede or his views, which, he was careful to tell me, no Norwegian could possibly hold. He took a fatherly care of me and saw me through the confusion of arriving at Petrograd at midnight. The journey passed easily, although owing to the loss of my luggage I had nothing at all to read. The luggage was sent home by sea, and one suitcase eventually arrived, while the other disappeared when the ship which carried it was torpedoed.

In Petrograd I took advantage of a kind invitation which Robert Wilton had given on my way out, and asked myself to stay with him. He generously took me in at his large flat in Pochtamtskaya 20 facing the square before the Isaac's Cathedral. His wife was in England, his elder son in the British Army in France, and his younger son preparing to become an officer in the Russian Army. His flat was covered with dust sheets and only in partial use, and he himself was very busy. But he encouraged me to stay and to do what I liked. Peking had opened my eyes to what beauty a great city can have, and now when I looked at Petrograd I was, in a different way, enormously impressed. Much of it was then painted a dark red colour, with sinister suggestions of blood, but there was something superbly inhuman about this city built of granite by Italian architects among the marshes of the Neva. In their own country Quarenghi and Rastrelli could never have found patrons like the Tsars to build on so enormous a scale or to let their imaginations rip in inventing new forms of architectural splendour. The canals with their graceful bridges, the long, wide vistas down the main streets, the spire of the Admiralty, the forbidding and yet noble expanse of the Winter Palace, belonged to a world which was equally distant from London and from Peking and excited my sharpest curiosity. I had intended to spend only a few days there, but difficulties about the next stage of the journey meant that I spent nearly a month, and passed many happy hours in the Hermitage which was the first large museum I had seen, and offered to my delight Greek objects, notably vases, gems, and gold-work, such as I had not imagined to exist. Here too I had my first proper introduction to the great masters of painting and saw what vast possibilities lay ahead for exploration. I was fascinated by the large, rich, dark churches with their endless flow of worshippers, the mysterious singing behind the *eikonostasis*, the prostrations and the kissing of holy pictures, the sudden emergence of a glittering procession from its place of hiding.

Wilton was a man of much charm and kindness. He had lived for many years in Russia and absorbed the Russian instinctiveness and ease. He told me much that I wished to know, and at a time when rations were very short indeed, he looked after me much better than I deserved. As a patriotic Englishman and a devoted lover of Russia, he longed for the victory of the allies and did his best to help it by his own efforts. He had recently been as a correspondent to the Russian front in Galicia, where he had taken part in a battle with such ardour that he was awarded the Cross of St George. He took the Russian people as he found them and liked them for being what they were. He was convinced that the average soldier in their army was better fed and better clothed than at home, and he had a deep respect for the self-sacrificing courage which he had seen at the front. He had many friends, but his own sympathies were with those Russians who had no grievances against the Tsarist régime, and claimed that in Russia personal liberty was in some ways greater than in any other country. He saw Russia through aristocratic eyes, and made no criticisms of it. He was a friend of the painter Ilya Repin, who was later to be idolized as the first exponent of Socialist realism. He had also an amusing and engaging young friend, Kornei Chukovsky, who had just been to England and returned with a taste for all things English. Chukovsky was later to become a famous scholar as well as an inspired writer of books for children, and at this stage he was rich in fancy and humour and totally unpredictable in what he said and did. He spoke of a friend of his, called Vladimir Mayakovsky, whom he regarded as a genius. I hoped to

meet him, but never did. Wilton introduced me to a number of
people and, together with others who had known my parents in
China, I led an agreeably social life. It was from these that I began
to learn more about the real condition of Russia and what agonies
it was suffering.

At first sight Petrograd was not much more down at heel than
London. It was better lit, and the museums and galleries were
open. People of course were shabby, as they were in England, and
the buildings needed a coat of paint. But this was not what
mattered. Every day from dawn to darkness interminable queues
lined the streets for food. There was notably a shortage of bread,
but everything else was in hideously small supply. As the patient,
pathetic people waited for food, which in the end they might
never find, Cossacks rode up and down the line and occasionally,
for no clear reason, cracked a whip at someone. My mind went
back to Newchwang and the summary treatment of the Chinese by
the Russians, and I felt that they had not changed, despite the vast
propaganda made in England about Holy Russia. The organization
of everyday life, which had never been a strong point in Russia,
had come near to breaking down. Wilton was reticent on the
matter, as he did not like to seem in any way defeatist, but others
were more outspoken. At one tea-party I was amazed to hear
views that were quite new to me. The Empress was spoken of with
utter hostility and something like hatred as 'the German woman'
and treated as a national danger. The Tsar was mentioned with
pity and contempt and said to have no will of his own. But more
important than either was a third person whose name I heard for
the first time – Grigori Rasputin. I was enthralled by the lurid
tales, not all untrue, of this monster. Everyone seemed to loathe
and fear him, and believed that because of his fabulous hold on
the Empress and his corrupt appointments the war could never
be won and might easily be lost. This was chilling enough, but
behind it lay something vaster and vaguer, a mood not quite of
despair but of fatalistic acceptance, a belief that something appalling would happen and that nothing could be done to stop it.
There were those who spoke of revolution as inevitable and
thought that it might do good, but most saw it as the end of a

world, the annihilation of all that they had known and of themselves with it. I felt that I was witnessing the last days of Byzantium
before Mehmet the Conqueror broke through the walls, and that
the situation was literally hopeless.

Years later I was to get a remarkable sidelight on this astonishing state of affairs from a friend of my father. Nicholas Gibbes
went to St Petersburg, as it then was, about 1906 and ran a school
for the daughters of the Russian aristocracy. He did this so well
that he was appointed tutor to the Tsar's children in 1910 and
stayed with them to the end, being in the next-door house in
Ekaterinburg when they were murdered in 1918, and it was only
by an oversight that he was not murdered with them. He was
soon afterwards rescued by the White forces and brought to
Harbin, where my father found him a post in the Customs
Service. He held this for some ten years, and then had a call to
become a priest in the Russian Orthodox Church. In due course
he came to England, where he was an archimandrite and lived in
Oxford. He survived until 1963, and I saw him quite often. He
was devoted to my father and usually came to see him when he
was with me, and if we stayed up late enough, we could get
Gibbes to talk. As tutor he had lived in the precincts of the palace
at Tsarskoe Selo, and he came to know the imperial family
intimately. Though Rasputin was usually about, Gibbes did not
meet him for some time and was eventually surprised to get an
invitation to meet him in the city. He went, and Rasputin set out
to be pleasant to him. The next morning Gibbes was woken by
all five of the Tsar's children bursting into his room and saying,
'What did you think of our friend? Isn't he wonderful?' Gibbes
marked that with the Emperor and Empress Rasputin kept himself
well in hand and that his table-manners, which were much complained of by his critics, were those of a decent peasant. Gibbes
had no doubt of Rasputin's extraordinary powers over the little
boy's bleeding attacks from haemophilia, and confirmed the talk
that Rasputin could always cure them and once did so by speaking
to the boy over the telephone. He liked Rasputin's daughter, who,
he said, was the only link between the princesses and the big world.
They never went to dances, but she did, and they would question

her at length about her clothes and who was there and what dances she danced. Gibbes gave the impression that the girls were so cut off from any society, so ignorant and so innocent, that they seemed to be almost half-witted.

Gibbes became very fond of the little boy, who was high-spirited and much resented the restrictions put on him in case he should cut himself and start to bleed. He would take too many risks and was not easy to control. Even in his last days he played his own little game of outwitting his parents. On his dead body nails and tintacks were found in his coat-pocket, kept there simply because they were forbidden. Life in the huge palace was incorrigibly domestic and dull. The Empress, who was shy, anxious, and neurotic, was not easy to live with, and though the setting was magnificent, the life was drab, from the poor food and the incompetent service to the narrow round of nursery amusements. The Tsar turned all his charm on Gibbes, whom he liked and trusted, but Gibbes witnessed more than once his extraordinary double-dealing with his ministers. They would come away from an interview convinced that the Tsar would keep them in office, only to find on returning home a letter from him saying that they had been dismissed. The Emperor and Empress had a few toadies, but almost no friends, and were on poor terms with most of the Romanov family. They had little idea of what happened in the rest of the palace, and one day when Gibbes and the boy were exploring it, they came on a room where two men were breaking crockery with hammers. The explanation was that the imperial family ate from special porcelain which was reserved for them; if a piece was faulty, it could not be used by them, nor by anyone else. So two men were kept whose only task was to smash such pieces. In Tobolsk and later in Ekaterinburg the imperial family was much restricted and had very little to do. The Tsar would read through a newspaper from beginning to end, and when he had finished, would start again. They all played theatricals, and the Tsar was an excellent actor, especially in such parts as the more ineffective country gentlemen in Chekhov. Gibbes was an extraordinary survival from this extraordinary world. As he walked the streets of Oxford, in the full dress of an archimandrite, with a gold pectoral cross and a tall staff, nobody knew who he was or what he had once seen.

Other disturbing information came from some English airmen who had been teaching Russians how to fly and had recently been at the front. They may have exaggerated what they saw, but they were quite uninhibited in telling of it and extracted from it a comic horror. They spoke of the tragic shortage even of rifles and how soldiers sometimes had no weapon but a walking-stick, how supplies came with dangerous irregularity and were never enough, how high-ranking officers kept mistresses and minions at their headquarters, how Russian soldiers flung away their lives with useless extravagance. They purveyed also the gossip of the army, of ammunition which fitted German rifles but not Russian, of Jews burned to death in pogroms conducted by Russians in the occupied districts of Galicia, of fearful incompetence in completing the railway to Murmansk, of munition factories destroyed by enemy agents. They told of the most appalling events in an insouciant spirit as if they were all part of the grotesque absurdity of war. They liked the Russians very much and appreciated their generosity and gaiety, but with the assurance of British youth they felt that they themselves would do the whole thing much better. Nor were their stories much exaggerated. These things happened and in due course became generally known. But they confirmed my doubts about the stability of Russia. In my innocence I decided that, if the incompetent Tsarist system could be removed and succeeded by a democratic régime, all might be well, and I waited for this to happen. It did, in the following spring, but the sequel was not at all what I had anticipated.

While I absorbed this menacing drama, there was much else to do. I made friends with a young Russian who was an ensign in a Guards Regiment, and he helped greatly to make my life enjoyable. He took me to dine in his mess, and this solved the problem of food shortage and meant that I did not devour too many of Wilton's rations. The only danger was that my friend's fellow-officers would in the course of dinner get so excited that they would shoot the electric bulbs in the chandeliers and plunge us into darkness. The solution was to advance early to the *zakouska* and eat all you could before the fun began. My friend had a sister of remarkable beauty, who from the first moment I saw her obsessed my thoughts. She was extremely intelligent, warm-hearted, natural and quick on the uptake. She had much fancy and humour, and unlike some Russians, did not bother to talk about her soul or even about mine. While I was enraptured by her, she became very fond of me, and we passed most evenings together, with or without her brother, whom we both loved. While Russia was sinking into some primeval chaos, Petrograd offered in its theatres what must have been the highest level of the applied arts in the history of man. Chaliapine was singing at the opera; the old ballet was at its fantastic summit of skill; Chekhov was played very much as he is still played in Moscow. We went to everything that we could, and I soon understood why Chaliapine said, 'If I were not the greatest singer in the world, I should be the greatest actor', for it was his acting in *Ivan the Terrible* and in *Boris Godunov* which first revealed his genius to me. Though the music added enormously to it, it was in the combination of voice and gesture that his unique magnificence lay. The ballet had not yet been completely transformed by Diaghilev, and its most inspired exponent, Nijinsky, was away, but this too was at an incomparable level. To enjoy such spectacles in the most delightful company possible was so enthralling that I have never regained its delight. My friend had an unerring instinct for the arts and in her gentle tactful way did much to remedy my brutal ignorance. I drank in every word that she said, and still treasure it. These evenings were of an unalloyed happiness. Nothing harsh intruded on them, and I was absorbed in a magical delight. After I left Russia we wrote constantly to each other, but early in 1918 letters ceased to come from her, and many years later I learned that she had died in the Revolution, probably from starvation.

At the end of September it was time for me to go home. Wilton with his usual skill fixed my exit-visa and got me a ticket from the Finland station, which was some six months later to be the scene of Lenin's triumphant return to Russia. My journey was uneventful, and I had much to think about. I saw Wilton again, a few years after the war, when I met him casually in a London street and had a talk with him. He had joined Kolchak and told me that they had come near to victory at one point. Then Kolchak was murdered, and the whole enterprise fell to pieces. The French political agent attached to him is said to have telegraphed after his death, 'Enfin on m'a débarrassé de ce morphinomane syphilitique.' Wilton was much too good a man to work for Kolchak, but he was driven by his loyalty to the old Russia which he loved and from which he had absorbed so much in manners and outlook. He died soon afterwards.

4

The Army

Before I went to China I had consulted Edward on what branch of the army I should enter. He strongly advised the Royal Field Artillery, on the grounds that it was less uncomfortable than the infantry and that my small acquaintance with horses might be useful. I took him at his word and on arriving back in England set about to implement my plans. I visited family friends at the War Office, who indicated that all would be well, and I waited to be sent to a Cadet School. But the delay was longer than I expected, and rather than hang about at Putney doing nothing, I went to Oxford and kept the Michaelmas Term. The place was full of cadets, among them some school-friends, and undergraduates were confined to people waiting like myself, invalids, and a few Americans and Indians. I had to join the OTC and this took up a large part of each day. I also attended some lectures, but I do not remember what they were. I made a few friends, chiefly through the OTC, notably Langdon Muirhead and M.F. Barrow, both of whom were to be killed, and Tom Armstrong, who was to become a prominent and much loved figure in the world of music. I knew that this was but a shadow of the real Oxford, but I was quite content to have what I could before the call to service came. I did not even hear of the small group of intellectual undergraduates who still maintained a scholarly life due to their physical infirmity, or Irish origin, or other reason, and it was only some years later that I learned that I was in Oxford with three men who were to win various kinds of prominence, E. R. Dodds, Hugh Last and R. Palme Dutt. Most of the dons were on some sort of national service, and there was hardly any social activity, except at tea-time after the afternoon's drill. I had seen Oxford very little before, and it was not looking at its best, but it laid its hold on me, and I formed a picture of it which I found comforting in the months to come. If in its diminished present state it could be as good as this, what would it not be when it returned to full activity after the war?

I got my call-up at the beginning of 1917 and began my service as an officer cadet at what had been in peacetime a territorial headquarters in Handel Street, Bloomsbury. There I spent a month, and loathed it. We were quartered in derelict houses in Hunter Street opposite the now demolished Foundling Hospital. I felt rather as I had in my first term at Cheltenham, except that this was an even stranger and much more irrational world. But whereas then I had been alone in my misery, I now shared it with most of the other cadets. Some of them had come straight from public schools and, though conditioned to hardship, were not ready for it on this scale. Others had served in the ranks, and complained that what was expected of us now would never be expected in any decent regiment. We got up at 6 a.m. and cleaned out stables, where, since there were almost no brooms or spades, we did the 'mucking out' with our hands. We then rode horses bare-back among the trams and traffic of St Pancras and neighbouring areas, and there was always a danger that you might fall off – and what would happen then no one could foretell. From 8 to 9.30 we had breakfast and devoted every minute of the rest of the time to our 'turn-out'. Rough army boots had to be brought up to a dazzling pitch of polish, and even the part under the instep had to be blackened. Lanyards and cap-bands had to be blancoed. Worst of all, steel spurs had to be burnished, and this might take half an hour. Shaves had to be conducted with extreme precision, and all signs of dirt removed from uniforms. At 9.30 we were inspected with pedantic care. One officer had a genius for the smallest niceties and made us lift up our feet, as if we were horses, to see how the heels of our boots looked. Any spot of dirt meant confinement to barracks, and though I managed to avoid this, I more than once came too near for my liking. After this harrowing ordeal, which took about half an hour, we got down to the business of the day, which consisted of gun-drill, riding-drill, and little else. Most of the instruction was conducted by NCOs, and we seldom saw an officer after the first parade. We soon realized what kind of a place it was, and the sharpest critics were those who had come from the ranks and knew what they were talking about.

Our commanding officer was a regular soldier in the Royal Horse Artillery, 'the cloud of dust', and wore the famous and, so we were told, much coveted round buttons, as for some obscure reason we also did. His opening address set the tone for the course, and we knew how we stood when he said, 'I don't care how good your shooting may be. If you haven't got a good turn-out and fat horses, you're a bloody rotten battery.' He was a brave soldier, who had been badly wounded, and believed every word that he said, but disrespectful Australians made derisive comments. They had been in Gallipoli and in France and did not underrate the importance of shooting guns as they should be shot. When he inspected us, I was in the front rank, and he said to me, 'Have you ever been on a horse?' Knowing the danger of the smallest pretence to any accomplishment, I said firmly 'No, sir', and he replied, 'Funny. You look as if you had.' I may have had a little experience of riding, but not nearly enough to admit it, nor was it of a kind that would have helped at Handel Street, where the big event of the day was the riding-school. It was indoors and rather cramped, and the jumps were not far from a stone wall. There had been accidents not long before, and the matter had been taken up in *John Bull* by Horatio Bottomley, whom for this reason I have never been able to condemn as he deserves. We were at the mercy of a bombardier, who was reputed to have been a sergeant-major but reduced for some violent outbreak in his cups. He had certainly the authority and the confidence of a sergeant-major, and since we were merely cadets, he could do what he liked with us. After trotting us round the school, he would take us over the jumps. The horses were old and overworked and none too willing to jump, but getting them to do so was not made easier by his habit of mocking you as you were preparing to kick your mount over, 'That poor old horse has been trying to get over that jump for five minutes, and you won't let him.' If anyone fell off, he marked it with cries of 'He's going ... he's going ... he's gone.' At intervals he would halt the parade to impart more general instruction in a harsh, strident voice, and would tell us how to behave when speaking to our superiors, 'If it's an officer or a sergeant-major on parade, say "Sir!"; if it's a sergeant say "Sergeant"; if it's a corporal say "Corporal"; if it's a bombardier, say "Bombardier". It's all a matter of form, gentlemen, and it's got to be done.' And done it was.

Our other chief activity was gun-drill, which we did in the grounds of the Foundling Hospital. We practised coming into action as it might have been done at Omdurman, and became wonderfully agile at flinging eighteen-pounder guns round with their trails in the air and slamming breeches with noisy gusto. In this there were perils, since if you closed the breech too quickly you might cut off the fingers of the man who was loading. It was amusing to shout words of command in the best regular manner, to show how deft one was at tossing a heavy bit of machinery, to get warm with work in the extremely cold air. There were also disadvantages. That winter there was a lot of snow, which did murder to our steel spurs and meant that another hour in a crowded day had to be spent in getting them back to their right glory. The old soldiers regarded the whole thing as fatuous and pointed out that this was not at all the way in which guns were really brought into action. Nor was it intended to be. It was 'all a matter of form', and that is what mattered. The aim of Handel Street was to instil into us a smartness on parade which in due course we could instil into others. The old regular army had been built on this principle, and its survivors, who taught us, passed on their methods. The assumption was that, if we could respond with speed and smartness to any command, we could face any crisis in battle. The matter was well summed up by the sergeant-major when he said, 'Just you do what you're told, and you'll be all right.' If our reactions became automatic enough, we should be good soldiers. What was not in anyone's mind was that we were being trained to be officers and to take decisions in unforeseen circumstances. That was left to the actual business of war, which had very little to do with what we now learned. We concluded that the army was run by lunatics and that the wisest course was to humour them by doing what they wanted.

The routine at Handel Street was physically most exacting, and in the evening I was by no means alone in wanting to do nothing but go straight to bed. One Australian told me that for a whole month he had never thought of a woman, and this was unique in his life. No doubt bodily exhaustion was as good a way as any other to break us in. But it was reinforced by threats that if we did not do well we should be returned to our units. I was not sure what my unit was, but suspected it was the East Surrey Regiment, and did not fancy the idea, but my companions who had been in the ranks insisted that it was far better than being a cadet, and anyhow there was not the slightest chance of anyone being sent to them, for the huge daily list of casualties consisted largely of subalterns and we should all be needed to take their places. In this case a very ill wind might bring us a bit of good. Fortunately after a month we were transferred to much better quarters and conditions on Lord's Cricket Ground. We lived in the pavilion, where there was ample space for beds and we had excellent washing-rooms, which had been in short supply in Hunter Street. We had edible army food and were so hungry that we hardly noticed what we ate. Our riding-school was the holy precinct which used before the war to contain the cricket-nets. The atmosphere was quite different from that of Handel Street. Officers not only appeared on parade but even gave instruction. It was clear that they knew what they were talking about, and equally that they were not regular soldiers. Their aim was to make us understand how to make the guns hit their targets, how to read maps, how to treat mechanical breakdowns. We were allowed to abandon our steel spurs for nickel, which took only two minutes to clean, and the whole strain was vastly less exacting. Moreover with the spring the weather improved, and life began to assert its claims. By now we all knew each other pretty well, and though there were some cadets who were disliked for giving themselves airs or boasting or being 'knowing', a remarkable tolerance reigned. The common comment was that when we moved in a body anywhere it was 'as sheep led to the slaughter', and the irony only half concealed a real solidarity which was no longer founded on a hatred of our instructors.

Among us were some Australians, all of whom had seen active service and were quite unlike either the public school boys, or the men from the British ranks. I got to know and like three of them very much. Their names were Bourne, Marsh, and Freeman, and they delighted me by their total contempt for spit and polish and their professional knowledge of soldiering. They were magnificently outspoken, and their remarks had a vigour and point which were lacking in most of the English complaints. Bourne was older than the others and had a wealth of experience and anecdote. He insisted that Gallipoli was child's play in comparison with the Western front and that though the flies and smells were odious, they were nothing like as bad as Flanders mud. He knew all the tricks of military life and enjoyed the role of an old soldier. Once, we had fallen in and were standing at attention, when Bourne smartly stepped three steps forward, broke wind loudly, and stepped smartly back. This was the correct drill for such a need, but he alone knew it. The sergeant in control was on the point of explosion but not sure enough of himself to say anything. Freeman and Marsh were less unusual, but had many attractive qualities. All three were notably hostile to anything which savoured of pomposity or humbug. They suspected that the British were given to these, and they punctured them with deadly aim at their first appearance. They were themselves totally candid and full of self-mockery. Their comments on life were rich and racy, and nothing was beneath their attention. They found me less inhibited than some of the other English cadets and gave me every help in our more difficult duties, notably when we drove teams of six horses with limbers and guns on Hampstead Heath. Some of the jobs, especially that of wheel-driver, when one's leg was battered by the driving-shaft, were extremely painful, and the horses had a tiresome habit of getting their legs over the traces, but the Australians were willing to take them on while I did something less exacting. One day we were driving our teams in Regent's Park, when the Germans staged a daylight raid and dropped bombs some miles away from us. We were passing by the Zoo when it happened, and as the animals began to howl, our horses bolted and nothing could hold them. Bourne, who was in charge of my team, was not in the least dismayed, and said firmly that we must let them have their heads and all would be well. He was quite right. After a few minutes of frenzied galloping, for which their physique was ill prepared, the horses quietened down. Our instructors were horrified by what they regarded as a disgrace to the Royal Regiment, and we were paraded and addressed as if we had done something unspeakable. But the Australians were not standing for that. With calm candour they explained what had happened and that nothing could have prevented it. The parade was dismissed, and the whole matter was hushed up.

At Lord's, as at Handel Street, there was a riding-school, but it was conducted by a man of genius who turned it into uproarious farce. His name was Hance, and my brother had been under him when he was a sergeant-major at Woolwich. He had now been commissioned and had plenty of scope for his unusual gifts. After we had fallen in and mounted our horses, he would suddenly appear from nowhere at a canter, with his cap at a jaunty angle and the air of a man who had lunched well. His opening remarks were encouraging, 'This is not a riding-school, gentlemen. This is HHH – Hance's Hell House.' He soon got us going and varied the drill with a series of surprising interventions. As we were trotting round, he would shout 'Ride, halt!' and canter up to some cadet and say, 'I say, cadet, you're not a bloody fool, are you? You're not a f...ing idiot, are you? Ride, walk march.' In a similar manner he would say to some unfortunate victim, 'You're not a cadet. You're an old Piccadilly prostitute on a night-commode.' More riotous fun began when he gave the order, 'Quit your stirrups! Drop your reins!' and put us over the jumps. The horses were better than at Handel Street and usually managed to get over, but of course if anyone fell off, Hance made the most of it. He would pretend that they were dead and say, 'We often kill them here,' and then turning to his bombardier, 'When did we kill the last one, bombardier?' 'Last Tuesday, sir' came the pat, untrue answer, and all went on merrily as before. Not everyone enjoyed Hance so much as I did. The Australians took up a line that he could not ride and knew nothing about horses, and of course their manner of riding was not at all like his, as he did not fail to point out. The Englishmen who had been in the ranks complained that the whole thing was useless and absurd, since at the front horses did nothing but walk, and were lucky if they could do that, while the public school boys accepted it as part of the universe into which they had been born.

After three months at Lord's we all spent a month at Larkhill on Salisbury Plain and even learned how to fire real shells from real guns. Our treatment improved as we got on, and in July we were commissioned. I do not remember that anyone failed, and the prophets were right who had said that the casualty lists would see to that. I had leave and spent it at Clevedon where my grandparents had moved to be near my Aunt Mabel, and was delighted to see my grandmother so well settled. She was still very much herself and ran her new household with her old skill, gorging me on all the things that I most liked. Rationing was a worry to her, but she was otherwise serene and happy, as indeed was my grandfather, who could now devote the whole of his day to photography. It was the last time that I saw my grandmother. In February 1918 she received a telegram from Brazil saying that my Uncle Edward had died. She had always loved him most of her children, and the shock was too much for her. Within a few hours she was dead. She is buried in the churchyard of the old Parish Church at Clevedon, on a little hill looking over the Bristol Channel, and the inscription is more apt than such inscriptions are wont to be, 'Her husband praises her. Her children arise and call her blessed.'

Waiting to be sent to France I was posted to a depot camp near Hindhead. It was not much of an affair, with a large number of officers recovering from wounds before going back to service and troops of poor quality who needed a good deal of supervision. I

missed the gaiety and the disrespect of persons which had so enlivened Lord's, and I had no notion of how to behave in an
Officers' Mess. I began by talking too much, as I had as a new boy
at Cheltenham. I also said the wrong things. On one fatal occasion
I quoted from a story then in circulation the phrase, 'Cries of
"Order!" and "Chuck the sod out!"'. I did this in all innocence,
attaching no precise meaning to the deadly monosyllable, but
after dinner the Officer Commanding, who was known as 'Tin
Prick', told me that I had exceeded the bounds of decency and
must pull myself together. I apologized humbly, and an uneasy
peace was patched up. After this I was more wary. My lot was
lightened by a fellow-officer who was recovering from wounds
received in France, and was not only an inexhaustible mine of
information on recondite subjects, but an encouraging counsellor
on army life. I asked him what one did about being frightened in
battle, and he wisely said, 'You'll find that you are usually able to
hide it.' We were both present at an inspection by a formidable
general called Brunker, who was, I think, Inspector-General of
Artillery. He ordered a battery to be brought into action, which
was done correctly except that one sergeant was out of place.
Brunker rode up to the officer who was in command and said,
'Have you ever read *Field Artillery Training*?' 'Yes sir.' 'Read it
again. It's written by far cleverer men than you are ever likely to
have met.' None the less I found this camp a bit dreary and began
to think that the front might be better.

I went to France at the beginning of September 1917 and found
my way on a long train journey, in which I slept on the baggage-
rack, to B Battery, 298th (Army) Brigade, RFA. Army Brigades
were a recent invention of GHQ. They were detached from their
original divisions and put directly under the command of an army
or even higher. This was said to be deleterious in such matters as
decorations and paternal attentions from the big brass, and the
familiar cry went up that we were 'nobody's child'. But this had
advantages. It meant that no divisional bosses fussed us, and we
were left to ourselves, though at times we might be all but forgotten and left too long in the line. My battery had originally
been a territorial unit from Essex, but in the course of years kept

very few of its original members. It was a typical New Army concern, and it suited me down to the ground. It prided itself on never shirking its duties in action, but also on not fussing about minor details when it was out of the line. Our major was a veteran of the Boer War, a man of calm courage, humour, and tolerance, who expected us to do our own jobs without being chivvied. The battery was recovering from the Third Battle of Ypres, to which it was soon to return, and was at the moment short of officers. One, who was on the way home for good, kept me up for a large part of my first night telling me how ghastly fighting was and how bad I should be at it. I resisted his attacks on my morale, but felt that there might be something in what he said, though I hated him for saying it. Apart from the major there was a captain, whose nerves were wearing a bit thin, but who was in his unwelcoming way quite friendly, and a senior subaltern who was admirable in battle but a bit rough out of it. I was soon joined by two more subalterns, whom I had known in my training, Humphrey Campbell Jones, who had been a scholar of Eton, and Bill Saunders, who came from Surbiton. I liked both very much and was fortunate in that we all three survived and kept together to the Armistice. Campbell Jones had an engagingly arrogant manner and rigidly refused to do anything that he thought unnecessary; Saunders was elegant and gentle and did not mind being treated as a butt when he wrote long letters to his girl at home. The three of us worked together and helped each other as best we could with no nonsense about seniority or prior claims. It was a nice party, and we got on well. Somewhere in the background was Brigade GHQ, with a sardonic colonel, a competent and courteous adjutant, and two younger officers.

I joined my brigade at St Momelin, near St Omer, and we spent a few days cleaning up and refitting and were then sent back to Ypres, where despite enormous casualties and very poor advances the British Army was about to be hurled again at the Germans. When we arrived, things were comparatively quiet, and since September was a dry month, even the salient provided places where it was possible to walk and at times to take guns and transport. In October the colossal attacks began again, and with them came the rain, which always accompanied our attempts to advance. The salient reverted to a bog, an unbroken waste of mud pitted every few yards with holes full of greasy, scummy, slimy liquid and more often than not of decomposing bodies of horses or men. It became more and more difficult to get the guns into position or to keep them on the right lines after each shot, since the recoil drove their trails into the gluey clay. It was impossible to make dugouts, since water lay a foot or two below the surface, and we had to do our best with mackintosh-sheets, ammunition-boxes, and corrugated iron. The first duty of a subaltern was with the guns, and, though this was dangerous and filthy, it had its compensations. There were companions to talk to, and there was plenty to do, especially when we had to work out barrages and then fire them in the unintelligible offensives which came every few days. A second duty was to go forward to an observation post and see that the guns were firing at the right targets. This had its perils, since, if the posts were to be of any use, they had to be in full view of the enemy. Luckily they tended to be captured concrete pill-boxes, which were safe from almost any shell except the largest. Their disadvantage was that after recent fighting they were seldom free of dead Germans, who had begun to decompose and stank loathsomely and on whose field-grey uniforms sprouted a soft, grey fungus. I insisted that they should be dragged out and usually did it myself, stopping my nose and shutting my eyes. The third duty was taken in rotation and meant that you went back to the wagon-lines, which were some miles to the rear and where living was not too bad in a tent, but every night ammunition and supplies had to be taken up to the guns, for the last part on rickety, slippery duck-boards in pitch dark, broken only by the tremendous firework display which went on all night on both sides and by the explosion of shells. It was easy to lose the way, and still easier to lose the poor pack-animals. Horses tended to give up at the first wound and die, but mules, which were surer of foot and more tenacious of life, struggled to the last, even if they kicked and bit while doing so. For me this was worse than duty at the guns because I was left much more to my own devices. I had indeed an excellent NCO with me and men whom I now knew well and who did their best to get laughs out of an obscene situation, but I had to make my own decisions and felt my responsibilities a little nagging.

As everyone except GHQ knew, the trouble with Ypres was simply mud. It was this which made all advances so hideously slow and therefore murderous, which meant that even slight wounds might gangrene and kill, that supplies were ruinously hard to bring up, that morale was damaged by everyone being perpetually caked in mud, that sleep was never easy and often impossible. On a more solid terrain the huge attacks might have done much better, and the question that worried us was why the supreme command insisted on attacking here of all places. We felt that they must have a reason, and we never dreamed that they had never seen the battlefield and did not know what it was like. It was with relief, almost with exultation, that in November towards the end of the battle of Cambrai we had orders to go south to take part in it. The journey was slow, and we arrived after the main fighting, when the Germans had counter-attacked and gained important ground on our right, while our left held. We were stationed on the left in a deep German dugout by the village of Flesquières, and had never known such comfort. There were rabbit-wire bunks to sleep on and a solid cover of earth overhead. The only nuisance was rats, but fortunately a small gas-attack did for them. Intermittent fighting went on, and during one German attack I was at the bottom of a deep sap telephoning, when the only entry was blown up by a large shell, and I found myself buried. I went on mechanically working the telephone, and after a few minutes a voice answered and asked who I was. I said 'Bowra', and found it was Campbell Jones, who with his usual efficiency collected a few men and dug me out. I was beginning to feel a bit queasy and loose in the head, but I had put on my gas-mask, and it may have made some difference.

After this we spent some two to three quiet months, mostly on the high ground behind Gouzeaucort. Battle had abated while the Germans prepared for their next blow, and we made ourselves comfortable in an excellent dugout. There was still a certain amount of shelling, but one soon learned how to avoid it, since the methodical Germans tended to pound away at a single target for some minutes, and if you were clear of the first shell, you might avoid the rest. In the mess we played very bad bridge, not much better poker, and made incessant use of a portable gramophone which was supplied with records sent from England, mostly from the wonderful revues of the time and much featuring the inspired songs of George Robey and Violet Lorraine. An occasional well-known aria from Verdi or Puccini was the utmost concession to highbrow tastes. The ground was hard and easy to walk on; supplies presented no problems, since they could be brought up by day, and the change of situation confirmed our view that what was wrong with Ypres was simply the mud.

At the end of February we moved south to where the British Army had taken over from the French, and ended up opposite St Quentin near a place called Jussy. The country was desolate, having been devastated by the Germans when they made the calculated retreat called 'Alberic' in the spring of 1917, and we lacked anything in the way of comforts behind the line. In March I went on leave to England, and spent most of it with my Aunt Mabel. I got back to the railhead on the evening of 20 March. My batman met me with a horse; there was a moon and a thin mist. On getting to my battery wagon-lines I was told, 'The Germans are attacking tomorrow morning, and you must go up at dawn to the battery.' At 4.30 a.m. a high-velocity shell whistled over our flimsy roof and burst near by. I at once got up, collected a few items of equipment, and rode up to the battery, which was in reserve. An attack had begun. It was the first stroke of 'Michael', of the 'Kaiserschlacht', by which Ludendorff hoped to cut off the British forces from the French and drive us into the sea. Shells were falling heavily on all the roads and cross-roads, but I cut safely across country. I was lucky to start when I did, since a few minutes later a large shell fell on our flimsy mess and totally destroyed it with everyone and everything in it. At the battery things were fairly quiet till about noon when the mist began to lift and the first parties of Germans, moving in small groups, came into range. We fired at them and did some damage, especially as they seemed rather slow and tired after their efforts. But when they came nearer, we packed up hurriedly and retired, and this was the normal routine for the next few days – taking up positions, engaging the enemy if possible, then limbering up and retreating. It was extremely wearisome, as we hardly got any sleep. Much of the movement had to be done at night and was costly in both men and horses. On the third night we had settled down with a sense of relief when a staff-officer in a state of wild excitement arrived and told us we must move off at once since the Germans were only a few minutes away. We found bridges intact, and this enabled us to get over the local canals. Though the Fifth Army command was savagely criticized at the time and afterwards, we kept in touch with our superiors and received intelligible orders. We got our guns away safely and must have inflicted considerable damage with them. At one point I was told to deal with some Germans who were said to be using the cathedral at Noyon as an observation post. I was sure that they were, but at first I had qualms about firing on the noble Gothic building which was in full view from my post on a small hill. Then I remembered that Noyon was the original home of John Calvin, and my qualms vanished. I felt that nothing could be too bad, even after some four centuries, for this enemy of the human race, and I set to work with care. I fired a plus and a minus, and my third shot fell neatly into the middle of the church. The retreat lasted for some ten days and had many nasty moments. More than once we seemed to be on the point of being surrounded by the enemy, but we always managed to get away. After a few days the strain and the pace slackened, and it was a wonderful relief to see French troops, with their guns laden with all sorts of equipment including bird-cages and gramophones, coming into action as we turned northwards towards Amiens.

We took up our position to the west of Villers Bretonneux, and the cathedral at Amiens was in full view behind us. The Australian and New Zealand Army Corps had just come up and filled the large gap in the front. They began by taking Villers Bretonneux in the middle of the day, when the Germans were guzzling the wine in the many undamaged cellars. I had an excellent, if rather exposed, view of a consequent operation, and watched the Anzacs clearing the Germans out with bayonets. Many years later I found that almost immediately opposite me was Heinrich Brüning, who was to become Chancellor of the German Republic and was then a major in a machine-gun unit. He wisely retreated at once and formed a view of the Australians, which he never retracted, that they were the finest troops in either army. They were indeed a remarkable body of men. I had already learned some of their ways when I was a cadet, and I now knew that I was right to admire them. I met my old companion Marsh, who told me that Freeman was well but that Bourne had been invalided out. The Australians had marked idiosyncrasies. They did not salute British officers, and they were liable to 'scrounge' any property which they found unguarded, especially horses and ammunition. Behind the lines their discipline was notoriously lax, and hard tales were told of what they did to harmless French villages. But in the line it was another story. They were men of magnificent physique, trained to life in the open and entirely at home with both animals and machines, and when they went into action, they shirked nothing and were determined to win. Soon after we joined them, they did a tidying-up operation by the small town of Corbie, and I saw it from a neighbouring slope and arranged that our guns did what was wanted. It was before dawn, but there was a moon, and I had a front seat for the whole action. After a small smoke barrage the Australians advanced at a leisurely pace with fixed bayonets and dug the Germans out of their trenches. The action was a complete success and a happy omen of others to come.

At this time we had the misfortune to lose our battery-commander, who was severely wounded in the back and sent to hospital in England. He was some years older than the rest of us and stood the hardships of the retreat with a humorous patience, being particularly pleased when Brigade HQ lost their portable lavatory seat, with a back and arms, to the enemy. Our new major, a podgy, pudding-faced man, was quite young and came from a regular division of which he was proud more for social than for military reasons. He thought us undisciplined colts and imposed a number of routine duties in which we saw no point. We did what we were told, and were studiously polite, calling

7. The author, Sylvester Gates and Leslie Hartley, at Garsington, 1924

8. The author with the Wadham VIII in 1924

9. Reading party at Hartland Quay, 1925, including Cecil Day-Lewis, Rex Warner, and the author

10. John Sparrow and the author at Naas, 1926

12. Evelyn Waugh at Villefranche, 1930

13. John Betjeman at Uffington, 1934

11. Hugh Gaitskell on the Lido, 1927

14. Alan Blakeway in Greece in 1936

him 'Sir' on every occasion. But we reserved our gayer moments for ourselves, and in time he began to feel that he was out of things, and modified some of his stiffer pretensions. There was plenty to do, and in splendid weather we lay between Villers Bretonneux and Amiens, getting ready for our revenge on the Germans. Though the news through April, May, and June was uniformly bad, we were certain that our next move would be not backwards but forwards, and for this we waited. We spent some time behind the line training in the green unspoiled country by the Somme. We even bathed in the river, despite the perils of occasional shells and even more of hand-grenades which the Australians threw into the water to stun the fish and bring them to the surface. In our spare time we were sustained and delighted by newspaper accounts of the Pemberton Billing case, in which Mr Justice Darling dealt most ineptly with allegations of a 'black book' which contained the names of 47,000 people said to be perverts. We did not see it as an example of the hysterical spirit which was rife in England, but took it all as a splendid joke. It did much to restore the morale of the British Army at a dark period, and we tried to believe that it was organized by the government for this purpose. But not even Lloyd George would have dared to do that.

We had our reward on 8 August 1918 when the Anzacs and Canadians attacked the German line east of Villers Bretonneux. We were behind the Australians and much closer to their infantry than we were usually allowed to be. The ground was cluttered with field-guns and immediately behind them were the howitzers varying from 4.5 inch to 9.2 inch. On 7 August there was a nasty moment when a casual German shell hit a dump of ammunition which went on exploding for about half an hour, but the Germans drew no conclusions, and on the next day the attack caught them by surprise. Our job was first to provide a moving barrage for the Australian infantry, and at this we were now quite expert, and the ammunition was much more reliable. Then, we were to move forward behind the attackers. Since they advanced according to schedule, we followed without trouble. Tanks were at last sent into action in large numbers on dry, unbroken ground with a proper appreciation of their value. The Australians claimed that they had found out how to use them with full effect and were rightly proud of it. No pockets of enemy troops were left in hiding, and the clearance was done with a prodigious zest. The Australians pushed ahead with such speed that they captured a divisional headquarters at its lunch and, realizing the difficulty of looking after so many high-ranking prisoners, made it impossible for them to get away by the simple expedient of cutting off all their breeches-buttons. By the end of the day all the objectives had been reached, and we settled into new positions with a wonderful sense of having done something at last. This was one of the few days in my military life when I felt the terrifying fascination of battle. The sinister silence before zero-hour, the sudden, simultaneous, deafening start of the barrage, the emergence of the tanks and their accompanying infantry, the struggle, always successful, to take well-held positions, the decisive advance forward, all contributed to a wild exhilaration in which we conducted our duties with fits of laughter and uproarious jokes.

After this splendid day we knew that the tide had turned and that we should win the war. We had never thought that we should lose it, but we thought that it might last for years. The end came much sooner than we anticipated. After 8 August there was much heavy fighting, and we had serious losses. But we moved steadily forward. We lost both our major and our captain from wounds. Their places were taken by two men, both in their early twenties, who added to our gaiety and solidarity. The new major, called Brown, was an ideal commander. He never took anything too seriously and knew exactly what his men could do and what not. He always stood by his subalterns, as when Campbell Jones, in an exhilarated moment, was rude to the Brigade Commander on the telephone and given a terrific dressing-down, but Brown bravely insisted that it was not really deserved. When I had been sent forward with two guns to support the attacking infantry, now, alas, no longer the Australians, the authorities left us without supplies or orders for two days. My men were tired out and at their wits' ends, but I sent word to Brown, who went at once to the

Brigadier and saw that we were relieved. Brown was a man of much fancy and charm, who indulged certain eccentric tastes, such as pornography. He had a book called *The New Lady's Tickler*, which he read aloud with an ecclesiastical unction and mocked for the pomposity of its style and the absurd periphrases which it used for physical actions and parts of the body. When I recall these readings, I cannot but see a certain likeness between this ridiculous work and some parts of *Lady Chatterley's Lover*, and that is perhaps why I have never been able to treat the latter seriously. Brown's conversation was entirely his own. He liked improprieties, but spoke of them in a language so brilliantly inventive that it was impossible not to laugh. He was, I suppose, badly educated but he had a natural love of words and when by accident he discovered Fitzgerald's translation of Omar Khayyam, he was fascinated by it and could talk of nothing else for days, finding its nihilistic philosophy much to his taste. I met him once after the war in a train, and, though he was now married, he was exactly the same and gave me a lot of spicy gossip on the peacetime activities of our colonel who had got himself attached as a Gentleman Usher to the court at Buckingham Palace. As Vice-Chancellor I met him there in 1952, when I went on a delegation from Oxford to pay our loyal respects to the present Queen on her succession to the throne. Brown would have much enjoyed the spectacle of this disillusioned man acting as usher to a party of dons.

When the Armistice was announced, we were at a small town called Sains du Nord. It was a dark dreary day, and though everyone felt an immense relief that the killing had stopped, there was an uneasy fear that the Germans might resume hostilities and an obsessing certainty that all the dull routine of looking after horses and kit would have to go on. Nor did the Battery Sergeant-major make things easier, when, after the manner of his kind, he said, 'Now that the war is over, we can get down to real soldiering', since everyone knew what that meant. Brown made me approach the local authorities, who rose to the occasion. Bottles of wine were produced from middens and wells, and though the ration was naturally small, everyone felt it was a royal occasion.

We moved forward after the Germans and ended up near Charleroi, where we had good billets and had to devise means to diminish the appalling boredom which lay ahead. Brown fixed up games for the troops, and I had to play football with them. We also had lectures, and Brown spoke brilliantly, if fancifully, on 'Chinese tortures'. We spent Christmas Day in some comfort and not only introduced the local *curé* to whisky but joined him in singing *Adeste fideles* in Latin. Campbell Jones and I knew the words, while the others improvised sounds with irreverent ingenuity. At the end of the year I was sent on a course for education officers at Oxford, and though I attended the full course and much enjoyed it, I took the opportunity to get myself demobilized at the end of it and so severed my connection with the army.

The war taught me a great deal. I was eighteen when I joined up and not yet twenty-one when I was demobilized; so I was still at a very impressionable age, and the impressions I received were forcible. I found that in this life of action, which called for immediate decisions and was spent entirely in the company of other men, it was both necessary and possible to maintain some sort of inner life. My fellow-officers were quite happy that I should read books instead of talking and never made fun of me for doing so. When the front was quiet or we were behind the lines, I read a good deal. Whenever I could, I bought French books and devoured almost the whole of Anatole France, whose low but kindly view of humanity was well fitted to army life, and I had books sent out from England. I saw that in my classical education I had an asset of which I had hitherto made nothing, and I read Homer, Virgil, and Tacitus. I was of course hampered by a lack of dictionaries and commentaries, but Exton had taught me better than I thought, and I was able to puzzle the texts out, even if I often did so wrongly. This was a useful lesson. At school I had idled, but now I saw that to do nothing was insufferably boring, and I formed a habit of reading in almost any circumstances, which I have managed to keep. Neither noise nor discomfort disturbed me, and in the end I covered quite a wide range. I also kept up, to the best of my ability, with modern works, especially English poetry. I made some discoveries, and on one leave bought on a single occasion Thomas Hardy, *Moments of Vision*, W. B. Yeats, *The Wild Swans of Coole*, and T. S. Eliot, *Prufrock and other Observations*. The last both puzzled and fascinated me. I could not get the lines out of my head, but was not certain what significance they had for me. I wrote about this to my friend Barrow, who replied that they were the real thing. He was himself a poet, and the last letter I got from him before his death, contained a short poem which ended,

> Love? No, for the crows call us,
> And all things are mixed in the perhaps
> Of a nescient eternity.

I was still not at all sure what I liked or admired, and tried to extract the best from any author that I read. This habit I have never quite lost, though I realize that it is a grave disqualification for anyone who wishes to write about literature or claims to be in any respect a critic. The blessed word 'evaluation' was not yet lying in ambush to spoil my pleasure.

This inner life was in no way incompatible with the extrovert duties which had a first claim on me. Many of these were pure routine and could be conducted without any great effort. More interesting was their human side. With some of my fellow-officers, as I have indicated, I formed ties of real affection, and only for one or two did I feel anything like dislike. This I managed to conceal under a mask of correct behaviour. With the other ranks relations were more formal but in the end hardly less intimate. Our soldiers came from all parts of Great Britain and from very different backgrounds. In moments of danger or excitement or even of frustrating tedium they would relax their restraints and tell me about their families and their jobs in time of peace. On the surface they had developed what seemed to be a callous indifference to death, and if someone was killed, might say 'He's had it', or 'There's another gonner', but this was their defence against feelings which they might otherwise not have been able to master. They looked after one another with protective care, and more than once I was saved from damage by some gunner telling me peremptorily to lie down because a shell was on its way towards us. Beneath their endless grumbles, punctuated all the time with the same inevitable adjective, lay a powerful desire to get their jobs done and to remain themselves in doing them. They looked after the wounded with a total disregard of their own safety and showed a motherly kindliness in getting them back to the dressing stations. I remember no case of a man shirking his job, even though it might seem to be and often was futile and dangerous. Equally they never made any show of enthusiasm. One young officer showed an exemplary keenness in his desire to kill the enemy, but he was thought to be showing off and never won the respect of his men or the liking of his colleagues.

In later years I have often been asked why we went on as we did, without objecting to the often murderous tasks to which we were assigned. After all, the French mutinied in large numbers during the Chemin des Dames – why did not the British during Third Ypres? To this I have no clear answer. I certainly do not think that our soldiers were kept to their task by the sinister printed notices which came far too often from GHQ, saying that someone or other had been sentenced to death for cowardice in the face of the enemy and duly shot. It is true that once or twice men were so shaken by a bombardment that they quivered all over, but it was not their fault, and they were properly sent back to base. Even if someone had shown real cowardice in battle, I doubt if we would have done anything about it. Courage is not a thing to be commanded at will, and nobody pretended that it was. Nor do I think that many were moved by high ideals of what we were fighting for. The violation of Belgium and the first German atrocities belonged to past history. They might have incited some to join up at the start, but they were now forgotten, and the poor 'Jerries' were regarded as men very like ourselves, doomed to an unnatural and hideous existence. It was true that we had to kill them, but they had to kill us, and we could call it quits. What held soldiers to their work was an almost unconscious conviction that to shirk was to let one's fellows down. A comfortable wound or a nice transfer to the rear was an act of God, much to be welcomed, but any deliberate attempt to get away was not to be seriously thought of. This sense of solidarity and of its worth was a lesson inculcated by the war, and it extended to all ranks. Before I joined the army I had lived in a very select and privileged class, knowing nothing and caring very little about the ways of other men. The war opened my eyes to the basic similarity of human beings and the absurdity of artificial distinctions between them. Even paternal care meant very little, for though it was my task to look after my men, it was usually they who looked after me, and were more capable of dealing with a sudden crisis than I was.

Against these valuable lessons which I learned from the war must be set its endless menaces. As I saw more of its realities, I found that, instead of becoming hardened to them, I disliked them more and more, and though I accepted fatalistically the possibility of death, I was increasingly frightened of being gravely wounded with no hope of rescue as one died slowly in agony. I managed to control and hide my fears, but the memory of the carnage and the filth has never left me. Yet, the war did me a lot of good. It greatly extended my horizon, reduced my conceit, and formed in me a love for the comradeship that comes from living with other people and sharing their interests and their work. All this I owe not to the army but to the war. In peacetime I could never have endured the army, and I am grateful that my experience of it was confined to war, when I found its fantastic improvisations vastly preferable to the spit and polish of Handel Street.

5

New College
1919–22

I had in the army built up an imaginary picture of Oxford as a place for which it was worth fighting. My war aim, such as it was, was to get back to a life which I saw in highly romantic colours and in which I hoped to find the freedom of spirit and speech which had been impossible at school and only partially possible in the army. I imagined myself as mixing with other young men who shared my interests and with whom I would be on terms of equality and frankness, neither side having to make concessions to the other. If I had known more about Oxford before 1914, I doubt if I should have indulged such a daydream. In those boisterous years the privileged young relieved their ebullience in outbursts of violence. Philip Sassoon was chased out of Balliol by young aristocrats with whips, and at New College it was a common amusement on summer evenings to take the furniture from a man's room and burn it. The victim need not necessarily be unpopular or have come from the wrong school; what counted was the thrill of incendiarism. Nor should I have liked certain conventions which then governed undergraduate life, such as that men should confine themselves to others of their own year and that it was proper to dress up in full finery on Sundays. I knew nothing of these oddities and nurtured my fancies without them, and there was no reason to think that I should be justified. But I was. My fancy became a reality, and my life as an undergraduate was all that I could have hoped, and more.

Though I was demobilized in February 1919, I did not come properly into residence till April for the summer term, which even at the time seemed to enjoy unbroken days of sunshine from start to finish. I had rooms in the old quadrangle of New College and despite many shortages found them entirely comfortable. I did not complain, as the Rhodes scholars did, that I had to walk some distance across the open to get a bath or that I had to pay for it when I got there; I was quite happy to eat breakfast and luncheon in the Junior Common Room, and I found the dinners in Hall good and remarkably cheap. I felt no insult to my personal honour in having to be in college by midnight or in not being allowed to walk on the grass in the quadrangle. I suffered from none of the conflicts which Kipling depicted at the time in his poem *The Clerks and the Bells*. It is true that after living for two years in the open air, I went to sleep at all hours of the day simply because I was indoors, but I made up for it by staying up later at night. After a long sojourn in devastated countrysides the buildings and the gardens of the college were an unfailing astonishment and delight. But what enthralled me was the number of young men of about my own age among whom I made friends. There were a few survivals from before the war, but they ate apart and were known as the Brontosaurs. They did not attempt to revive pre-war habits, and if they had, they would have met with a poor response. There were also boys who had come straight from school, but we did not feel any gap between them and ourselves. If we wished to forget the war, they did not wish to hear about it, and both parties started from the same point of hoping to get the most out of Oxford. They too had suffered hardships and restrictions at school and were only too glad to be rid of them.

My immediate circle consisted both of ex-soldiers and of boys straight from school. Cyril Radcliffe had been a subaltern in the Labour Corps and published a volume of poems called *Spring's Highway*, which reflected with much dexterity the influence of A. E. Housman and Austin Dobson; Hugh Francis had had a tough time in the army but nothing daunted his ebullient gaiety or his devout Anglo-Catholicism; Eric Strauss, who wore a monocle and was a convert to Roman Catholicism, had been badly wounded in the infantry; Idris Deane Jones had been in the Air Force and was still suffering from a serious crash; Henry Price had also been in the Air Force but seemed to survive it unscathed; Anthony Steel had been commissioned in the RASC and served in France and Germany. On the other hand Roy Harrod had not got beyond being a cadet; Amyas Ross came from Repton, where he had been a brilliant pupil of two very unconventional school-masters, Victor Gollancz and D.C. Somervell; Stephen Tomlin, who came from Harrow, was more mature than most of his elders and soon established a remarkable ascendancy over some of them; his friend Hew Anderson was essentially an artist, but insisted that he must first learn philosophy. We did not form a set, and I had other friends outside those I have named, but most of these I saw every day, or sat with at meals, or visited in the evening. These were the first people I knew at all well, and they set the tone for my undergraduate life at New College.

In the years immediately after the war undergraduates managed to combine seriousness with frivolity without letting either spoil the other. Politics could not fail to be of interest. My own ideas were chaotic, but I had been deeply impressed by the intrusion of Woodrow Wilson into European affairs and saw him as a possible saviour of a distressed world. I had very little against the Germans, whom I regarded as fellow-sufferers with myself, and I abominated the hysterical cry of 'Hang the Kaiser!' In the 'coupon election' of 1918 I voted for an Asquithian Liberal, who of course failed to get in. My friends at New College held very various views. Strauss posed as a diehard Conservative, and Cyril Radcliffe saw all politics in a wider unity of some monistic metaphysic. But Harrod, Francis, and Deane Jones were of the radical left, while Ross claimed to be a Bolshevik and inveigled me against my better judgement into speaking at a college debate in favour of the detested Soviet régime. I did it badly, and could only argue that Russia, as I had seen, was in such a mess that revolution was inevitable. I made a poor impression on the more respectable members, who thought me, not without reason, frivolous. Ross was an impassioned and ingenious debater, in full revolt against existing institutions, but though everyone liked him, he was dismissed as a fanatic. Abler and better informed was Harrod, who instilled into me the view that the war was quite unnecessary and could easily have been avoided. From this shock I have never fully recovered.

We were all more or less convinced that another war could not come in our lifetime and that there was no need to punish Germany too savagely, since anyhow she must be ruined and it looked as if the military domination of Prussia was finished. Nor did we feel that France should be too generously indulged with compensations. Few of us regarded Bolshevist Russia as dangerous, and in this we differed from our Conservative friends who were already in a panic about her. As soon as the terms of the Versailles Treaty were known, we were bombarded by talks about it. Some were well-informed but too technical to arouse much response, as when the speakers pointed out the danger of including three million Germans in Czechoslovakia or of breaking up the Austro-Hungarian Empire. Randall Davidson, Archbishop of Canterbury, preached in St Mary's Church from the text, 'Mercy and truth are met together; righteousness and peace have kissed each other', but despite his elegant language did not show what this should mean in practice. Far more stirring was the revivalist eloquence of George Lansbury, who spoke with passion on the need to translate the Sermon on the Mount into action and on the wickedness of punishing the Germans. It is a tribute to our various upbringings that we welcomed him with our hearts, if not with our heads. We longed so eagerly for peace and were in so strong a reaction against war that we allowed our thoughts to be swayed more by hopes than by realities. Our trouble was that we knew nothing about the Germans and believed that defeat would teach them wisdom. It was not for some years that I saw that it had done nothing of the kind.

Though we complained of French policy and did not understand what strong reasons lay behind it, we were more interested in home affairs, and though we distrusted Lloyd George, we believed that he was right to demand that England should be a fit country for heroes to live in. Not that we thought anyone a hero, but because we thought that social reform was anyhow overdue and more than deserved by a generation which had given so much for its country. At first this meant little more than a considerate discussion of social questions. Roy spoke with an old-fashioned rotundity at the Union, but the rest of us, especially Ross, were content with the New College debating society, which allowed a decent measure of frivolity. But as the first shock of peace wore off, and the Coalition Government revealed its seamy side, feelings grew stronger, and political disagreements sharper. In May 1920 the men of the Oxford bus company went on strike, and it was thought that they had good cause. Deane Jones was passionately concerned. He felt that this was a test case for the post-war world and that he must do something about it. The strikers staged demonstrations in Oxford, and Deane Jones went into action. He jumped on to one or two buses run by blacklegs and threw off the conductors. Fortunately the police did not see him, and he came home flushed with victory. The news spread quickly, and two nights later after dinner I saw marching towards his room, which was beneath mine, a group of about ten of the more gentlemanly members of the college. I sniffed trouble and quickly summoned Roy Harrod and one or two others and warned Deane Jones. It was just in time. The party marched solemnly into his room, and the ringleader made a pompous speech about 'dragging the name of the college in the dirt'. Deane Jones answered with contemptuous disdain, and for a few minutes impolite words were exchanged. The ringleader then said, 'Enough of words. Let's get to work', but he was too slow. Before he had finished Deane Jones, with a magnificent leap, fell on him, and brought him to the ground, where he proceeded with some effect to pummel him. The others did not know what to do and looked sheepishly on, but next to me was a man whom I thought insufferable; so I went at him with my knees and fists and brought him down. Roy also did some useful work. The row might have become worse, but the door opened and the senior science tutor, A. F. Walden, entered and said with impressive authority that at the Warden's orders we must stop at once. How he knew what was happening

I do not know, nor do I believe that the Warden had given any orders. But it worked, and the invaders walked out. We had no more trouble from them and even took advantage of their humiliation to make them withdraw their candidate for the presidency of Junior Common Room. This was the only affair of its kind in my time as an undergraduate. Deane Jones had put himself in the wrong by his violent behaviour, but what my friends and I resented was the decision of a self-appointed body of judges to inflict punishment on him. This smacked of the days before the war when unpopular or socially incorrect undergraduates were beaten up by their richer contemporaries, and this was why we minded it so strongly. The row was soon forgotten. In later years Deane Jones did not like to be reminded of it, but at least he had nothing to be ashamed of in his handling of his chief opponent.

Politics was not really our first interest. More often we talked of other matters which lay closer to what we were actually studying but did not necessarily belong to it. The visual arts took a larger place than literature, but our tastes were conventional. We had scarcely heard of Corbusier or the Bauhaus, and were much more at home with the Impressionists than with Picasso. In fact most of us were more concerned with the past than with the present. I went to Provence in 1920 and to Italy in 1921, where I was overwhelmed first by Florence and then by Ravenna. Very few of us had travelled in our boyhood, and we enjoyed to the full the pleasures of surprise, since picture-books were rare and not very good, and we kept on discovering buildings and paintings of which we had never heard. Music did not mean much to us, though Strauss played the piano and composed a 'March of the Catholic Gentlemen' and a jazz version of 'Abide with me'. What we really liked were general ideas, which could be analysed and discussed and made to provoke concrete questions. The new psychology was beginning to seep through and gave a new dimension to talk about character and behaviour. Einstein's first views on relativity were in circulation, and raised fascinating doubts on the nature of Euclidean space on which we had been brought up. But we could not discuss it very carefully because we were not scientists or mathematicians. Our ignorance of science was dismal, but we were uneasily aware that we ought to know more. Ross, who was an eager advocate of new causes, deluged us for a time with eager accounts of Major Douglas's credit theories, no doubt because they seemed to offer some escape from the communism which he was beginning to find burdensome.

The forum in which ideas were most fully discussed was the New College Essay Society, which had about fourteen members and met once a week on Saturdays in the Michaelmas and Hilary Terms. It had a Latin ritual, invented at the end of the last century, and a loving-cup of mulled claret was passed round after a paper had been read and before the discussion began. The papers read had seldom any direct relation to the course a man was taking and tended to represent some other interest which he nurtured more or less secretly. This added to their originality and their personal appeal. Henry Price, who was our most able philosopher, read about Byzantine history; Deane Jones described the architecture of Santa Sofia; Roy Harrod read about *The Lady from the Sea*, which was less about Ibsen than about himself as the only son of a widowed mother. I read rambling papers on 'Theocracies' and 'The Comfortable Life', which provided pegs on which I could hang titbits of amusing or recondite information. The papers produced good discussions, which were formal in the sense that the speaker stood up in front of the fire-place and made a short speech. This prevented what happens so often in debating societies – the decline of discussion into random and aimless talk. The members had their own ways of speaking. Cyril Radcliffe commanded even at this time a perfect control of his sentences, never hesitated for a word, and knew exactly what degree of sentiment to strike; Roy Harrod employed the eloquence that he practised in the Union and punctuated his speeches with such phrases as 'I dare aver' or 'if you will permit the observation'; Henry Andrewes, who was rather older than the rest, spoke with much feeling and handled philosophical matters in a manner not usual in Oxford, with oracular pronouncements such as 'We are gradually moving from individualism to individuality'; Strauss, who had anti-intellectual leanings, introduced his own kind of Catholicism when he said that in Heaven 'we shall laugh with

God at God'; Gordon Catlin, who drew upon a wide range of knowledge on political science, would throw out such remarks as 'History is cognized change'. Most of us had been maturing our own thoughts too long in solitude, and now had a chance of bringing them to the light. We took it greedily, and though what we said was very seldom important, it was part of the business of growing-up and laid the foundations of what we were later to be.

We did not discuss each other, anyhow to our faces. Roy had some friends at Christ Church who did this ruthlessly and spent much time and talent on analysing one another. We rejected this as indecent, and though we gossiped with avidity, we did not like the idea of humiliating one another. Nor did we report unpleasant things that we heard other people say about our friends. This, like mutual analysis, was regarded in some places as healthy criticism, but not by us. We thought it offensive, but more deeply we were too unsure of ourselves to feel that we could take it quietly. What we did discuss was our work, not merely for its own sake but for its impact on us. Apart from Strauss, who, having abandoned the idea of becoming a diplomat on the grounds that 'nowadays you can't even make a war till you're fifty', was reading medicine, with a view to becoming a psycho-analyst, most of us were reading for either Greats or History. We were for the most part entitled to start on our final schools without preliminaries and nearly everyone did. I had made up my mind to do Literae Humaniores, but I havered with extreme indecision how to do it – should I do the full course of Mods and Greats, or should I go straight for Greats? Mods was rather looked down upon, since it consisted only of Greek and Latin language and literature, while Greats offered the alluring prestige of philosophy. I began by going straight for Greats, and was sent for tuition to H. W. B. Joseph, a most formidable and unusual man. He was short and stocky, had a large head, and a pronounced jaw. He was totally devoted to the college and gave to his teaching an energy and care which would have destroyed most other men. His aim was to make his pupils think correctly, and this aim he pursued with no care for their vanity or self-respect. He insisted that words must be used with absolute precision, and before you had read two sentences of an essay he began to point out the contradictions in them. He himself had an astonishing gift for formulating fully shaped sentences which contained no such contradictions, and he expected us to do the same. We could not, partly because we had not drilled our minds to do so, partly because his use of words gave them meanings different from ours. He treated me as he treated everyone else, and I was paralysed, as I had been when I first went to Cheltenham. I was unable to answer his questions, and this, which was really a total lack of self-confidence, he mistook for conceit, and became even more merciless. He was particularly hard on any kind of metaphor and when told in the discussions on Einstein that 'space was warped', he answered, 'But what is it warped in?' I had thought that philosophy was a far-ranging, generous discussion of large matters such as the nature of knowledge and of being, and Joseph had his views on these, but you had to find out the answers for yourself and to use his language in doing so. I was no good at this and did not yet see that it was largely a matter of linguistics, of mastering a special vocabulary. I floundered with my own very imprecise language and was totally foiled and humiliated. In the wonderful summer term of 1919 my weekly visits to him were increasingly dark episodes to be faced with fear and anxiety.

Towards the end of the summer term I decided that this would not do, that I must make a decision of some kind or other. To read another school was absurd, since after all I had a decent knowledge of Latin and Greek and would be spendthrift not to use it. At this point I met in the street an odd, engaging character whom I had known since Cheltenham days. His name was A. S. Owen, and he had been both a boy and a master at Cheltenham and took a kindly interest in Old Cheltonians at Oxford. He had become a don at Keble before the war and had taken me out to a dinner and a theatre more than once when I was in the army. He was delightfully unkempt and ungainly, and deserved the nickname of 'the Crab' from the way he swung a malformed arm. But he rejoiced in it and there came the rapturous moment when he would say 'Call me Crab', and you did. He never succeeded in having a proper shave, and his face was marred by cuts and little tufts of hair, while his waistcoat carried many signs of his breakfast and his cigarettes. He was a good scholar of the old school and in his dry way highly cultivated, with a memory which seemed to forget nothing and emboldened him to contradict you on points on which you were quite certain. But he was generous and kind and not lacking in worldly wisdom. On the fateful day when I met him, he asked me what I was doing, and I told him 'Greats' and explained why I was unhappy about it. He at once told me that I should go back to start, do Mods, and think of becoming a don in that subject. I was not so sure about the ultimate aim, but the immediate plan was clearly right. I went to see Joseph, who was not welcoming. He first told me that if I went on with Greats I might possibly get a second class, and he seemed to think that I should be content with that. He then argued that since Mods would be in the following March, I should have to do five terms' work in two, but I pointed out that there was to be a special Mods in the summer, and that I was sure I could do the work by then. He denied the existence of such an examination, but I showed him the notice in the *University Gazette*, and with no good will he gave in. An enormous load was off my mind. I could now go back with confidence to Greek and Latin literature in which I was deeply interested, and I was determined to work as hard as possible at it. The splendid summer term ended with the removal of its one dark spot, and I knew where I stood.

At this time the Senior Common Room of New College was still suffering from losses in the war. Four Fellows had been killed, and since three of these were tutors in Mods and Greats, the classics were particularly hit. Joseph remained as a prodigious performer, but he was not well assisted, since the surviving ancient history tutor, Percy Matheson, was past his prime and the Mods tutor was still in Singapore. But the vacancies were gradually filled, and the Senior Common Room took shape in my eyes. The Warden was Dr W. A. Spooner, who was now seventy-five years old, but showed no signs of decrepitude or of being different from what he had always been. He was small with very white hair and a cherubic, pink face. He was very short-sighted and read with a magnifying glass. Though he was responsible for the word

Spoonerism being added to the language to describe the transfer of initial consonants between two words, as in 'half-warmed fish' for 'half-formed wish', I never heard him make one, and he was sensitive to any reference to the subject. Once, when at a College Gaudy a Judge of the High Court made a ponderous joke about 'New College' and 'Kew knowledge', Spooner replied sharply, comparing himself with Homer and Shakespeare to whom works not their own were attributed and arguing, that if the same was done to him, 'I err in very good company'. Once after a bump-supper we serenaded him and stood outside his window calling for a speech. He put his head out and said, 'You don't want a speech. You only want me to say one of those things,' and immediately withdrew. But he had a genius for making highly unexpected remarks, and in my belief he did it deliberately as an embarrassment game. When a new Fellow called Stanley Casson had been elected, Spooner went up to him in the quad and said, 'I want you to come to tea today to meet Mr Casson.' 'But I am Mr Casson.' 'Come all the same.' He played the same kind of joke on undergraduates, but it was always tinged with a measure of kindly wisdom. When Roy was depressed about his work, Spooner sent for him and said, 'You mustn't think that you are not what you once were. That's all. Good morning.' In the same way in my first summer term he sent for me and asked how I was getting on with my work. 'Not very well,' I said, 'I don't understand what Mr Joseph says,' and he comforted me greatly by replying, 'Neither do I, but it doesn't matter.' When Strauss had moved to medicine, Spooner played a complicated trick on him. 'I get good reports on your work from Mr Knight.' 'But I am not going to Mr Knight,' said Strauss. 'Oh yes, you are. I get very good reports on your law from him.' Strauss retired dumbfounded.

Spooner was a kind of Lob, with a touch of fairy-blood. He moved in his own world and had an elfin clairvoyance into our characters and doings. I cannot think how he did it. He had no spies, and he was much too blind to see what we did, but he none the less knew. Ernest Barker, who was then a history tutor, ventured the suggestion that he was like Edward the Confessor, but the evidence seemed inadequate. There was certainly something saintly about him, in his inspired innocence and his complete lack of malice or self-righteousness. It was impossible not to love him, and though you never felt quite safe in his company, you knew that he wished you well and went about it in his own peculiar way. There were innumerable legends about him, but among them I cherish most one which told that once when preaching to the boys of Winchester College, he delivered by mistake a sermon meant for a country parish, which contained the words, 'All of you have hands horny with toil, and some of you are mothers.' That after all is a nice description of Wykehamists. He stayed on till after I left New College and then retired to north Oxford, where I lunched with him shortly before his death and found him as spry and as unpredictable as ever, pushing his successor, H. A. L. Fisher, before him into the dining-room, saying 'Seniores priores'. Compared with Fisher, Spooner certainly seemed to possess the gift of eternal youth.

Among the professorial Fellows of New College were three men who call for some notice. D. S. Margoliouth, professor of Arabic, was hardly known to me, but had a fabulous reputation as an Arabic scholar, and the story was that, when in the war he lectured in Arabic in Cairo, in the morning he spoke the modern language, and that was admirable, but in the evening he spoke ancient Arabic, and then it was 'like attar of roses'. He was now in his decline and devoted his gifts to finding cryptograms to prove that the Homeric poems were after all written by Homer. Younger and more fascinating was J. L. Myres, professor of Ancient History. He wore a pointed beard like an Elizabethan seaman and had very bright eyes and a provocatively rapid speech. In the war he had been in the RNVR with not very specified duties in the Aegean. He commanded a tug which he took where he wished, and conducted raids on the Turkish coast. Once when he was sailing out of the harbour of Samos, one of the British warships there signalled to him, 'Does your mother know you are out?' Myres was a man of eager curiosity who saw the past in a full setting of archaeology, geography, anthropology, and ethnology. I attended his lectures with a bemused fascination. He was not easy to follow or even to hear, and I felt that if only I could shake his beard after each lecture, all the lost words would fall out of it. He gave a broad and enlightening background for ancient history, and illuminated it with many happy phrases, as when he spoke of the 'nobler stone-fruits' of the Balkans, or urged us to study the ethnography of cherry-brandy. As a young man he had gone to Greece in 1894 only to hear that Schliemann, who had excavated Troy and Mycenae, was dead, 'and I felt that the spring had gone out of the year'. In this electric flow of ideas Greek history itself tended to get lost, and Myres was less interested in its details than in its background. A third eminent professor at New College was the mathematician G. H. Hardy, whom I knew simply because his rooms were above mine and he used to raid my cupboard for tea-things and other necessaries. He looked remarkably young, still played games, and organized an annual cricket match between the Fellows and the choir school. He was a Wykehamist, but had come from Cambridge of which he was a rare and fine product. He had disapproved of the war, taken a part in the campaign to reinstate Bertrand Russell after he had been deprived of his lectureship at Trinity, and was a staunch atheist, who liked clergymen. He was a keen reader of detective stories, passionately interested in cricket, and an admirer of good looks in undergraduates. He was a little remote despite all his playfulness, but it was impossible to speak to him even for a short time without appreciating the remarkable edge of his intellect and the crisp neatness of his words.

In a less exalted atmosphere moved the tutors, and among these I was brought into contact with only a few. My friends who read history were at first taught by Ernest Barker, and claimed that he was a genius. He spoke with a strong Lancashire accent, but was thought to have learned it after he came as a scholar to Balliol from Manchester Grammar School. Anyhow he indulged it freely, and his remarks got much of their savour from it. I met him chiefly at undergraduate dinners to which dons were invited and was amazed at the risks which he took with sentimentality before his critical and ironical audience. He had in his youth written poems in the manner of *A Shropshire Lad*, and when he was asked about them, he said, 'Before I was married I read poetry, but since I've been married I've lived it.' At the end of the summer term of 1919 he made a speech in which he said, 'It's been a golden term written in letters of gold in a golden book' – all this in the finest Lancashire. The wonder is that nobody was embarrassed. He had once been a classical scholar, referring to Greek as 'the language that I love best', and he had a good memory for Greek poetry which he quoted with force and feeling. Unfortunately for his pupils he left New College at the end of the summer of 1920, and they were relegated to less unusual tutors.

Though there were almost no scientists in my immediate circle, I came early to know one of the most remarkable in his genera-tion. J. B. S. Haldane had in 1919 been elected to a Fellowship at New College in physiology. Before the war he had taken first classes first in Mathematical Moderations and then in Greats, but, as the son of the famous physiologist J. S. Haldane, he had studied physiology in his spare time and helped his father in conducting experiments on each other. He had been a soldier through the war and much enjoyed being a bombing-officer. He had been seriously wounded more than once and sent to the East, where he picked up some Arabic and indulged his taste for the study of religions. He was very large, with a fine head, beetling eyebrows and bristling moustache, and a deep, rather slow speech. At Eton he had been known as 'the giant sloth', and it suited his appearance. He was most unusually gifted. He was able to make science intelligible by apt parallels and comparisons or striking remarks, such as 'Einstein has proved that Kant was right' or that the Houris of the Muslim Paradise have their virginities perpetually renewed 'like female guinea-pigs'. He recited poetry in various languages and at times wrote it with distinction. When I moved on to read for Greats, I learned quite as much from him as from any of my tutors. In philosophy he was a Hegelian, like his uncle, R. B. Haldane, the former Minister for War and Lord Chancellor, but from this he moved into Marxism, which he claimed helped him in scientific research. But he was keenly aware of the problems that concerned Oxford philosophers and had his own answers to them. In ancient history he illuminated subjects by extraordinary insights as when he claimed that Diocletian instituted a kind of hereditary syndicalism, or suggested that the blond peoples who immigrated into the Aegean did not survive because they could not sweat enough. To the Essay Society he read a paper on science and the future, which was to be published later in an extended form as a small book called *Daedalus*. It was a dazzling forecast of the future, seen more by a physiologist than by a historian, and I have never heard anything so thrilling read to any society young or old.

Haldane was already a man of the left, despite the emphatically right-wing views of his remarkable mother. It was with him a matter both of the head and the heart. He thought capitalism a messy and wasteful system, which called for a complete recasting, and, despite a certain gruffness and intolerance of stupidity, he was distressed by suffering. This did not prevent him from admitting that he had much enjoyed the war, but he also admitted that it was an appalling waste of everything. We liked and admired him, and he was very easy in his relations with us, never retiring into any donnish dignity or discouraging us from saying what we thought. In 1922 he moved to Cambridge as a Reader, and the change was far from happy. He was a member of Trinity, but the governing body did not elect him to a Fellowship because they thought him 'rather a bore' – a comment which came from misunderstanding his manners. Even worse, he was cited as a co-respondent and deprived of his post by a body ridiculously called the 'Sex viri'. The proceedings were instigated by a Proctor called Hunkin, who afterwards became Bishop of Truro. Fortunately Haldane appealed and was reinstated, largely, it is said, through the influence of Arthur Balfour. But the embittering experience drove him into the Communist Party, where for a time he felt at home, until Lysenko was forced on biologists by Stalin. This was too much for Haldane, who left the Party and eventually found a new home in India. Before going there he wrote to me and quoted the line of Virgil which haunted Savanarola,

> Heu, fuge crudeles terras, fuge litus avarum
> (Alas, flee from the cruel lands, flee from the
> greedy shore).

When in 1964 he had an operation for cancer he wrote an admirable poem about it and sent it to me with a letter in which he said,

The verse, I think, opens up a new line in literature, namely comic verse about cancer by patients with that disease. Jokes about one's imminent death have been common form at least since Thermopylae, though the finest collection known to me is in Njal's Saga. But people seem to be more frightened in bed than in battle, perhaps because they are not so busy. This should be stopped.

In a year cancer killed him, but I am sure that he faced it with his usual courageous curiosity.

Another don, who was later to become a much loved friend, was Alic Smith. After working in the Scottish Office for thirteen years he was brought back to New College in the summer of 1919 to help Joseph in the teaching of philosophy. Though he had not worked at it for a long time, he was given a load of teaching which would have broken most men. He was a highly cultivated man who made his rooms charming with fine pieces of furniture and had excellent manners and a fluent conversation. At this time, as Dean of Chapel, he was responsible for our attendance at it. The governing body of New College was prepared to let ex-soldiers off roll-calls at 8 a.m., but that was about their limit. Otherwise they seemed to think that these veterans were not unlike schoolboys, or perhaps they did not think at all but assumed that what had been must always be. They had irritating rules about having to pay charges if we came into college after 9 p.m., and if we came in after midnight we were in danger of expulsion. Among their other errors they insisted that we must attend chapel once on Sundays. A large number, including myself, had no intention of doing so and wilfully abstained, knowing that there was safety in numbers. We were all summoned by Smith, who made a little speech which I recorded at the time,

I see that you have not been attending chapel on Sundays. Now the college rules say that you must. But I am prepared to give you exemption for one of the following three reasons – first, that you do not approve of the principle of compulsion, second, that you go to some other place of worship, third, that you do not believe in the Christian religion. For any of these I am prepared to give you exemption. There is a fourth reason, which is not so good, that you cannot be bothered to come, but I am prepared to give you exemption for this also. I shall therefore ask you if you wish to be exempted, but I shall not ask for what reason.

This was indeed the true spirit of liberty such as I had hoped to find at Oxford and been too often disappointed in missing. We took Smith at his word, and there was no more compulsory chapel for us.

After deciding to read Mods I saw that I must do a lot of work in my long vacation. Fortunately my parents and two sisters came home during the summer term, and my father soon afterwards bought a house at Ightham in Kent which we kept till my mother's death in 1960. I had at last a proper home, and was very comfortably provided with two attic rooms, which had a wide view of the North Downs and were isolated and quiet. Here I read my texts and led a healthy, tranquil life. My parents went back to China in 1921, but lent the house to some old friends, called Moorhead, who were extremely kind to me and asked me to stay whenever I liked. I took grateful advantage of this and found them most friendly and companionable. In these conditions I managed to work regularly in vacations and had more time to enjoy myself during term, though even then I was not shy of disappearing into the charming New College library where silence was compulsory and visitors could not find me. I much enjoyed the large mass of Greek and Latin literature which was laid down for us. We had to read much more then than candidates now do, and it was a new satisfaction to read the masters in bulk and not in snippets as at school.

When I came up for the Michaelmas Term 1919 my tutor was Henry Ludwig Henderson, who had returned from Singapore, where he had been in the censorship. He had a German mother and was in many ways more German than English. He had a round face and a round head, closely cropped white hair, a slight moustache, an upright carriage, and a long stride. Many years later I was to detect a striking facial resemblance between him and Heinrich Himmler, but at this happy date nothing of the kind entered my mind. He spoke English perfectly but with the German guttural *r*. He was not an energetic or inspiring tutor and gave the impression that, having won some prizes as an undergraduate, he thought it sufficient effort for a lifetime. I am not aware that he ever published anything, and his lectures, though competent, were not very up to date. Yet he did his work as he thought that it should be done and taught us as no doubt he had been taught himself at the beginning of the century. Humanly, he was more interesting. He had excellent manners, and an admirable taste in food and drink. He frequented the theatre and public lectures. Above all he was opposed to reform, and the mere hint of it turned him purple and nearly speechless. His emotions were easily aroused, both in admiration and in disapproval. His chief interest was in good-looking young women. He would make up to them with an undisguised sentimentality and was heard saying to one, 'Do you never think of the moths which flutter round the candle?' He liked to convey the impression that in his youth he had been rather a dog, and his love of the past came out when he was on the committee for a college ball and entreated, 'Please don't forget to put in some old-fashioned waltzes.' He never married, and this seemed odd in one whose interests were so single-minded. He may of course have tried and failed, but Alic Smith in an unusually intimate moment once asked him about it, and he replied, 'It's because I like only the fluffy ones.' He survived for many years and eventually died, most appropriately, on Boxing Day, 1963, at Monte Carlo.

Fortunately Henderson was not my only tutor for Mods. In the next two terms I was sent with two other undergraduates from New College to Gilbert Murray for Greek composition. Murray was Regius Professor and as such not allowed to give private tuition, but an exception was made because of the shortage of tutors. We were fortunate indeed, and this was my first acquaintance with this remarkable man. We did proses and verses for him and sent them to him in advance. He corrected them before we arrived and gave them back to us, discussed our versions, and then showed us his own. It was a most exciting experience, for he made us better every time. Of course he corrected our mistakes, but his real power was more subtle, consisting of such comments as 'I like that' or 'I prefer mine here'. And his own versions were wonderful. He would give us foggy and turgid bits of English and expect them to be turned into lucid Attic, as he himself did, and enabled us to understand what he meant when he said that Greek composition was the best training that he knew for the mind. He was capable of a gentle irony, as when one of us had handed in rather a wooden set of Greek hexameters, he said, 'Have you been reading Quintus Smyrnaeus lately?', as if the young man was likely to spend his time on this dull, late writer and feel his influence. Under his enchanting guidance I became quite competent at this elegant art, and felt myself much more at home with the Greek language as it really was. His lectures, on Homer and Aeschylus' *Agamemnon*, were by far the best that I heard. He had a charming, musical voice, and he read the majestic Aeschylean choruses with a full sense of their magnificent rhythm. More than this, he really explained what the play was about. He had considerable experience of the stage, and ideas on how the *Agamemnon* must have been acted, but beyond this the poet in him responded to its imaginative and emotional sweep, and he rose to its lofty occasions. So when Clytaemnestra summons Cassandra into the palace, he said, 'She wants another victim' – just that, and no more was needed. He provided the inspiration that transformed what might have been rather a dull grind into an exalting and exciting experience. He made Greek poetry live and compelled us to feel that we must spare no effort to get at its essence, to understand it fully, and see how it worked. Not only was this just what we needed after war-service but it was quite different from what most of us had had at school.

I took Mods in the summer of 1920 and got a first class. The Crab was delighted and justifiably took much credit to himself. I could now move on to Greats with a fresh confidence and a determination that this time I would not be defeated by Joseph, and in the end despite many set-backs I was not. I had one or two advantages. My friends, Roy Harrod and Cyril Radcliffe, were taking final schools a year before me, and I was able to pick their brains. While Cyril formed his own generous metaphysics from such writers as Bosanquet and Bradley without much reference to what was being taught at Oxford at the time, Roy was troubled. At Westminster he had read some philosophy and formed views of an English empirical kind, which was beginning to have a new lease of life under Bertrand Russell, but was not at all liked by Joseph, who was a latter-day schoolman with a touch of Neo-Platonist and temperamentally opposed to empirical views. Roy was able to stand up to him, but the struggle took too much of his time and prevented him from developing his own ideas as he would have liked. He was depressed to think that this was what Oxford philosophy had become. He would have chosen to make philosophy his profession, but he felt that his training did not really fit him for it. So he took History after Greats, got a first class in a year, and became one of the earliest dons at Oxford to specialise in economics, for which he has over the years won a wide renown. I learned a great deal from him, as I shared some of his convictions and saw that, when Joseph carved up Bertrand Russell, he was not answering him in his own language and scored too many unfair points. We were not impressed when he ended a lecture fifteen minutes after the hour with the ironical statement, ' "So far," says Mr Russell, "all is plain sailing." We will continue the voyage next week.' Judged by his own standards Joseph was a consummate performer. He once asked me, 'If we see a train getting smaller, what is it that gets smaller?', and of course all my attempts at answers were wrong, but the real trouble was that the question prejudged the issue by the way in which it was put. No wonder that William James once called him 'a myopic ant'. For me his methods of controversy bore some resemblance to family croquet in which you invent the rules as you go on and accuse your opponent of breaking them.

I decided that the right way to deal with Joseph was to learn his own peculiar language on the principle that writing essays for him was not ultimately unlike doing Greek prose for Murray. One must be clear and unambiguous and see that the words had an exact meaning. I practised this with occasional success but more often I was defeated. But I did not despair and in the end formed my own little philosophy from an odd mixture of doctrines and presented it in what I hoped to be fool-proof English. I knew quite well that I was not born to be a philosopher, but I thought it a useful training and could not believe that it was completely beyond my powers. I had also a second advantage. Alic Smith taught me in alternate terms. He was at first hard pressed to keep abreast with what he had to teach and cannot have been more than a week ahead of such pupils as Radcliffe and Price, but when I came to him, he was more firmly established, and I gained much from him. He was a highly civilized and cultivated man, who liked philosophy because it enabled him to express his ideas on many interesting matters, including the fine arts. In this he presented a marked contrast with Joseph, who was at heart a rather simple man with a touching affection for Victorian poetry, but whose visual sense could be judged by a hideous carved Indian mantelpiece which occupied a large part of one wall in his room. More than this, Smith understood his pupils as Joseph seldom did, unless they were Wykehamists cast in the same mould as himself. Smith saw at once that my intermittent dumbness was not conceit but distrust of myself, and he set about not to drill me into submission but to make me share his speculations with him. His expansive, leisurely manner was very unlike Joseph's masterly concision, and there was no danger that he would suddenly snap some deadly question at you. He had no very decided views himself, but that made him all the better as a teacher.

I dished up to Smith what I learned from the lectures of H. A. Prichard, who shared many of Joseph's views but was a more fascinating character. He wore rough, shabby clothes, and had a dirty moustache and closely cropped hair. In lecturing he tied himself up in knots or began to climb the mantelpiece. There was no doubt of his passionate commitment to his subject, He went through fearful self-lacerations to find the right ideas and the right words for them. One term he lectured on 'What do we see?' He began hopefully with the idea that we see colours, but he abandoned it in the third week, and argued that we saw things. But that would not do either, and by the end of term he admitted ruefully, 'I'm damned if I know what we do see.' This was magnificently humble, and I attended every lecture by Prichard that I could. From him I picked up a smattering of ideas and a manner of writing which Smith spotted at once but did not mind. I even listened to Prichard on moral philosophy. He had very eccentric views on duty, which had to be obeyed without hesitation but was never in the least explicable. Since his examples of it were getting up early in the morning and having one's hair cut short, it fell short of my ideal of a good life. Not that Prichard himself did not suffer in trying to decipher its messages, and we all read with avidity an article which he had written called 'Is moral philosophy based on a mistake?' But, as Jack Haldane pointed out, it was not the kind of mistake that we hoped.

Philosophy was only half of Greats, and though it was the half which we discussed among ourselves and was thought to present the stronger challenge to our wits, we had also to study ancient history. In this I was from the start greatly interested, but few of my friends were. I was drawn to Greek history as an essential background to Greek literature, and to Roman for its own sake, as a study of an imperial world not unlike that in which I had been brought up, and my curiosity about it was enhanced by what I had seen of Roman remains in Provence and Italy. Unfortunately the teaching of ancient history at New College was poor. The chief tutor was Percy Matheson, whose appearance reminded me of a camel outside the walls of Peking. He was personally most kind to me and towards the end of my course tried to persuade me to become a master at Parramatta School in Australia, but he was past his prime as a teacher and beginning to forget what he once knew. He had few illuminating insights into the ancient world and did not help me to find pegs on which to hang ideas. Nor were things any better when Stanley Casson was brought in to help him. Casson had a good record as a practical archaeologist in the field and knew modern Greece well. But he was not a historian and did not spend much time in trying to become one. Cyril Radcliffe and I used to invent quotations from an imaginary Greek historian called Aristomenes of Tauromenium, and Casson would either nod his head knowingly or say, 'I had forgotten that.' His actual post was University Reader in Classical Archaeology, but in this too he had his critics. When his appointment came up for approval by Congregation, Hugh Last, of St John's, who had just taken his M A, spoke against it with some force, and though it went through, it was not an encouraging start for Casson. However, he survived the blow and wisely gave up teaching ancient history, which he should never have been asked to do.

These scholastic activities were varied by much social life. In those days excellent luncheons and dinners could be given in one's rooms from the college kitchen at an enticingly low price, and were the most agreeable way of seeing one's friends. I had a scholarship of £80 and my father gave me a generous allowance of £350 a year. So I spent what I could on this kind of entertainment. We talked a great deal of nonsense, knowing that it was nonsense and enjoying it for that reason. For this Strauss had a pre-eminent gift. He could be deliriously amusing in flights of pure fancy, and was the leading spirit in a group consisting of himself, Roy, Stephen Tomlin, Hew Anderson, and myself, in writing poems in what we hoped to be the most modern manner. Fragments of them still remain in my memory, such as

> Waltzing moonward wistfully

or

> Filmy, fly-blown, Papal toe,
> Benedicamus domino

or more brutally,

> O buttercups have buttocks,
> And so have daffodils,

We proposed to call ourselves 'the Five' and to publish the collection as *Nights of Sulphur*, dedicated to the Knights of Malta. This of course was done for amusement, but the results were not alien to the poetical manner of the time, and we could not be accused of not knowing what was happening in literature. If we were not creative writers ourselves, we were sufficiently interested in such writing to be able to make fun of it. Though parody is now much deplored and thought to have no value as criticism, we agreed with Aristophanes and Proust in finding it a salutary and illuminating exercise.

This kind of frivolity provided a relaxation not only from our work, but from inner tensions which were the result of the war and had begun to show themselves by 1920. Even Cyril Radcliffe, who knew exactly what he wished to do and set about it with quiet determination, had lost dear friends and needed something or someone to take their place. Under a gentle irony he hid a desire for some peaceful, secure affection and hoped to regain the happiness which he had enjoyed in his childhood with his remarkable mother and three brothers. Strauss was much more troubled. He had suffered gravely in the war, and still suffered from his markedly Jewish appearance, enhanced by an eye-glass. He found some assurance in the Roman Church and adopted from a Jesuit friend a condescending attitude towards Anglicans and a conviction that the troubles of undergraduates need not always be taken very seriously. His gift for nonsense helped him much more. But there were moments when his defences were down and he was a lonely, pathetic figure. He almost clamoured for help and affection, and it was impossible not to like him. But it was not easy to know what to do, since in his intimate moments he always besought one to join the Roman Church, and this spoiled everything. Roy, who was a little younger than myself, had uneasy complications with his mother. In the nineties she had been a successful novelist, the friend of Henry James and Oscar Wilde, and even now in her majestic ruin she had a high style and an old-fashioned, emotional manner of talking which was as remote as the great queen herself. Roy was angelic to her, but she was a fearful drain on his vitality, and made awkward scenes with him in front of others. She hated poverty and old age, and longed for the glorious past, and Roy was expected to revive it. To some extent he did. We were asked to meet her, and I found her excellent company, but at times Roy was almost worn out by her, and this was all the worse since he was battling for his intellectual independence with Joseph and needed all his force for it. Deane Jones presented a different case. He was the son of a Nonconformist clergyman in Birmingham and had been badly injured in the head when he had a crash in an aeroplane in the Air Force. He found his anodyne in work. He was a passionate student of history, which engaged all his imaginative and romantic instincts. But he had also the remnants of a Nonconformist conscience, which, since he had lost his religion, found an outlet in politics, and it was this which forced him to take so active a part in the bus-strike.

Nor was I myself short of troubles. I was for some time not sure what I wished to do after Oxford. My father wanted me to go to the Bar but would have settled for my becoming a civil servant. I was convinced that I should not go to the Bar, since I had no gifts for it, and I thought the civil service a bit dreary. I had meditated on the Crab's suggestion of becoming a don, but I did not see in what subject, and I was not convinced that I was good enough. Despite a bold front to the world I was aware of many deficiencies and could not see that I was any better than many people whom I knew. In different ways we were to solve our problems, but we all had them, and they were for the most part the result of the war which had broken into our lives and so upset our balance that we had real difficulty in regaining it. Nor was this trouble confined to those who had actually been in the forces. The bad teaching and the moral strain at schools did quite as much harm. Stephen Tomlin, who was unusually gifted and clever, believed neither in himself nor in Oxford, and after a few terms of aimless indecision suddenly packed up his bag and left. On being asked about it, Warden Spooner said, 'Mr Tomlin will not recur.'

Among my New College friends hardly anyone had a dominating interest in modern literature. Anthony Steel was an exception, and was himself more than a promising poet, but work kept him to his books. My own interest took me outside New College to other places, where I made friends of rather a different kind. Leslie Hartley at Balliol seemed much more mature than most of us. He had a winning smile, a quiet, humorous detachment, a keen observation of life, and already wrote with an unusual skill. He waged a quiet war with the dons of Balliol who did not appreciate his full merits and felt that he should work harder. Actually he worked quite hard enough, but did not make a parade of it. He was well abreast with modern literature and knew about T.S. Eliot and the Sitwells, but his chief personal claim was his gift for intimacy and understanding. He treated literature as part of life and wove its themes into his private relations. Leslie's series of distinguished novels still bear the imprint of his personality at this time, with its humour, its scepticism, and its sudden, scintillating moments of anger or delight. Another gifted friend was Eddy Sackville West, who was at Christ Church. He was already a first-class musician, but he was now more interested in the other arts and pursued them with an unflagging zest. From him I first heard the name of Marcel Proust, but also of other French writers, who were hardly even phantoms to me. He had a taste for the so-called Decadents, but so had I, and he strengthened and helped me to enjoy it. He was a frail, elegant little figure, who went out with a stick and muffler, and at times fell into fits of melancholy. But he had an indomitable will which refused to admit defeat, and he countered his blackest hours by a delicious sense of fun and a ringing laugh. Through him I met David Cecil, who was much tougher-minded, being trained in the grand tradition of his family that anything may be a matter of discussion and that, if it is, it should be discussed for all that it is worth. He did not go so far as his uncle Hugh, afterwards Lord Quickswood, who said to the present Archbishop of Canterbury, 'I think that controversy, particularly acrimonious controversy, is one of the privileges of a civilized life', but he liked gay, good-natured argument and was unusually adept at it, having at his command a sharp intelligence which punctured most forms of nonsense. He was extremely quick at taking a point and making the most of it, and had an eager curiosity about all kinds of human behaviour. Though he had strong convictions on religion and politics, he never forced them on you, and was much too tolerant to make you feel that your own opinions were absurd. He had an excellent taste in books and a gift for making you share his likes, but he was also a serious historian who was able to compete as an equal with the more obvious professionals in the subject and had a special talent for making the past live when he spoke of it.

Modern literature had to be relegated to spare time, but I

managed to read substantially in it. It was an age of remarkable achievements, and there was always something good and new crying for attention. Thomas Hardy was still alive and writing the poetry which forms so splendid a second chapter to his life. When the OUDS put on a selection from *The Dynasts* in the spring of 1920, he came to Oxford and was given an honorary degree. I went to see him get it, and he was just what he should have been – small and frail and old, with a fine head and large, innocent eyes. He carried himself very well for his eighty years and looked like a very good, rather shrunken English apple. Hardy embodied a splendid past, but his poetry struck us as entirely contemporary in its themes and its manner. If the living tradition of English letters had him at its head, it gave signs of creative invention in almost every generation from his to our own. Joseph Conrad was still writing, and though he seemed to be losing some of his earlier impetus, we found much to like in *The Shadow Line*, which had come out during the war, and were not ashamed of responding to the more romantic parts of *The Arrow of Gold*. Though the war had stimulated its own literature, this was soon seen to be less relevant to us than what had been written in defiance of it. If in these dark years the English language was enriched by W. B. Yeats' *The Wild Swans of Coole* and was to show results in T. S. Eliot's *The Waste Land* and James Joyce's *Ulysses*, we were soon to see that in other countries war had fostered equally powerful works which had almost nothing to do with it, from the astonishing poetry of revolutionary Russia to the greater part of Proust's *A la recherche du temps perdu*. In all directions discoveries were to be made and were nearly always rewarding. It was as if on coming back from the battlefields we found that literature had been accumulating in our absence and now challenged our full attention. So abundant were the riches available that it was easy to assume that they would continue to flow on this scale and that, whatever Europe had lost in human lives, it had kept its creative spirit and showed no signs of slackening it.

I did not visit Cambridge or come to know anyone there until my last year, when I formed a lasting friendship with George Rylands, who had just come up to King's from Eton. From some survival from the nursery he was called Dadie, and he made an enlivening impact by his rich array of gifts. He was very good-looking, abounding with health and energy, and full of delighted excitement at his discovery of University life. At Cambridge, unlike Oxford, clever undergraduates went in for acting, and Dadie made a mark for himself first in the *Oresteia* and then in *Troilus and Cressida*. What distinguished his acting was his unusually keen perception of poetry and his ability to speak lines with a full sense of their worth. Literature was his first interest, and when he moved from the classics to English, he put into its study a passion and an insight which I had not yet encountered. He had a powerful capacity for enjoyment at all levels, and imparted it generously to others. Yet under his gaiety and sympathy and quick understanding of other people, he had a hard, clear intelligence which saw things without illusions and made him a most capable man of affairs. If at a party nobody was more amusing or lively, he could also be an enchanting companion *tête à tête*. He had a devouring interest in the doings of his friends and gave them just the support and the comfort that they needed. He could, when occasion called, be sharp, and sometimes, when his feelings were outraged, formidable. He did not wish to be a scholar in a narrow or technical sense and was quite content to carry in his head large masses of English literature on which he had many original and illuminating ideas. I learned far more from him about English than from anyone at Oxford, and he had the great advantage that he did not talk in our philosophical jargon but applied his keen mind to making books more enjoyable through his capacity for divining an author's mind and seeing what he was trying to do. When I came to know him, I began to see why Cambridge has produced so many more first-class poets than Oxford.

In extending my circle of friends beyond New College I inevitably came into contact with two dons, who had a name for being interested in undergraduates. F. F. Urquhart, known universally as 'Sligger', was a history tutor at Balliol. The nickname was said to be a corruption into pre-war dialect of 'the sleek one', and Sligger in his youth had apparently provided a model for the chief character in Walter Pater's painful story *Emerald*

Uthwart. Sligger was primarily a Balliol figure, but he spread his net outside, and I came to know him well. He was cultivated but not highbrow, and his influence was largely due to a tolerance and a gentleness which he extended to a number of highly strung young men much in need of them. He would calm them down, give them unobtrusively good advice, and help them in their troubles. One met all sorts in his rooms, where he gave little dinners at which nobody ate or drank too much. He talked about interesting matters, knew quite a lot about art, and insisted provocatively that medieval sculpture was better than Greek. In the vacations he wrote innumerable letters which contained agreeable pieces of gossip and sage, but not too sage, observations on life. In the Long Vacation he would entertain parties of undergraduates in a chalet which he owned on the slope of Mont Blanc in the French Alps. Here the living was rather Spartan. Work was the order of the day, broken by a piece of chocolate in the middle of the morning and occasional walks up or down the mountain. He asked me several times to go, but I refused, feeling that I should work better at home and that the rest of the programme did not appeal to me. He had been a Roman Catholic since birth, but though he was regular in his duties, he never let his beliefs impinge on his personal relations except with other Catholics. Nor do I think that he liked them more than other young men. His chief friend before the war had been Walter Monckton, who was to rise to notable heights at the bar and in politics, and Monckton had just the qualities which Sligger liked – an easy manner, a wide interest in human beings and a good judgement on them, and above all a calm inner life which sustained him through a varied and exacting career.

Very different from Sligger was R. H. Dundas, known first as Robin and later simply as D. He was a tutor in ancient history at Christ Church and at this time held the responsible post of Senior Censor. I did not know him, and cannot remember that I had heard of him, when one day I received a postcard, which said, 'Have heard a lot about you both for and against. Come to dinner next Friday. 7.10 in my rooms. Black tie. Gown.' I made inquiries and, finding that my Christ Church friends liked him, accepted. It was the beginning of a friendship which lasted for some forty years till his death. He was a heavy man with a fine, large head, and he had a way of speaking in short clipped sentences which contained much insight in a few words. He was greatly interested in the young and knew that they had their private difficulties. So he would suddenly ask a lot of intimate questions. Some people objected, some laughed, most told him the truth and were relieved by doing so. He was able to know young men from the inside and truthfully said, 'I'm a motherly soul.' If his brusque manner belied this, his friends found it out soon enough. He was an excellent tutor, who hardly published a word, but he inspired his pupils with a love for the Greek past. It was his tragedy, and theirs, that three of the best of them, Humphry Payne, Alan Blakeway, and Robert Beaumont, all died in their thirties, but he must have known how much they owed to him and how grateful they were. He often asked me to dine at the high table of Christ Church, where I drank champagne from a silver goblet and met such heroic figures as Aurel Stein, the explorer of Chinese Turkestan, and Arthur Evans, the discoverer of the Minoan civilization of Crete. At one of his lectures, which were dry but informative, Dundas played a little trick on me. I had lent him a book on Chinese references to the Roman Empire, and he suddenly quoted from it, saying, 'I owe this to Mr Bowra of New College, now present.' I was embarrassed and delighted. He had a house outside Stirling in Scotland, of which he had changed the name from 'Christian Bank' to 'Laurel Hill', and there he spent a large part of his vacations with his splendid old mother and an unmarried sister, who in many ways resembled him. I once stayed there, and we did a motor tour of the western Highlands in bright autumn weather. Dundas was as careful of his own driving as he was critical of his sister's, especially when she drove on to the grass verge of the narrow road, 'You've done it again.' He kept very careful accounts and apportioned the cost of drinks on the strictest rules of distributive justice. With him at Edinburgh I met Lord Haldane, who smoked a cigar by holding it on a gold pin and told me, 'You won't mind getting old, except that sometimes after a good lunch you will find that you can't get up.'

Not all my friends treated their work seriously. Some sought pleasure, and if they did not invariably find it, that only confirms what the moral philosophers have always said. Philip Ritchie, of Trinity, was a most engaging, amusing, fanciful, and self-indulgent man, whose interest in the vagaries of his friends occupied much of his time. But he too had his troubles. He was devoted to a young man who was determined to take Holy Orders, and Philip was appalled by the mere suggestion of it. He set out to undermine his friend's faith, read a lot of anti-Christian literature, and became an expert on the highest criticism of the New Testament. But it was all of no avail. The friend laughed and remained perfectly friendly, but none of these arguments had any meaning for him. For him religious faith was unquestionably real, and it was absurd to dispute its validity. After a long and futile siege Philip gave up, and spent his unusual talents on amusing himself and others. He had a whimsical talent for satirical fancy and created a team of Aunt Sallies from various worthy characters. He knew French literature very well and was an ardent lover of music. But he was unhappy. In his hatred of accepted religion he showed a religious zeal in propounding a dark nihilism and at one point put his precepts into practice by trying to kill himself with a large number of aspirins. He woke up in the morning feeling very ill and vomited most of his dose. A little later he was visited by W. Hadley, then Master of Pembroke College, Cambridge, and the father of an old friend. Hadley could not make out the situation but was a little perturbed and reported to his son, 'Your friend Phil looked in very poor shape.' Philip was in so violent reaction against what he thought to be a dishonest and disgusting world that he found himself without any real aim. He sought consolation in Communism, and appreciated not only its atheism but its hostility to many established institutions. But he was far too much of a hedonist to submit to its puritanical demands and far too sceptical to accept its dogmas. He was more than usually extravagant and not only spent a lot of money on recognized pleasures but wasted a lot on gambling. Yet he kept an unusual distinction, which gave dignity even to his absurd efforts to raise cash from moneylenders on the prospects of his father's will. He died young from an operation for tonsils, but despite his apparent gaiety he did not wish to live. The war had taken something out of him and unfitted him for survival. When he died, it was found that he had in a bank a substantial sum of money which he had forgotten.

No less unusual was Peter Ralli, who came to New College with £3,000. During his three years he spent most of it, largely in giving delicious dinners, to which he often asked me. He had very black hair and a very pink face, and looked rather like an old-fashioned Dutch doll. He was wonderfully perceptive and entertaining, and a most rewarding waster of time. His chief energies were given to horse-racing, and he did no work at all. When he took History finals in 1922, he answered very few questions, and those briefly, one example being the single sentence, written in a huge, flowing hand, 'Her subjects wanted Queen Elizabeth to abolish tunnage and poundage, but the splendid creature stood firm.' He was, of course, ploughed, but it did not trouble him. After going down he was stricken by a long, incurable illness, and I used to visit him as he lay in bed. He was quite unchanged and never complained, but, being rather out of things, was avid for every kind of news. He made his nurse lay bets for him, and treated her with an intimate mockery which she adored but could not begin to understand. When he died, he had come to the end of his small fortune, from which he had derived and given enormous pleasure.

A friend of Philip and of Peter was Bob Boothby, of Magdalen, who was not at all like either. At heart he cherished ambitions of political success but for the moment he was out to enjoy himself, and succeeded on a handsome scale. He did in fact get a degree by throwing himself for his last term at the mercy of L. B. Namier, who candidly told him that he must simply learn the answers to certain questions, which he proceeded to tell him. Bob announced early, 'This is so good that it can't last,' and made the most of it. He had inexhaustible energy; he was very intelligent and perceptive, especially about people, but also about politics; he had a fine appearance with black hair and dark eyes, a beautiful voice and a natural gift for eloquence, a capacity for enlivening any conversation by his acute or reckless comments and a most winning generosity and warmth. Yet though he enjoyed himself to the limit, he knew what he was doing. He wished to go into politics, and for this a good degree was not indispensable. On the other hand even undergraduate politics have their uses for the aspiring politician, and Bob made a place for himself at the Chatham Club and spoke with skill at dinners when cabinet ministers were present. He presented himself as a bit of a swashbuckler, but this deceived only those who did not know him. To them his political gifts were already obvious, nor was there any doubt of either his courage or his sincerity. His hatred of cant and his love of the good life had already made him an independent conservative, and such he has remained ever since. His indiscretions were part of his candour; his romantic optimism was the reflection of his ebullient temperament. He has had a remarkable career, and though his greatest successes have not been in the strict order of political promotion, he has won a wider renown and had a bigger influence than many who have held high office.

In looking back on my undergraduate life I find a credit and a debit side. On the credit side I managed to combine work and pleasure without much difficulty, and the pleasure was lively and various and by no means a waste of time. I made friendships which have lasted through my life, and I formed tastes, notably for Greek literature, which have been central to my happiness ever since. I also managed intermittently to develop other tastes in literature and the arts. I do not regret certain refusals which I made, such as to join the OUDS, or to speak at the Union, or to participate in political clubs. On the debit side I have misgivings. I was not nearly so sure of myself as I should have liked, and this made me present a brassy face to the world and pretend to be more hard-boiled than I was. Just as this deceived the innocent Joseph, so it put other people off, usually to my loss. The trouble was that at school and in the army I developed a mocking, cynical way of treating events because it prevented them from being too painful. I had formed such a habit of this that I kept it even at Oxford when it was no longer necessary. Such a habit has many uses, and I was by no means alone in my cultivation of it, but it is not in the end a satisfactory system, since it may hamper easy and

unstrained relations with other people. In a few years I realized
that it was not always necessary to be on guard and that nothing
was to be lost by giving myself away. When Dundas told me that
I had mellowed, I felt that I was on the right path.

Though at the time my generation thought that it was different
from preceding generations at Oxford and that the war had, both
for better and for worse, set us apart, we were wrong. Warden
Spooner put his finger on the essential point when he said,
'Undergraduates recur', and this was true of us. Where we differed from our predecessors and successors was not in the nature
of what we got out of Oxford, but in the degree in which we got
it. We were so delighted to be there that we squeezed everything
that we could from it and took more than a full share of its
multifarious enjoyments. If most of these were too transitory and
too local to be worth recording, that is not to their discredit. The
jokes of undergraduates may be deliriously amusing at the time
but make little impact outside their original context. If after
dinner-parties we played highly imaginative charades, or wrote
what we thought to be inspired *bouts rimés*, that was all part of
our youthful ebullience and calls for no special mention. If such
things still happen, they differ from our own relaxations only in
that they may possibly be snatched with less avidity. In the same
way, though we had our troubles and attributed them, reasonably
enough, to the war, young men always have troubles, and our
only peculiarity was that we saw fairly clearly what ours were.
Despite these small differences we found in Oxford what eager
and lively young men have always found – a pause between one
kind of life and another, the stimulus of warm and intimate
companionship, the zest for the passing moment which inspires
hilarious comedy and is yet able to combine it with a fundamental
seriousness and to gain much from the combination. Like other
undergraduates at other times, we were hindered by ignorance
and inexperience from dealing with some situations which would
present no problem to maturer people, but we had ample compensation for this in the exhilaration which transformed even the
daily routine into a series of unique events, each of which had its
own dramatic character.

6

First Years at Wadham

In my last undergraduate year I realized that I must make up my mind about what I was going to do afterwards and get the kind of post that suited it. I was now sure that I wished to be a don. My father did not like the idea, and wrote to me that 'the traditions of our family are not scholastic but administrative'. This was not quite true, since my great-uncle Fred had been a distinguished scholar, but I gave thought to it and decided that a scholastic life must inevitably involve administration and would be all the better for it. He accepted this and encouraged me to go on. The next problem was a job. I would have been happy with one either in ancient history or in Greek and Latin literature. In my mind they formed a single subject and were not very different aspects of the ancient world, which had a first claim on my affection. It happened that at this time there were no posts vacant in ancient history at Oxford, and, since it was a subject neglected in other universities, I gave up hope of one, and decided that it must be literature. In this there were two posts vacant, one at Worcester and the other at Wadham. For the first I had to make formal application, and got testimonials from Spooner and Henderson; the second was to be decided without formalities, and was more difficult to assess. However, two good friends were working for me behind my back. The first was Murray, who had not only taught me but also examined me in Mods, when he was impressed by a paper I had

done on Roman Poetry and wrote at the time, 'Let me congratu-
late you on your Roman Poetry paper. It was quite remarkable.'
This stood me in good stead. Murray thought that too many
classical scholars were bored with the subject by the time that they
came to Oxford and that I might be able to give them the fresh
start which they needed. He talked to the Warden of Wadham and
to the ancient history tutor about me. My other unseen ally was
the Crab, who was an old family friend of the Warden, and painted
a picture of me as not only a good enough scholar but likely to
take trouble with the undergraduates. This was important, since
the post as lecturer in classics was combined with that of dean,
which meant being responsible for discipline in college.

The governing body of Wadham, with whom the election lay,
consisted of eight members including the Warden. They were
divided on a matter of policy. Some of them thought that since
the post about to be vacated was in the classics, it was right that a
classical Fellow should fill it, especially as most scholarships were
still given for classics. Others, led by Professor F. A. Lindemann,
thought that this was a good chance to get a young scientist and
that the classics could be taught by a retired master from Winchester, who had settled in Oxford, and though not a Fellow,
would be a competent teacher. The election was to be decided in
the penultimate week of the summer term, and though I do not
know what the inner manœuvres were, the college records give
some facts. There were two candidates, myself and a scientist, and
after a long discussion, no conclusion was reached, and the meeting was postponed for a few days, when eventually a vote was
taken. Three votes were given for the scientist, three for me, while
two Fellows abstained. The Warden then gave his casting vote for
me, and I was elected to be Fellow, lecturer in classics, and Dean.
The Warden came round to tell me the news, and I wrote to the
Provost of Worcester withdrawing my application there. I soon
got a note from Warden Spooner saying, 'I am very glad that
you have got work', which hit the right nail on the head, and
Joseph, rather charmingly, said to me, 'I think you are going to
the most beautiful college in Oxford.' I wrote to my father about
what had happened, and he seemed to be pleased, though he was

not very sure what it meant. I had finished Greats, and all I had to do now was to wait for the results. They came out at the beginning of August, and I heard that I had been awarded a first class, with specially good marks in the Ancient History and Logic papers.

Wadham was very much the college I wished to go to. It was remarkably beautiful, with its original buildings intact and a garden, which, though less majestic than that of New College, was more intimate and more satisfying. It was small, with some 125 undergraduates, and that meant that my duties as dean would not be too burdensome. It had had periods of great brilliance in the past, notably in the middle of the seventeenth century when under John Wilkins it helped to bring the Royal Society into being, and in the nineties of the last century when a galaxy of F. E. Smith, J. A. Simon, C. B. Fry, F. W. Hirst, and A. A. Roche had all been up more or less together. If now it was a bit diminished, that was all the better, since it provided a powerful incentive to getting something done. It had many incidental advantages. Because of the small number of Fellows, the services were good and the servants attentive. I had a pleasant, sunny set of rooms on the second floor and an excellent scout, Walter Sims, who came to the college when I did and at the time of writing is still with us. The chef, Albert Tuck, was in some sense a Cambridge man, since his father had been the head chef at Emmanuel, and it was said that young Tuck would do no good unless he got away from him. He moved to Oxford and stayed at Wadham for many years. He visited me every morning to ask my needs, and was an excellent cook, who liked to provide special lunches and dinners. The cellar was well stocked, and the Senior Common Room butler, Pollicott, was the best servant I have ever known, setting a splendid standard of style and efficiency and mercilessly driving his underling. In these respects Wadham kept the ease of the nineteenth century. Since I lived in college, everything was done for me, and though there was very little plumbing, and that not very near, I did not mind. To me this was luxury, and I was deeply relieved not to have to worry about house-keeping.

I liked my colleagues. They fell into two groups, the old and the young, divided by almost a generation. The Warden, Joseph

Wells, was a man of unusual sweetness and simplicity. He had a pink cherubic face, and a slight fault in his speech due to an operation which he had had for cancer in the tongue at a time when such operations were extremely risky. He was a good Christian and a good Conservative, and did not like those who held other views, but since he very seldom suspected anyone of it, this did not impair his abundant charity and good temper. He had done a great deal for the college and was loved by its old members. In his quiet way he had an impressive authority, and it was told that once, when he heard a fearful row at night in the back quad, he walked up in the dark and said, 'If you don't stop at once, I shall light a match.' They stopped. He had a touch of fairy-blood, not to the same degree as Warden Spooner, but not altogether unlike. He announced, 'Women, even if respectable, are always a nuisance', and once when he broke a recent resolution of the college, he said blandly, 'I know we made that rule, but surely we never meant to keep it', and in his way he was right. He was generous both to the college and to impecunious undergraduates, and he was devoted to his wife and small son. Mrs Wells was an unusually clever and stylish woman who had taken a first class in History and combined a warm heart with an agreeable wit. It was tragic that when Wells became Vice-Chancellor in 1923, she fell ill and, after suffering for two years, died. Even in her last months she was an unfailing support to him, but her illness was a cruel drain on his strength, and from her death he never fully recovered.

The Sub-Warden, F. A. Dixey, came to Wadham as a scholar in 1874 and remained there almost continuously from then on. He was a physiologist and an expert on butterflies. He was also Bursar, in which he was assisted by a clerk, F. S. Gee, who had taken an MA from St Catherine's Society and stroked its eight when in 1904 it bumped Wadham in the nadir of its rowing days under the captaincy of Hewlett Johnson, afterwards famous as the 'red Dean' of Canterbury, and sent us to the bottom of the river. Dixey had been a keen Volunteer, and his churchmanship took the form of singing in the choir of St Barnabas. He had a rich repertory of stories about the past, especially about Benjamin Parsons Symons, who was Warden from 1831 to 1871 and did much harm to the college, out of which he made nearly £200,000. Dixey, who came up after his resignation but before his death, had struck his legend at the source and threw a searching light on what a Victorian head of a college might be. Once a young BA thought that he was exempted by his status from attending chapel. Symons sent for him, and the man explained, 'I thought that as I am in my thirteenth term I did not have to attend', and Symons answered, 'Is there no longer a God in heaven because you are in your thirteenth term?' Symons attended the coronation of Queen Victoria and in speaking of it to some undergraduates said, 'I couldn't help wondering what all those people were going to have for their breakfast', to which Mrs Symons added, 'The dear Warden is of course referring to their spiritual food.' Symons was much harried by a colleague called Ross, who was a little mad. Once, in chapel he shook his fist at Symons and said in a loud voice, 'Bloody, bawdy villain.' Symons was proud of his sermons and printed one of them and sent it to all his colleagues except Ross, who that evening in Common Room, complained, 'Nine and twenty years have I known thee, yet thou didst not give me a sermon that I might make merry withal.' Symons never admitted that he was wrong. An undergraduate was found drunk, and Symons abused another, quite innocent man for it, who said that his name was not that by which Symons had called him, but Symons would not admit it, 'You're drunk still. You don't even know your own name. Go to your room at once.' Dixey's stories of Symons conveyed the clerical ferocity of Victorian Oxford in its heyday, and made me glad that I had not lived in it. He himself showed another side of that paradoxical age in the gracious way in which he presided over the Senior Common Room with a genial tolerance for his younger colleagues, to whom in a rash moment he said, 'You don't drink as much as your grandfathers spilled', but whether this was said in derision or praise we never knew.

The third figure in the elder trio was some years younger. J. F. Stenning, who had been a member of the college since 1886, taught Hebrew and Theology to the few undergraduates who took these subjects. He may once have thought of taking Holy

Orders, but had never done so, though he remained a practising Christian. He was a good scholar, but not content to be merely that, and he combined his college post with being Secretary of the University Chest, which was then a part-time job and vastly easier than now. In the war he had commanded an infantry cadet battalion in Oxford, and for this he was awarded a CB and a CBE. He had also commanded the OTC when for a short time I was in it, but he never remembered this, and, since he had once spoken rather sharply to me, I thought it prudent not to remind him. He was very polite and gentle and conservative in a pleasant way. For a time he was chairman of the caucus which chose the Conservative candidate for parliament. Later, when Lindemann wanted the nomination, Stenning opposed it, and Lindemann did not get it. Stenning tried to make it up by asking Lindemann to tea in the garden, and mentioned that the Judas-tree was in full bloom. 'I should think so', said Lindemann, and the reconciliation was not a success. Stenning was not a full-blown Victorian like Wells and Dixey, but a man of the nineties who set a high value on good manners and a good appearance and interpolated 'Don't you know?' into his sentences.

After him came the newer Fellows. Of these the most striking and most brilliant was Theodore Wade-Gery, who taught ancient history. A man of noble appearance and resounding voice, he had, despite very short sight, fought through the war and shown remarkable gallantry, but his letters at the time never mentioned fighting and were mainly concerned with the wild flowers which he found at the front. Before the war he had tried both the civil service and schoolmastering, but, not liking either, had with the assistance of Arnold Toynbee become a Fellow of Wadham in 1914, only to join the army at once. In 1922 he was beginning to make up for lost years and to impress himself on Oxford as a teacher. He was both a scholar and a lover of literature, and still wrote poetry. He was an excellent talker, rich in ideas and fancies, ironical and humorous. He did more for Greek history in these years and later than anyone else at Oxford, and he strengthened me with his enthusiasm and sparkling intelligence. With him I produced my first book, a translation of the *Pythian Odes* of

Pindar, published by the Nonesuch Press in 1928. I wrote the first draft; he then took it in hand and improved it beyond measure; and finally I did a little tidying up. It was a lively delight to work with him and to enjoy the keenness of his mind and the delicacy of his perception. But he was primarily a historian, and felt the need for some large and complex subject to engage his full powers. He found it in the inscriptions of the Attic tribute-lists, and on these he set to work like a bulldozer as he drove his way through complex problems of text and interpretation. But behind this he kept his love of the Greek poets and always had something new to say about them. If his main published work was ruthlessly scientific, it was founded on his imaginative vision of the Greek world.

The history tutor was Reginald Lennard, who had been a lecturer before the war and was elected to a Fellowship after it. He had to shoulder an almost impossible burden of teaching and was expected to instruct a large number of pupils in the whole of history. The wonder is that he did it remarkably well, trained his pupils into first classes, and was much liked by them. He had been educated at home and had lively suspicions about the products of public schools. He also indulged in some scepticism about the classics, and when he enlarged upon this at lunch, it was liable to lead to a certain coldness. As the son of a clergyman, he was an agnostic, and though he was highly conservative in most matters, he was politically a radical. For this reason Wells was a little distrustful of him. He kept a cottage at Lower Heyford, where he organized concerts which were much appreciated by the villagers. The players were all amateurs, but among them were young men who rose to be Air Marshals and high civil servants, including two secretaries of the cabinet. He also cultivated an agreeable eccentricity of liking to swim in unfamiliar lakes and rivers and had accumulated a list of them which amounted to several hundreds and covered many parts of Europe. Despite an insufferable load of teaching, he wrote a number of books and articles with a distinctive elegance and solid learning.

Very unlike Lennard was our chaplain and tutor in philosophy, Frank Brabant. He looked frail and ascetic as if he were the original of some image of a medieval bishop, with a fine sensitive face and a slim frame. He was deeply religious, but did not expect others to be and was always rather surprised if they were. He thought that religion had little to do with morality, which was quite a separate affair and much less important. He had an excellent sense of fun and enjoyed the human scene with a detached gaiety, but his emotions were easily aroused, especially by theological controversy, into which he would enter bravely even on the tow-path during Eights Week, when his antagonist was a Low-church clergyman who coached the eight. In philosophy he cultivated an old-fashioned idealism, which fitted easily into his religion, and he was little interested in the new realism which was then in fashion. Intellectually he was more attracted by history, especially by that of France in the nineteenth century, on which he did some fine research. I once suggested that Brabant might like to teach some history but was discouraged by Lennard who said that he did not believe in having 'a dual-purpose short-horn'. Brabant kept a car and drove it badly, even by academic standards, which, from myopia, or self-righteousness, or loquacity, or absorption in other matters, are notoriously low. Once when I was with him, he drove straight into a cow and knocked it down, fortunately without damage. When the man in charge of it said quite mildly, 'Look out where you are going', Brabant said fiercely, 'Mind your own business,' and drove on. He was to find a wider and more satisfying field for his faith when in 1931 he went as a missionary to South Africa and worked among Bantus. Though in England he was a romantic conservative, in South Africa he became an outspoken and uncompromising adversary of Apartheid. He had in him something of the saint with its unexpectedness, its detach-ment, and its humour.

Brabant formed a lasting friendship with my friend David Cecil, who joined as a History don and colleague of Lennard in 1925. In his years at Wadham he was an enormous asset. He really liked and believed in Oxford and was quite independent in his attitude to it. He found much to amuse him, and expressed his views with wit and pungency. He was writing *The Stricken Deer*, which won him a considerable fame, but though he had a fine, sensitive imagination, he tempered it in ordinary affairs with a hard commonsense. He liked college life and took its differences and divergences with a light-hearted realism. He believed that undergraduates should be treated as if they were grown up and not tormented by ridiculous minor regulations, and if they got into trouble, he spoke up for them. In this he followed the tradition of his family. His uncle Hugh, later Lord Quickswood, was, when a don at Hertford, called to a meeting to consider the expulsion of a man who had been found paralytically drunk in the middle of the day, but, though everyone else was in favour of strong action, Lord Hugh argued, 'I see no difference between eating too much and spending a sleepless night and drinking too much and feeling a little giddy.' David was not so ruthlessly logical as this, but he knew what undergraduates were like and did not take too elderly a view of them. He was entirely natural with them, treated them with an easy familiarity and won their respect and affection. If they were tongue-tied, he would galvanize them into speech by provocative remarks, and if they were too cocky, he would deflate them almost without their knowing it. His pupils, who went to him with some awe at first, found that he was delightfully companionable and friendly. He took a lively part in their societies and provided a civilizing influence of a kind which they would never have met in their ordinary lives. He soon moved from History to English and established himself as one of the liveliest and most stylish members of the faculty. When he left in 1931 to get married and to have more time to write books, Wadham became a much duller place.

The number of Fellows at this time was completed by F. A. Lindemann, Professor of Experimental Philosophy in the University. He came in 1919 after a sensational career as a research pilot for the Air Force, and his position was anomalous, since he was both a Fellow of Wadham and a Student (which is the same thing) of Christ Church. He had just before my arrival moved to live in Christ Church, which he felt to be more suited to his social claims, but he had a vote on our governing body and sometimes dined with us on his unsavoury vegetarian food. He had a name for being brilliant and amusing, but, when as an undergraduate I met him, I did not like him. He had a sneering, superior manner and made too much ado about being a scientist, as when he told me that he could make me a Beethoven by an operation on my brain. This was nonsense, and I found it pretentious and silly. Nor did my first contacts with him at Wadham make me like him any more. I thought him a Philistine, a snob, and a Pharisee, and in a sense he was all three. He cared for none of the arts, except for music, and of that he was rather ashamed. He longed and liked to move in the very best society and was relentless in getting himself into it. Once arrived, his part was that of the famous scientist who knew all about everything and was delighted to lay down the law. His origin was complicated. The family came from Alsace and had opted to be French in 1871, but he himself had been born at Baden-Baden, and of this he was deeply ashamed, blaming his mother for it and concealing it from his entry in *Who's Who*. His pursuit of dukes may have been due to his desire to feel secure, but later I began to think that he really regarded himself as their equal. He was very well off, and this may have accounted for his delusion. His Pharisaism came out in his unbending puritanism towards undergraduates who got into trouble. He had himself been by no means virtuous in his younger days, and many of his friends were lax enough in their morals. He was not a Christian, though his stern line about sexual behaviour might suggest that he was. His god was respectability, and when this was outraged, he was implacable. An unfortunate undergraduate got a girl with child and married her, as was then thought the right thing to do. But he was an exhibitioner of the college, and exhibitioners were forbidden by the statutes to marry. Brabant and I saw an easy solution – the college should pay the same amount of money as a grant but not as an exhibition. Lindemann made a fearful scene and proposed the following motion,

that it being a prerequisite under Stat. IX 3 for the payment to an undergraduate from the Exhibition Fund that he shall have shown by his conduct that he deserves such assistance the Governing Body declare that he has not fulfilled this condition if he has admittedly recently committed fornication.

The proposal excited a fierce debate, which was not made easier by Lindemann's sneering righteousness, and at one point David said sharply, 'You seem to prefer the Mosaic to the Christian dispensation.' The motion was not carried, and the young man was given a grant, but his marriage was not a success.

If Lindemann presented these unfavourable aspects, there were other sides to his character which were more agreeable. When he took over the Clarendon Laboratory, it was almost moribund, but in time he built it into one of the best physical laboratories in the country. He was extremely helpful to his staff and his students, and without exception they liked him. He would encourage them without interfering unduly with them, see that they got jobs, and keep an eye on their careers. Even his snobbery had its bright side, since it made him a life-long friend of Winston Churchill and enabled him to do valuable work for him both before and during the Second World War. In time I found that even his contemptuous attitude to the classics was half a pose. Though he never saw what Wade-Gery and I saw in them, he was willing to discuss historical matters and to offer new scientific techniques in, for instance, the dating of archaeological finds. In time I came to like him, and he even came to like me. He was entirely devoted to the University, and was an excellent ally in any common cause. Even better, if you supported him on an issue, which did not mean very much to you, he would support you on another, which meant very little to him. He maintained his cynical, deprecatory air, but it hid real feelings, and it is odd that so clever a man did not see how much support it lost. Into all his activities he infused an atmosphere of crisis and drama, and this made any association with him exciting and amusing. Under it all he was a lonely man, and though he was much loved by some families, such as the Birkenheads, he would have liked more. He had built himself into a hard man of the world, and found himself tied to its requirements. In politics he was an unregenerate diehard, whose views would have been more at home among French royalists than on the English right, but on vital matters he followed Churchill, and this turned him into a national asset.

The variety of types in our Senior Common Room led to

moments of comedy. Lindemann was in his early days holding forth about Dreyfus and produced a more than usually absurd story that Dreyfus was guilty of selling information not to the Germans, but to the Russians, and since they were allies of the French, the point had to be hushed up. There was no evidence for this, and it was sadly typical of Lindemann at his silliest that he should tell it. That night A. C. Clark, Professor of Latin, was dining. He was the gentlest of men, and almost incapable of saying a harsh word, but he turned purple and said in his funny voice which went up a semitone at the end of each clause, 'That is the most abominable story I have ever heard.' On another occasion a clergyman was dining with Wells and told him that he had been on a conference which had decided that imperialism was un-Christian. Wells was deeply shocked and said, 'But surely St Paul approved of the Roman Empire and would have approved of the British.' Then from across the room came Wade-Gery's voice, 'On the other hand the author of the Apocalypse showed an admiration which was more tempered.' Wells fortunately did not hear. Wade-Gery had a genial friend called Sidney Marsh, who had been in the Royal Navy and in his retirement ran a boys' club in the East End. He used to bring his troop of boy scouts to Wadham for Whitsun when they encamped in the Warden's garden. All went smoothly so long as Wells was Warden, but the wife of his successor, Stenning, was a Christian Scientist. Marsh was an evangelical Anglican of a familiar naval kind, and when he saw a book by Mrs Eddy on her table, he said, 'You don't believe this rot, do you?' Mrs Stenning did, and reasons were found why Marsh should no longer make use of the Warden's garden for his scouts.

Wadham had some famous and fascinating old members, whom I met in my first years. The most astonishing was Frederic Harrison. He was ninety-two, and his first question to me was, 'When did you come up to Oxford?' I told him, 'In 1919,' and he answered, 'I came up in 1848.' So indeed he had. What is more, he had toured parts of Europe in that year of revolutions and had vivid memories of Paris after the fall of Louis Philippe. He remembered the accession of Queen Victoria when he was seven years old. He was playing with his bricks when his father came in and told him that the king was dead. He asked who the new king was going to be, and his father said, ' "We are not going to have a king, Frederick; we are going to have a queen" . . . I said, "It's come to that, has it?" and went on playing with my bricks.' When he came up, there was no north Oxford and you walked straight from Wadham into fields and market-gardens with relics of earth-works built in the Civil War. He must have known Oxford at the summit of its beauty when it was still a small town and the newest building was the Ashmolean Museum, designed by C. R. Cockerell, and the Gothic Revival had as yet embarked neither on its richer fantasies like Butterfield's Keble nor its shoddier bits of hackwork like Waterhouse's blocks at Balliol, or Scott's at New College. But he told me that in his time colleges were spoiled by creepers, which made it impossible to see either their outlines or their details. Incidentally he provided a link with a still remoter past by a neat chain of circumstances. He had as an undergraduate met Routh, President of Magdalen, who died in his hundredth year soon afterwards. Routh had in his boyhood met an old lady, who had in her girlhood seen Charles II exercising his spaniels in Magdalen Grove.

More formidable and more fascinating was F. E. Smith, then Lord Birkenhead and, when I first met him in June 1922, still Lord Chancellor. My first impression was of someone larger than life, with a tall, muscular frame, a rich complexion, and the well-preserved and well-tended hair of a young man. Among his cronies he naturally talked about the past, especially about games, which he had played well and still enjoyed. But there was much more even at a first meeting. He was then, as always, extremely kind to me, spoke to me as an equal, asked questions about Greek and Latin, and displayed his deep love for the college and for Oxford. In repose his face was meditative, often grave, at times almost sulky, but the moment he spoke it was alive with expression. He spoke with effortless fluency, but always with a literary flavour, which was even more marked when he made a speech. Then the famous voice rolled out the majestic periods, the ironies and the mockeries, the unashamed sentiment, and the sheer fun, which made him the delight of every audience. I never saw him use a note or hesitate for a word, and, though often enough at a speech at a college dinner there was no need for him to make much preparation, I suspect that he made some and that he had the full shape of a speech in his head before he delivered it. Birkenhead drank what seemed to be a great deal, especially brandy, but it had no perceptible effect on his words. He remained equally coherent through the evening. At the time and later some people said that he ruined himself by drink. If it weakened his resistance to illness, as it could have, this may be true, but reliance on it carried him through his career. He was not a man to go without anything he liked, and he had a particularly strong liking for convivial company in which everyone spoke freely. He combined the life of a man-about-town with that of a hard-working politician and lawyer. After an evening out, he would work on a brief or a speech for the next day, and in this he needed stimulation. He could not have done so much without it, and it was the price for leading so crammed a life. Though he was outspokenly ambitious, he refused to give up his pleasures, and one liked him all the more for it.

In many ways Birkenhead remained young till his death, and he was always at ease with the young, whom he encouraged and treated as equals. He moved effortlessly from one mood to another, from blithe ribaldry to attentive seriousness, from story-telling to easy intimacy. He understood people very well, and though he may not always have managed his own life with prudence, his advice to others was wise and well weighed. He asked me about the college and talked seriously about it, and invited me to dinners which he gave in Oxford and at his house at Charlton, where I met his delightful, gifted, humorous wife, and his young family. His son, Freddy, took after him in his sharp insight and his love of words; his daughter, Pamela, in her ebullient candour and her loyalty to her friends. Towards the end of his life, when he was much more ill than I knew, I sent him a copy of *The Oxford Book of Greek Verse*, of which I was a co-editor and for which I had written the Introduction, and I received the following letter in his firm, fine hand,

Dear Mr Bowra,

I am very grateful indeed to you for sending me the Oxford Book of Greek Verse, the introduction of which I have read with the greatest interest.

You must attribute my delay in replying to my illness. I have been far from well for six months and have for the last six weeks been under the charge of maladroit and expensive medical advisers: I have been quite unable to deal with business.

Let me say that I am honoured by the book which you have sent me and that I am delighted that the College to which I am so devoted is again passing through a period of well deserved distinction.

Yours sincerely

Birkenhead

This short letter contains much of him – his courtesy, his generosity, his style. I hardly expected him to acknowledge the book, but in his last illness, when the writing of a letter must have cost him a painful effort, he wrote in this way with more than one characteristic touch.

The antithesis of Birkenhead in many ways was his contemporary, and in some sense rival, Sir John Simon. Simon was equally tall but less heavily built and quite bald; he was equally ambitious, but less frank about it; he was never exuberant, never indiscreet; even when he told you something that 'must not go beyond these four walls', it was usually common knowledge; he allowed his wineglasses to be filled but hardly tasted of them. He was an excellent speaker, clear and persuasive, with an apt taste for words and some well-chosen touches of sentiment, but he was not provocative, and his few jokes lacked frivolity. Birkenhead liked him as an old friend, but could not refrain from teasing him. He usually managed to speak before him and to put in some mocking touch. At a college dinner, when Simon was making large sums at the bar and Birkenhead was temporarily out of office, he began, 'Sir John Simon, whose presence here this evening is costing him a thousand pounds . . .' and on another occasion, 'The law is an arid but remunerative taskmistress. In me you see an example of its aridity, in Sir John Simon of its remunerativeness.' He went further than this in ragging the eminently respectable

Simon, 'My dear Simon, when you came here, you were an innocent boy. When you were here, you learned things that you now prefer to forget.' Poor Simon, who lacked humour, could not imagine what these things could be but felt that there must be something somewhere. Birkenhead treated Simon in this deflating way, partly because he was an old friend, partly because Simon's combination of righteousness and success was not altogether to his taste. He felt that there was some humbug somewhere, and he took a shot at it. Simon accepted it politely, but was not happy. He was not without vanity, and he disliked ridicule. So when Birkenhead made fun of him, he had to pretend to like it and think it characteristic of an old friend, but it took the edge off such pleasure as he hoped to get.

Whereas Birkenhead seemed not to care what duties tomorrow might bring and was prepared to give himself wholly to the present moment, Simon seemed always to be looking ahead and economising his strength. In conversation he could be most interesting, especially in set-pieces like an account of Curzon lecturing the cabinet on the dangers of retreat from the Dardanelles and quoting at length Thucydides' account of the disastrous Athenian retreat from Syracuse – only to be told that the greater part of our forces had already been safely evacuated. Simon was something of an artist with words and quoted poetry with feeling, but he never gave the impression of being spontaneous. He seemed, despite his obvious politeness, to be preoccupied with something else, and this impression was enhanced by his habit of calling by the wrong name even people whom he knew quite well. In concentrating on success Simon repressed his more human side, with the result that in the end he never won the success which he desired so avidly. He held most of the high offices of state, but he was never Prime Minister, nor was there any likelihood that he would be. He was thought to be a cold fish and, worse, to have no very strong convictions. The first charge was not quite fair. He was deeply devoted to his first wife, and her early death was a shattering blow to him: he was hardly less devoted to his second wife, who must often have embarrassed him in later years when she became a little queer, but he always treated her with the utmost consideration. It is harder to say how seriously he treated his political principles. He resigned from the cabinet in 1916 on the issue of conscription, and this meant that he was out of office for many years, but he rather spoiled the effect by saying later that he had been wrong. Even his speech on the General Strike, which denounced it as illegal, lost something by looking too much like the special pleading of a lawyer. Later when he supported Chamberlain in the policy of appeasement, he appeared to do so largely from a desire to trim his sails to the prevailing wind. Simon longed to be thought a strong man, and struck powerful gestures when he read a lesson in chapel or prepared to drive from a golf-tee, but, though from a safe position he was capable of a formidable pose, he lacked real conviction. Perhaps, like other gifts, it had been dried up by ambition, or perhaps his experience at the bar meant that he saw problems from too many angles and was not able to decide which was really right. For many years I found him a little difficult to talk to. All would begin promisingly, but then, as his fine turns were exhausted, there was nothing more to say. In his last years I got to know him better. After he ceased to be Lord Chancellor in 1945, there was very little more that he could reasonably want, though he approached me in 1948 about becoming High Steward of the University on the death of Lord Sankey, and was duly appointed. In old age he paid more attention to others. Despite his placid exterior he had a certain pathos. He longed to be liked, to be admired, to please, but somehow he failed, and he knew it.

Two other men, C. B. Fry and F. W. Hirst, had been contemporaries of Birkenhead and Simon, and neither had really been a worldly success. Fry, after being the greatest athlete of his age, might well have settled into a comfortable and well-remunerated post in business, but he chose to run a training-ship and did it very successfully. He may at moments have felt a twinge of envy for his old friends who had done so much better, but if he did, he did not show it, and what I liked in him was his detachment. His line on Birkenhead was that he was a 'card', a man who was always ready with the right words in any situation, however awkward, and had a fabulous gift of the gab. He himself combined his work with a large number of interests, and you never knew what he would take up next. He kept his magnificent figure into old age, and he was a lively, ingenious, and somewhat innocent talker. When Wade-Gery and I were translating Pindar, he asked, 'Has anyone here heard of Pindar?' and was astonished that we had. He had as an undergraduate got a first class in Mods but a fourth in Greats, and this irked him. He claimed that it was because he was made to read 'a fellow called Mill', whom he could not endure, and that if only he had been told to read F.H. Bradley, he would have done very well. There may have been truth in this. Fry had a keen sense of literature and Bradley's impassioned dialectic would have appealed to him much more than Mill's dry arguments. Fry had been to India to work with his old cricketing friend Ranjitsinhji and had many original comments to make on it. He was fascinated by the caste-system and asked what you could do when people believed that your station in this life was determined by your behaviour in the last, and wondered whether there might not be something in it. Fry believed that dancing and singing were better training for the body than physical drill and, being in complete control of his own limbs, liked to demonstrate what could be done with them. He noticed what people looked like and gave much pleasure when he congratulated Wells on the good looks of his Fellows. He was eager and natural, and though perhaps he lived on a manic curve, of which I never saw the downward trend, he was happier than Simon and lasted much longer than Birkenhead.

Hirst was the best scholar of the party. He was throughout his life a Gladstonian Liberal, and it is significant that, when Gladstone gave the first Romanes Lecture, Hirst attended it, but Simon was too busy tubbing on the river to go. Hirst's heroes were Gladstone, Morley, and Campbell-Bannerman, and to the pure essence of their gospel he remained faithful. His delightful and warm-hearted wife shared all his interests, and, being free from financial worries, he led an independent life as a Liberal thinker. The older dons did not approve of him, since he had been against the war, and that was enough for them. They got round it by saying that he was a bore, which he was very far from being. This troubled him not at all. He was at his ease with all sorts of men, talked freely and engagingly from a wide knowledge, and had his own observations on Birkenhead, whom he liked for his warmth and loyalty, and whose style he savoured with pleasure. The best example of it, in his view, was when Birkenhead, describing how he once climbed into college, was very precise on the placing of the ladder, 'It was midway between the chapel and another humbler but not less necessary building', but he was also delighted by Birkenhead's comment just before a general election when it was suggested that Baldwin ought to go – 'I see no point in swapping donkeys when crossing a stream.' Though Hirst was strongly against war for financial and moral reasons, he was a keen student of it and had his preferences among the great captains, while he claimed that Churchill did not understand the rudiments of strategy. He was delighted when he was made an honorary Fellow of the college, and attended the dinner for Simon when he was appointed High Steward. Simon was telling one of his stories, when he was interrupted by Hirst saying, 'That was the man who kept his secretary in a grandfather-clock.' Hirst was a fine representative of a Liberalism which had often been a characteristic of Wadham, notably with Wilkins, who was Cromwell's brother-in-law, and with Frederic Harrison and his Positivists, and he combined it with a rich humanity and a delighted interest in the common scene.

These fascinating characters were no more than occasional visitors, and for ordinary life I had the society of my colleagues. Between us we had to administer the college and were responsible for its welfare. Wadham at this time was extremely poor, and suffered from it. Until about 1870 it had done well enough with its ownership of agricultural property, but even then it had been much injured by the outrageous Symons, who was much more interested in making money for himself than for the college. But after 1870, with the arrival of cheap food from the United States and the increasing depression in the countryside, Wadham went from worse to worse. Farms were sold to bolster up other farms, and then these had to be sold to get enough money to keep the place going. There had been a very slight improvement after

1919, but the college was still desperately short of funds with too small a number of Fellows and of Scholars. The latter meant that we competed on bad terms with richer colleges who examined for scholarships with us but afforded more awards and therefore attracted more candidates. The candidates we got were good, but there were not enough Scholars in residence. The other younger Fellows and myself felt that something should and could be done about this, but we were hampered by the inbred defeatism of our elders. They had been brought up to accept the college's poverty as a decision of Providence and could not believe that anything could alleviate it. In these movements Lennard, who was something of an economist, was the leading spirit. Our first efforts were not successful. We decided to sell a large area of land at Southrop and did so at what we thought was a good price, only to discover soon afterwards that it had been sold again for almost double to a speculative builder. We had made something on the deal, but not nearly enough and had exposed our lack of business capacity. Fortunately another attempt to get money by selling our first four folios of Shakespeare failed because the price offered was not enough even for our unambitious demands.

A new and more promising opportunity then presented itself. The Rhodes Trustees, who commanded large resources and had put by a lot of money in the war, were eager to build a centre in the middle of Oxford, where land even then was extremely scarce. Wadham had an unusual asset in the farther part of the Warden's garden, which went right up to South Parks Road and was not so much a garden as a paddock with some fine trees. It was a piece of country in the middle of Oxford, but it was not in fact much used, and, if left as it was, might have led to nasty remarks about us. The Warden had to pay for its upkeep from his none too large salary. The Rhodes Trustees made approaches, and after a long and serious discussion we agreed to sell $1\frac{1}{2}$ acres for £30,000. This was for those days a very good price, though now it would be four or five times as much. We were still left with substantial gardens, and the part kept by the Warden was quite as much as he could manage. Dixey voted against the deal, and later Birkenhead told me that he was very distressed to hear about it as

he had used the far part of the land to read in when he was working secretly for his schools. But Wells was for it, and his advocacy
carried the day. We improved our finances by a neat sum, and
were able almost at once to elect another Fellow. Looking back
on it I have no doubt that we did the right thing. If we had not
sold this piece of land, we should have been much slower in that
improvement in our finances which led to a notable improvement
in academic results. Moreover, if we had kept the land, we should
either have had to turn it into a proper garden open to the public,
which would mean that we did at our own expense something
that brought no special advantage to us, or we should have been
compelled to sell it to some buyers less accommodating than the
Rhodes Trustees and might well have had a science laboratory
there instead of Sir Herbert Baker's attempt to combine a Cots-
wold manor-house with hints of African imperialism in a circular
'heröon' surmounted by a copper bird of Zimbabwe. Once we
had taken this step we began to move forward, and though the
process was slow, our virtue was rewarded when a few years later
Sir Algernon Methuen, the publisher, left us money for scholarships which eventually amounted to some £70,000. Methuen,
like Hirst, was not loved by the older generation. It was claimed
that he had changed his name, which indeed he had for family
reasons, and there was nothing wrong in that, but the real reason
for disapproval was that he was on the list of men whom Asquith
had decided to make peers if the Parliament Bill failed to pass the
House of Lords. The Methuen bequest provided us with a large
number of scholarships, and by the late thirties we were beginning
to show some results from them.

College meetings, at which the Warden and Fellows made their
decisions, had their comic side. On the whole everyone behaved
well within limits. Accusations of corruption and the like were
lacking, but there were undercurrents of feeling which at times
became noisy. Lennard, who chose his words with skill, had a
somewhat mannered way of speaking which Wade-Gery called
'the dishonest voice' or 'the Low Church voice', and when Lennard
was reaching his climax, we heard the fatal words uttered *sotto
voce* with damaging effect. On the other hand Wade-Gery, who

could be equally eloquent, had his own critics. A charming science don, who came in January 1925, T.C. Keeley, hardly spoke at all for his first year, but then, after a very fine display by Wade-Gery, said simply 'Bosh'. He was however repaid with equal derision when the discussion turned on the use of certain earth-closets by women servants, and he said, 'I suggest that as the women fall in they be replaced by men.' Wells was always sweetness itself and got out of his occasional slips with guileless charm. Once we found that he had admitted two candidates for entry whom the tutors had turned down, and when we asked about it, we got the answer, 'I am afraid that I must have omitted the word "not" from my letter.' Whenever figures were in question, Lindemann used to produce a pocket slide-rule and announce results which no one could question, rather as in the Second World War he did to confound the critics of area-bombing.

When Frederic Harrison died, he left us his ashes, together with those of his wife, in an urn to be placed in the chapel. After some debate it was agreed that as he had not been a Christian, they could not go in the chapel, where anyhow there was no room for them, but might go in the ante-chapel. The urn, with a Latin inscription by Wade-Gery and myself, was fixed in position. At the last moment Lennard suspected a clerical plot, but his query 'Nothing ecclesiastical, I hope?' received a reassuring answer. A distinguished party gathered in the ante-chapel. Among the speakers was Birkenhead, and in the front row was Sir Thomas Jackson, the architect, aged eighty-seven. Birkenhead began, 'We are met today on a solemn and memorable occasion to welcome to their last resting-place the ashes of a very distinguished Englishman, of a very distinguished Oxford man, of a very distinguished Wadham man, the ashes of no less a person than Mr Jackson.' At this point Jackson perked up and wondered what could be happening to him, but Wells in a loud voice prompted 'Harrison', and Birkenhead, quite unruffled, continued, 'the ashes of Mr Harrison.'

College meetings had also their distressing side. In 1931, both David and Brabant left us, and while we elected a layman to do philosophy in Brabant's place, we elected as chaplain and lecturer in English a very able man from Hertford called Humphry House. He had rather a saturnine appearance, and, having only recently decided to take Holy Orders, was still a deacon. For the larger part of 1932 I was abroad on Sabbatical leave and came back at the end of the year to find that a serious crisis had arisen and been settled in a most unsatisfactory manner. Humphry had lost his faith and decided that he could not become a priest or continue to be chaplain. He had then, most unwisely, resigned his Fellowship, which he could reasonably have kept as lecturer in English without being chaplain. I arrived too late, but did my best to revive the issue. I proposed that Humphry should be elected a tutorial Fellow, since there was plenty for him to do, and he was an unusually able man. I found against me the solid ranks of unbelievers led by Lindemann, who seemed to think that to lose one's faith was as bad as to lose someone else's virginity. I was strongly supported by Wade-Gery, but our new philosopher, Ian Gallie, who after a year at Cambridge was conscientiously anti-God, joined the majority, and the cause was lost. It was a humiliating and distressing defeat, a victory for the Pharisees, and I made up my mind that in due course it should be put right. Humphry had a hard time, and it was not until after the Second World War that he was appointed a University Lecturer in Oxford. I gave him rooms in college, and my colleagues, then much replenished by younger men, saw his value so clearly that they elected him to a Fellowship. An ugly wrong was at last righted, but Humphry's health had been undermined by army-life in India, and he died, still quite a young man, a few years later.

My main duty was to teach classics for Mods. I was supposed to teach up to eighteen hours a week, but my quota did not always reach this, and in the summer term was nearer nine. I had some very good pupils. At the beginning the top scholar, who came from Wolverhampton Grammar School, was a tall fair-haired man called Norman Brook. He had beautiful handwriting, a very clear mind, and a gift for sorting a difficult subject into its main elements under the right headings. He was doing the archaeological background of the Homeric poems as a special subject, and since I was myself working on Homer, I was able to help him and discuss my own tentative speculations. He mastered the whole thing with ease and expressed his views with a mature clarity, and I was not surprised that in due course he became head of the Civil Service and secretary of the Cabinet, with whose services Churchill, on his return to office in 1951, refused to dispense. In my first years I was fortunate in having a number of lively and gifted pupils – Herbert Parke, who in his delighted eagerness for the subject was a natural scholar, and in due course became Vice-Provost of Trinity College, Dublin; Rex Warner, whose remarkable gifts and promise were hampered by a breakdown in his third year, when he was said to see the transcendental deduction of the categories lying in solid blocks across the room, but who was, when I taught him, the ideal pupil, since he had been badly grounded at school and found in Greek and Latin all the charms of novelty; Cecil Day-Lewis, who was already a poet and applied his literary gifts to the translation of classical texts with an adventurous originality. There were many others who had lively touches of individuality and got much out of a drill in noble works of literature. There were of course dullards, who were extremely difficult to teach, since they treated every attempt to help them as an affront to their dignity and endured it with a resentful silence. There were others worse than this – young men who had been stuffed at school and come to hate the subject. Murray had warned me of them, and more than once I saw how right he was. Sometimes they could be won by the appeal of something absolutely new, but more often it was a losing battle and I tried to get them to take some other course. There was one particularly painful case. He came from a poorish home, and at the start I had hopes for him because he wrote good Greek prose. But he hated the classics, and Greek prose more than anything else. I tried all my stratagems, but without success, and was relieved when he got no worse than a second in Mods. He then moved to 'Modern Greats' and seemed quite happy in it. Later he became very odd and wrote general history with a strong Fascist bias. Unluckily for him he could not find a publisher, and he died with his grand design unrecognized.

I had from time to time to examine for the University in Mods, and on my first occasion in 1927 I had an unusual excitement. Our chairman was E. E. Genner, Fellow of Jesus, a puritanical man who neither smoked nor drank and tended to order his colleagues about as if we were on parade. Among the candidates was a man from Jesus whom we will call Jones. His papers were remarkably good, and he got such high marks that we awarded him an undisputed first class. Genner displayed becoming modesty about having taught him so well, but gave no hint that he did not think very highly of him. Later, after the list had been published, a man wrote from Brighton to say that on looking at the composition papers set in the recent Mods he saw that they were the same as had been sent him before the examination by a Mr Jones from Jesus and that he had on request written versions of them. Slowly the whole story came to light. Jones had stolen a complete set of proofs of the papers from Genner's room, copied out those which concerned him, and then returned the originals. The compositions were done for him by the man at Brighton, but the other papers, such as the unseen translations and the prepared books, he wrote out himself with the aid of dictionaries, cribs, and every other kind of aid. He took them with him into the examination room, and at the end of each period handed in the appropriate paper. Once he seems to have felt that had gone wrong, and he tried a different plan. He removed a pile of scripts, including his own, from the room of an examiner, took out his own and substituted a new one for it, and returned the whole lot when the examiner was not in. The examiner noticed that some scripts were missing, but when he came to correct them, found them all there, and assumed that he had made a silly mistake. This explained why in his prepared books Jones was very knowledgeable about quite small points which he seemed to have memorized *verbatim* from such editors as Jebb. We thought that he must have a photographic memory, but he had simply copied out the passages with very few changes. The matter went to the Proctors, who looked very carefully into it and proved that Jones had cheated on a colossal scale. His name was erased from the class-list, and he was expelled from the University. I am ashamed to say that my other colleagues and I were secretly not displeased that Genner had been shown up not only as grossly careless in his treatment of examination papers, which should be kept locked up, but in his smug acceptance of Jones as a good scholar, when he must have known that he was not. Jones made a noble attempt the following October to come up to Exeter as his own brother, but his scheme was unmasked, and he was not accepted.

In the twenties and thirties young dons were asked out to formal dinners by their elders, especially by heads of colleges. At such parties you wore a tail-coat, white waistcoat, white tie, and stiff shirt, and on arrival you were given a card telling you whom you were to take in. Once you had identified her, you offered her your arm and marched solemnly in. This was seldom justified by the dinner which followed and tended to consist of white soup, white fish, white chicken, and blancmange, but it was common form and had had its own dignity. At dinner you had to avoid controversial topics of conversation, such as religion or politics, and were usually reduced to travel, which was not likely to inflame dangerous passions. After dinner you were shifted rapidly from one person to another, until at ten o'clock the senior lady guest would get up as if stunned to find that it was so late and you would all troop out together, refusing on the way offers of a much-needed 'night-cap'.

Among heads of colleges H. A. L. Fisher, who succeeded Spooner as Warden of New College in 1925, was always an encouraging friend to me. He looked a little remote and stiff, and it was said that he began too many sentences with 'When I was in the Cabinet . . .' Actually I never heard him say these words, but if I had, I should have been delighted, since I much enjoyed his reminiscences of politics. He had two heroes of almost diametrically opposite gifts. One was Lloyd George, whom he admired as 'the most dynamic figure since Napoleon' and to whom he remained unswervingly loyal; the other was Arthur Balfour, whose mind he regarded as the finest he had ever encountered. Fisher had a talent for coining memorable phrases, as when, after visiting Quebec, he described it as 'a fragment of the *ancien régime* frozen in the ice-floes of Canada', or said of a book by a colleague, 'I think it excellent and only wish that it had been written in English.' He was a Victorian agnostic, but his sense of duty made him attend college chapel on Sunday evenings, where he maintained a fine aloofness as if he had no interest in what was happening. When Spencer Leeson became headmaster of Winchester and evangelized many of the boys, Fisher was deeply shocked and complained that 'their minds are rotted by piety'. He compared New College at this time very unfavourably with what it had been twenty years earlier; then he would find Vinogradoff talking to Maitland, 'but now when I go into the Senior Common Room, what do I find? A mausoleum, a morgue.' As a young man he had studied in Paris and listened to Taine and Renan, and he always cherished ideals of elegant scholarship which were alien to those who had studied in Germany.

Another impressive head of a house was the Reverend F. Homes Dudden, Master of Pembroke. He was tall and handsome, and when I was Proctor in 1930–1, he was Vice-Chancellor. He entertained on a fine scale, and I much enjoyed his benevolent condescension as host. He had as a young man been involved in the Aesthetic Movement of the nineties and was reported as having said, 'I think that one ought to live beautifully.' Now he was not only an epicure, but so far as a Christian priest can be, an Epicurean. He attached much importance to his comforts and would allow no business, however urgent, to interfere with his afternoon tea. He had liked being rector of Holy Trinity, Sloane Street, where his sermons on climbing the stony path with torn and bleeding feet were much appreciated by his well-to-do congregation. He said of it, 'It was a parish with no poor, and I much prefer a parish with no poor.' Later he said to me, 'Of course as a Christian I believe in survival after death, but personally I should much prefer extinction.' He was a considerable scholar who wrote large books in a fine rotund style worthy of the eighteenth century, to which spiritually he belonged. He was also a very able Vice-Chancellor. A crook had been appointed by the government to be head of a university department and took advantage of his position to squeeze large sums of money out of gullible firms. Dudden saw through him and got rid of him, and in the end the University was liable for much smaller damages than I had feared. The cause of much of the trouble was that poor Wells had in all innocence encouraged the crook and heartened him to go ahead as if the University were behind him.

As Proctor I was *ex officio* a member of the Hebdomadal Council, which is the real governing body of the University, and on one occasion two of my revered mentors caused me some trouble. Murray had told Fisher that undergraduates used motor-cars for making love. Why he did so, I do not know, but there was in him an unpredictable streak of puritanism which broke out from time to time. Fisher took up the case with eloquence. He enlarged on the melancholy way in which motor-cars disrupted the unity and self-sufficiency of Oxford, and would not be deterred by arguments that they were helpful in visiting the surrounding country or in taking young men to sports-grounds. He persuaded Council to instruct the Proctors to forbid their use by undergraduates. Fortunately this was beyond the powers of Council, as my colleague and I pointed out. He then said that Congregation must pass a decree to the same effect. This was perfectly in order, but we announced that, if it were proposed, we should veto it. Though this seldom happened, it was in accord with the statutes, and all we had to do was to stand up together and say without any explanation, 'Nobis procuratoribus non placet'. Fisher flinched, and in a spirit of compromise a committee was set up to see what could be done. On it the Proctors sat, with Dudden, who was sceptical of the whole affair, in the chair. On it was also a Fellow of University College, A. S. L. Farquharson, who had rather a tragic life at home and compensated for it by a puckish humour. Early in the discussion he said, 'You know, Mr Vice-Chancellor, that if they wish to commit fornication, they can do so just as well by train.' We kept our faces, but Dudden saw that the whole thing was discredited, and little more was heard of it.

7

The Next Generation

A generation of undergraduates at Oxford lasts for three or four years, and then its place is taken by another which is very little interested in it and shapes its own schemes of work and pleasure. On moving from New College to Wadham in 1922 I still knew a few men younger than myself and through them I met some of their juniors and successors and so kept contact with undergraduates other than my own at Wadham for the next few years. I got a great deal out of it and through it formed some friendships which have lasted ever since. The post-war generation had come to a close and was succeeded by something quite different. With the new arrivals of 1922 a dominant note was struck by a small and gifted party of Etonians, who set out unashamedly to be aesthetes and to revive some glories of the nineties. In 1919 aesthetes hardly existed, but the new set arrived well heralded. At Eton they had produced a paper, *The Eton Candle*, which was very consciously *avant-garde* and had the support of the Sitwells, then coming into a deserved renown. The new set was in full reaction against the drabness and the discipline which the war had enforced on schools and which were still maintained when there was no excuse for them. The aesthetes were out to shock and to amuse, and had a confidence lacking in my own generation. They were not troubled about their work, and though some of them later matured into original scholars, this was not their aim at the

time. They were splendidly courageous in defying their un-
cultivated contemporaries, who were first amused by them and
then admired them. Beneath all their fun and fireworks they had
a real devotion to the arts and knew a lot about them. But on the
surface they displayed a taste for the unfamiliar and the unexpected
and devised ingenious ways of showing their originality from
luncheons at which lobster Newburg was served for fifty guests
in what looked like a tin bath, to singing Victorian ballads or
growing cactuses or giving dances in country barns extravagantly
decorated for the evening. They added a brilliant touch of colour
to the Oxford scene, and if they were sometimes scandalous, they
were usually entertaining.

By common consent the two leading aesthetes were Harold
Acton and Brian Howard, both Etonians at Christ Church, but
very different in manner and character. Harold had passed much
of his life in Italy and had good manners such as none of us had
ever seen. He was tall and well built, with fine eyes and a rich,
rumbustious laugh. He dressed very carefully in a dark suit and a
grey bowler-hat, and carried a rolled umbrella or a decorative
walking-stick. He spoke fluently with a notable sense of fun and
drama, mixing agreeable flattery with keen observation and utter-
ing outrageous sentiments with a careless gaiety. He had a welcoming warmth and a talent for captivating the most unlikely
people. To Roy, who was his tutor in economics – of all things –
he read eloquent essays which were not always quite on the
academic point. He had also his moments of brilliant comedy,
though his intention was not merely to amuse. He used to stand
on a balcony of Meadow Buildings at Christ Church and recite
The Waste Land through a megaphone, and though many
laughed, some were impressed. He would also throw open his
window and address any young men who happened to be passing, 'Come in, boys. You're ripping fellows. Come and see old
Acton. It's only old Acton the aesthete.' If they came in, he was
magnificently courteous and made them like him at once. His
long friendship with the great scholar Jackie Beazley and his wife
began with a typical courtesy on his part. The Beazleys kept a
goose at Christ Church, and one day Mrs Beazley was exercising

it in Tom Quad. Between them they more or less filled the path, and when Harold came in the opposite direction, he not only jumped over the goose, which was to be expected, but at the same time took off his bowler in salutation, and Mrs Beazley knew that he was a true gentleman. Unfortunately the goose died, and the Beazleys were deeply distressed. One evening in hall an old classics don, S. G. Owen, who was renowned for his greed, said to Beazley, 'How's your goose? I suppose you are fattening him for Michaelmas.' Beazley, with a look of anguish, said, 'He's dead. Many worse men are still alive.'

Brian Howard was of mixed origin, partly Jewish and partly American, and looked much more exotic than Harold. He was slim and dark, with a finely modelled face, bright, black eyes, and long eyelashes. If Harold was welcoming, Brian was aloof and self-contained. He spoke with marked mannerisms, emphasizing each point as he made it and choosing his words for their unusual flavour, often with a hint of inverted commas when he dropped into colloquialisms. He addressed one frequently as 'my dear' and sought more to dominate than to please. He suffered from social ambitions. At Eton he had cultivated the sons of noble houses, and he kept up with them at Oxford. They could not quite make him out, but accepted him as a bird of paradise, and recognized that he knew much of which they were ignorant. With them he assumed a paedagogic, even moralistic tone. He would chide them for their stupidity, their dull opinions, their flat vocabulary, their young women. While they did not resent his chiding, he wished to be like them, and for this nature and his upbringing had not intended him. He took to hunting and rode in a steeplechase with notable courage but little success. He once asked me to a dinner at which every guest except myself was a peer and made a speech beginning, 'My lords and gentleman', with a strong stress on the final syllable of the last word. When the Surréalistes first appeared on the horizon, he gave a party for them and during it led me aside and said, 'My dear, all that they are trying to do is to write without any *effort*, and we all know what that leads to.' He made no secret of his sexual tastes, and this proved his undoing. He was much too outspoken to be a welcome guest at the grand houses of his friends, and one by one they dropped him. He managed to live more or less happily, preferably with some simple young man who did not understand him but admired him for being unlike anyone else. In the Second World War he was in the RAF as an AC2 and bore it with patient courage. Once when the food was being inspected by an officer, who asked, 'How's the grub?' Brian with utter calm replied, 'Perfectly delicious, sir.' He was not above spreading doubt and despondency, and his place for this was the Ritz bar where 'other ranks' were forbidden to go by Air Force regulations. One day, when he was doing this on no mean scale, an Air Vice-Marshal came up to him and said, 'Come, my man. You can't do this. What's your name?' 'Mrs Smith to you, my dear', replied Brian. After the war he lived in the south of France with a friend, of whom he said to me, 'Shakespeare and boats, that's all that he likes, Shakespeare and boats.' When the friend, to whom he was deeply attached, died, Brian at once killed himself with a poison which he kept in readiness for such a thing happening. He left no lasting memorial and made very little use of his unusual talents. He had a striking, if disturbing, personality, and might have been an artist if he had not been brought up among pictures by his father in what he called 'that mausoleum, my home' and come in the end to dislike them because of this association.

Known to Harold and Brian but not really a member of their set was Cyril Connolly, who came up in 1922 from Eton as a scholar to Balliol. I soon got to know him better than the famous aesthetes. He was slim and slight, with a rather large head, a fine forehead, eager, questing eyes, a face that registered every change of feeling, and a soft hypnotizing voice. At Eton he had not only won prizes for history but made himself so agreeable to the 'bloods' that of their own accord they elected him a member of the Eton Society, known as 'Pop'. At Balliol he reacted strongly against his earlier career. He no longer wished to keep in with 'bloods', nor had he any desire for a rich social life. His work had lost its charm for him, and to make up for it he applied his acute and sensitive intelligence partly to finding a select circle of close friends, with whom he could live in intimate ease, partly to extending his knowledge of literature and of foreign countries, which took him away from the inhibiting routine of home and provided food for his hungry imagination. He had lost his old stance and was looking for another, and this meant that at times he was unhappy, unsure of himself, and in need of support.

Sligger was from the start kind and generous to him, but though he calmed some of his worries, he did not give him quite the incitement that he needed, or discuss with sufficient knowledge or insight the subjects that absorbed him. Cyril was fascinated by the Greek poets and by some of the moderns, notably Yeats and Eliot, and since these tastes coincided with mine, we had much to say to each other, and our friendship expanded quickly. He needed affection. He was the only child of a retired major, who was a world-authority on snail-shells, and a mother whose claims on him were more than he could accept and from whom he had to escape for long intervals. His standards were high, and too often a promising friend revealed limitations which put Cyril off. His worries over personal relations occupied much of his time and kept him even further from the mass of his contemporaries. Nor did Balliol appeal to him. He managed to secure a quiet room in a far corner of it, but seldom frequented its open spaces. It was a little too hard, too worldly for him, and it had almost nothing to offer as he explored his sensibility. Though he had a great capacity for enjoyment, he could be exacting about it. If you asked him to luncheon or dinner, you had to be careful that he would like the other guests. He usually did, since he was not so much intolerant as too expectant, but if his expectations were not realized, he might be deeply depressed as if some unique opportunity had been missed.

Cyril had a vivid talent for comedy, which could transform the actual scene into farce, create imaginary myths about dull people, and thrive on a firm distinction between those who were real and those who were not, the latter being in a majority. When Proust burst upon us, Cyril devoured him and turned him to his own purposes, comparing himself with Swann, Sligger with Françoise, a great friend with Albertine, a socially pretentious young man with Odette, the Morrells of Garsington with the Verdurins, and David Cecil with the Duchesse de Guermantes. From his reading of Proust he learned how to analyse his feelings not in the scientific way of the new psychologists but with imagery and choice parallels from literature. He was extremely quick to notice changes of mood or small betrayals of character, and on them he would build bold edifices of speculation. He used his derisive mockery for the dull, the gross, the pretentious, the prosaic, and what he liked was a sensitivity as delicate as his own or an elegance which satisfied his sense of style. When he was happy, he was excellent company, amusing and amused, outspoken without being brusque, very quick to take a point and enrich it. I have never known anyone of his age who was in so many ways mature and yet kept the freshness, both sad and glad, of youth.

Cyril was in love with words, with good literature, especially with poetry. He composed Greek epigrams about his private concerns and inscribed them on the walls behind the pictures of Sligger's chalet. In his vacations he wrote long, descriptive, and highly diverting letters about his impressions and his adventures. They were completely spontaneous, the fruit of his busy thoughts, and though from sheer youth some of his judgements might be hasty or even absurd, the final effect was extraordinary. Through them he trained himself, without knowing it, to be a man of letters. He was trying to master the world for himself and in the process made endless discoveries. He was an observer and a critic, but he had also a poetical imagination, and his gift for words did not fit into any conventional category. This meant that as yet he fell between the opposite poles of a poet and a theoretical thinker. He was too critical to think that he could write poetry, but he was too much of a poet to become the studious history scholar that Sligger wished him to be. He thought things out in his own way by a series of illuminating insights and a stern faithfulness to his own feelings. He preferred the particular to the general and kept his eye on the individual object or situation until it yielded all that he wanted. Whatever troubles he might have and whatever uncertainties he might feel about his own decisions, he clung to his belief in the art of words and found in it a central security. At times this meant that his standards were a little too high for his friends, and he was disappointed with them as he might be also with himself. He was poorly armoured against shocks, and satire did not always give him an adequate relief from them. But his love of literature sustained him and set the direction of his life.

An intermittent friend of Cyril's was Kenneth Clark, of Trinity, henceforth called K. He too was an only son, but of rich parents, and had been brought up with a callousness which only the rich dare to show to their children. Much of his childhood had been spent in solitude, and he had learned how to adapt himself to it and even to like it. But for the rest of the time, when he was not at school, he had to follow the merciless routine which the Edwardians imposed as a kind of penance on themselves. At the appropriate time of year you shot or hunted or yachted or went to Monte Carlo or did the London season; if you did not conform to this, you were a 'rotter'. K recalled the parties at his parents' house in Scotland, where, as he said, the purple-faced, gross men 'looked like barons of beef', and a servant was kept whose sole task was to iron the newspapers. Even yachting was governed by strict rules, and there was a special concept of 'going-ashore clothes', and of course the yacht never stopped at the places you liked, because of the wind or for some other inscrutable reason. K was brought up in the manner of his class, played billiards and golf, and shot. He took it patiently, and neither liked nor disliked it. His self-indulgent, bored father and his rather prim, critical mother paid no special attention to him, but this meant that he matured his own resources and found out for himself what his tastes were. In exhilarated moments he would sing snatches of opera; he liked good food and drink, and knew about them; he cultivated young women at a time when there were few about, but kept them from his friends, since they did not yet form part of the Oxford scene and he was not sure how they would be received. He had a keen sense of absurdity, told excellent stories of strange characters whom he had met, and was always ready to laugh at himself. This essential gaiety was rather at war with his appearance and manner. He was always neat and trim, and by some he was thought to be a bit too prim, too reserved. This was a protection which he had formed for himself in his strange up-bringing, but it was completely at variance with his character.

K had been to school at Winchester, where he had not been very happy but had found consolation in his remarkable head-master, M. J. Rendall. Rendall was a passionate enthusiast for Italian painting and lectured on it to highly appreciative school-boys. He may not have known very much, but his delight was infused with a romantic glow, which he made them share. K certainly owed something to him, but Rendall did no more than foster what was already there. K knew from an early age what he wished to do and where his tastes and talents lay, and he set to work with a happy determination. When he came to Oxford he had already a remarkable knowledge of painting and other visual arts. Nor did he confine himself to any limited period. His natural responses were such that he could follow them instinctively and know that he was right. He loved pictures for their own sake, would look at them with concentrated care, take in their points, and come to his own decision about them. But he had another, equally valuable gift. He liked ideas and the exchange of ideas, and he related his vivid aesthetic experience to other matters historical, social, and literary. He read a great deal, not only about art, and placed his inquiries in a wider setting. He was already both an aesthete and a scholar, both a connoisseur and a student of civilization.

After taking his degree K went to Florence to study with Bernard Berenson, and soon afterwards married Jane Martin, who had been much admired in my time at Oxford and was not only unusually pretty and warm-hearted but shared K's devotion to the arts. In the early days of their married life John Sparrow and I stayed with him at a nice little house at Settignano, just outside Berenson's villa 'I Tatti'. I was introduced to the Master, but naturally enough he was not interested in me, and I was rather disheartened by the touches of resentful disparagement in his talk. Though the house was overheated, it was notable inside for its pictures and books and outside for the formal variety of the Italian garden. It reflected one of the more positive sides of the Aesthetic Movement and showed what judgement and knowledge were needed to put its gospel into effect. The society was cosmopolitan and quarrelsome. Into it swooped Lady Colefax, the famous hostess, whose house at the corner of a street in Chelsea was known as 'the lions' Corner House'. Later she was to become an intimate friend of mine, but even at this time I was impressed by her solid knowledge of the arts and her sturdy sense in practical affairs. Vernon Lee, still spry and energetic and dressed apparently for an otter-hunt, dropped in on us to make inquiries about 'the famous lion-huntress'. The Austrian painter, Viktor Hammer, played the bagpipes and painted a picture of Jane which made her look like a Florentine of the *quattrocento* but failed to catch her vivid attraction. There was of course much talk about painting, but I learned more from K than from any of his elders. Among others was a young Frenchman, who was said to be wonderfully up to date on the arts. We asked him about contemporary French painters, and he said that only one was really good. When asked what he painted, he said, 'He paints only bulls. He likes only bulls.' Too much conversation turned on how such and such a painter or writer was now rated, as if his shares were quoted on the Stock Exchange, but K and Jane, though deeply involved with the Berensons, paid no attention to this and put in long hours of work in the Uffizi, from which they always returned with some new discovery or discrimination, though I myself remained unable to distinguish between Gaddi and Daddi.

Closely allied to the Etonian aesthetes was a man who had little in common with their startling flamboyance, but made a powerful impression on me from the very start. At school Henry Yorke had joined with Brian Howard in inviting 'Pop' to a repast, and regaled them with a barrel of oysters. He was unusually dark and compared not inaptly with an olive. He looked and was more mature than his schoolfriends of the Eton Art Society, and though they both respected and amused him, he was not deeply involved with them, but went his own purposeful way. He intended to write novels, and this aim he realized when he became known to the public as Henry Green. At Oxford he studied English with C. S. Lewis for his tutor, but the combination was not happy. Lewis, though highly cultivated and well read, did not much like young aspirants to literature and was much more at home with the past than with the present. Nor were Henry's tastes likely to please him. Henry disliked Shakespeare, whose imagery he found unpleasing, and thought nothing of Lewis' gods, Sidney and Spenser. Though he was strongly drawn to Anglo-Saxon poetry, it was not from Lewis' love of its emotional impetus, but for its concise and expressive syntax. At the other end he was a keen admirer of George Moore, who was still alive and active. Henry not only liked the 'melodic line', which Moore pursued in his later narrative, but found the autobiographical books wonderfully witty and amusing. He treated Moore's malicious innocence as a lucid vision of people that resembled the independence which he himself sought. Henry had a taste for the bizarre, the incongruous, and the unusual, and disliked anything that was conventionally pretty. We used to walk along the tow-path, not where it goes by fields, but where it passes through the gas-works to the railway station, and the bleak, black scene gave him much satisfaction. At one end of it was a small weir with a cascade which Henry would watch with intent interest and compared with a woman's silk underclothes. His judgements on people were swift and sharp, but seldom wrong, the conclusions of a powerful and perceptive mind. It might have no very great range but within its limits it worked with a piercing insight, stripping men and ideas of their disguises and going straight to some central point. He was already writing his first novel, *Blindness*, and this unusual subject revealed the strange originality of his outlook. In it he had already begun to exploit some of his linguistic idiosyncrasies, such as a taste for crisp, pungent sentences.

Henry did not finish his course at Oxford. He was irritated and bored by C. S. Lewis, and wanted material for his next book. So he went to Birmingham and worked as a mechanic in a family firm which made apparatus for bottling beer. Lady Ottoline Morrell hoped that this indicated a humanitarian desire on his part to know as a social reformer working men's life from the inside, but such was not Henry's motive. He observed working men keenly and closely as an artist and learned a great deal about them, which he turned to excellent effect in his second novel, *Living*. He had his rewards, as when he found that a forge-worker knew the whole of Byron by heart. Birmingham provided the break that Henry needed before he settled down in London, but he was much more interested in complex and leisurely circles of society, and it was in these that he found his later themes. He was fascinated by young women both in general and in particular, and while he marked with amused detachment their adroit efforts not to commit themselves on debatable matters and their competitive jealousy in the matter of clothes, he was sharply aware of their physical appeal. Once he was with me and a beautiful girl in my room, when she said something rather silly. In a moment of light-hearted irritation I lifted her up and threw her to Henry, who caught her, but what thrilled him through all his being was that sparks came out of her underclothes. On leaving Birmingham he married and settled down to the family business in London, but spent much of his spare time in writing a distinguished series of novels, which reflected not only his concern with a special section of society but his gift for translating his fears and anxieties into strange forms of fancy. He had always had an excellent ear for turns of speech, and just as he admired Moore's talent for patter, so he made himself a master of it.

Henry was the younger son of well-to-do parents. His father, Vincent Yorke, was a prosperous businessman and a director of the Westminster Bank, but had in his day been a good classical scholar and a Fellow of King's College, Cambridge. From him Henry inherited his appearance and some of his intellectual powers, but his other gifts came from his mother. Mrs Yorke, who had been born a Wyndham and brought up at Petworth, was a remarkable example of how a personality will fulfil itself despite its education or lack of it. When she was a girl, she thought, as she said, 'of nothing but horse and dog', and she still kept her outdoor tastes and bred horses. They did not do very well, and she said ruthlessly of one, 'We had to put him under the grass.' She talked the clipped language of her time and class and not only dropped the *g* from 'huntin'' and 'shootin'', but managed somehow to drop it from words which did not contain it, as in

'Cheltin'ham' and 'Chippin'ham'. She was extremely quick and clever and witty and scored one off with great brilliance. Once I told her that Sir Philip Chetwode, whom she knew, had complained of the architect who built him a house in the Avenue Road, 'You can see the feller's never built a gentleman's house. There's no brushin' room.' Mrs Yorke was not much amused and merely commented, 'How like Sir Philip to want a brushin' room in London.' I often stayed with the Yorkes at their house across the Severn from Tewkesbury, and she kept us all up to the mark. When John Sparrow was there, she referred to him as 'That clever Mr Partridge', and when Evelyn Waugh came, after staying at a mansion nearby, she welcomed him, 'Well, Evelyn, you must tell us all that's happenin' in the county.' She could be most unexpected in her comments, as when speaking of some cousin who was said to have appeared as a ghost, she said, 'How like her to come troublin' everyone after they had got rid of her', and on a famous scandal, in which a man's wife had turned against him, she pronounced a final judgement, 'How absurd of her to cut up rough so late in the day. After all we've known about his goin's on with the footmen for years.' She was delighted when Henry got married, and was very fond of his wife, but added to me as an afterthought, 'I wouldn't have minded almost anyone, except of course a Roman Catholic', and at the wedding she was heard discussing Henry's latest book, 'But I don't know what he was doin' leavin' out the definite articles.'

Another pupil of C. S. Lewis, who got on even worse than Henry with him, was John Betjeman. He was slight and not very tall, and had a wonderfully expressive and mobile face, which changed from moment to moment, and a certain elfin quality. The first time I met him he talked fluently about half-forgotten authors of the nineteenth century – Sir Henry Taylor, Ebenezer Elliott, Philip James Bailey, and Sir Lewis Morris, but this was not done for effect. He was fascinated by the Victorian age and was already busy exploring its bypaths. He had just come from Marlborough, where the Master, Cyril Norwood, who looked like a policeman in an early Chaplin film, had given him a majestic warning, 'Oxford is a very delightful place. I only hope that you do not find it too delightful.' Unfortunately he did, but that added enormously to his charm. He was carried away by the place, by its memories, by the extraordinary variety of human beings whom it sustained, by its outspokenness and lack of inhibitions. Part of his genius lay in his exuberance. He took everything as it came, made the most of it, and then asked for more. He transformed any party by his warmth and gaiety and his gift for interesting others and for being interested in them. He had indeed his black moments. He too was an only child, and his relations with his father had ups and downs. Ernest Betjeman was stone-deaf. He designed objects for Asprey's but also had ambitions to be a country gentleman and wore sporting suits with loud checks. John would be taken on fishing parties, which he loathed, especially when he was told, 'Don't talk. You're disturbing the fish.' His father's friends could not make him out, nor could he them. His father wanted John to follow him in his own work, but John was determined not to. The social life which intoxicated him at Oxford was an anodyne for his family conflicts, and for that reason he flung himself all the more excitedly into it.

John was already a learned man when he came to Oxford, and there he greatly extended his learning. He did very little work for his schools in English, and C. S. Lewis, who had an Ulsterman's austerity of judgement, thought him a pretentious playboy. John's handicap was that the field of learning which he was to make very much his own lay outside the scope of any Oxford curriculum. His speciality was the architecture of the nineteenth century in Great Britain and Ireland. For places abroad he had no use, if only because it was not easy to get afternoon-tea in them. But for British architecture of all periods he had a passion, which found its climax in the nineteenth century and especially in the Gothic Revival. He knew all about Scott, Street, Waterhouse, and Butterfield, visited their numerous churches, and was always excited when he found something built by one of them. If he was driving a car, he would take both his hands off the steering-wheel, wave his arms and cry, 'Phew! Gothic!' Victorianism was much in fashion, and the more prescient aesthetes collected wax flowers, antimacassars, and Doulton images of the great queen and her consort. But John went much further in the range and depth of his knowledge. It was a passion that he indulged to the utmost. His more serious friends sometimes asked what it all meant. Was it a prolonged joke? Or did John really like the Gothic Revival, which in those days was still viewed with distaste? Nor was the question easy to answer. John's interest may in the first place have begun as a bit of a turn, but even then his curiosity was genuinely aroused and he found a real excitement in it. Later, despite all his jokes, it was serious, and he really looked for what the Victorian architects were trying to do and discriminated firmly between them and their different abilities and accomplishments. The Victorian age appealed to something deep in him. Its security, its religion, its sense of a social order were what he wanted for his own happiness, and in it he found an unlimited field for his lively and inquiring mind.

John was unusually sensitive and all too easily wounded, or discouraged, or depressed. If anyone said something callous or Philistine or false, it would haunt him for days, and in perfect honesty he would build up the speaker into a kind of Antichrist and persuade his friends to share his horror of him. Then, without telling anyone, he would call off the campaign and think no more about it. He made his friends with extraordinary ease, and always extracted something original from them. He sometimes imposed on them unsuitable roles of his own invention. He was liable to tell some perfectly worthy don that he was 'the obscurest don in Oxford', and this was meant as praise. He had a lively affection for the peerage, not with Proust's sense of it as part of history, but because it was anomalous and unusual and very unlike the Betjeman household in Church Street, Chelsea. For him it was a survival and an oddity and, as such, fascinating. To many of his friends he attached nicknames or labels. One charmingly melancholy man was 'the Sarcophagus', one young peer 'Cracky' and another 'little Bloody', a young woman 'Goldie Legs', a clergyman 'Father Folky'. He enlivened the human scene by inventing roles for its inmates. John surmounted his troubles by creating comedy around him. He was out to amuse and be amused, but into both activities he infused an unusual power. Just as he made endless jokes about the Gothic Revival, which he loved, so he did about his friends, and they were delighted. It was not an age when people said 'To be serious . . .' and then assumed a solemn voice, and of this John was anyhow incapable. By throwing an air of absurdity round his subject he made himself an original artist with his own peculiar message for the time.

John had from an early age wished to be a poet, and at Oxford he became one. There he wrote some poems, which may now be classed as 'Juvenilia' but have his authentic note and are true records of his highly personal vision, notably *Death in Leamington*, *The Arrest of Oscar Wilde at the Cadogan Hotel*, and *Hymn*. When he showed them to me, I saw how original they were and how much more they were than merely funny. The first, by treating an insignificant event in a dim place, increases its pathos by the note of absurdity. The second, which deals with a highly dramatic theme, makes it more disturbing by its careful realism and its keen eye for what really must have happened. The third is closer to satire, but none the less reflects John's ambivalent attitude to some aspects of Victorian religion, especially in its eagerness to dignify its churches and its ineptness at doing so. The union of strong feelings and a touch of comedy or satire was already the basis of John's poetry. The incitement of laughter and tears not in succession, as with Dickens, but in the same moment at the same thing, as with Charlie Chaplin, is a creation of our age, and though John exploited other themes and greatly extended his range both in rural landscape and in suburban ecology, he kept his gift for conveying pathos and comedy in one breath.

Like Henry Yorke, John did not complete his career at Magdalen, though his end was not entirely deliberate. There was a ridiculous examination, called Divinity Moderations, which could be taken at any point in a man's career but had to be passed before he could enter for his finals. It was dishonourably easy and consisted of the Gospels and the Acts of the Apostles in English. John, who knew the Bible very well, took the examination more than once, and consistently failed. The explanation is that unconsciously he wished to fail, that he had no desire to take his finals, for which he had done very little work, and found instinctively a way out.

His father cut off his allowance, and for a time John did various jobs, seldom rewarding and always ill paid. The best was when he was on the staff of *The Architectural Review*. He, the editor, and anyone else who happened to be present, played a game called 'Architectural Consequences'. You first drew the ground-floor of a building and then folded the paper back, leaving only two small side lines visible, and passed it on. The next man drew the first floor, and the man after him the second. It was highly enjoyable and produced some remarkable designs for buildings in the Hispano Suiza and Rokokokola styles. In his various avatars John extended his acquaintance and his experience, and though he saw himself as a hack and said so in *Who's Who*, he was not discouraged from writing poetry. It provided the centre of his being, as he had always meant that it should. Almost from the start he knew where his gifts lay and remained faithful to them.

John was liable to fall in love, and some of his first devotions were misplaced. He picked up a waitress from an Oxford restaurant and took her out to look at churches, but gave her up when she did dance-steps up the aisle. At the other extreme was a very dutiful, plain girl, the daughter of a clergyman, who appealed to his clerical tastes. She bicycled over to see him in Oxford and wore a strangely unbecoming raincoat. She had already written long and embarrassing letters about her home life and its duties, but the raincoat was too much. Some of John's friends saw her in it and pointed it out, and that was the end of her. Much more serious and infinitely more rewarding was when he fell really in love with Penelope, daughter of Field-Marshal Sir Philip (later Lord) Chetwode. She was extremely attractive, amusing, warmhearted, protective, and loyal, and radiated energy like a dynamo. At first John's passage was not easy. Lady Chetwode quite liked him but said, 'We ask people like that to our houses, but we don't marry them.' The Field-Marshal could not make John out and counselled Penelope to marry him, 'if you are sure he's your man, but weigh carefully all that your mother says'. In consequence the engagement went on and off, and prospects were bad when Penelope joined her parents in India, where Sir Philip was now commander-in-chief. Then she came back, and they were married, and a new long chapter in John's life began; for his wife was as vital and as gifted in her own way as he was in his.

Lady Chetwode was in due course able to digest John into her ample system, but the Field-Marshal did not find it so easy. In the first place he found it difficult to remember his name. It was not common and anyhow not the kind of name to be found in a cavalry regiment. Once, after Penelope's marriage, she said something to the butler, who replied 'Yes, Miss Penelope', only to be interrupted by the Field-Marshal, who exclaimed, 'She's not Miss Penelope. She's Mrs Bargeman.' Nor did he quite know how John should address him. 'Sir' might be all right, but did not seem intimate enough. So he sought for a solution, 'You can't call me Philip, that wouldn't do. You can't call me father – I'm not your father. You'd better call me Field-Marshal.' So that was settled. The Field-Marshal shared with Penelope a passionate interest in horses. They were his chief love and the main basis of his success in the army, and my old Commanding Officer at Handel Street would strongly have approved of his care for them. Penelope kept a beautiful white-grey Arab horse, called Moti. He was very well bred and well trained and was sometimes brought into the sitting-room in the farm-house at Uffington, which the Betjemans now rented. As often as not he had marks of lipstick on his neck, and he was very much one of the family. The Field-Marshal wrote copiously about his health, on the need for an occasional bran-mash, a purge, and other details of diet. Penelope rode him brilliantly to hounds and took him for long trips over the downs with a light buggy, which often upset. She herself still looked very young and caused a flutter among hunting people by her stylish riding and her beautiful mount. The following conversation took place on the hunting field with an elderly gentleman who approached her,

E.G.   Where did you get that nice horse?
P.   Inja.
E.G.   And what were you doing in India?
P.   Staying with my father.
E.G.   And what was he doing there?
P.   Commander-in-Chief.

Yet though Penelope had ample memories of imperial splendour in Delhi and vaguely felt that India belonged to her, she did not complain about having to live quite modestly at Uffington. She was a first-class cook and turned some of her super-abundant energies to feeding her friends. She liked village life and soon became a dominating figure in it, lecturing to the Women's Institute on such matters as the making of *soufflés,* or pre-Muslim architecture in India.

John had always been religious, and in time his beliefs settled into a High Church pattern, though he kept some affection for such Low Church establishments as Holy Trinity, Gas Street, Oxford, where there was a gas-burner at the end of each pew and evening communion was celebrated once a month. When they were first married, Penelope was aware of his proclivities and admired him for them, but was herself sunk in the religions of India, whose holy men had made a powerful impression on her, and about whose temples she was volubly knowledgeable. Concessions were made to all tastes, and after Sunday supper she would play the piano and lead hymns with a fine *bel canto*, while the rest joined in. They were largely chosen for their emotional richness, and the Reverend John Bacchus Dykes was a favourite composer. When the German maid, Paula, burst in to clear the remains of the meal, Penelope would dismiss her abruptly, 'Aber, Paula, Sie können nicht einkommen. Wir haben Gottesdienst.' ('Paula, you can't come in. We are having a religious service.') But in the middle thirties Penelope began to turn her thoughts to Anglicanism and was soon well ahead of John in the vigour of her practices. Indeed, as Adrian Bishop, who was at Uffington at the time and had recently passed through a remarkable conversion, wrote to me, 'Penelope is practising mysticism, but the Kingdom of Heaven is not taken by storm.' The upshot was that she now added religious duties to the many others that she conducted at Uffington. For a time she even played the harmonium for evensong at the neighbouring church of Baulking. Her playing was unusual, even in a country parish, since her improvised voluntaries were often based on secular works like German folk-songs or Offenbach's *Goddesses three to Ida went.* For a time all seemed to go well, but one dark morning she received a letter,

Baulking Vicarage

My dear Penelope,

I have been thinking over the question of the playing of the harmonium on Sunday evenings here and have reached the conclusion that I must now take it over myself.

I am very grateful to you for doing it for so long and hate to have to ask you to give it up, but, to put it plainly, your playing has got worse and worse and the disaccord between the harmonium and the congregation is becoming destructive of devotion. People are not very sensitive here, but even some of them have begun to complain, and they are not usually given to doing that. I do not like writing this, but I think you will understand that it is my business to see that divine worship is as perfect as it can be made. Perhaps the crankiness of the instrument has something to do with the trouble. I think it does require a careful and experienced player to deal with it.

Thank you ever so much for stepping so generously into the breach when Sibyl was ill; it was the greatest possible help to me and your results were noticeably better then than now.

Yours ever

F.P.Harton

Penelope accepted the decision with the utmost grace and good temper, remained on excellent terms with the Hartons, and was delighted to receive a copy of H. V. Morton's *In the Steps of the Master*, inscribed, 'With grateful thanks from the Vicar and Churchwardens of Baulking'. When war came, John was appointed to a post in Dublin, and Penelope went also, taking Moti with her. He lived to the ripe age of thirty-two and was buried at Belgarde Castle where a tombstone records his memory.

Like the Betjemans in the strength of his personality and the originality of his genius was Evelyn Waugh, but he was more formidable and more complex. I hardly knew him when he was an undergraduate and did not really become a friend of his until he had already published *Decline and Fall*, which I had not read. He had bright, piercing eyes which he fixed on you with a critical stare. I was fascinated by his unfailing choice of the right

word even in casual talk, his heart-warming laugh, his unlimited
curiosity about people, and his talent for creating comedy from
the events of every day. Soon after I met him he had a bitter blow
in the break-up of his marriage. He had just received his last
wedding-present and was half-way through writing *Vile Bodies*.
In the next few years I saw quite a lot of him, and even after he
married again I found no difference in his friendliness. The better
I knew him, the more I appreciated his rich character and his
quite outstanding gifts. He was the best company in the world,
not only devastatingly observant but appreciative, scholarly, and
generous. Though later he might be thought to present a very
different figure to the public gaze, it contained elements of his
earlier self. He was above all an artist, self-critical and keenly
conscious of what he owed to his art. He liked the precise, careful
paintings of the Victorians and had already written a book on
Rossetti. At school he had trained himself to draw with a firm,
confident line, and it was for this that he was known at Oxford.
When he moved from drawing to writing, he was from the start
most scrupulous and perceptive in his choice of words. He
abhorred shapeless exuberance and, like all good craftsmen, was
much concerned with the tools of his craft, notably with grammar
and correct usage. If slips were pointed out to him, he never complained. He was both a comedian and a satirist, who had Saki's
taste for violence, and his own gift for making it funny. He would
not have been so effective if he had not at heart been a moralist.
He may for a time have lived in defiance of his principles, but he
was still impelled by a strong sense of right and wrong. His demon
might turn both into preposterous fancy, and it was characteristic
of him that if you told him some lurid piece of news, he would
say, 'Horrible, horrible. You couldn't please me more.' With
such fundamental convictions, no matter how much he flouted
them, he was fated to turn to religion, and his adherence to the
Roman Catholic Church in 1930 was inevitable. At school
at Lancing, he had at first been an Anglo-Catholic and done
duty in the chapel, where once, when arranging the altar-cloth
with Tom Driberg, he said impatiently, 'If that's good enough
for me, it's good enough for God.' Later at school and at

Oxford he lost touch with religion, but when the break-up of his first marriage caused him agonizing distress, he found in Catholicism the consolation which he needed and adopted it in the determination to be as orthodox as possible and to translate the elusive demands of the *mens catholica* into a coherent code of conduct.

In the later twenties Evelyn led a very varied social life, if only to console himself for the collapse of his marriage. He liked the company of young women and took them to night-clubs, though he never danced. His terms of praise were unusual. Very high was 'Nice short girl' – Evelyn was conscious of being himself on the short side – or of Nancy Mitford, 'Nice cheap girl to take out for the evening. Costs you only eighteen and six for an orangeade at a night-club.' Eddy Sackville West met him at a country house, where he was about to take a pretty girl for a walk. It was an unusually hot day, and Evelyn was carrying a heavy overcoat. Eddy asked about it, and Evelyn answered, 'I hope it may prove useful as a groundsheet.' He claimed to be much distressed that a couple whom he liked had no child, and pretended to start an elaborate plot to provide them with one, assuring me that the chauffeur had told him, 'You may take it from me, sir, that it's not her ladyship's fault', and that he knew of a firm which for substantial fees had done much to replenish the shrinking ranks of the aristocracy. If he felt that someone was unduly praised, he could be undeniably sharp. When Robert Byron, whom he had known at Oxford, was beginning to make a name for himself as a writer, Evelyn was sceptical. He said to me, 'Robert has found a new word – verities', and when Peter Quennell told him, 'None of our generation has made good except you and Robert', he snapped back, 'Robert has not made good.' Yet though he said harsh things about his friends, they were not intended to wound. They were his ruthlessly honest conclusions, and he would not have thought of holding them back. As a host he denied nothing to his guests, and he had many engaging ways of showing his generosity, as once when he called on me bringing half a dozen bottles of champagne and said, 'I thought that these might prove useful before dinner.' His 'atrocities', which were much quoted, were usually directed against those whom I did not like, and I felt privileged that I was not the victim of them. They were his way of clearing the mind of cant, and they did it very effectively.

Evelyn's taste for horrors was matched by his dislike of sentimentality, or of anything that he thought sloppy or silly, and this included many liberal and humanitarian causes. He saw them as governed not by firmly based principles but by uninformed weakness. His likes and dislikes were supported by a body of doctrine which on its own assumptions could not be contradicted. His imagination had been so captivated in youth by the art of an earlier generation that he could not endure to see it changed or its place taken by other, quite different manners. Modern painting stirred his contempt and mockery, and though he much admired P. G. Wodehouse and Ivy Compton Burnett, he owed almost nothing to the work of contemporary novelists. In time this isolation was to become more obvious, but even in the twenties Evelyn had the roots of it in him. The spectacle of the curmudgeon which he at times presented to the public was largely an act, which it amused him to play, but it was built on something real. He longed for some home in which he could regain the blitheness and the security of childhood, and for one deceived year of marriage he thought that he had found it. When the dream broke, he still sought it. Despite his hard-boiled attitudes, he was incurably sentimental about this. He wanted warmth, children's games, children's talk, the enclosed universe of the nursery. He longed to marry again, but since he was now a Roman Catholic, his first marriage stood forbiddingly in the way. His only hope lay in an annulment, and this after a long delay was secured. Then he had to find a suitable wife, and since his demands were very exacting, this was not easy. He fell in love, but not with the right girl, and from this he suffered acutely. The faint, water-colourish girls, to whom his imagination drew him, were not what he really wanted, and he put his defeats brilliantly and bitterly into *A Handful of Dust*. Fortunately at last all went well, and in 1936 he married a young woman, who provided him with the home and family that he had always desired, and not only appreciated his very unusual gifts but made affectionate fun of him in a quiet, whimsical way. The new Evelyn began to emerge, but it was a development of the old.

After marriage Evelyn bought a house at Stinchcombe in Gloucestershire and settled down to the life of a country gentleman who is also a writer. The house was Georgian and not too large, on the lower slopes of the Cotswolds, and had a certain amount of land. Inside were charming evidences of Evelyn's taste. There was a fine Victorian painting, called *Into the cold world*, of a woman in full widow's weeds taking her small son into a snowy blizzard from an empty house. A whole story could be reconstructed from the details, and much whimsical ingenuity was spent in doing so. Two other pictures, of roughly the same period, were called *Then* and *Now*, the first displaying a party in a coach being held up by a highwayman, the second travellers in a train with muffs and foot-warmers. Evelyn commissioned a third called *To-day*, which is of people in an aeroplane being burned to death. In the ground floor lavatory was a fine array of paintings which Evelyn had brought back from Ethiopia. They depicted with a combination of early Christian formality and observant realism the defeat of the Italians by Menelik and did not shrink from showing how the Abyssinians mutilated the enemy and hung the trophies so obtained round their necks. It was noticed that a learned Jesuit, who came to stay with Evelyn, spent rather a long time in the lavatory and was thought to be held by its artistic treasures. On Sundays the whole family and its dependents went to early Mass and came back hungry for breakfast. For dinner, even on Sunday, we dressed, and Evelyn produced majestic pieces of Victorian silver to decorate the table. The wine was generous and good, the food simple. At Oxford Evelyn was reported to have said that he would like to spend his days in a country rectory. Allowing for schismatic differences, Stinchcombe provided something of the kind. The furniture was consciously Victorian and suggested that it had long been in use and chosen more for its durability than from any pursuit of fashion. At Stinchcombe Evelyn realized at least part of his early dreams and settled down to raise a family.

So far I have spoken of friends who were directly concerned with the arts, either as practitioners or as critics. Hugh Gaitskell was not quite like these, and did not at first sight fall into any obvious category. He had a winning voice and manner which soon revealed an unusual character. He had not enjoyed his school-days at Winchester, and at Oxford he found just the encouragement to be himself that he needed. He had plenty of energy and moved without embarrassment in a number of different circles, though he was careful to keep his friends in compartments and not to take risks by mixing them carelessly together. This was because he was exploiting different possibilities in himself and was not yet sure where his real disposition lay. He was entirely spontaneous and natural, and whether he was being serious or enjoying himself, he put everything into it. He had a variety of interests, including modern painting and psychology. He skilfully sought out some of the best-looking girls in the women's colleges and liked to dance with them, but he was equally at home in male society, where he would fling himself delightedly into any controversy and say exactly what he thought. His friends took their troubles to him, and he not only entered into them as if they were his own but gave excellent advice and help. He had no sense of social distinctions, and this was not the result of intellectual conviction but the cause of it. He was a natural democrat who took people on their merits, and he judged merits by much more than academic standards. What really drew me to him was his obvious goodness, his gentleness and compassion, combined with a sprightly vitality and an unfailing honesty. He was all of one piece and seemed to have no inner conflicts which he could not solve. He lived largely for his friends and gave quite as much to them as he got from them. He was in no sense a prig, not merely because he had a bursting sense of fun, but because he never struck an attitude or tried to present himself as other than he was. Most young men slip more or less unconsciously into poses, but Hugh's integrity was such that he never did.

The basic unity of Hugh's character settled his way of life. He was not ambitious for any ordinary kind of success, but he was too serious and too public-minded to shirk the chances provided by Oxford for training himself. At the start he showed his determination by deciding to take the new and somewhat mistrusted course of Philosophy, Politics, and Economics, to which the name of 'Modern Greats' had ingeniously been given. If philosophy never meant very much to him, economics and politics meant a great deal. He was never boring about his studies and did not talk 'shop' unless he was certain that it would be welcome, but 'Modern Greats' was a solid, even a central part of his Oxford life, and he managed to work hard at it without sacrificing other interests. It provided him with the firm foundation which he needed to justify his instinctive convictions. As soon as he began to think about the world around him, he found that it wounded both his feelings and his intelligence. His natural tenderness was outraged by the sordid and brutal conditions in which a large part of the population lived; his sense of order and decency was appalled by the jungle of a competitive system in which the few had too much and the many too little. He read Marx but was not impressed by him, thinking Marxism too mechanical to be right and too inhuman to deserve any devotion. Nor did the applied Christianity of George Lansbury make any appeal to him. He had abandoned Christianity at school and never reverted to it. Its religious side did not touch him, and he found its ethics too vague and too subjective to inspire any practical course of action. Soon enough I learned what a hold politics had on him and noted that when he talked about them, he did it with all his attention and indeed with those gestures which were to become so familiar in later years, when he knocked down a flimsy argument or rammed a point home. His mind was fully at work and in control of the subject, and yet so quick on the uptake that he could deal at once with any fresh or unforeseen point. The charming young man had become a formidable debater.

The strength of Hugh's convictions was revealed in the General Strike in May 1926, when he insisted on helping the strikers at a time when most undergraduates went off far too cheeerfully to London in the hope of breaking them. With quiet determination Hugh and two or three friends stayed in Oxford and did all that they could on the other side. The strike caught me quite unawares, and when it came I was at a loss what to do. I could not go strike-breaking, as this might involve violence and savoured far too strongly of the worse sides of army life; nor could I join Hugh, since I thought that the strike was lamentably ill-judged and likely to do more harm than good to the coal-miners. I could not understand why the government refused to negotiate with the strikers and got a bad mark from Warden Wells for saying so, but I felt that negotiations were possible and should be tried. Fortunately the new Master of Balliol, A. D. Lindsay, thought the same and, following a lead set by the Archbishop of Canterbury, Randall Davidson, organized parties to collect names in favour of some kind of negotiations. K and his friend Bobby Longden and I set out in K's car and collected a number of respectable signatures, and I do not remember that we were ever dismissed curtly or rudely. We had our happy moments, as when I rang the bell at the door of the Catholic Bishop of Portsmouth and was told, 'Well, sir, he's brought someone back and he can't see you', and this suggested many fanciful explanations on the lines of David Garnett's *The Sailor's Return*. K and Bobby told a nice story that I said, 'We are, of course, expecting much from prayer', but I do not think that it is true. Suddenly, to my enormous relief, it all came to an end and was very soon forgotten. It is true that soon after it I had a painful passage of words with Lindemann, who had been busy with Churchill on the deplorable *British Gazette*, but he was so flushed with his journalistic glories that he did not very much mind. If I had not already met Hugh, I should not have been so concerned as I was. At least he made me treat the whole thing seriously and try to do something about it.

With K I met John Sparrow, who had come up with a remarkable reputation to New College from Winchester, where as a boy he had already published a scholarly edition of Donne's *Devotions*. He looked very young and had the appearance of a very bright schoolboy who also played games, and this was what he was. From the first moment he was charmingly at his ease and responded with remarkable readiness to a wide range of openings. In one way he was unusually mature, not merely in his knowledge but in his control of it, but he had also the gaiety and the humour of youth, the zest for new topics and the freshness of outlook to enjoy them. He was already possessed by a love of scholarship, but he was more than a mere scholar. For a young man of his age he had not only a close and well-founded knowledge of English and Latin poetry, but a very keen perception of it and a discriminating judgement on its merits. His scholarship was his response to his love of poetry, his way of adjusting himself to an experience which played a leading part in his life. Having decided in his modesty that he could not be a poet himself, he set out to know about poetry, and this was a driving passion. Yet this striking gift was accompanied by others which might sometimes fortify it, but at other times were less easy to combine with it.

John had a sharp, analytical mind, which could make observations and distinctions beyond the reach of most people. When he applied it to literature, it was in the field of careful scholarship. His intelligence found a new and more demanding claim when he began to study philosophy with Joseph. He took readily, even eagerly to it, suffered no frustration or humiliation, and liked Joseph for his own sake, detecting a childlike simplicity behind the merciless logic, and recognizing in this a likeness to himself. Joseph enjoyed at this time an Indian summer when he was almost taken up by his pupils, but what John admired was the uncommon resourcefulness and dexterity of his mind, which seemed to flinch from no formulation, however complex. At the time I felt that Joseph's influence on John was deleterious. He seemed likely to crush the poet by turning him into a logician, and that of a not very sympathetic kind. But underneath the new manner the old love was still at work, and John needed something like Joseph's discipline to satisfy his eager intelligence which sought for a foolproof foundation for his thoughts. The drill in logic certainly took away some of his ready responsiveness. His intellectual conscience told him that he must not tolerate slipshod thinking, and at times he would puncture it in not too courteous a spirit. Yet this too was part of growing up and might have come without Joseph, though the manner and the method would have been different. But the gap between the lover of poetry and the young logician widened, and it became more difficult for John to bring the two together. What saved him was his zest for life and enjoyment.

John combined sensibility and intelligence with a taste for action. He not only played football but liked footballers. It was his reaction against the over-cultivated scholasticism of Winchester, with its aridity and restraint, but it was also his nature. He liked to mix among strange people, to discover engaging qualities in them to which others were impervious, to savour many sides of the mixed microcosm of Oxford. He was a friend both of John Betjeman and of Hugh Gaitskell, and his taste for enjoyment was not unlike theirs. On one occasion he climbed into New College after midnight, which was a grave offence, and was roundly dressed down by H. A. L. Fisher, on the principle that 'a college is a fortified place' and that he had 'pointed a pistol at the heart of the University'. Joseph liked him as a good pupil, but also felt at times a need to chide him for his lapses. John took it all in his stride. Without seeming to work, he did quite enough, not always on the sly, and he was able to master any subject in a short time. He got first classes, and though for a time he had to abate his English studies, he never lost his hold on them or his love of them.

John knew that he wanted a life of action, of engagement in affairs. He could have been a don in classics, philosophy, English, or law, but preferred to become a prize-Fellow of All Souls and to go to the bar. As a Chancery lawyer he could apply his sharp, subtle mind to sorting out complex problems into their essential components. He settled happily in London, where he hoped to keep up his literary interests and enjoy, with no regard for social distinctions, a wider range of acquaintances than in Oxford. Yet the bar exacted its price. It developed, at the expense of his more imaginative gifts, the bleaker side of his mind and hampered him in pursuing his other loves. Nor were some of his mentors ideally suited to him. He absorbed too easily their sceptical outlook and yielded too readily to their treatment of him as an ingenuous child who would soon know better. He remained charming and gay and enormously companionable, and when I went abroad with him, he was very much his old self, greatly enjoying anything from picture galleries to German night-life. But when he was back in London, the difficulties became greater. He did well enough at the Bar and could in due course have taken silk. The trouble was that what really engaged his fullest and most delightful powers, his love of literature, had to take a second place and become a pastime instead of a central interest. Worse than this, the Chancery bar lacks the drama and variety of the usual law-courts and forced John to exert his driest and most abstract talents. Whereas scholarship was a natural outlet for his literary passions, the law was a hindrance and worse to them. They lived on, but there was now a real split between them and the bleak technicalities and argumentation which were John's profession, and too often the second tended to smother the first. This was mainly on the surface, but at times it went deeper and was more disturbing. John was conscious of it and sought to keep a balance, but though he looked back with longing to the unregained Paradise of his boyhood, most of his time had to be given, not always unwillingly, to dry and unrewarding tasks. Nor did he fully regain his early balance until he joined the army as a private soldier in September 1939.

The last intimate friend whom I made in the twenties was more unusual than any that I have yet mentioned. Isaiah Berlin was born in Riga of a well-established family of Russian Jews, who migrated to England when he was a small boy. From a very early age he had been bilingual in Russian and English and combined a European background with a lively attachment to the English scene. From St Paul's School, where he was entirely happy, he came to Corpus and became early in his career a legendary figure, not indeed on the prodigious scale that he was to be in Washington in the Second World War but still to a degree unusual for Oxford. Corpus was small and intimate and lively, and Isaiah was much more at home there than he would have been in a larger college, though it did not hamper his forays into wider territories. The New Aesthetes were fading away, but their last survivors won his applause for their courage. Nothing could restrain his adventurous curiosity or hold him from exploring the University. The first thing that everyone noticed in him was the rapidity of his speech, which matched an equal rapidity in his thought. Some of us talked fast enough already, but Isaiah talked even faster, and at times I found it hard to keep up with him. Not only did this reflect an extremely supple and lively mind, but it was almost indispensable in his eager exploration of almost every human element that he could find. He kept a touching affection for Russia and its language, and though in general he did not appreciate poetry any more than he appreciated the visual arts, he liked Russian poetry, and since at the time I was struggling to make some acquaintance with it, this first brought him to my notice. A friend introduced us, and we talked about the Russian poet Alexander Blok, whom I was trying to translate. Blok appealed to Isaiah, and he was glad to know that he appealed to me also. I devoured Isaiah with greed and knew that someone very remarkable had emerged to keep the vanishing twenties up to their first promise. I had met no Russian since 1916 and was delighted to be carried back to that golden time.

Isaiah was prodigiously intelligent, not merely in the swiftness of his mind but in its range and capacity and depth. He moved easily among philosophical abstractions and mastered their language in a very short time. He had an admiring affection for his tutor, W. F. R. Hardie, who afterwards became President of Corpus, and much appreciated his gentle modesty and whimsical humour. Isaiah did not belong to the newest class of philosophers, who had discovered Wittgenstein and were inspired by a young genius in A. J. Ayer of Christ Church. Isaiah picked his own path and found in philosophy a wider range of interests than they did. This was because he was, in an unusual way, a highly cultivated man. If his main love in the arts was music, on which he was immensely knowledgeable, he had a passionate curiosity about movements of thought and ideas and an ingrained respect for the claims of the artist or the thinker. He did not take civilization for granted but treated it as something to be examined and analysed and assessed. He had already an ample knowledge of European thinkers, some of them hardly known at Oxford, and talked intimately about them, as if they were friends whose virtues and foibles he knew from personal contact. Though he was proficient in the Oxford technique of handling philosophical problems, he supplemented it with much else that was less abstract and brought it into closer touch with human beings. His sense of history and his taste for people enabled him to see thinkers, past and present, as working, not in some curricular vacuum, but as active forces in a world of passions and convictions. With such a disposition he could not fail to be interested in politics, but here too it was not quite in the usual way. For him it meant partly the Russian Revolution and the troubles of Palestine. Though he was always against Stalin and saw very early where his maniacal intolerance would lead, nothing could diminish his affection for Russia or his sympathetic understanding of it. In the same way, though he would never himself have migrated to Palestine, he felt its struggles as his own and knew that it was his own kin who were suffering from the indecisions and vagaries of British policy.

Isaiah had an insatiable interest in human beings and an unlimited capacity for getting to know them. How he managed it was always rather a mystery, but there was no doubt of the range and variety of his acquaintances, or of his close ties with them. Nor did he seek them merely from curiosity; he really liked most of them, and even those whom he did not like added to his private comedy of manners. This was right, for he was understanding and kind-hearted. In trouble he would give excellent advice to his friends and take enormous pains to help them. At the time, when we knew far less about Proust than now, Isaiah was compared with him for his gift of making friends in the most unexpected quarters. But even then one fundamental difference was clear – Isaiah was not a snob. Oxford provided him with the milieu that suited him best, and he stuck to it. He liked to discover foreigners, preferably Russians, but also German refugees, and to present Oxford to them in a series of lively and illuminating paradoxes. He had an incorrigible sense of absurdity and retailed anecdotes which have passed into the local folk-lore and still evoke hilarity. But he combined all this with a strong moral sense. He was not intolerant or narrow-minded, and towards his friends he could be very broad-minded indeed, but he had fixed principles which determined his own conduct and his estimate of others. Certain kinds of what he called *pourriture* repelled him in the arts, and he found them alike in Rilke and in César Franck, and he was quick to detect any traces of this in those around him. This gave him an authority which everyone recognized and respected. He was plainly so good a man that he must be heard with attention, and he was. When in 1932 he became a Fellow of All Souls, he remained in outlook and habits a thorough European, but it was comforting to think that only perhaps in England could he be this happily and successfully.

Yet despite the wide range of his interests and connections Isaiah entered very seriously into the academic life of Oxford and moved within its orbit without undue excursions outside. He was soon joined at All Souls by the remarkable John Austin, and Isaiah felt more drawn to him than to the new school of Logical Positivists. Austin went his own way and thought out his problems for himself. His original and powerful mind was seldom satisfied with any solution, and certainly not with current solutions. His passion for the truth allowed him to make no concessions in pursuit of it, and in discussion he was a formidable and tireless adversary. At times he seemed almost too sincere to be quite human, but he tempered his austerity with a charming humour and an unexpected kindness of heart. He knew instinctively when someone was troubled, and could say just the right thing to him. He liked Isaiah's truthfulness and vivacity, and on most matters they agreed. In its higher reaches All Souls at this time was beginning to have a dubious reputation in politics, but the younger Fellows, especially Isaiah and Austin, countered these unpleasant tendencies by refusing to accept the opiates offered by such senior Fellows as Sir John Simon and Geoffrey Dawson. Oxford had begun to become politically minded on a scale greater than for many years. Isaiah belonged to this new generation and enlarged his horizon as he saw in many parts of the world ugly forces at work to destroy the civilization which he valued so highly. In 1932 he marked the portent of future betrayals in Simon's handling of Manchuria; he recognized the deadly implications of Mussolini's invasion of Abyssinia; like many others, he regarded the Spanish Civil War as a test of human values, and Eden's non-intervention policy as an unconvincing piece of hypocrisy. His life was centred on Oxford, but from it he looked around and marked what was happening elsewhere. Politics were very far from being his only, or even his chief interest, but he could not and would not refuse their challenges, and in this respect he was typical of the new generation which had come to maturity during the depression and been horrified by the forces of savagery which it brought to the surface. Much though he enjoyed the intimacies of personal life, enriched by philosophy and music, he was increasingly troubled by violence abroad and supine indifference at home, and he and his friends helped to create a new seriousness at Oxford without impairing its traditional relaxations or its intellectual detachment. All Souls was exposed to the intrigues of high-placed 'fixers' who regarded it as their legitimate sphere of influence and tried to plant their agents in it, not always unsuccessfully. The younger Fellows resisted them, often at the cost of offending their seniors.

8

Wider Vistas

Undergraduates, whose business is often to study literature, cannot fail to be interested in living men of letters and to seek the man behind the mask. I certainly did and was thrilled to meet any writer whose books I knew. A friend of mine at Christ Church, Victor Cazalet, lived near us in Kent in a large house, which was famous for its house-parties. He was a chatty, friendly man, an all-round athlete, who had been a prominent figure at Eton and was much liked, if sometimes made fun of, at Oxford. He was, like his parents, an unashamed collector of celebrities, whom he generously introduced to his friends. In the summer vacation of 1921 he asked me to his home to meet Rudyard Kipling, who was interested in Oxford, because he had lately become a Rhodes trustee, a post which he treated very seriously, but soon abandoned because Philip Kerr, later Lord Lothian, whom he regarded as a dangerous radical, was made secretary to the Trust. When I met Kipling, his once vast reputation had dwindled, and the imperial creed which he preached with such fervour found few adherents. He was already 'the Kipling whom nobody read', but he was my father's favourite author, and I myself was well acquainted with his books and full of curiosity about him. He had the famous face, so often and so truthfully depicted by Max Beerbohm, with the bushy eyebrows, the cleft chin, the receding forehead, the bristling, provocative moustache. But behind the thick spectacles was a pair of bright blue eyes, and his manner was unexpectedly friendly. He did not look at all well, and ate and drank very little. In fact he suffered from a duodenal ulcer, but though he was intimate with some of the leading doctors of the day, none of them diagnosed it, and it was not till some years later that a general practitioner in France saw what the trouble was, and then it was too late to operate. When I met him, Kipling's mind was still fixed on the war. He had lost his only son in it, and he may have had bitter regrets at using his influence with Lord Roberts to send a boy of seventeen, whose eyesight was as bad as his own, into the Irish Guards to be killed in the insane massacre at Loos. Most of the young people present had been in the war and had no desire to talk about it, and Victor had lost a much loved brother in it. But Kipling brought up the subject, and we had to respond. In retrospect I can see that at this time he had begun to shape in his mind some of his later, remarkable stories about the war and its effect on those who took part in it.

Kipling did not express any general ideas about the war and would probably have thought it wrong to criticize the generals, though he let off a few nasty cracks at Lloyd George. But he knew about the topography of the battlefields and was, as one might expect, full of curiosity about weapons. He had at his finger-tips a number of technical words, which he seemed to enjoy just because they were technical, but, hearing that I had been a gunner, he asked me about guns and especially about the buffer by which the eighteen-pounder gun is enabled to recoil after firing. He talked with assurance, but about an out-of-date buffer, worked by oil, instead of about the new kind, worked by compressed air. For a minute or so I was rather lost, as when he asked what we did to stop leakages, which made no sense with the air buffer. Then I saw what he was after, and told him about the change to air. He seemed to be greatly interested, not so much in how the machinery worked, as in what the pieces were called and what effect on range and accuracy the new buffer had. He talked in a quiet voice and was most friendly and attentive. When the subject was exhausted, he turned to politics, in which he seemed to dislike everyone and to think all British policies wrong, and his language became coarser and cruder. He still hankered for some severe punishment for the Germans, though he did not specify what it should be or how it should be exacted. But what particularly exasperated him was Zionism. He called the Jews 'Yids', and had nothing too bad to say about Arthur Balfour, who had been the successful advocate of a national home for the Jews in Palestine. Kipling had the traditional English taste for Arabs about whom he knew very little, but whom he may have liked on principle, because they were Muslims, like some of the best troops in the Indian Army. He gave the impression that his views were formed less on reason than on rather hysterical emotions. Despite his courtesy, there was a note of violence in what he said, and I felt that fundamentally he was less sure of his opinions than he liked us to believe, and that his over-emphasis on certain matters was necessary to counter his chameleonic adaptability.

Very unlike Kipling was another Nobel Prize winner whom I met in the summer of 1931. Paul Valéry had been awarded an honorary doctorate by the University. In the evening he dined at All Souls, where I had some talk with him. I had to do my best in French and was greatly flattered when he said that I talked the language *admirablement*, though I knew that this was just politeness. Just as our talk was beginning to be interesting, Humphrey Sumner, who was a tall, Victorian-looking historian, insisted that the distinguished guest must be initiated into the ancient custom of playing bowls on the lawn. It was a dark, cold, damp June evening, and the last thing that Valéry wanted was to play bowls. He made a few perfunctory and unsuccessful efforts to take part but then sighed as if he had had enough. Sumner did not grasp the situation; so, rather impertinently for a guest, I took Valéry inside and continued our conversation. Even now he seems to me to have had the finest intelligence I have ever met. From him came a flow of sparkling ideas in limpid and lucent French, and no subject seemed to lie outside his scope. He talked not as a poet but as a thinker, though his thought was highly imaginative and inspiring. Poetry was among his subjects, and he insisted that nowadays the one thing that all poets sought was 'surprise', and that this was equally true of himself. Though he talked with sustained brilliance, he never overplayed a paradox or tried to impress, but was throughout completely natural and unaffected. He asked me what I wrote, and I told him that I had recently published a book on the *Iliad*. He asked me to send him a copy, and this I gladly did, to receive by return a picture postcard of himself with the following text written on the back,

Dear Mr Bowra,

I was very charmed of making acquaintance with you. I now know an ex-proctor is not so a dreadful one I was supposing – as I know now, by personal experiment, that a doctor is not so a clever and learned man people is fancying him.

Please to accept all my thanks for sending me your book on Iliad. shall read with much interest. Excuse me for writing in English and think me yours sincerely

Paul Valéry

who will preserve the best remembrance of Oxford and of yourself.

Kipling and Valéry were meteors to be seen and marked and not to be seen again. More available in Oxford was a remarkable writer of a younger generation who played a vivid part in our lives. Elizabeth Bowen published *The Hotel* in 1927, and Leslie Hartley praised it in a weekly paper. She was to follow this by other books written with a fine, forceful feeling for words and flashes of disturbing insight. Her husband, Alan Cameron, was an education officer in Oxford. He had been gassed in the war and, though his health slowly deteriorated, he battled heroically for it. They lived in a charming small house in the Old High Street in Headington and added a very distinctive note to our lives. Alan was an attentive host who had much interest in academic and intellectual matters, which he saw the more clearly because he was not attached to the University. Elizabeth was born from the Anglo-Irish ascendancy and had been brought up by a widowed father in a large Georgian house in Co. Cork. She was tall and well built and had the manner of someone who has lived in the country and knows its habits. She was handsome in an unusual way, with a face that indicated both mind and character. Unlike some Irish, she did not talk for effect but kept the conversation at a high level and gave her full attention to it. She had a slight stutter which added force to her remarks. She had the fine style of a great lady, who on rare occasions was not shy of slapping down impertinence, but she came from a society where the decorum of the nineteenth century had been tempered by an Irish frankness. With all her sensibility and imagination, she had a masculine intelligence which was fully at home in large subjects and general ideas, and when she sometimes gave a lecture, it was delivered with a force and control of which most University teachers would be envious. Though she was entirely at home in the modern world and deeply committed to it, she had her roots in a more spacious and more assured society.

Elizabeth could have been head of a women's college at Oxford or Cambridge. She had the right presence and authority for such a post and would have left a lasting impression. But she was a creative artist, and this demanded her full attention. The artist came out in her quick perceptions, her ready responses to people's behaviour, her fine style even in small matters, her assumption that writers owe special obligations to one another, and her belief that writing is a vocation to be treated with the utmost seriousness. Though academic society is not usually very favourable to creative artists, since its own purposes are of a different kind, she fitted uncommonly well into Oxford because she believed in it. This was helped by a historical insight lacking in many historians. Her feeling for the past and for places which embodied it was enhanced for her by living in Ireland, which has ruins from almost every century from the fourth to the twentieth. With her I visited the ruins of Kilcholman, where Spenser wrote *The Faerie Queene*, and of a large Italianate mansion which had been burned in the 'troubles'. The first was no more than a ruined tower, but standing on the edge of the wild country, it recalled how dangerously near Spenser lived to the Irish whom he feared and hated, while the second, which had trees growing through the drawing-room floor and ferns on the staircase, recalled to Elizabeth her own girlhood with its alarms and atrocities. She would survey such sights with a historian's impartiality as well as a novelist's commitment, and each reinforced the other. This sense of the past enhanced her affection for Oxford. The ancient buildings and the relics of a traditional way of life confirmed her conviction that learning was founded in some fundamental human need. Her father had been a scholar, and she had a real respect for scholarship and its practitioners. She saw that in its own strange way it is as difficult as a creative art and calls for a like care and concentration, and that though its rules may be unfamiliar, they make it both exacting and rewarding.

Some five miles from Oxford is the village of Garsington, and in its centre is the Manor House, a stone Jacobean building which has beautifully escaped the ravages of time and the attentions of restorers. It stands back a little from the road, and on each side of its wide gravel entry is a tall yew hedge. Behind the house is a rectangular pool, surrounded by statues and more yew hedges, and from here in the twenties was a wide view over unspoiled country, though now Lord Nuffield's enterprises have created a large drab fog of factories. This was the home of Philip and Lady Ottoline Morrell. Philip came from an old Oxford family, and was a tall, distinguished looking man, with a ready flow of well informed talk. He had once been a Liberal member of parliament, but had opposed our entry into the war in 1914, and for that reason been thrown aside. His wife had been born a Cavendish-Bentinck and was a half-sister of the Duke of Portland. While Philip was, not very fairly, said to look like a grey bowler-hat, Lady Ottoline was noteworthy by any standards. She was tall and even stately, with bright copper-coloured hair and a heavily powdered face, and she wore clothes remarkable for their brilliant colours and original design. Her face, painted more than once by Augustus John, was even more remarkable. She had a prominent, large nose, a jutting chin, and a highly expressive mouth. She spoke with a curiously nasal tone and at intervals shot out a red tongue and licked her lips with it. She had early rebelled against the discipline of her childhood at Welbeck and decided to devote herself to encouraging the arts. She would refer to 'the wicked, wasted lives' of those with whom she had been brought up and cultivated to a high degree painters and writers and, somewhat hesitatingly, scholars. In the war she and Philip had found work on the land for conscientious objectors, with whom they had a natural sympathy, and in the early twenties their house was a place of pilgrimage for young men from Oxford. The Manor House had been decorated with imaginative taste. The panelled rooms were painted red or blue or grey, and there were some excellent modern pictures. It was very much a place to be seen and enjoyed, and both host and hostess encouraged us to visit them.

The fascination of Garsington lay partly in not knowing whom you would find there. There were the painters of the then younger generation – Mark Gertler, sombre and serious, but supremely honest and devoted to his art; Stanley Spencer, torn between apocalyptic visions of what might happen to living men and women on the Day of Judgement and domestic duties, such as giving the children their baths; Gilbert Spencer, gay and amusing and uninhibited, with a passionate admiration for his brother, and himself an excellent draughtsman. Then there were the writers – Aldous Huxley, gentle and humane and omniscient; W. B. Yeats, shocking the more serious-minded by his stories about spooks; James Stephens, a little Irish gnome, who goggled before Yeats' dominating genius and broke into exclamations of amazement and admiration; Walter de la Mare, much troubled that Coleridge should have given to his Abyssinian Maid so clumsy an instrument as a dulcimer; Lytton Strachey, with his red beard and long spidery legs, talking in a falsetto voice; and, less commonly, Virginia Woolf, remote, beautiful, and ethereal, but flashing suddenly into keen comments on human foibles. Among dons were two from Cambridge, John Sheppard and Goldsworthy Lowes Dickinson. Sheppard, who was not yet forty, already had white hair, walked with a stick, as if he were an old man, as indeed I thought that he was, and punctuated his remarks with loud laughs, but under a rather forced buffoonery he had a very sharp insight into people and sometimes took even Lady Ottoline by surprise. Dickinson was grave and gentle and serious, much troubled by the state of the world and seeing everywhere portents of evil to come. He was a passionate advocate of peace and worked hard for the League of Nations, for which he had invented the name. His sweet reasonableness made it easy to understand why he had so great an influence at Cambridge, though I found his interpretation both of Greece and of China rather too sentimental for my taste. Some of Lady Ottoline's older friends, notably Augustus John and Bertrand Russell, I did not meet with her, but their unseen presence was usually discernible, since she could not keep her worship of them concealed for long.

It was a household in which dramatic events were frequent. A young man whom the Morrells hoped to help by getting him to look after their chickens, suddenly cut up rough, hired a taxi and went off with his own belongings and the Morrells' chickens. A housemaid, when asked by Lady Ottoline to fetch her boots, did indeed fetch them but then threw them at her. When Lytton Strachey was staying in the house, a party of Asquiths arrived and settled down to tea. Lady Ottoline left the room, and when she came back it was empty except for Strachey. She asked what had happened, and he said in his piping voice, 'There's been a row'. There had, about the war, and the Asquiths had retired in a dudgeon. A gifted young man, who was in love with the Morrells' beautiful daughter, was asked to stay, only to receive a note in his bedroom early in the morning ordering him to leave the house at once. Though the Bloomsbury set liked to guy Lady Ottoline and told all sorts of tales about her, these usually had their origin with her. She had a sharp sense of absurdity and was not shy of being her own butt. At one time the clergyman at Garsington was a little mad, and when Philip and Lady Ottoline, who was a keen Christian, were sitting in the front pew, he said in his sermon, with an unmistakable reference to them, 'We sing "Nearer, my God, to Thee", but what if the Lord our God is a flaming, fiery furnace?' She would recall her girlhood at Welbeck when she gave Bible-lessons to the servants, and commented, 'It was hard to preach the gospel of Christ to fifty footmen chosen for their good looks.' Once she and Philip took Siegfried Sassoon on a motor-tour in Italy. They had a nasty turn when they hurt a child and only just escaped an ugly demonstration, but nothing serious happened when Sassoon, presumably bored and irritated, went up to the roof of the hotel and pushed a large block of stone into the street. Lady Ottoline told of these disasters with much spirit and was not at all above presenting herself as a comic figure.

Lady Ottoline could be sharp about her guests. If anyone left the room, she was ready with some damaging comment. Of a young man who fancied himself at home in all the arts, she said, 'It's really a form of vulgarity'; of a genial and courteous man, 'He's rather an old pussy cat, isn't he?'; of Ethel Sands, who had been a friend of Henry James, 'She's very *nulle*'; and, alas, of myself, 'He's not so clever as he thinks he is.' All this was an astringent training for the young writers, Henry Yorke, Cyril Connolly, Peter Quennell, Harold Acton, and Anthony Powell, who came out from Oxford and saw that they must keep themselves up to the mark. At times Lady Ottoline would ask odd questions, and it was hard to say how seriously she meant them to be taken. So to Anthony Powell she said; 'Mr Powell, do you prefer spring or autumn?' He thought, and said 'Autumn', to which she replied, 'At my age you'll prefer spring.' In moments of crisis she was capable of bold improvisation. Desmond MacCarthy's wife, Molly, once entered the room and found her embracing Henry Lamb, by whom she was greatly attracted, and with perfect self-command she said, 'I was just giving Henry an aspirin.'

Lady Ottoline was in her own eyes a thorough democrat, a woman of the left, and her opinions played a large part in persuading her husband to vote against the war. A myth, probably apocryphal since it is told in various forms about others, but true in essence, says that once when she was speaking for him at a parliamentary election, she said, 'I love the people. I married into the people', and she certainly liked to be a Lady Bountiful at Garsington. But she was still keenly conscious of her origins. I remember a hushed moment when she came into the room and said, 'Portland's downstairs.' She then went out, and we were not allowed to see him. On the other hand her relations with his family were not easy. When one of his sons came to Garsington to visit his aunt, he received a stern reproof from his mother saying, 'Do you wish our happy home to run with blood?' Philip and Lady Ottoline visited the ex-Kaiser at Doorn, and she came away thinking him a genius and a saint, which seemed a bit too much for this adroit actor of many parts and was perhaps prompted by the knowledge that most of her countrymen would be horrified.

She worked hard to find a suitable husband for her daughter and decided that money was probably better than birth. So young sons of stationers and brewers were asked out and made much of. She would place them carefully by name at the tea-table, but as Leslie Hartley observed, she took less trouble with the rest, and on one occasion said to him, 'Anywhere, Mr Hartley.' Once there was a Spanish duke in the offing, and Lady Ottoline, acutely seeing that he liked to dress up as Napoleon, insisted on charades after tea. It happened that at this moment Philip's mother was dying, and he came into the room at intervals with increasingly bad news. Lady Ottoline consoled him with a few words, and then turned to us, crying gaily, 'Go on! Go on!'

In the middle twenties the Morrells left Garsington and moved to a pretty little house in Gower Street in London, where Lady Ottoline continued to give large teas, but something was missing. The surroundings lacked the beauty of Garsington, and there was not the same atmosphere of crisis. Lady Ottoline continued to collect writers and painters, and did not seem to mind that Aldous Huxley had put her, all too recognizably, into *Crome Yellow*, and D. H. Lawrence into *Women in Love*. I was often asked to Gower Street, and on one occasion it was not an invitation but a summons. Lady Ottoline wished to talk to me on a personal matter. I could not imagine what it could be, and hurried up in eager curiosity. Lady Ottoline was alone, and over luncheon suggested that I should marry a young woman whom I knew and liked but did not find in the least attractive. I explained this as best I could, and Lady Ottoline was deeply disappointed. She seemed to think that she had only to speak the word, and I would obey. I do not know even now what put the idea into her head. It might have been pure benevolence, since the young woman was well off, and Lady Ottoline may have wished to do me a good turn, but somehow I did not think that she liked me enough for that. Or had the young woman spoken to her about me? She was not of that kind, and I can only conclude that Lady Ottoline was acting on some obscure prompting, some sudden inspiration which she herself did not fully understand.

If Lady Ottoline enlarged my horizon in many unfamiliar ways, it was still more enlarged by another household not far from Oxford. At New College I had a friend, Sylvester Gates, who was not only very clever and handsome but under a calm exterior nursed an appetite for adventure. At Winchester he had been a close friend of Anthony Asquith, whom I met with him. Puffin, as he was called, was delightfully forthcoming and friendly. He had been brought up in a social turmoil of which I had no inkling and in which he must have found it difficult to keep himself intact. Somehow he managed to do so, and though at times he had to disappear to remote plaes to ge t any work done, he was an invaluable member of hiscfamily circle. His sister, Elizabeth, had been married a few years earlier to the Rumanian prince, Antoine Bibesco. Sylvester was d evoted to her and asked Cyril Radcliffe and myself to meet her at lunch. She was quite outside any orbit I had ever moved in, and I was not at all at my ease with her, but I was fascinated by her talk and her laugh. She had just come back from Washington, where her husband had been Rumanian ambassador, and she had much disliked it. She maintained that all Americans were bores, and she told stories to illustrate the point. She had an agile verbal wit, which turned easily into epigram and paradox, and this did not always go down very well with Americans. Once at a dinner in Washington she said, 'The only reason why generals win battles is that they have generals against them.' After a slight pause an American lady answered, 'But, princess, of course they have generals against them.' She knew everything about American politics and told how in 1916 when C. E. Hughes, thinking that he might be elected President of the United States, sent his wife to visit Mrs Wilson at the White House. Mrs Hughes was shown round by Mrs Wilson, and, being rather enthusiastic, said, 'To think that I may be sleeping here in a few weeks' time', to which Mrs Wilson replied, 'My dear, you mustn't believe everything they say about the President.'

Marcel Proust, who was an old friend of Antoine Bibesco, said that Elizabeth was 'probably the most intelligent woman in the world'. When she talked of politics or books, she had an unusual grip and kept her paradoxes in control. On many people she had excellent things to say and spiced them with illuminating anecdotes. Sligger's sister, Lady Tyrrell, had just gone to Paris where her husband was ambassador. She was rather a dowdy old thing, but Elizabeth reported that she was a great success with the Faubourg St Germain, who said, 'Elle n'a pas ce côté night-club qu'avait Lady Crewe.' It must have been these gifts that made Elizabeth's husband nag her to write. She wrote some stories, poems, and a play, but they lacked the sparkle of her talk and were too elaborate to be a public success. They also embodied other qualities of hers which made me uncomfortable. She saw herself as a centre of love and admiration, of yearning desires and breaking hearts. Of these she talked freely, especially when I was alone with her. I could never grasp what they meant. The conversations reported seemed too good to be true, and I could not believe that her admirers, some of whom I knew, spoke a language so like her own at its most ambitious. I listened with sympathetic attention, but felt that it was no good. If there was any truth in what she said, her imagination had transformed it into her own image, and the process must have been the answer to some inner need. She wished to be loved at the highest level and seemed to believe that she was. In her childhood she may have been rather neglected. Her mother had infinite things to do, and her half-brothers and half-sister felt that she was not quite one of themselves. When she was born, the nurse told them to think of the nicest thing in the world, because they were going to have it. After a conclave they decided that it was a green parrot, and when they were told that it was a baby sister, they were deeply disappointed. She may too have suffered from her sardonic husband, who had a remarkable gift for deflating others. Once when he asked me what I did, and I told him that I taught the classics at Oxford, he said, 'That is like some disgusting vice . . . like onanism.' This was not at all my notion of it, and I did not pursue the subject. He made fun of his wife, and though she bore it with equanimity, she must have felt that something was wrong, and this may have driven her deeper into a dream-world, in which she was the enchanting princess surrounded by ideal lovers and wondering which she ought to choose.

Elizabeth was extremely generous, and through her and Puffin

I was often asked to the Asquiths' house, 'The Wharf", at Sutton Courtnay some ten miles from Oxford. During term this meant dinner on Saturday or Sunday, but in vacation it might mean a stay of a few days. The house had once been an inn and stood on the corner of a main road. Behind it was a garden going down to the river, and there was also an annexe, the Mill House, next door. 'The Wharf' itself had no special claims to beauty and several to inconvenience. As Molly MacCarthy pointed out, everyone lived in a passage. There was a den reserved for Mr Asquith and a dark, not very welcoming room reserved for bridge, but the main activities took place in a room between them which opened on the garden and was the scene of endless traffic to and fro. The dining-room had Hepplewhite furniture and eighteenth-century pictures of London which were said to have come from 10 Downing Street. Mrs Asquith, the famous Margot, had excellent, if somewhat reckless taste. She would cut up good coloured prints to make them into lampshades or waste-paper baskets and slice fine stuffs to cover cushions. The food was wonderful – 'the cleanest cook in the world,' said Margot, and in summer the garden provided an escape from the pressure of life indoors. The week-end parties were large, and their members fell into two classes. The first, and vastly the more interesting, were members of the Asquith family and old friends of Mr Asquith; the second were an indeterminate mass who seemed to be asked because they played bridge. While the first might be a little alarming, they were always worth hearing, but the second had little interest, even for Margot.

In these unpredictable gatherings Margot was the most fascinating figure. She lived in a converted barn in the garden, where she had a large crucifix and slept in a Shetland shawl. She woke up very early and scrawled dozens of letters in pencil, and during the day she passed again and again from her quarters to the house, letting cold gales into the single sitting-room. She held herself astonishingly erect, as if she had been drilled in the nursery to do so. She had a large head, a prominent rectangular nose, and a face which in repose looked almost severe. Her voice was rather deep but had a winning quality and was superbly audible, no matter how many people were talking. What delighted me was her warmth of welcome, her eagerness to be kind to any friend of Elizabeth or Puffin, her assumption that you were a brilliant young man, destined to be Prime Minister or Lord Chancellor or Archbishop of Canterbury. Since she had known and liked Jowett, it was also all right to have a post at Oxford, since in time you were certain to become a national figure. She vastly preferred men to women, and with young women she was a little too bossy to be comfortable. She would look at their clothes, say, 'Darling, you look a perfect fright', and proceed to operate then and there, tearing a dress down the front, folding bits back, and fastening them with safety-pins. It was useless for the victims to complain, since Margot was quite certain that she knew how to dress and that almost nobody else did. She had a superabundant vitality and was always doing something. The household was run with extraordinary smoothness, and there were no crises such as enlivened Garsington. Margot, who had been brought up in large houses, knew all about them, and 'The Wharf' was governed on Edwardian principles. There was an air of extravagance about everything, and whenever I came away from it, I felt that I should go at once and spend money, so infectious was its spirit.

Margot was often accused of being an egoist, and in some ways she was. She not only talked about herself a great deal, but assumed that she was the centre of attention. But I liked to hear her talk, and she was undeniably the centre of attention. She was also gallantly and unashamedly religious. Though she had a perpetual feud with the local parson and once led her whole party out of church during a service, she was not much interested in the details of religious observance. Her Christianity was a form of charity, of being kind and considerate, of helping those in trouble. This she practised splendidly and was never afraid of outraging Pharisees by her championship of the rejected or the discredited. Yet she thought that she had a private line to God, who communicated more directly with her than with others. In particular she distrusted those who claimed to be religious in ways other than her own. Such was Mr Balfour, whom she could never quite fathom, and of whom she said, 'Arthur Balfour talks a lot about

God, but he has never felt the tug at the heart.' With religion
went her own kind of morality, which was not narrow or severe
but was never far from her mind and apparent more often than
not in her endless judgements on people. Though she rather liked
Lord Birkenhead, who made up to her with delightful dexterity,
she felt that there was something wrong, and decided, 'The trouble
with Lord Birkenhead is that he is so un-Christlike.' Her morality
took whimsical turns. Once Molly MacCarthy had taken D. H.
Lawrence's book *The Rainbow* to 'The Wharf' and left it lying
about. At about 7 a.m. it was brought to her with a pencilled note
from Margot, 'Darling, please send this book out of the house
before Violet or Elizabeth sees it.' Conversely, she might be un-
expectedly tolerant. When Eddy Sackville West was in one of his
dark moods, she observed, 'Poor Eddy! But after all his aunt tried
to poison him for the first ten years of his life.' At the other
extreme she would turn matters of common prudence into moral
issues, as when, on finding us drinking beer before lunch on a hot
day, she exclaimed, 'Drinking in the morning! No wonder you
are all as fat as pigs.' A lasting source of uncertainty with her was
the brilliant exterior which her Asquith stepchildren displayed to
the world. She felt that it indicated a lack of heart, and with her
that was a serious fault. It all came out in a rush, 'Misery, anguish,
blood, tears, starving children make the Asquiths laugh.'

Margot adored conversation and did not try to monopolize it.
Her technique was to start a subject and let others develop it until
she could break in with some brief and startling comment. Once
the famous sportsman Lord Lonsdale was being discussed. Margot
did not like him, and when someone praised his courage in the
hunting-field, she said, 'Jump? Anyone can jump. Look at fleas.'
She spent money with reckless extravagance and was often in
trouble about it, but she remained defiant in her attitude towards
it, 'Money! no more to me than almonds and raisins!' Though her
anecdotes about the countless people whom she had met were
always dramatic and alluring, it was not clear that they were
always true. She had a gift for improving upon events and would
tell how at the time of the Marconi Case Rufus Isaacs, who was
deeply and dangerously involved, lay with his head in her lap

sobbing for hours. It was just possible, but it was hard to imagine Isaacs, whom I met at 'The Wharf' and thought remarkably in command of himself, behaving quite like this. She was in a way fascinated by John Morley, whose conversation she thought almost the best she had ever heard. He had, in a moment of quixotic chivalry, married a totally unsuitable woman, and their son got into trouble. Margot then continued, 'I knew that it couldn't be *his* son – a little, slight, womanish man like that. So I asked him, "Whose son is he?", and John replied, "I don't know, and I doubt if she does." ' She gave an enthralling account of Queen Alexandra talking about the dog Caesar, who became a national hero when he followed the coffin of his dead master, King Edward VII, in the funeral procession. But, according to Queen Alexandra as reported by Margot, Caesar was not in the least fond of his master and behaved as he did simply from greed. Margot's accounts of politics had the same radiant, untrustworthy character, and when she began, 'When Mr Lloyd George ruined your father, children . . .', one knew that something good was on the way. She adored her husband and would even interrupt one of her own discourses and say in a commanding tone, 'Just listen to Henry!' She lived for him and his career. She was not wise or discreet, and at times she may well have done him harm, but if she did, it was from uncontrolled devotion.

Margot liked her guests to be fully employed. After dinner she organized them in fours for bridge. This I dreaded, since I disliked the game and was a very bad player, nor could I afford the losses which I usually incurred. Margot was vaguely aware of this and, if I lost, would suggest that with her as partner I should play another rubber in the hope of winning my losses back. Since she was herself a reckless player, this tended to lead to more losses, and I had to invent excuses for evasion. Financially harmless and much more amusing were other games, notably one called 'Analogies', in which all the party but one thought of some person and the one had to guess who this was by asking what kind of book or film or flower etc he was like. It did not matter if you did not know the person in question, for, as Margot said, 'You'll pick him up as you go along.' 'Clumps' was also in favour. Mr Asquith

played by the strictest standards and would answer nothing but
'Yes' or 'No', and then with the most careful precision, but
Margot played by flashes of inspiration – 'It's not Elizabeth? . . .
Then it's an elephant', and it was. In the intervals she kept rather
a stern eye open to see that not too much was drunk. She herself
was very abstemious, and though she did not object to men drinking and even thought it proper that they should, she was against
women doing it at all seriously. Once when someone was getting
a whisky for Elizabeth, Margot hissed loudly, 'Only lemonade.'
Nor was she quite happy about her husband's taste for brandy.
He clearly enjoyed it and found that it helped him through a
social evening, but Margot was uneasy, and had on her side the
butler Clouder, who remarked; 'Sip, sip, sip can't do the old man
any good.' Margot resorted to various ruses, always unsuccessful.
Once she was found pouring the brandy on the rose-bushes and
then filling half the decanter with water, but nobody was deceived.
She had after all brought her husband into a society where brandy
was drunk after dinner, and it was too late now for her to try to
reverse her own policy.

Mr Asquith presented an extraordinary contrast with his wife.
He had a fine head of white hair, which he wore rather long, a
rubicund complexion, legs a little too short for his body, and a
face which still indicated authority. His movements were slow but
dignified and matched his manner of speech. At a first meeting he
was rather restrained, as if he did not welcome the sight of a new
face, and looked at you as if he were sizing you up. When he
spoke, he had a little mannerism of jerking his head, and this
somehow added weight to his concise and well formed sentences.
He asked me about my work at Oxford and spoke with knowledge about Latin and Greek, both of which he still read for
pleasure. At first I thought that there was something to be said for
Birkenhead's comment, 'The old man wants to get out of politics,
but Margot sits under his tail like a horsefly, stinging him on', but
he was still concerned with them, and when Reginald McKenna,
who was an old friend, coquetted publicly with the Conservatives
about becoming Chancellor of the Exchequer and eventually
backed out, Mr Asquith dismissed him derisively as 'a figure of

fun'. His own views came to the front in the General Strike, when I took G. D. H. Cole over to talk to him. Both Margot and Elizabeth were much taken by Cole's good looks, but Mr Asquith was not impressed by his arguments and maintained his firm stand against the strikers. He thought that their gravest mistake was to antagonize the Press, and he said with perfect equanimity, 'After all, I have no reason to like the Press', but that did not shake him. Nor did he sympathize with the Archbishop's efforts to make a truce, though Margot did. Mr Asquith related her activities, 'Your mother then rang up the Archbishop', and treated it as rather a joke. I never heard him say anything against Lloyd George and formed a vague impression that, like Fisher and Balfour, he was fascinated by his primeval energy and clairvoyant insight. He was in these years having rows with Lloyd George about the Liberal Party funds. Margot, without consulting her husband, wrote Lloyd George a letter, 'Straight from the shoulder it was, the straightest letter I have ever written anyone.' Lloyd George came round the next morning to the Asquiths' house in Bedford Square. There he found first the butler, who took his hat and coat, then Mr Asquith, who said, 'You mustn't believe a word my wife says', and finally Margot, bristling with hostility. He put his arm round her neck, kissed her, and said, 'Darling Margot, I forgive you.'

Asquith was by now an old man. He presided over the table with benign dignity and maintained a high level of conversation. He had flashes of his old quickness, as when an American lawyer, describing to him the Sacco and Vanzetti case, began, 'I don't know, Mr Asquith, whether you are acquainted with our constitution', when Asquith interrupted him, 'The worst in the world.' He had much to say about the past, both recent and distant. He liked to recall that when he prosecuted Vizetelly for his translations of Zola, the French Press referred to 'la pudeur effarouchée de l'avocat Asquith'. He had known Mrs Humphry Ward and her husband, and told how a friend of the husband, on returning from years abroad, wrote to him asking him to dinner and added, 'P.S. If there is a Mrs H. W., bring her with you.' Knowing that Lord Chancellor Westbury had been at Wadham, he told me that when he had to resign because of allegations of nepotism, Queen Victoria, on receiving from him the seals of office, said, 'Now you see how much more important it is to be good than to be clever.' When he spoke about the war, he displayed admiration for Sir Henry Wilson for his vivid and amusing expositions before the Committee for National Defence. He also had a high opinion of Sir Archibald Murray, who had been sacked by Lloyd George for failure at Gaza. Asquith claimed that the failure in the first battle was due to Chetwode who withdrew the cavalry to water the horses at a vital point of the battle, and that Murray was not to blame, while it was he who with careful foresight laid the foundations of Allenby's later victory. He much enjoyed the witticisms of his daughters and particularly relished Violet Bonham-Carter's account of 'Sir John Simon's synthetic geniality'. Asquith showed no obvious liking for Simon and preferred more adventurous characters, including Birkenhead, whose eloquence he enjoyed, and of course, in spite of everything, Churchill.

The first time I saw Churchill was at 'The Wharf', when, draped in a noble dressing-gown, he was marching with firm determination to the bathroom, carrying a sponge of heroic dimensions. At dinner he talked without ceasing, and everyone listened. It was clear that he did not like to be interrupted, and his talk held us in thrall. He was much admired by the Asquith family, by Margot for being a devoted husband, by Violet for his powerful personality, by Elizabeth for his consistency in politics, which she elucidated with some ingenuity, and by Asquith for his prodigious vitality. He talked about the war and produced the bitter, ironical summary, not, I believe, for the first time, 'In the recent war we politicians had only two duties. The one was to persuade our admirals to put to sea, the other to persuade our generals to stop killing their own men. In both we were quite unsuccessful.' He had just agreed to join Baldwin's government, and none of the Asquiths thought this at all odd, least of all Asquith himself, who liked and was liked by Baldwin and thought that Churchill's place was with him. After dinner the two played chess. Churchill got out his pieces in no time, but Asquith was setting out his pawns with some deliberation, when Churchill said, 'Marshal your Baldwins! Marshal your Baldwins!' Asquith was delighted.

Early in my acquaintance with the Asquiths I met, at luncheon with them in London, John Morley. He was very old and frail, but still spry and quick on the mark. Margot had a protective affection for him, but thought him rather too high-minded and not sufficiently masculine. She led him to talk about Gladstone, and he produced two stories which struck a vein very unlike the reverential awe of his biography. Once, when Mr G. was speaking to a large audience, a drunkard kept on interrupting him. With perfect calm the old man addressed himself to him, 'May I ask you, sir, to extend towards me that same measure of generous tolerance which, were I in your place and you were in mine, I would extend towards you?' The drunkard was completely discomfited. On another occasion a visitor was telling Gladstone about a crank school which existed in 1812 in Devonshire, and its rule was that if anyone did anything wrong, he was not punished but all the boys in the school wrote home about it. So one day dear old Canon Denniston of Durham, who had six boys at the school, received six letters, each of which said, 'Yesterday Jones minor cheated', and on each letter he had to pay one and threepence. At this point Gladstone commented, 'But in eighteen hundred and twelve the postage from Devonshire to Durham was a great deal more than one and threepence.' His children, feeling that this was a little unkind to the story-teller, said, 'But, father, this is a funny story', and he said, 'I am perfectly aware of the humorous aspects of this story but what particularly interests me are the financial aspects.' This was truly a voice from the dead.

In 1925 I was, in a very minor capacity, involved in a matter which caused Asquith considerable grief. On the death of Lord Curzon the Chancellorship of Oxford University became vacant. Birkenhead took an active part in finding a successor and, having dismissed Lord Salisbury on the grounds that he had taken a fourth class in science and feeling that he himself, despite obvious claims, might not command enough support, gave all his assistance to Asquith, under whom he had been Solicitor-general and

Attorney-general, and whom he regarded as the greatest living Oxonian. He was helped by Lindemann and Roy Harrod, both of whom worked hard to collect names of supporters, while I did my best among my own acquaintances, most of whom signed without a qualm. An impressive list was formed, including the better heads of houses and a number of bishops. But in some circles there was an ominous silence. Wells, despite his affection for Birkenhead, explained that as Vice-Chancellor he could not take any part, but it was clear that he disliked the idea of Asquith, who had recently become Earl of Oxford. I began to see that others shared his views and was appalled when my old supporter the Crab set out the case against Asquith – he had never proceeded from his BA to an MA; he had no right to take the title of Earl of Oxford; he had piloted the Welsh Disestablishment Bill through parliament; he had presided over a Royal Commission on Oxford and Cambridge which had had the temerity to suggest some reforms. Since the Crab was a Conservative and his views were those of many in his party, I saw trouble in the offing.

The man who organized the malcontents was G. B. Grundy, a tutor in ancient history at Corpus, who had once done good work on the geography of the battlefields of the Persian Wars in Greece and claimed to have killed a man who threatened him in the Peloponnese. He was now past his prime and had a name for getting second classes for his first-class pupils, whom he encouraged to read no books but his own. He was an arrogant, self-satisfied man who paid no attention to what other scholars wrote on his subject and never revised his views in the light of new discoveries. As such he was well suited to find an opponent to Asquith, and he found one in the then Lord Chancellor, Viscount Cave. Cave, despite his high office, was not distinguished, and his chief title to fame was that he had been a follower of Carson in the Ulster troubles before 1914 and, like some other rebels, won a name for being a patriot. Cave accepted the nomination, and a suitable list of supporters was soon collected for him and published. It contained very few notable names, but some of the blacker heads of colleges were on it. Anyhow the quality of the supporters did not matter; what mattered was the quantity, and here Cave had the advantage. The electorate was Convocation, which means all Masters of Arts who by paying a small sum 'keep their names on the books' of their colleges. The majority of these lived outside Oxford, and many of them were clergymen, who no doubt kept in touch in the hope of getting college livings, and who had the advantage that, with much spare time on their hands, they could easily come to Oxford to vote. They felt that Asquith was not of their party, and, since they knew nothing about Cave, except that he was a Conservative, they assumed that he was their man. The result was that Cave was elected by a large majority. It brought no credit to the University, and Asquith was deeply upset. This was one of the few honours that he would have liked, for he was a most loyal son of Oxford. As usual, he did not complain, but I knew that he minded, and I felt ashamed of not having been able to do more for him. In fact, if he had been elected, he would not have held the office for long, since he died in 1928. So also did Cave, and was succeeded by Lord Grey of Fallodon, who had been sent down from Balliol for incorrigible idleness.

What I saw of Asquith convinced me that some of the common views of him were wrong. Even in old age he was an impressive figure, who made no concessions on points of principle and commanded respect from many people, including Churchill. He read widely, had a very retentive memory, and liked to talk of the bypaths of history. His analytical mind reduced complex problems to their essence without over-simplifying them. He had been the victim of extremely vicious attacks from the Press, but, though Margot minded them terribly both for his sake and for her own, he dismissed them with disdain. The defeats of his later years he took with philosophic calm and seemed to bear no grudges against the most faithless of his old followers. It was thought that his marriage had had a bad effect on him by taking him out of his proper social sphere and launching him into high society. Margot may have made him attend too many lunches and dinners, but her loyalty and vitality sustained him, while her vagaries amused him. He liked the smart set into which she had brought him, and found in it compensation for the austerity of his childhood and earlier years. His trouble was that he was an intellectual and believed in justice at a time when violent emotions swayed both the crowd and its leaders, and injustice followed. His loyalty made him trust his military commanders more faithfully than they deserved, while his modesty convinced him that in war the professionals must have a full say. He was punished for their mistakes, and they were exalted when he was derided. In the end it is not surprising that he was ousted and humiliated by Lloyd George.

I met Lloyd George twice, and on each occasion the impression was overwhelming. The bright, light-blue eyes would wander round the room, and then settle on you, while he turned on all his charm and vitality to win you to his side. Though he had very few real affections and almost no intimate friends, he liked to exert his power over everyone that he met, and the fascination was prodigious. He had a sixth sense which told him what would please you, and though he might make one or two false starts, he got there before you knew it. Most of his conversation was about politics, which was the dominating passion of his life. He was much more than a professional politician; he was a politician and almost nothing else. He saw politics as a complex and difficult game in which his job was to get people to do what he wanted, but he enjoyed every twist and manœuvre in it. All the resources of persuasion and cajolery were at his command, and if one failed, he would try another. He was a consummate actor who believed in the parts that he played at least while he played them, but he was also a creative comedian with an unsurpassed talent for mimicry. He would in turn be Woodrow Wilson refusing to do something, Asquith leaving a restaurant and failing to pick up his hat, a row of Japanese hissing and grunting at the Peace Conference, Balfour lecturing an imaginary Lloyd George on his treatment of Curzon, 'I think that if you were kinder to George, you would get more out of him.' His insight into character was deadly, and he spotted at once any weaknesses on which he could work. If he noticed virtues, it was because he could make use of them. Yet, while he talked to you, no doubts or misgivings assailed you, so riveting was the performance, so dazzling the speed and the agility of his mind. Yet in all the wonder-working two factors were constant. The first was his belief in democracy, which he might at times betray but to which in his fashion he remained faithful, if only because he was a man of the people and could never be anything else. The other was his taste for women. Sir Robert Ensor told me that even before 1914 one of his tasks was to appease husbands whose domestic felicity Lloyd George had violated, and the nickname of 'the goat' referred not to any 'giddy garden' antics but to his uncontrolled appetites and his skill in satisfying them. When he was Prime Minister, he was said to enjoy himself after luncheon in the Cabinet room. If anyone attacked him on the matter, he was ready with an answer. Lady (Nancy) Astor found out an affair of his long after it was well known to others and assailed him with the full armoury of American rectitude. He listened with quiet patience, and at the end said, 'What about you and Philip Lothian?' She was outraged and explained indignantly that this affection was not at all of his kind, that it was purely spiritual and high-minded, as indeed it was. Lloyd George, in a voice of the strongest moral fervour, said 'You ought to be ashamed of yourself', and that round was over. His wonderful sense of comedy enabled him to laugh at himself. He once took Hugh Allen, Professor of Music at Oxford, to a Welsh occasion when hymns were sung. Lloyd George himself sang with ardour and unction and seemed to share all the fervour of his countrymen, but, on leaving, he turned to Allen and said, 'Funny people the Welsh. They pray on their knees on Sunday and on their neighbours all the rest of the week.' Lloyd George was both less and more than human, and that was why nobody knew how to deal with him.

From Garsington and Sutton Courtnay I had fascinating perspectives far from my ordinary round. In quite a different way this happened at a less exalted level. In my undergraduate days Roy Harrod had a friend called Maurice Hastings at University College, whom I met and instantly liked. He came up wearing chain epaulettes, having been in the Indian Cavalry and looking like a young hunting squire. He read Greats but intended to take Holy Orders and was an assiduous attendant at the High Church establishment of Pusey House. He was an excellent talker and an admirable companion, who enjoyed expressing paradoxical views, but combined this with an unusual understanding of human nature and a fierce respect for learning and the intellectual life. At the same time he was a close friend of the distinguished athletes who were then at his college. He took Greats when I did, and to my surprise and regret got only a third class. Then he disappeared. I heard that he had given up the idea of Holy Orders and was doing something or other in the United States, though nobody seemed to know what. Then on a dark evening in the winter of 1925 I met him in Turl Street. We were both delighted, and that evening Roy and I dined with him in his private room at the Randolph Hotel. He had with him a young American wife, and was plainly doing very well indeed. She came from Massachusetts, where her family were paper-manufacturers, and aided by them Maurice had gone into speculative finance at the height of the American boom. He had made a lot of money, and since she too was very well off, he seemed to have solved some of his problems. He had an agreeable habit of shouting remarks when he got excited, and on this occasion, he stood in front of the fireplace and bellowed, 'You don't know how rich I am.'

Maurice had no intention of staying in the United States and was determined to settle as a country gentleman in England. For this purpose he rented houses not too far from Oxford, first in the Cotswolds, then at Rousham. He liked horses and became a master of foxhounds. Roy and I, and later John Sparrow, were constant visitors at his house and never knew what would happen. We were none of us in the least interested in hunting, but I had at least ridden a horse in the army, and Maurice would mount me and take me out. On one occasion the other guests were two young army officers who thought I was a dim don and treated me as such. When we went out riding, I pulled myself together and jumped over two low walls, while the subalterns went through the gates. At lunch they were distinctly more affable, and when after it we played poker and I won quite a lot of money, they treated me with respect. I have never played poker or jumped over a wall since. The company was always mixed and quite unpredictable. There were members of the hunting-set, who enjoyed

indoor games of an active kind. One was to blindfold everyone and then make them steeplechase over the furniture, which
was arranged like a racecourse. When John Sparrow failed to
take a sofa in his stride, a visiting M.F.H. jeered, 'I've never
seen such a clumsy fellow in my life.' Then there were the
Americans, mostly relations of Mrs Hastings, but also friends of
Maurice. They treated the whole thing reverentially as a supreme
example of gracious living, but they must have had some rude
shocks. The younger generation often became riotous and played
practical jokes such as climbing into the windows of visiting
ladies, hoping to be taken for burglars. I was appalled at what the
visitors might think, and suggested to Maurice that they must hate
us, but he dismissed my fears by saying, 'They are far too busy
hating themselves ever to hate you.' He had studied the New
England mentality with some care and especially its conscience,
which does not stop you from doing what you know to be wrong,
but at least stops you from enjoying it.

Maurice had been in the United States during the fantastic
boom of the twenties. This was also the period of prohibition,
which made it a matter of prestige and honour to drink too much,
especially hard liquor. He had both enjoyed and examined this
strange state of affairs and been oddly affected by it. The search
for excitement which had so clearly marked it had infected him.
He wished to get too much out of life, to combine as many different interests as possible, to startle, amuse, excite, deride, or encourage everyone who came his way. If on the one hand he gave
riotous parties, on the other hand he had powerful intellectual
and artistic interests. He knew a lot about music and painting,
and he kept up his earlier taste for philosophy. Religion for the
moment was in abeyance, but he invited High Church clergymen
to his house and engaged them in bellicose controversy. His ideal
of a man was that he should be able to deal with almost any situation and be at home with all kinds of people. This was certainly
necessary when I stayed with him and met the most wildly
assorted guests, and if I managed to talk to them, I got good marks
for 'coping'. Then in the Wall Street crash of 1929 and 1930 he
lost nearly all the large fortune that he had made for himself. His

wife was still well established, and he was not in need, but the sense of boundless possibilities had withered. He moved to an old house in Norfolk, where he turned himself into a learned scholar on medieval architecture. This filled a large part of his time until his death in 1965. I saw a lot of him, especially when his marriage broke up and he was living happily in quite humble circumstances and working hard on the accounts of St Stephen's Chapel at Westminster. He kept to the last his old fascination, even in his outbursts of agreement or disagreement, and he was still a most perceptive critic of human beings. He was a true man of the twenties, who kept some of its notions in a very different age.

9

Gilbert Murray

I have already told how much I gained as an undergraduate from Gilbert Murray's tuition and lectures, but I also came to know him well personally and was in some ways much influenced by him. When I was an undergraduate, he used to ask me to his house on Boars Hill, and later I was often a visitor, sometimes because I wanted advice, more often for the sheer pleasure of his company. Though he did not die until 1957, when he was ninety-one, his appearance did not change very much. He had a very distinguished bearing. The high domed skull of the scholar was matched by a fine, firm mouth and a remarkably resolute chin. He never lost his lithe and easy movements or his upright stance. He had no airs or affectations and was charmingly courteous to everyone with the true courtesy which comes from being really interested in others. If he asked you questions about yourself, his deep interest made you fear that your answer would be quite unworthy of him. He had a large repertory of tricks and diversions. He could walk up a ladder without using his hands and take off his waistcoat without taking off his coat. He played tennis into old age and was a master of adroit and amusing gamesmanship. He was a fast and fearless walker, who would go straight through a wood regardless of boughs or brambles, or step lightly along ice-edges or the brinks of crevasses in Switzerland. He had more unusual talents in reserve, as when he gave displays of thought-reading. He would go out of the room, while those inside thought about some event and fixed their minds on it. When he came in, he would look round, wait in a mood of great concentration for a few moments, and then get the answer in a series of steps. I once took part with his daughter Rosalind, his wife, and one other. He settled it in five moves with slight pauses between them, 'There's blood in it ... a crowd shouting ... it's in Paris ... there's a guillotine ... it's the execution of Marie Antoinette.' Even in conversation with him I felt that he had a clairvoyant insight into what I was thinking, so quickly did he adapt himself to my moods and catch the very tone of them.

Murray owed much of his eminence to being an authentic Victorian, who, like other Victorians, was compounded of curiously contradictory elements. He combined assurance and doubt, intellectual independence and intransigent prejudices, classical precision and romantic vagueness. For this his origins and background were partly responsible. He was born in the old 'governing' class, which found an outlet for its ambitions and its sense of responsibility in administering territories which were still colonies. His father, Sir Terence Murray, was President of the Legislative Council of New South Wales, and his brother, Hubert, was for many years an enlightened and highly capable Governor of Papua. But this orthodox lineage was tempered by a strain of Irish blood and membership of the Roman Catholic Church, which Murray forsook at the age of eleven when he came to England. There was an aristocratic distinction not only in his manners but in his dress. He wore very well-cut clothes, a stiff up-and-down collar with pointed ends, and kept his necktie in place with a gold ring. But he saw himself as a rebel, while his adversaries saw him as a crank. In his Australian boyhood he was horrified by the brutal treatment of the aborigines and formed his first sympathies for the oppressed, and his speech, which was much admired by Americans, owed not a little to a slight Australian twang, which mitigated what might otherwise have been too mellifluous an utterance. He could never be fitted into any accepted category. In the academic world he was suspected as a man of letters and a man of affairs, and in the world of politics he was always unmistakably a professor. Yet in both he moved on equal terms with his more strictly professional colleagues. He was sustained by a Victorian assurance and pursued his own ends with a confidence characteristic of his generation and his class.

Murray had a brilliant academic career. At Oxford, where he was a scholar of St John's, he won all the prizes, and as an infant prodigy of twenty-three he was appointed Professor of Greek at Glasgow, where he had to begin the day's work at 7 a.m. with prayers. He confounded the critics and appeased his own agnostic conscience by reciting the Lord's Prayer in Greek. Ten years later he was thought not likely to live long and retired to Surrey, whence he was lured to Oxford in 1906 and appointed by Asquith to be Regius Professor of Greek in 1910. He had used his years of leisure to real profit. He went to study Greek in Berlin with the magnificent Hellenist, Ulrich von Wilamowitz-Moellendorff, who records that he received a letter from Murray in 'elegant Attic', and Murray used to recall that when the German students made mistakes and the English (presumably himself) got it right, the great man would bang the table and cry, 'Nur die Engländer!' ('Only the English!'). It was at this time too that Murray began his translations and formed a friendship with Bernard Shaw, who put him as Cusins into *Major Barbara* and got Granville Barker to play the part with an uncanny verisimilitude. Euripides, who had never been a first favourite with English readers, won a much belated renown when Murray's versions were acted, and was credited with having played in Athens in the second half of the fifth century BC the kind of part that Shaw now played in London, except that he wrote tragedies instead of comedies. In the first decade of this century Murray's translations were almost the only new verse in English to command a large sale.

Murray's success came the more easily because he presented Greek poetry to the English-speaking public in an idiom in which it felt at home. The high Victorian manner, mellifluously romantic and consciously archaic, was still regarded as the right way to write poetry. There were indeed subterranean rumblings of revolt, but many educated readers took no notice of them and welcomed from Murray something that they liked and understood. Murray turned Euripides into the style of Swinburne and Morris: Swinburne provided a model for the choruses, Morris for the rest. In recent years sophisticated taste has turned against these translations, and critics tend to repeat, in rather less cogent words, T. S. Eliot's sharp little judgement that 'as a poet Mr Murray is merely a very insignificant follower of the pre-Raphaelite movement'. It is understandable that the young Eliot, in his ardent search for a cosmopolitan, colloquial diction, found nothing to help him in Murray's translations, which were regrettably reminiscent of his own first poetical contributions to Harvard periodicals. Yet Murray could hardly have done otherwise. A man who was born in 1866 and began to translate Greek poetry in the eighties would scarcely anticipate the dehydrated manner of H. D., which Eliot, oblivious alike of Milton and Arnold, recommends as suitable for Greek choruses. Even A. E. Housman, who fashioned his own idiom for *A Shropshire Lad*, translated them into a close pastiche of Swinburne, whose *Atalanta in Calydon* was in those days regarded as the nearest that English could get to Greek tragedy. If Murray had been a truly creative poet, he would no doubt have fashioned a different style, but in that case he would not have been content with mere translations. It was because his poetical talent was essentially derivative that he never altered his style. Swinburne and Morris, having done service for Euripides, were called in later for Aeschylus and Sophocles. At school I thought these translations wonderful, and even at Oxford, when Murray read them in his lectures, they still kept relics of their old magic. Later he lost some of his liveliness, but to the last he kept astonishingly close to the Greek text, which was all the more remarkable since he used rhyme throughout.

When he translated Aristophanes, Murray had another model. He was a cousin of William Schwenck Gilbert, the collaborator with Arthur Sullivan in the D'Oyly Carte Operas, and it was after him that Murray was christened Gilbert. He greatly admired the neat and skilful versification of these comic operas, and used his own adaptation of it for the *Frogs* and the *Knights*. These too have passed out of fashion, and modern versions are much less formal and less neat, but Aristophanes was a neat writer, and Murray did not betray him in this respect. These translations were a kind of tribute to his kinsman, whose Victorian jokes appealed strongly to Murray. Once at a party Gilbert was approached by a man who mistook him for a waiter and said, 'Call me a cab.' 'You're a growler', said Gilbert. 'Come, come, my man, you can't talk to me like that', said the man. 'Anyhow', countered Gilbert, 'nobody could call you a hansom.' On another occasion, when Gilbert was taking a trip on a pleasure-steamer on the Thames, they passed a new bungalow, and someone said to him, 'I suppose that's what they call a bijou residence', and Gilbert replied, 'Yes, and that's a he-Jew sitting in the garden and a she-Jew coming out of the door.' Murray much enjoyed quips of this kind, and found plenty of them in Aristophanes.

A serious criticism of Murray's methods was also urged by T. S. Eliot, 'Professor Murray has simply interposed between Euripides and ourselves a barrier more impenetrable than the Greek language' and he refers explicitly to one or two places where Murray adds images which are not visible to the naked eye in Greek nor easily inferred from it. The accusation is fair enough, and was indeed current in Oxford before Eliot gave his *imprimatur* to it. A story, apocryphal indeed, but not fundamentally false, tells that in a lecture Murray, on reaching the crisis of a play, said, 'I will read you my version, "Death, and a cold white thing within the house . . ." ' but those who followed in the Greek found no more than the emotive cries *e e â â*. Murray certainly adorned his originals, but he did so consciously and of set purpose, and was ready with his defence. In his view, English, after centuries of hard use, had lost the freshness which survived in Greek, and he tried to compensate for this by providing an emphasis which the Greek does not possess and does not need. It could be doubted whether he chose the best way to do this, but he had a case. If we stick too closely to the Greek and translate literally word for word, we get only the bare, dry bones and extinguish the living breath. The problem may be insoluble, but at least there is a problem, and Murray solved it to the satisfaction of his own generation. His translations were often acted with success on the commercial stage. They were not his most important contribution to Greek scholarship but in their day they did much to maintain its place in common regard.

Murray's view of the difference between English and Greek is characteristic of his complex nature. He, who added so much when he translated from Greek into English, would never have done the same thing from English into Greek. His own versions, whether in prose or verse, were of a matchless limpidity, which made the work of other renowned practitioners look stuffy and factitious. Though he never shirked the full implications of what an English passage meant, he took pride in making it as straightforward as possible in Greek. He knew that Greek abhors vague outlines, and he insisted that the translator must make up his mind what the words really mean and go boldly for it. So when he took Wordsworth's 'The world is too much with us' and put it, very appropriately, into Greek elegiacs, his version is astonishingly word for word, but each word has a sharper outline than its English equivalent, and the final effect is true to the authentic nature of the Greek language. This is not to suggest that Murray was neglectful of the many undertones in English poetry or that in his desire for clarity he made no attempt to reproduce them in Greek. On the contrary, it is his ability to unite clarity with a full feeling for poetry that makes his versions so remarkable. When, for instance, he translated Tennyson's 'short, sweet Idyll' from *The Princess*, he rightly turned it into hexameters in the manner of Theocritus. Though Tennyson flaunts his ability to make every sound support and strengthen his meaning, Murray does not fall behind him in making Greek do the same. If ever the poetry of one language has been transferred to another, it is here, and it could never have been done if Murray had not been awake, with all his being, to the essential qualities of Tennyson's lines and able to reproduce their spirit and their life in his Greek version.

The source of Murray's strength in scholarship was that he knew the Greek language and Greek literature extremely well. He must have worked incredibly hard in his youth and earlier manhood, and what he then learned he remembered for the rest of his life. He knew large tracts of Greek poetry by heart and had so absorbed them that he was entirely at home with them and understood them from the inside. In this he represented at its very best the English tradition of classical learning, which insisted that the language must be mastered as a living thing. This was why he did not need and did not much respect the German method of learning Greek from the outside, of approaching a text with an enormous apparatus of commentary and explanation. He thought that this was far less effective than a mind so well trained to the language that it grasped almost instinctively not only its plain meaning but its nuances and associations. At any meeting of a classical society, when a Greek text was discussed in detail, Murray was often first in the discussion with his recollection of exactly the right passages to show what those in question must mean. So, too, in handling the extremely complex metres of Greek lyric poetry, though he knew the modern technical terms and was quite in touch with what scholars had written to analyse the rhythms, he was ultimately guided by his own ear and made the words sound as verbal music, as they were meant to do.

In reinforcing scholarship with imagination Murray satisfied powerful elements in his nature and indulged alike his classical sense of order and his romantic yearnings, his delight in words for their own sake and his desire that they should make an impression on the world, his respect for the past and his wish to use it as an instrument of reform. Among professional scholars he had detractors. When Henry Jackson, Regius Professor of Greek at Cambridge, first saw in the Preface of Murray's *Ancient Greek Literature* the words 'To read and re-read the scanty remains now left to us of the literature of Ancient Greece, is a pleasant and not a laborious task', he scrawled in the margin, 'Insolent puppy!'. Rather more ambiguous but not ultimately more pleasant was the attitude of A. E. Housman, who had been a scholar of St John's before Murray and was in 1911 elected Professor of Latin at Cambridge. Housman claimed to like Murray, and Murray was certainly amused by Housman's abrupt manner of approach, as when Murray was standing as a Liberal candidate for a university seat in Parliament, Housman came up to him and said, 'I won't vote for you.' 'Why not?' said Murray, 'you must admit that I know some Greek.' But Housman merely reiterated, 'I won't vote for you.' Murray and Housman got on quite well because Murray took Housman's crudities with a humorous tolerance. But we must not argue too much, as some have, from Housman's unsuccessful attempts to persuade Murray to go to a music-hall with him. His motive was quite probably a malicious hope that Murray would be shocked, as he almost certainly would have been. Nor is it true that Housman never turned his savage pen against Murray. Once when reviewing a posthumous work by Murray's predecessor, Ingram Bywater, Housman wrote, 'It is the business-like performance of a good scholar who did not aspire to be an indifferent man of letters; and readers who wish to hear about the Greek spirit may leave it alone.' This is all too clearly aimed at Murray. The formidable editor of Manilius might himself write poems when the fit was on him, but he did not approve of scholarship and literature being combined in a single work. Even in Oxford some people regarded Murray as 'brilliant', and the word was not meant to praise. Yet Murray was attacked precisely for his outstanding virtues. It was idle, and worse, to expect him to conform to the demands of humdrum scholarship, for that would have wasted his superb gift for teaching and interpreting Greek. Yet by 1914 he had already established himself. The new generation looked on him as their master, and though he was sensitive to hostility and saw no excuse for *odium philologicum*, he was sure enough of himself to pursue his own way.

Even so scholarship was not enough. Murray had always been keenly and actively interested in politics as a radical who disapproved of the Boer War and advocated votes for women. He was vigorously abetted by his wife, whom he married in 1889. Lady Mary Howard was a daughter of the 9th Earl of Carlisle and came of a family noted for its aristocratic independence. Her remarkable and eccentric mother had been so shocked by the junketings of the British Association for the Advancement of

Science when it met at her home at Castle Howard that she ordered the family wine-cellars to be emptied into the lake and herself supervised the massacre, seeing that the top of each bottle was knocked off before it was drowned. Once, when she observed her husband helping himself to trifle at a tenants' luncheon, she called in ringing tones down the table, 'Don't touch it, dear. It might bring on the old craving.' Lady Mary, who was her mother's favourite daughter, inherited her strength of character, but combined it with a warm heart and a brisk intelligence. She had once been beautiful, but when I knew her, she seemed to have decided that, if she still had any claims to looks, she would make the worst of them. Unlike Gilbert, she took no trouble at all with her clothes, and, again unlike him, she had almost no sense of humour. With all her warmth and generosity she could be both bossy and censorious. If in a crowded bus she saw any man sitting, she would at once tell him to give up his place to a lady. Once when Gilbert was playing with his small granddaughters, they broke a croquet-mallet, and Lady Mary made an absurd fuss about it at lunch before the guests, but Gilbert said calmly, 'Yes, we were playing tricks.' She was wonderfully kind to refugees, and a small lodge in the garden usually housed some, but she could not refrain from keeping them in order. One unfortunate man was told to repeat to me a story which he had told her, and began rather laboriously, when she interrupted, 'Never mind. That will do for the present. Get on with your pudding.' She made friends with my Austrian housekeeper and would visit my kitchen and eat three or four raw eggs at a sitting. She was like her mother a teetotaller and a vegetarian, but eggs were not on the list of forbidden foods, and she never mentioned her clandestine indulgences to me. To both her creeds she converted Gilbert, who got round the first by saying, 'I like wine, but I don't think it's so good a drink as coffee' (he pronounced it 'korfi'). When guests were present, Gilbert used to carve the joint and say, 'Will you have some of the corpse, or will you try the alternative?' The sadder side of their economy was revealed when Gilbert, before going to bed, said in a plaintive voice, 'Mary, you've mixed the Horlicks too thick.'

Gilbert was deeply attached to Lady Mary and almost broken by her death after sixty years of marriage, but he could not refrain from making mild fun of her. After going to official dinners in London, he would, to her horror, regale her with accounts of the huge joints and the lavish alcohol which had been served. Once, when he told a particularly amusing story, she said, 'That's not true, Gilbert', and with a charming smile, he answered, 'I may have dramatized it in my mind', and proceeded to tell another. If she told him to put on his coat or take the letters to the post (she was obsessed by this), he would say quietly, 'No. I won't.' He agreed with her on many matters, and she supported him in his political activities. But when she became a Socialist, he remained a Liberal, and when she became a Quaker, he remained a reverent agnostic. He was not exactly, as Bernard Shaw said, 'a collector of religions', but he was deeply interested in them. What he disliked in Christianity was what he called its magical claims, but he admired holiness in whatever creed it could be found, and was a lifelong friend of Charles Gore, who became Bishop of Oxford and held advanced political views. Murray's personal admiration for Asquith and Grey modified his earlier radicalism, and it was largely from confidence in them that he supported the entry of Great Britain into war in 1914. He saw it as a crusade for what he most valued in western civilization, but once it was finished, he was determined that it should not happen again.

With men like Smuts and Robert Cecil, Murray worked hard for the League of Nations and for a machinery to make it effective. In England he was a pillar of the League of Nations Union and its president from 1928 to 1938. He would spare himself no trouble to make its objects known and would think nothing of going to remote places to explain them to small groups. He did the work because he believed in it, but he was rewarded by the pleasure which he found in its personal aspects. Though he cut an incongruous figure at official dinners as he sipped his barley-water and ate nut-cutlets, in council he carried considerable weight. But he always seemed rather too fine a creature for the rough and tumble of politics, no matter how high-minded, and his ability to see more than one side of a question was sometimes construed as an inability to make up his mind. Indeed, so far from being an implacable doctrinaire, as academic persons are supposed to be when they take to public affairs, Murray was unusually supple and resourceful. He enjoyed the intricacies of manœuvre and felt that concessions and compromises were inevitable if any progress was to be made. He was probably at his best at meetings of the International Committee for Intellectual Co-operation, which was a faint anticipation of UNESCO and dealt with cultural and educational matters on which Murray could speak with experience and authority. In the early days of the League he formed a deep affection and admiration for Fridjthof Nansen, who fulfilled his ideal of what a modern hero ought to be. Nansen not only looked like a Viking, but had been a leader in Polar exploration, and after the war had helped many displaced persons by the creation of 'Nansen passports'. The Murrays asked him to stay, but his behaviour was not what they expected. At breakfast, which was always at 8 a.m., he suddenly announced that he intended to go fox-hunting. The Murrays were horrified and tried to dissuade him on the ground that he had no suitable clothes. Nansen was not put off but toured a series of undergraduates' rooms at Magdalen until he got all that he wanted. Murray, who disapproved of hunting quite as strongly as his wife did, was delighted by this display of resource, but Lady Mary felt that there were cracks in her idol.

Murray embodied much that was traditional in English culture. Despite his affection for eccentrics and rebels and his own advanced views on certain subjects, he was in many respects conservative. He was extremely fond of literature, but his tastes were formed in boyhood and changed very little. Apart from Greek, which had a unique place in his affections, he liked the great masters of the classical style, such as Milton, Racine, and Goethe, and he remained to the last a devotee of the Victorian poets, especially Swinburne. Once when he went on a holiday in Switzerland, he took Ovid's *Metamorphoses* and Hugo's *Les Misérables* as his bedside books, but when Roy Harrod, who had been abroad with him and was judged to be 'rather serious', sent him a copy of Arthur Waley's *Tale of Genji*, he did not much like it. It seemed to him too refined and too limited in comparison with Greek literature. His most curious blind spot was for Shakespeare, on whom he went even further than George III in thinking much of his work 'sad stuff', while he positively disliked his frankness on physical matters. An ardent undergraduate, who was much distressed by Murray's low view of Shakespeare, played his last card on leaving the house and said, 'But surely you like *Twelfth Night*?' only to receive the answer, 'I think it's a disgusting play.' At the other extreme he much enjoyed the irresponsible frivolity of P. G. Wodehouse, though he claimed that it was more for the style than the matter. Indeed once, when Murray read aloud a book by Wodehouse in a hotel in Switzerland, he caused such uproarious hilarity that he was told by the proprietor that, if he did not stop, he would have to leave. For most modern poetry he had no great feeling. Yeats' later work meant nothing to him, nor was he much impressed by that of his neighbours Bridges and Masefield, though he was touched to hear that Robert Bridges' last words were, 'If Constance Masefield calls, tell her I'm not in.'

In morals also and politics Murray had unexpected limitations. Though he was a man of unusual charity, he was rather strait-laced on personal morals and even felt that J. M. Keynes was a doubtful accession to the Liberal Party because of his tolerant views. On the other hand he was a lifelong friend of Bertrand Russell, perhaps because in practice Russell was a keen exponent of marriage. Yet on this too Murray could avoid solemnity. When Anatole France was coming to Oxford, Bridges asked Murray, 'Is he a filthy fellow?' and Murray thought that in Bridges' sense of the word he was, but he was much amused. In politics Murray was the champion of more than one unpopular cause. Though he believed in peace, it was not in peace at all costs, and he was against appeasement in the thirties. More surprisingly, he had in him a strain of the Victorian imperialist, who thought that it was sometimes permissible for a 'higher' civilization to impose itself on a 'lower', and in 1956 at the end of his life he even gave modified support to Sir Anthony Eden in his Suez adventure. But in other ways he kept to his Liberal creed. He was never enthusiastic about Churchill, partly because he thought him a war-monger, partly because he could not quite forgive him for leaving the Liberal Party. He liked Baldwin and got on very well with him, quoting him as saying, 'Winston has one very good point. He can't tell a lie. I know because I have seen him try.' Murray much preferred more internationally-minded statesmen like Briand and Beneš and, despite religious differences, Robert Cecil. He always had a good word to say for Woodrow Wilson and deeply regretted his rejection by his own people. Murray would do everything possible to help the oppressed or the persecuted. He devoted much time and trouble to the Assyrian Christians when they were harried by new masters in the Middle East, and when Hitler came to power, he was among the first to organize funds to help refugees. He was at times depressed because he felt that the civilization in which he believed so strongly was threatened by a new barbarism, but he refused to give up the struggle and thought that even lost causes might produce results long after they themselves were forgotten.

Murray had an enchanting sense of humour. Those who knew him only from his books or his lectures might not have surmised his whimsical and original fantasy. He had an eager curiosity about all kinds of men and women and watched with delighted wonder their quirks and oddities. He told stories in a quiet, unassuming way and you never quite knew what to expect. An example of his art is this, 'I knew a learned Turk. He knew all about Cicero, and had read everything about Cicero. No one has ever known so much about Cicero . . . He hated Cicero.' He was greatly amused by the American ambassador in Cairo, who was said to have taken an Arab and an Israeli each by the arm and said, 'Now, why can't you both behave like Christians?' He much appreciated the innocent charm of A. C. Clark, who was Professor of Latin until 1934 and Murray's opposite number in the classical faculty at Oxford. The classical dons used to dine together once a term, and at dinner a cheap white wine was served. Lady Mary disapproved of this and persuaded Murray that he must do something about it. He went to Clark and said, 'I think we ought to do something about the wine at our dinners', and Clark replied, 'I quite agree, I quite agree. I should much prefer something fizzy.' Murray was delighted at his failure and reported it gaily to his wife. His letters and postcards usually contained some touch of humour or fancy. When I was associated with him in compiling *The Oxford Book of Greek Verse*, I asked him whether we should include anything from the stridently un-Hellenic poet Timotheus, and he answered, 'We'd better put him in. Otherwise T. S. Eliot might complain.' When he was eighty-seven he sent me a post-card on a point of scholarship and, after dealing with it, added a postscript, 'I'm getting terribly old, but don't tell anyone.' On his ninetieth birthday some of his old pupils gave him a lunch. I had written about him as a teacher in the *Oxford Mail*, and in proposing his health Dodds told of his own debt to Murray and how Murray had tamed him in his youth. Murray in his answer said, 'I think that, as Bowra says, I was a good teacher, and I think that I tamed Professor Dodds, for a young lady said to me the other day, "Isn't he sweet?"'

Murray's life was so rich and varied, and he himself was always so beautifully considerate and courteous, that some of his actions could be misinterpreted. When he supported the abolition of compulsory Greek, he did so because he really believed that Greek could survive on its own merits and that compulsion did it more harm than good. Some of his colleagues could not understand his point of view, and he argued his case so reasonably and so gently that he was accused of cowardice and treachery. C. R. L. Fletcher, who was a die-hard of the old school and had collaborated with Kipling in writing a *History of England* for schools, denounced him as 'that snake in the grass, Gilbert Murray'. The same kind of mis-understanding may account for a strange episode in his last months. His daughter, Rosalind, who was a convert to Roman Catholicism, introduced to him a priest, whom he liked. A little later, when he was very ill, she asked her father if he would like to be blessed by the priest. Murray consented and received the blessing. At once a rumour spread that after eighty years of apostasy Murray had repented and returned to the church of his fathers. I very much doubt it. Murray was extremely weak when he gave his consent and probably did so out of unwillingness to hurt Rosalind's feelings.

Anyhow this was the only concession that he made. After it, when he had recovered somewhat, he was walking in his garden with Hugh Lloyd-Jones, who was to be his successor's successor as Regius Professor of Greek. Murray pointed out two houses on the left and said, 'That one is a mental home, and the other is a Catholic community. So if anyone in this house develops either trouble, he has only to cross the hedge.'

Greek and his love of it provided the central thread in Murray's being. In it he found a universe which captivated him in his youth and kept his devotion throughout his life. What fascinated him in the Greeks was their active, positive, purposeful approach to existence. He would admit that they made appalling mistakes and sometimes failed disastrously, but he was convinced that this was inevitable in a people who attempted so much, and that what mattered was the intellectual and moral courage which inspired the attempts. In the Greeks he found a sane and generous ideal of what men ought to be and of what is most significant in their lives, a desire to create order out of chaos, whether in the self, or in society, or in knowledge, or in the arts. Murray, who himself loved the vagaries and varieties of human behaviour, saw that the Greeks had the same taste and exercised it with an unexampled range of response and appreciation. He liked their ability to turn from sublime gravity to ribald laughter, and was equally at home with Aeschylus and with Aristophanes. His gentle, compassionate nature was not in the least deterred by the dark stories of passion and slaughter which play so large a part in Greek poetry. He knew that such horrors exist and felt that we must not shirk them but follow the Greeks in asking what they mean in the souls of men and the scheme of things. Above all he liked Greek literature because it is concerned with action and expresses an extrovert outlook in which action is sought and honoured as the right end of man. He felt that this was healthier and more natural than any self-analysis, however acute, or any refusal, however sensitive, to face the hard facts of reality. Indeed just because he was himself unusually sensitive, he liked the Greeks for turning their sensitivity to serious purposes beyond any immediate, self-sufficient exercise. The Greeks presented something which he believed to be needed by his age – a resolute determination to understand the place of man in the universe and to see where his true potentialities lie. He had his own vision of the full life which he learned from the Greeks, and it was this that he imparted to others. It was impossible to know him without loving him, or to see him without being revived and encouraged and inspirited.

10

W. B. Yeats

In the spring of 1917, when I was a cadet in London, the Crab asked me to lunch with him at the Savile Club, where, instead of sitting at small separate tables, the company sat at one long table. I was on the Crab's right, and on my right was a stranger to whom the Crab did not introduce me. He was tall and quite heavily built. His hair was turning grey; he had a fine straight nose, and dark eyes, which had that look of peering into infinity which is the privilege of the short-sighted. He carried his glasses on a black ribbon and manipulated them with a ceremonial care. He had no notion who I was, and did not ask, but began to talk freely. He spoke with a marked Irish brogue, and his choice of words was as striking as his sentences were well fashioned. He talked about the past, and, rather to my surprise, about Oscar Wilde, whom he had known and of whom he had much to say in praise and gratitude. I could not imagine who he could be, but did not dare ask the Crab until lunch was over, and the courteous stranger had disappeared. 'Oh', said the Crab, 'he's a poet called Yeats.' I found the Crab's nonchalance a little disturbing, especially since he was himself a cousin of J. M. Synge. I had read Yeats' early poems as far back as 1914 and thought them wonderful. Of the new poets he was the one I admired most and knew by heart, and I was not troubled by any nasty doubts that what I liked in them was their essentially romantic quality, their dream-laden themes and their caressing rhythms. I had also read quite recently a few of his later poems in *The Little Review* and *The New Statesman*, and though I saw how very different they were from the earlier, I was strangely moved by them, especially by *The Wild Swans of Coole*. The moment I knew who the stranger was, everything fell into place. Later I understood why he talked about Wilde. He was at this time turning over in his mind the memories which were to appear later in *The Trembling of the Veil*. What he gave to me was the rough material for the remarkable passages on Wilde which he was shaping in his mind for this book.

After the war Yeats and his wife lived in Oxford, in Broad Street opposite Balliol in a house now demolished. I used to see him walking about, with a distant, abstracted air, wearing a grey, floppy hat and what was more a cravat than a tie. But I did not dare to approach him on the flimsy excuse of having met him once at the Savile Club, nor did any of my friends know him. But one evening A. P. Ryan of Balliol asked me to come to his rooms, where Yeats was going to read his poems. He was, as always, courteous in a stately, old-fashioned way and treated the small company of undergraduates with a fine consideration. He had with him a volume of his verse, which I cannot now identify. The pages were still uncut, and Yeats took out from his pocket a small paper-knife and cut them with careful gravity. He then read some poems, first from his earlier period, then from his latest, including *The Wild Swans of Coole, Easter 1916*, and *Solomon and the Witch*. The whole evening was a revelation. In reading Yeats emphasized the rhythm, which was of first importance, since it showed how the poems ought to sound and how far he had travelled from his earlier, easier and much slacker rhythms. But what I had not expected was the tone in which he read. It was not sing-song nor yet incantation, nor had it that rather too prophetic tone which he adopted in later years. Yeats stressed the rhythm as much as he could. His voice was very much the same in speed and volume as when he spoke, but different in pitch. He seemed to be carried away by his poems and to wish to convey as much of his feelings as possible. Yet the feelings were under full control, even in *Easter 1916*, when he began with a low, level voice and did not make it recognizably louder on reaching the end of the stanza, 'A terrible beauty is born'. His method was quite unlike the dry manner which was already becoming common in reading poetry and was to be popularized by T. S. Eliot. Nor was it like the public recitation favoured by young Russian poets today and intended to hold large audiences in a new communal art which has something of a dramatic performance. Having himself no ear for music, Yeats sought to put another kind of music into his reading. His method stressed what the poems had to say in all their depth and breadth, and though very few readers could take such risks as he did, there was no question of his being histrionic or trying to get more out of the poems than was in them. He was now at the height of his powers. He had perfected his new style and used it for matters of pressing urgency to all of us.

In the later twenties I met Yeats quite often, sometimes at Garsington, where he liked to enunciate at their full value the words 'the Lady Ottoline Morrell', and where he could say what he pleased, even at the cost of shocking some of the more austere visitors. Then I met him in Ireland, when I was staying with my friend Pierce Synnott at Naas in Co Kildare. A guest in the house was Mrs Hinkson, who had in her youth been a friend of Yeats and won, under her maiden name of Katharine Tynan, a place for herself as a poet in the Irish literary revival. She was getting old and her eyesight was very bad, but she was full of life and comments on life. Like others of her countryfolk, she liked to put small pin-pricks into reputations, and though she had once liked Yeats and he had admired her, they had drifted a little apart. She had sold his letters to her, and that may have caused some slight chilliness. Still she recognized his greatness, even if she did not admire him as much as I did, and she sent Pierce, John Sparrow, and myself to Dublin armed with an introduction to George Russell, known as 'A.E.', who was one of Yeats' oldest and closest friends. We called on A.E. at his room in Merrion Square, and Yeats came in a little later. With A.E. he was more at his ease than at Garsington and talked freely on a number of matters, on the new Irish coins which he hoped would be as beautiful as the Greek, on the preposterous prohibition of divorce in Ireland, on the machinations of D. S. MacColl to prevent any of Hugh Lane's pictures from going to Dublin. He was beginning to find that politics, into which he had been lured after the establishment of the Free State, had its own faults and corruptions, and some man had incurred his displeasure, 'He may have been an honest man, but I have never seen anyone look less like an honest man.' He talked too of Edward Martyn, whom George Moore had guyed in *Hail and Farewell*, but who treated all Moore's gibes with complete disdain; of Maud Gonne, who was the great love of his life, watching a British battleship and hoping it would blow up; of how attractive Mrs Hinkson had been in her youth and how attached he then was to her.

With old friends, like A.E. and Lennox Robinson, Yeats, whose name A.E. pronounced to rhyme with 'Keats', was less elaborate and less formal in his talk than when he was among people more or less strange to him. He had then his noble set-pieces, which were too good to be unpremeditated, and no doubt he made use of them more than once. In particular there was the story of himself and a Persian poet, next to whom he was placed at an official banquet. Neither knew a word of the other's language; so the talk, as Yeats emphasized, was conducted decorously through an interpreter. It ran something like this, 'I asked the poet what poetry he wrote, and the Persian replied that he used to write love-poetry, which was so beautiful that it became a model of decorum and was studied in all the girls' schools of Persia, but that was a long time ago. So I asked him what he wrote now, and the Persian replied that now he wrote useful poetry.' (At this point Yeats' voice became indignant.) 'So I asked what might that be. And the Persian replied that he went as the representative of Persia on the League of Nations, and sent all his reports in rhyme.' A long and fascinating saga turned on George Moore, and much of it Yeats published later in *Dramatis Personae*, but I recall one small episode which he did not record. Speaking of 'the infinite malice of Moore', Yeats said that Moore would look for the weak point in everyone, but could not find one in A.E. He was much disappointed and complained that there must be a fault, and he would find it. Then one day he turned up triumphantly and said to Yeats: 'I have found out what is wrong with A.E. He neglects his wife', and with this he was content.

In these set-pieces Yeats may, more or less consciously, have followed Wilde, whom he had known in his youth and who liked to tell stories, though not quite of this kind. In his less formal talk Yeats was much freer and not at all above trivialities, though even these he managed to make dramatic by his presentation of them, as when he announced with indignation, 'I was so cold last night that I had to put the carpet on my bed.' As in his poetry he made a personal mythology out of people whom he had known and presented them as symbols of various ways of life, so in his talk he did something of the same kind. Hearing that I was going to be Proctor, he was reminded of his father's old friend, Frederick York Powell, who had been Regius Professor of History at Christ Church and on being asked to be Proctor said, 'No, no. The older I get the harder I find it to distinguish between right and wrong.' Yeats enjoyed telling how, when he went to Stockholm to receive the Nobel prize, Anatole France was also there 'with three mistresses and four parrots'. Yeats was not averse to general ideas but used them largely to give depth to particular episodes or to explain certain people. In the same way, when he read the Greek philosophers in the translations of Thomas Taylor, what he looked for in them was examples and images to confirm his own beliefs. Though his views on painting were what we used to call 'literary' and he thought that its subjects should be symbolical, he had been well instructed in its technique by his father. If something was on his mind because he was going to write about it, he would try the phrases out. Just as in 1917 I heard him describe how the harlots danced in the street at the conviction of Wilde, and he put it later into *The Trembling of the Veil*, so in the thirties when he was thinking about his Introduction to *The Oxford Book of Modern Verse* he said, 'I met Father Hopkins several times at my father's studio, but I don't remember a word of what he said', and in due course this became 'Fifty odd years ago I met him in my father's studio, on different occasions, but remember almost nothing. A boy of seventeen, Walt Whitman in his pocket, had little interest in a querulous, sensitive scholar.' Again, on Bridges he said, 'Every line a platitude, every poem a masterpiece', but wrote, 'Emptiness everywhere, the whole magnificent.' The strength of these final versions comes from long brooding on a single point and a resolve to enrich it beyond its first impact.

In 1931, when I was Proctor, I was entitled to put up a name for an honorary degree, and I put up Yeats for a Doctorate of Letters. The older and less transient members of Hebdomadal Council, with whom the decision really lay, tried to persuade me to wait for some special occasion, but, since I had no trust in their willingness to go on with the matter once I was off Council, as I soon would be, I insisted on a vote being taken then and there. Rather to my surprise the degree was approved and was duly conferred in early June. The ceremony was in the Sheldonian Theatre, which had then not been restored to its present brilliance, but none the less appealed to Yeats, who said, 'What a beautiful building! The colour of ivory and of old books.' The ceremony was held at a meeting of Convocation, at which usually there is only a sparse attendance, but on this occasion several hundreds were present, for after the conferment of the degree there was to be a debate on the proposed abolition of Divinity Moderations, or 'Divvers', the absurd examination which had brought John Betjeman's career at Oxford to an untimely end. Yeats naturally thought that the crowd had come to see him, and was delighted. He looked magnificent in his scarlet gown, with his white hair, and his eyes, as Beazley said at the time, 'like an eagle's'. He did not stay for the debate, at which, I am glad to say, the young philosopher Gilbert Ryle united with Kenneth Kirk, soon to become Bishop of Oxford, to attack 'Divvers' and succeeded in getting it abolished.

That evening I gave a dinner for Yeats in our old Senior Common Room, which I thought he would like, since it is a fine panelled room of 1680 with carved swags by the school of Grinling Gibbons. I asked to meet him Kenneth and Jane Clark, John Livingston Lowes and his wife, who were visiting Oxford, Wade-Gery and his wife, Elizabeth Bowen, John Sparrow, and my young, beautiful and extremely lively friend, Nancy Mitford, who had somehow persuaded her ogre of a father to let her out for the evening. After dinner I made a very short speech in which I said that the University which had expelled Shelley had now tried to make amends by honouring the greatest poet of the age. When I said this, Yeats nodded. He did not make a formal reply, but from his chair said simply: 'A man may perhaps say a few words after a few minutes of warning but none after no warning at all', and this was agreed to be right. We then moved to my rooms, where Yeats read some of his poems. He began with some later ones, notably *In Memory of Eva Gore Booth and Con Markiewicz* and *A Dialogue of Self and Soul*. He introduced them with short explanations and comments, as if he thought that otherwise we might not fully understand them. He followed with some earlier pieces, beginning with *The Cap and Bells*, in which he said that he still delighted, but when he came to the words 'a flutter of flower-like hair', he interrupted himself and said, ' "Flower-like" is a *cliché*. I should not write it now.' Then Mrs Lowes, who was delightfully emotional and impulsive, asked him to read *The Man who Dreamed of Fairyland*, but met with a stern refusal, 'I will not read it. It is a bad poem.' Fortunately he proceeded with *The Happy Towland*, and all was well. He even read *The Lake Isle of Innisfree*, but explained that it was full of faults. When he went away, Yeats said to John Sparrow, 'No emperor does himself so well as an Oxford don', and I felt that at least the more material side of the evening had been a success.

A few days later I received the following letter,

42 Fitzwilliam Square
Dublin
June 10

Dear Mr Bowra,

I got back to Dublin last night and this morning have sat at my table and got out my letters and thought whom I should thank. You first of all certainly. That was a very charming evening at Wadham and especially charming to me, because you showed that you understood and valued poems that I like and that have not been much noticed. Henley told me once that he never knew if he had written well or ill until somebody told him that he had. I have not written verse for some months, and it may be owing to you and your friends that I am eager to write it. I thank you and thank them.

Yours
W.B.Yeats

In the uncertainty of his own judgement on his poems Yeats resembled other poets whom I have known. Though he took enormous trouble and was a ruthlessly exacting critic of himself, he was not sure how the result would appeal to others, and he felt that, if it did not, he had failed. He needed an approving audience to complete the process of creation, and in this he was like Boris Pasternak, who in his later years felt that he was writing in a vacuum, and was amazed when he found that I had written about him. The same was true of Edith Sitwell, who treated the foolish and frivolous things said against her as personal insults. She felt that she was being attacked in the most sacrosanct part of herself and deprived of that extension of personality which a right appreciation of her poems would give her.

I continued to see Yeats in the following years in London, Oxford, and Dublin. In London he made much use of the Athenaeum, of which I too was a member, where he would carry an attaché-case full of papers and spend much time in the library. I used sometimes to interrupt him, but he did not mind, since he would ask my opinion on whatever was in his mind at the moment. Often it was to do with the selection of poems for *The Oxford Book of Modern Verse*. Though he listened to what I said, he did not act upon it, and I could not persuade him to include either Wilfred Owen or Isaac Rosenberg. When the book came out, it reflected not so much his whimsical taste as a truth, which has long been clear to me, that poets are very seldom good judges of other poets. Just as Yeats said of Housman, 'I like only his humorous poetry', so Bridges, about 1923, said of Yeats 'Poor Yeats! He's finished.' Yeats was far too busy with his own creative problems to pay attention to the problems of others and their ways of solving them. His admiration for Lady Gerald Wellesley may have been largely due to his great affection for her, but there was some truth in his claim that she was trying to do the same kind of thing as himself.

Yeats was not in the least 'cosy'. His genius for words was an obstacle between you and any easy intimacy. They turned everything into a high occasion and encouraged you to ask for more of the same kind. He claimed, truthfully enough, that he was a shy man, and also that in company he adopted a mask which was not his real self, but this was not quite true. Rather, he made the most of his thoughts and feelings by adapting them to a public world, but the magnificent choice of words was the rough material from which he made his poetry. It had some of the same intensity and bore the marks of his creative personality. Nobody else spoke as he did, and it was impossible to imagine him speaking otherwise. He gave to his words an emphasis which hinted how carefully he chose them, and yet there was no hesitation in his flow. It could even have moments of singular charm. Once when a very pretty girl was leaving the room and standing for a moment by the door, he said, 'Stop! How sad it is to think of you standing there looking so beautiful – and yet I don't love you.' She was enchanted, and Yeats, who much admired good looks, meant exactly what he said.

Yeats' conversation sometimes turned to spiritualism, and he made no excuses for it. His attitude towards it has troubled some of his admirers, who cannot understand how a man of his sharp intelligence can have believed such twaddle or written so splendidly about it; for after all *All Souls' Night*, which is concerned with necromancy, is probably the finest poem ever written in Oxford. A way of escape is to claim that through séances and dreams Yeats found, as the spirits told him, images for poetry and that this was his way of exploiting his unconscious self. But this was not the impression he made on me. He talked freely about spirits and was convinced that No. 4 Staircase at Wadham, where I lived, was haunted, and he spent an evening on the roof of the New Buildings of Magdalen looking for elementals. The large structure which he made of spiritualism and developed with such eloquence in *Per amica silentia lunae* meant very much to him. It was his armoury against the scientific spirit and his alternative to the Christianity which had long lost all meaning for him. It may seem absurd today, but it was much in the air in his youth, notably in Paris, and he clung to it, just as Rainer Maria Rilke felt the presence of ghosts as he laboured in solitude at his later poetry. Yeats' spiritualism may lack adherents, but that is because it was an essentially private religion. He made it for himself without reference to common creeds, which might seem equally absurd if they had fewer believers. Yet his credulity provided Yeats with ways of dealing with odd situations. Once, when he had muddled an engagement with me, he insisted on giving a party for me and was firm on his need to do so, 'I am laying a ghost and this requires an exact ritual.' This might be merely a manner of speaking, but it came from one to whom it meant much more than to most. Equally he was capable of using his spirits for what might be ironical purposes. Once on being asked if he liked a much praised man, he answered, 'I used to like him, till I saw that wherever he went he was followed by two small green elephants, and I knew that he was a bad man.' Was there a twinkle in his eye when he said it? Or did he believe that there was something so sinister about the man that it could be explained only by supernatural elements?

Another point on which Yeats has been increasingly criticized in recent years is his political views, and he has been accused of being a Fascist. The accusation is not preposterous, but it is wrong. His interest in politics was of a cosmic kind. He liked to discern vast movements in history and, though he was deeply involved in particular issues when he was an Irish Senator, he still saw them from a lofty detachment. This is why so much of his political poetry passes beyond politics into prophecy and vision. But his inability to fall into any ordinary party was dictated by his special position. As an Irishman he inherited a dislike of England, which, though he lived here for years, he never quite overcame. But as an Irish Protestant, a member of the old Ascendancy, he hated the idea of a new Ireland run by Roman Catholic priests. The first explained his condemnation of the First World War and his description of it as 'bloody frivolity'; the second explained his failure to find the place of honour which he would have liked in a liberated Ireland. If for a time he supported the ridiculous O'Duffy and his Blue Shirts, it was because he rejected equally the two parties which competed to govern Ireland, but he soon turned against O'Duffy, and towards the end of his life made fun of him, saying that his was the only contingent which went to fight for Franco and came home with more men than it went out with. Yeats, like others of his generation, was a romantic who dreamed of a world on which industrialism had not set its blight. He hoped to find it in Ireland, where its finest qualities would be embodied in a few country houses, like Lady Gregory's, and the arts and fine conversation would be practised in a way worthy of the Renaissance. In this search he naturally failed, and he was left with a grievance and a sense of defeat. He would have liked to be a national figure, as Stefan George tried to be in Germany. Yeats more than once asked me about him, and saw in his cultivation of a few gifted friends something that he would himself like and which would revivify Ireland. But it was no more than a fancy, and he never took it very seriously. Indeed, when I told him that George's circle had disintegrated under the Nazis, who stole its slogans and set its members against one another, he said that he was not surprised.

In 1934 I wrote, for some society, a paper on Yeats, and thought that in due course I might include it in a book on him and other poets of what I called the post-Symbolist generation. In the end I incorporated it in *The Heritage of Symbolism*, which for various reasons did not come out till 1943. On K's advice, I sent a copy of it to Yeats, and received the following answer,

> 17 Lancaster Gate Terrace
> W.2
> May 31

Dear Mr Bowra,

I am now almost well again and am able once more to write to my friends. Your essay is excellent. I have little to criticise except perhaps in the early pages where you have followed too closely careless statements of my own. I don't think I was really much influenced by French Symbolists. My development was different, but that development was of such a nature that I felt I could not explain it, or even that it might make everybody hostile. When Symons talked to me about the Symbolistes, or read me passages from his translations from Mallarmé, I seized upon everything that at all resembled my own thought; here at last was something I could talk about. My symbolism came from actual experiments in vision, made by my friends or myself, in the society which called itself 'The Hermetic Students', and continually talked over by myself and my friends. I felt that these investigations were private, and felt also, and indeed still feel, that one can only explain oneself if one draws one's illustrations from accepted schools of thought. Furthermore, I felt, that unaccepted schools, however profound, are incomplete because isolated from the rest of knowledge. There was however one book which influenced me very greatly, it has just been edited by Le Galienne [*sic*], it was the younger Hallam's essay on Tennyson. It was only the first half of the essay which influenced me, and in that he defined what he called 'aesthetic poetry'. By 'aesthetic poetry' he meant exactly what the French mean by 'pure poetry'. It may interest you that an English critic was probably the first to make that definition.

I think the only other point is that I dont like disparagement of the Nineties. People have built up an impression of a decadent period by remembering only, when they speak of the Nineties, a few writers who had tragic careers. They do this because those writers were confined within the period, the writers who lived to maturity are the principal writers in prose and verse in England today. No, I am overstating, for several of the best verse-writers emerged some ten years later. The Nineties was in reality a period of very great vigour, thought and passion were breaking free from tradition.

On page 7 you say 'his uncles were spiritualists' it would be more true to say 'his uncle and certain cousins accepted the village spiritualism and had themselves visionary experience'.

I look forward to your book for I am full of curiosity about certain of the writers you are studying, Stephen [*sic*] George, for instance. Ignorant of languages I have always had to get much of my knowledge from such books as yours. A single quotation is sometimes an illumination.

Yours

W. B. Yeats

I took Yeats' advice about the nineties and about the spiritualism of his relations, but I regret that I did not make more of his difference from the French Symbolistes. I was not quite convinced about it, but felt that, though he went very much his own way, it was partly determined by Symons' translations and that it was very much in accord with the spirit of the time in more than one European country.

A little before this I heard that Yeats was coming to Oxford to address some society, and wrote to him asking him to lunch.

Rather to my surprise, I got a very formal and indeed curt note refusing. When I looked more closely at his not very legible writing, I found that the letter was addressed not to me but to a man whose name had the same number of letters and whom Yeats did not like. It looked as if he had misread my signature, which was more than forgivable, and confused me with the other man. I decided to do nothing, but I soon found that my surmise was right. Yeats had made a mistake, and when he discovered it, was much distressed. How deeply, I realized when a copy of his *Collected Poems* arrived with the following poem inscribed in his own hand on the front page,

> To Maurice Bowra
>
> Sound words from Yeats to Bowra: he
> Asks pardon for stupidity
> Committed in the month of June,
> Hand laid on heart declares the moon
> The Almighty and Devil know
> What made a sane man blunder so.

Nor was he satisfied with this. He insisted that he had been very discourteous and could make amends only by giving a lunch for me in Oxford, to which I must ask the guests. Unfortunately, circumstances were for a time against us. He fell ill, and I was in the United States, but in May 1938, we were able at last to arrange it. It took place in Wadham, and I asked a few of his admirers to meet him. Before we sat down he made movements with his hands to exorcise any ghosts who might still be lurking around to cause trouble. Though he had aged rapidly in the last year and stooped and walked slowly, he was as eloquent and as courteous as ever. He talked about the diatribes which he was writing in *On the Boiler*, deplored with irony his ignorance of Erse, explained how he wished to write poems which would catch the spontaneity of traditional ballads, and claimed that he could read nothing but boys' books about the Wild West. Before going away, he insisted on paying for luncheon, and was candidly pleased that it cost so little. He then departed for the Mitre Hotel and I never saw him again.

11

Classics at Oxford

The classical course at Oxford differs from that at any other university. It is a survival from the past when the study of Latin and Greek was regarded as the base of all humane education, and that is why its title is *Literae Humaniores*, which means 'Humane Letters'. Though changes have often been made in it, it still keeps the basic structure that it had in the nineteenth century, when it was the main course at Oxford, and even now, when it is only one among many, it differs from most in the wealth of study at a high level which it offers. Unlike most Oxford courses it takes four years instead of three. For his first five terms a student works for Classical Moderations, or Mods, and this means that he studies Greek and Latin literature in breadth and depth. For the next seven terms he studies Greats, which is a combination of ancient history, both Greek and Latin, with philosophy, both ancient, that is Plato and Aristotle, and modern. It is thus an education in the study of classical antiquity in a full sense with an important extension into today. The whole course requires a good preparation before anyone can start it. He must have enough command of the ancient languages to be able to read them in bulk and to know what the texts mean. If he can do this, he will, when he finishes, have had a training which exercises his mind in three quite different directions, first in ancient literature, which introduces him to a world unlike his own, second in ancient history, which is a stiff discipline in the use of evidence and the assessment of historical facts, and third in abstract thinking, both in interpreting the works of philosophers and in forming some kind of philosophy for himself. This rich, if exacting, training was intended to develop the full man, and so far as any course may be said to do this, it does. It teaches a man to think in more than one way and, if he masters its techniques, his mind should be so disciplined that he can apply it to all manner of subjects, which need not have any direct connection with his studies. In the nineteenth century it was the chief glory of Oxford education, and in the twentieth it has kept its prestige and its appeal to young and vigorous intelligences.

My task at Wadham was to teach for the first part of this course and to deal exclusively with Greek and Latin language and literature. This I was happy to do. I still had some hankerings for ancient history, but was satisfied that it was in the last resort indispensable to the study of Greek literature and that I should anyhow have to spend some time on it. I had to teach over a wide field and keep as abreast as I could with new additions to knowledge, but for my own specialized satisfaction I could concentrate on what I liked. In teaching my duties were twofold. First, I had to teach the actual languages to young men who were already well grounded in them, but still needed instruction in their finer points. The fascination of this lay in the vast difference between Greek and Roman ways of expressing their thoughts and our own. A literal translation into English is more than likely to miss some essential point, and, conversely, before English can be put into Greek or Latin it must be reduced to its essential meaning and rid of much superfluous or indeterminate matter. The ancients did not think as we do, and that is why their languages are more difficult to master than modern European languages which have a certain common basis in structure and habits of thought. The linguistic fascination of the classics lies in trying to find proper equivalents for them in our own tongue. But this was only a preparation for a second duty, the full understanding of the classics. Their literary forms are not the same as our own and must not be treated as if they were. There is no real modern equivalent to Homer or Aristophanes or even to Plato, and though we naturally compare

15 Ernst Kantorowicz   16 J. D. Denniston

17 Penelope Betjeman, with Moti, being painted by Lord Berners at
Faringdon House

18. The tercentenary of the University of Budapest in 1935. Admiral Horthy is in the right foreground, and the author second from the right in the front row

Shakespearian tragedy with Attic, the differences are as great as the similarities. Even in authors who look much more like our own we have still to reckon that their basic assumptions are often alien to us and that we must not judge them by our own standards, but try to understand what theirs were. The classics contain much that concerns a common humanity and reveal it on every page, but to get its full worth we must allow for the endless differences between the ancients and ourselves, and it is largely this that makes them so fine an instrument of education.

The study of the classics is essentially an attempt to extend our experience by absorbing that of a single Greco-Roman society which is both like and unlike our own, and the study is conducted largely through a close attention to a series of literary masterpieces which centuries have canonized as such. But this does not mean that we must not form our own judgements about them or ask whether they deserve their reputation. I had my own likes and dislikes, but it was not for me to convey these dogmatically to my pupils. I did indeed discuss them, but more often than not struck disagreement, which delighted me. We certainly did not regard the classics as models in every respect, and some of the best scholars I have known could make out a good case against Euripides for his uneven composition, or Plato for betraying the free spirit of Athens. Our discussions were based on much more than questions of technique, though we did not neglect these, and we really tried to extract what was of permanent value in our reading. Yet our methods were not those of modern criticism as it is, for instance, applied to English literature. We did not set authors in an order of priority or mark their different works as good, bad or indifferent. This was partly because we knew that we could never grasp in their full appeal what these works meant to their first public and that we must maintain a certain modesty before them. We lacked the confidence, and the knowledge, by which modern critics condemn whole authors or reject on the strength of their own prejudices works which have long been admired and loved. We were much less eager to find out what was bad than what was good, and it was this that we sought and sometimes thought that we had found. Nor, once we had come

I

to a decision, did we think that it must be imposed as a dogma and that any disagreement with it must be marked by abuse and rancour. One advantage of studying the Greeks and the Romans is that they are so far from us that even when we are most excited by them, we must have certain reservations about our knowledge of them.

Since classical scholarship is concerned with the study of texts, it is of primary importance that these texts should be established and edited with the utmost care. Though this has been done since the Renaissance, there seems always to be something new calling for attention, and a good text is regarded as a proof of a good scholar. The foremost maker of texts at Oxford was A. C. Clark, Professor of Latin, who edited the speeches of Cicero with unusual learning and insight. He was a gentle, modest, much loved man. A bachelor, who hardly left College precincts except to visit foreign libraries for the manuscripts in them, he maintained an enchanting innocence which inspired remarks in his very noticeable voice, which was at once high and staccato. He said of himself, 'I am a conservative, a conservative, in everything except textual criticism', but his conservatism never drove him to abate his courtesy or his delightfully individual comments on life. These might take strange forms, as once when he was crossing the Isis in an overloaded punt which began to ship water, a man laid hold of his arm, and Clark reported, 'It was a liberty, a liberty. So I struck at him with my umbrella.' He liked to pay compliments to young women and told how on a sea-voyage he met an American girl who complained that she had been 'devoured by bugs', to which he replied 'Fortunate creatures!' He was appalled by the thought of the Russian Revolution and refused to call St Petersburg by its new name of Leningrad. Part of his indignation concerned his fellow Ciceronian Tadeusz Zielinski, who wrote a letter in Latin to Clark saying that he had been thrown on the streets with his daughters, '*singulis vestimentis*, which I took to mean, with only a chemise'. Once Clark was visiting a college farm, and the party witnessed a bull servicing a cow. Clark turned to Alan Blakeway, who was with him, and said, 'Blakeway, *omne animal post coitum triste*. There was, Blakeway, a firm of solicitors in

London called Mann, Rogers, and Greaves.' Clark kept a bust of Cicero in his room and lectured with much feeling about the Renaissance Humanists and their predecessors such as Servatus Lupus – 'Preserved Wolf, or Wolf Preserved' – and Petrarch, and how, when he first met Laura, 'she had violets in her hair'. Though he lived in a very small world, Clark made the most of it, and when in 1934, he was ill with 'a growth or gathering' and decided that, though it meant living with a brother-in-law, who was 'rather short-tempered', he must resign, he was universally regretted. He did not like to interfere with the work of other scholars, but he always gave help when asked for it and set an example of a disinterested love of learning. It was not surprising that, when he presented himself at the Berlin State Library and was shyly introducing himself, the official said, 'Ihr Name ist bekannt' ('Your name is known'), and admitted him at once.

If the leading figures in the classical course were Murray and Clark, there were two or three others who might not be so centrally placed but added greatly to its distinction. Sir Arthur Evans was, when I became a don, already over seventy. He had large private means and lived comfortably on Boars Hill, but he was still active in Oxford, and I saw something of him. Having unearthed and restored Knossos at his own expense and revealed the unknown world of Minoan Crete, he was now busy writing his monumental *The Palace of Minos*, but this did not prevent him from maintaining many other interests. In 1882 he had been condemned to death by the Austro-Hungarian authorities for taking part in a rebellion, but the sentence was commuted to expulsion, and even now the old fires were still alive. He was driven by a demon which made him both formidable and lovable. At a committee, of which I was a member, Evans blew up against an old scientist, Arthur Thomson, and said, 'I move that Professor Thomson be not allowed to speak again.' This was hard practice, but it was Evans' way of dealing with his opponents. He was liable to treat intellectual differences as challenges to battle, and when A. J. B. Wace did not accept his views on the Mycenaean civilization and was in fact right where Evans was wrong, Evans saw that he never held a proper position in England and had to spend many years as a professor in Cairo. I myself nearly got into trouble when early in my career I tried to trace back some elements in Homeric Greek to Mycenaean times. Evans was much concerned and spoke to me severely, but forgave me, and good relations were restored. What fascinated me about him was the passionate, undivided concentration which he would give to any new object which came his way. He had an enormous knowledge and an extraordinary visual memory, but these were infused by a bursting excitement when any new problem called for solution. This might mean that sometimes he was deceived by clever forgeries, notably of Mycenaean gold rings, but it made any visit to him rewarding, since it was impossible not to catch his enthusiasm. He kept his powers into extreme old age and on his ninetieth birthday on 8 July 1941 welcomed a party of friends who went to pay honour to him. He seemed remarkably spry and talked about a new Roman road which he had discovered. Very soon afterwards a man in the Intelligence Corps, with Greece as his special province, who liked to be a bit of a 'know-all', told him that the Germans had destroyed Knossos. Evans was stricken to the heart, believing that his life's work had been ruined. He died three days later, and the tragic irony was that, so far from destroying Knossos, the Germans had taken pains to see that nothing was damaged.

Much younger than Evans, but still thirteen years older than myself, was J. D. Beazley, who was first a Mods don at Christ Church and then in 1925 became Professor of Classical Archaeology. The gods gave him every gift – a charming, rather fey appearance, a visual memory as good as that of Evans, eyes even more perceptive and a finer sensibility, a natural delicacy and subtlety in words, and a mind capable of organizing a vast mass of material into a noble, intellectual structure. As a young man he won every classical prize and wrote very promising poetry. It was to him that his friend J. E. Flecker, wrote the lines 'To a young but learned archaeologist', begging him to give up archaeology for poetry. But Beazley was a dedicated scholar, whose powerful poetical instincts found satisfaction in precise, creative scholarship. He had a full command of Latin and Greek literature, and through this moved to Greek art. His life work has been the study of Greek vases, on which he has done as much work as half a dozen men, all at the highest possible standard, in which no point of method or of organization is at fault. His unsurpassed achievement is to have sorted out almost all extant Attic vases, of which there are several thousands, and ascribed them to individual painters and schools. He has done this in so thorough and faultless a way that it need never be done again, and indeed calls only now and then for additions as new vases are discovered. This would have been impossible if he had not had an astonishing aesthetic perception of Greek drawing and a very wide and scholarly knowledge of Greek culture. His sensibility has kept his mind at work, and the result is scholarship in the finest sense – the study of a noble subject by an extremely gifted man. The subject might be thought to be limited, and some think that Beazley might have extended his scope. But it is precisely because his subject is well defined that he is able to pour into it all the riches of his knowledge and direct them towards a single, majestic end.

Beazley did a great deal more than write his great books. He was an excellent lecturer, with a quiet manner and no histrionic effects, but a delightfully apt choice of words and a mastering intelligence which brought what seemed a mass of disparate materials into a single, illuminating pattern. Though he wrote much less about Greek sculpture than about Greek vases, he was an expert on it and illustrated both arts with just the right parallels from Greek literature, but without the false analogies that are sometimes drawn between them. As a young don he would sometimes sit in Common Room with an abstracted look and was plainly thinking about some point of scholarship. Yet he was not in the least remote, but always friendly, responsive, and abounding in fancy and gaiety. His curiosity was as wide as his reading, and he welcomed and enriched any fresh topic of discussion. His delicacy of mind was matched by an equal delicacy of feeling. Though he had probably done more work than almost any living scholar, including much that was laborious and mechanical, it did not in any way impair his freshness or his spontaneity. He never put on the airs of a great man, as lesser scholars often do, and he took his frustrations and setbacks with a charming humour. Once a book of his was brought out with illustrations done in a way of which he disapproved. He said to me, 'All my life I have fought against illustrations being done in this way, and now they have done it to me. I am like a respectable abbess who late in life is caught out in fornication.'

Further out on the fringe of classical studies was R. M. Dawkins Professor of Byzantine and Modern Greek. He had had a curious, career. After going to school at Marlborough, which he hated and where his unusual gifts passed completely unrecognized by his masters, he could not afford to go to a university and spent six years learning to be an electrical engineer and became far more proficient than would be conceivable to anyone who knew him in later years. In 1897, when he was twenty-six, the death of his parents brought him a small legacy. On this he went to Emmanuel College, Cambridge, where despite his bad schooling and long absence from academic work, he took two first classes in classics and was elected to a Fellowship. In 1907 a cousin, John Doyle, who had been a Fellow of All Souls, bequeathed to Dawkins a substantial fortune, a large Victorian house in Denbighshire, which is said to be the original of Llanabba in Evelyn Waugh's *Decline and Fall*, some hunters, and a pack of foxhounds, though what Dawkins did with both of these is a matter for fanciful conjecture. Dawkins spent much of his time in Wales, formed a large library, and, being an excellent botanist, gave much of his time to the garden. Until the outbreak of the First World War he was chiefly concerned with archaeological excavation and made a name for himself in Crete and Sparta. From early in 1916 he served in Naval Intelligence, and his special sphere was the eastern half of Crete, of which he knew every detail.

Dawkins' first and strongest love was for language. He had once studied Sanskrit, and from ancient Greek he moved to modern. He liked to discover rare words and enjoyed all variations of dialect. He was excited by the survival of spoken Greek both in Pontus and in southern Italy and did pioneering work on the first. Yet he was by no means a mere linguist. He had a wide taste in literature both ancient and modern. In his time he had been a friend of Norman Douglas, whose curiosity he shared in travel, botany, folk-lore, and recondite information, but whom he also liked for his defiant individualism. Another acquaintance was Frederick William Rolfe, who called himself Baron Corvo. Rolfe borrowed money from Dawkins and requited his generosity with insults and slander. Dawkins did not much mind, since he felt that originality of this kind must be tolerated and humoured. Even in old age he kept up with modern literature, and his predilections were not governed by fashion. He liked especially what was sprightly or satirical or well written, and made many discoveries outside the usual range. When he was appointed to his chair in 1920, he was the first holder. It had been founded in memory of Ingram Bywater, and, though the salary was small, the duties were light, and this suited Dawkins, who did not need money and liked leisure for his own work.

In his later years Dawkins worked hard on folk-tales. He had collected them for years in Greece and now began to publish them, supplying when he could parallels from other languages. In this he was an exponent of the comparative study of literature, which was almost unknown in Oxford, but he himself would disown what he thought too pretentious a name. He had a special taste for the lives of Byzantine saints and claimed that they were better evidence for Byzantine life than any historians. He had himself studied their modern equivalent on Mount Athos, which he valued less for its treasures and libraries than for the actual life which survived in it. In the generous range of his learning he was a scholar of an old-fashioned type, who combined the enthusiasm and the scope of the amateur with the careful attention of the professional, and though he loved details, he always saw their relevance to more comprehensive issues.

Dawkins, who took much trouble to see that his published work was neat and accurate, took none with his appearance. He would not notice if he wore an odd pair of socks, and his hats were survivals from a remote past. He had red hair, which was thinning and turning grey, bright blue eyes, and what seemed to be an inability to keep his limbs in control. He would fidget and writhe in a chair, play with it, and often break off bits. He had a high voice and an even higher laugh, which would erupt suddenly in an explosion. His letters were written on an archaic typewriter, and in each line the words soared up and down like a musical score. He liked learning because he found it enjoyable; he had no pompous apologies that it was a duty or a vocation, and he made derisive fun of those who claimed to be 'pure' scholars, above the claims of literature. He was extremely kind to the young and totally free of cant or caution or pretence. Though he was generous with his money, he used to pretend that he was not, 'I was very poor when I was young. That's why I'm so mean now.' He was quite uninhibited in his comments on people. When he first came as a fellow to Exeter, L. R. Farnell was rector, an erudite scholar of excellent manners, but wanting in humour. Dawkins delighted in his lack of self-criticism, notably when he referred to his book, *The Attributes of God*, as 'my attributes' and later retired to a house called 'Windy Brae'. His successor, R. R. Marett, gave no less pleasure. He was a breezy swashbuckler with a talent for romance at short notice. Expatiating on the fine portrait of himself by Henry Lamb, he said, 'The mouth's all wrong. It's the mouth of a liar and a boaster.' Dawkins dismissed a dry and rather disagreeable Cambridge scholar as 'A toady . . . a toady', and the careful scholarship of E. A. Barber evoked the single exclamation, 'Callimachus!', as if nothing more damning could be said. Dawkins lived to be eighty-three, and though at seventy-six he broke his thigh and it refused to mend, he lost nothing of his sprightliness. I last saw him walking round our garden on a fine summer afternoon in 1955. He walked slowly with two sticks, carefully examining the flowers. A few minutes later the Lodge rang me up to say that 'a Mr Dawson' had 'passed out' on the road. I went down, and there in the middle of Parks Road lay Dawkins – dead. He had thrown away both his sticks, and his face had lost the strained look which painful movement gave to it. His bright eyes were as blue as ever, and for the moment he looked again like an untidy schoolboy at Marlborough.

In the twenties Greek flourished more abundantly at Oxford than Latin. No doubt this was partly because its appeal was basically stronger and because Murray had set a direction in which its study could be furthered. A. C. Clark produced a few excellent pupils, but he was too modest to advertise his wares. Moreover, the study of Latin was hampered by a barely visible but by no means inaudible presence operating from Cambridge. A. E. Housman was the greatest Latinist of his age. He excelled at editing difficult Latin texts, which called for the highest degree of knowledge and judgement. In his first years he was thought rather wild, and the learned W. M. Lindsay did not really approve of him until 1927, when he wrote a postcard to a friend: 'Housman has at last made good. His Lucan is A 1.' But Housman was, as A. C. Clark said, 'daemonic', and whatever he touched revealed his extraordinary mastery. He was a perfectionist and expected other scholars to maintain the same very high standards as himself. In reviewing books, especially editions of Latin poets, he pointed out, as was his right, the faults and flaws, but he did so in a wounding and humiliating way. Several Oxford Latinists suffered from him. In Robinson Ellis, who had been Clark's predecessor, Housman found – after his death, it must be admitted – 'the intellect of an idiot child'. He was hardly less brutal to the living, to Cyril Bailey, H. W. Garrod, and E. A. Barber, who may not have been men of genius, but were not such frauds or ninnies as Housman suggested. Still Housman stood for a grand ideal of scholarship and might have been forgiven but for two things. First, his jokes, which were often extremely funny, were not inspired by the book immediately under review but thought out in advance for general use, and this rather discredited their integrity. Second, though he could be very rude to those whom he did not know or did not like, he was sometimes unduly polite to his friends. Thus when A. C. Pearson, of Cambridge, produced a not very good text of Sophocles, Housman praised it as the work of 'an acute grammarian, a vigilant critic, and an honest man'. This was high praise, but by Housman's usual standards it was not deserved.

Nobody likes abuse on these terms, and Housman undoubtedly discouraged Latin studies by making them appear to be too difficult for anyone but a genius like himself. His appearance was unexpected. He looked like a retired major, with a neat moustache and a good carriage. His underlip hinted at ferocity, and nothing hinted that he was the author of *A Shropshire Lad*. I heard him read a paper on 'Prosody and Method' to the Oxford Philological Society. It was a masterly performance and annihilated some modern errors about Latin metric. There was only one characteristic outburst in it, and that was when he said that a misinterpretation of a line of Propertius was made in 'the frame of mind in which Tereus ravished Philomela, concupiscence concentrated on its object and indifferent to all beside'. This of course was a joke, and since it was aimed at a German whom none of us knew, it went down well. In the discussion Housman was quite polite, until Henderson suggested that the reason why Germans made such mistakes was because they were not taught to write Latin verses as we were. Housman snapped back, 'The English make mistakes just as bad.' I met him twice at Cambridge and was rather frightened, since Beazley had said to me, 'You'll find he says nasty things about your friends.' On the first occasion he said nothing; on the second he was quite genial at first and talked about Hardy's poetry, which, rather to my surprise, he liked. Then he turned to the topic of Murray and was not exactly nasty, but sarcastic about his political views and his teetotalism. He himself liked food and drink and sometimes came to feasts at his old college of St John's at Oxford, where on one occasion he horrified Hugh Last by exchanging dirty stories until a late hour with Henry Stuart Jones. Another guest, who heard them, said that the stories were of no artistic or human merit. I once read a paper at Cambridge when he was present, and he asked me a very pertinent question. I did my best to answer it, and afterwards wrote explaining the point as I saw it. I got a letter back saying, 'You are probably right.' I could not have asked for more and felt that I had not done badly.

One of a Mods tutor's tasks is to teach Greek and Latin composition, and he cannot do this unless he is himself a competent composer. So six of us formed a club which met at tea once a fortnight during term and discussed a version sent in beforehand by a member. The meetings were both entertaining and instructive. I learned much that I could pass to my pupils and gained more confidence in my own capacities. Many of the pieces we discussed were straightforward enough and could be used in the daily round, but sometimes we were more adventurous and aimed at less immediate ends. John Barrington-Ward, of Christ Church, seemed able to write in almost any Latin style and to provide several alternatives for a single phrase. Thomas Higham, of Trinity, had a delightful touch in both Latin and Greek and produced a complete translation of Meredith's *Love in the Valley* into Theocritean hexameters. I myself audaciously turned Coleridge's *Kubla Khan* into a Greek chorus. But the inspiring figure and the most accomplished all-round performer was J. D. Denniston, of Hertford. He took very great pains and achieved delightful and illuminating results. He believed that you cannot claim to know a language unless you can write it, and insisted that a proper understanding of classical literature is impossible without the exact discipline given by composition. He was not, however, an uncritical advocate of composition as it was taught at schools and universities. He felt that its practitioners, including some of the most famous, tended to move away from actual usage as it may be seen in classical texts to effects which were inbred and artificial and might look attractive but were fundamentally unsound. He believed that the first duty of anyone who translates from English into Latin or Greek is to reproduce as exactly as possible the meaning of the English as a Roman or a Greek would have expressed it. His primary aim was scientific. Once this demand was satisfied, he was more than ready to give a place to elegance, but he would never allow it to be treated as a substitute for exactness.

In his love of the Greek language and his desire to understand its workings Denniston had for long been interested in those short and finicky little words known as particles, and he set out to write a comprehensive book about them. With prodigious industry he read the whole of Greek literature down to 320 BC, analysed its use of particles, and recorded his results in a series of immaculate notebooks. He read slowly and carefully, determined always to find out exactly what a sentence meant and what the particles did for its meaning. If he was in any uncertainty, he could consult all available commentaries or send postcards to anyone who might be able to answer his questions. As he collected his material, he would classify and arrange it until the whole mass fell into order and was presented to the world in 1934 as *The Greek Particles*. The great contribution of this book to learning is that it enables us to understand more fully and more precisely a very large number of passages in which particles play a part. Even so innocent-looking a word as *kai* receives forty pages, which show how various its workings are, and justify a story that Denniston was once heard saying to a pupil, '*Kai* of course *can* mean "and".' His work settles the meaning of many passages in which an insufficient knowledge of particles had permitted interpretations against Greek usage, and for countless others it provides a new precision.

Denniston did much more than this. He liked difficult subjects which he could dissect and clarify, but he also liked to discuss wider aspects of Greek literature and to formulate what exactly a Greek play means in its whole effect. He insisted that wider issues of this kind depend on a complete mastery of the details, and he had little use for scholars who thought that there was some short cut to understanding Greek without grappling with its difficulties. He liked to talk 'shop', and I spent many absorbing evenings with him doing so. His range was large, and he was quite as interested in what I was doing as in what he was. He had an engaging candour and was incapable of saying anything that he did not believe. This sometimes took the form of a truculence, which was partly good-humoured play, partly the natural reaction of a high-minded man to what he thought foolish or wrong, as when he said of a distinguished foreign scholar who did not think out his views carefully, 'He suffers from sclerosis of the intellect.' When he entertained friends at home, he liked dispute and controversy, and it is characteristic of him that, after an old friend had spent a week-end with him without provoking any strong disagreement, Denniston said, 'This has been a most disappointing week-end. We seem to have been in complete agreement on almost everything.' Ultimately a man of strong beliefs, he was a life-long Liberal and a keen supporter of the League of Nations Union. He was passionately devoted to music, to which he listened with a face of agonized attention. Yet with all his humour and irony and intellectual passion he was a simple man. He knew what he wanted, and it was to be a good Greek scholar, and this he wanted because he loved the Greek language and Greek literature. He thought that if they meant so much to him, they might mean equally much to others, and those who came into close contact with him saw that he was right.

Though I knew very well that I had nothing like Denniston's linguistic equipment for the study of Greek, I agreed with him about its purpose. The task of a Greek scholar, we both thought, was to revive as best he could for the modern world the inner life of the Greeks by a close examination of their literature. Though I liked technicalities of interpretation, I was also drawn to rather wider assessments of Greek poetry and hoped to deal with them in a well-informed way, and in fact to continue in a limited sphere what Murray was doing, but with more apparatus of fact and detail. I was immensely impressed by the work of the German scholar Wilamowitz-Moellendorff and especially by the skill with which he related literature to history, but though I could not ever begin to rival his enormous learning and brilliant insights, I had an uncomfortable feeling that he did not always give to the actual poetry the consideration that he should, and I hoped that on a much less ambitious scale I might try to do the same kind of thing, but pay more attention to the poetry. I knew that on such a matter it is impossible to come to any final conclusion and that every generation judges such matters differently, but I thought that I might remove some of the obstacles which stand between us and the Greek poets and, by placing them in their historical context, show more clearly what they were trying to do and how they did it. This was more history than criticism, but I could not keep criticism out of it, and I was at least sure enough of my own tastes to express them with confidence. My first serious book, *Tradition and Design in the Iliad*, which came out in 1930, had faults of youth and inexperience and was blessed with a sharp review in *The Times Literary Supplement*, but it has provoked profitable controversy and still attracts some readers.

I concentrated on Greek poetry because it was the most powerful and richest poetry that I knew, and because it called for introduction and explanation before it could reveal its full compass. I was aware that this was not the purest or most objective kind of scholarship, and particularly that it was of a kind that Housman and his followers despised. This did not much trouble me, since I preferred Murray's example to Housman's, and anyhow had not the first elements of the right equipment for work in Housman's manner. I must make the best of what endowment I had and follow my own tastes, and I had at least an acquaintance with some poetry outside Greek and was fascinated by the subject in general. I found that by comparing Greek with other literatures I was able to see more clearly how different it is and what its unique virtues are. Greek poetry has richer forms than almost any other, and its very structure in metre and rhythm is far beyond the range of most modern languages. Classical studies in Great Britain have owed much to their close connection with our own living literature. In the past they have inspired many of our best poets, and even in recent times, when they have lost some of their predominance in education, they still exert an influence, if only by contrast and contradiction.

The writer of books on Greek literature finds more than one attraction in his work, but first comes the purely scholarly impetus, the desire to find out the facts and to get them as right as conditions allow. This calls for hard work and hard thought and usually for the study of much modern inquiry. Murray told me that A. W. Verrall thought the last largely otiose and called it 'stuffage', but it cannot be neglected. Agreeable though it might be to approach a subject without asking what anyone else has said about it, the chances are great that you will miss something which really concerns you or equally that your work will be useless because it has already been done by others. To master all the relevant modern material is never easy and sometimes impossible. To read, for instance, all that has been written about Homer would take many years and might easily destroy all interest in him. In such a case, though selection may be a second-best policy and lead to omissions and mistakes, it may at least save the book from dying before it is born. The establishment of facts is a scholar's duty, and there is no ultimate reason why he should do any more. Many scholars are content with it, enjoy the detective interest for its own sake, and are content when a point is decisively settled. This is what satisfies editors of texts and writers of specialized articles. Such work provides the foundation of all other work on the classics and without it no progress would be possible. It has also the advantage that it calls for almost no judgements of value and that it moves in a more or less scientific world. Some of its results may not at first show their relevance to wider studies, and some may be useless, but on the whole this is the kind of thing that scholars enjoy and do for its own sake. It was what I tried to do when I edited the text of Pindar, or wrote technical papers on limited, but not unrewarding topics.

A pre-eminent example of this kind of scholar was Edgar Lobel, who was ten years older than myself. He was of foreign origin, but not, to my disappointment, connected with an emporium called Lobel and Lindemann, from which I once bought a pair of shoes in Bucharest. For years he was an assistant in the Bodleian Library, where his work was hard and underpaid, but, though he once had Harold Macmillan for a pupil, he never took a teaching post. Lobel applied his scholarship to editing papyri which contained fragments of Greek literary texts discovered at Oxyrhynchus in Egypt by A. S. Hunt and B. P. Grenfell. He began with the new fragments of Sappho and Alcaeus and proceeded to other poets. The work was of the most exacting kind. The papyri were not at all easy to read, but Lobel mastered their idiosyncrasies and printed exactly what he found in them. They were always in fragments, most of them tiny, and it was often difficult to piece these together, but by examining the structure of the actual papyri Lobel was able to do so. Above all they demanded a knowledge of Greek at the highest level, and in this respect Lobel was the finest Greek scholar of our time. In due course he was found a post as University Reader and enabled to give all his time to his work. He did not even have to lecture, and when the faculty board tried to make him do so, he was supported by Wells as Vice-Chancellor in refusing. The result was a series of impeccably edited fragments, many of which might consist of only a few letters, and very few amounted to a complete line. This work was conducted in a strictly scientific spirit. Lobel rejected anything that tried to make Greek easy or agreeable and tended to dismiss works of this kind as 'pig-wash'. He had a tall and handsome presence, a rich, fruity laugh, especially when he laughed at his own jokes, and a number of fanciful stories. To anyone who was genuinely interested in papyri he gave time and trouble and at times he would discuss, though he would not write about, problems of history. He was in his own line as distinguished as Housman and had the same desire for perfection in his work. His misfortune was that many of the papyri which he edited were too broken to make sense or to reward the enormous care which he took with them.

At the same time not everyone thinks that this kind of learning, however indispensable and satisfying, is all that is needed. Murray certainly did not, nor did the leading German scholars of his and the preceding generation. Though they were heroically industrious and neglected no *minutiae*, they formed large conclusions on many aspects of antiquity. Yet it is these conclusions which are most debated and in their very nature lack the finality of a purely technical study. The scholar who wishes to organize a mass of details into a comprehensive unity is faced by the prospect that it will evoke less assent than dispute. There is certain to be in it a subjective element, due to his own predilections, or the incompleteness of the evidence. From this scholars like Housman and Lobel shrink. They prefer knowledge to opinion and think that they are closer to it in pure scholarship than in hypotheses and value judgements. Yet, if all scholars were of this opinion, the classics would long have ceased to be a living force. To make contact with a world so remote in time we require more than texts; we require interpretation and other aids by which this lost world can be brought to life, and this is where the historian of literature comes in. He must indeed master his material and muster his facts, but he must relate them to some embracing scheme which gives them significance. The pure scholar may scoff at this as below his dignity, but at least it helps to maintain the respect in which his subject is held. Nor is this kind of work necessarily easier than his. Even popularization at quite a low level calls for unusual gifts, which good scholars often lack, and at a higher level, when it does not deserve the harsh implications of its name, it calls both for intellectual and for artistic talents. A work of this kind must be both learned and attractive, and its presentation of facts must be infused by a sense of their relevance to living readers. By such methods the ancient world is made relevant to modern situations and enabled to reveal its claims to our own very different society.

I myself, in the intervals of trying to do more serious work, enjoyed popularization at more than one level, and though I treated it seriously and took much trouble with it, I knew that it offended some austere souls. For this very reason I was delighted when Edmund Blunden suggested to the Clarendon Press that the *Oxford Book of Greek Verse*, of which I had been a co-editor, should be followed by an *Oxford Book of Greek Verse in Translation*, and Thomas Higham and I were asked to undertake the job. It took some three years to do, but I found it most enjoyable, and Thomas was an ideal collaborator. He was both creative and critical, and took ceaseless pains to sift out the good from the less good. We agreed at the start that we could not and should not do it all ourselves but would use the best translations we could find. We examined many volumes of versions and extracted anything we liked from them, compared different specimens, and eventually either chose what we thought the best or decided that something new would have to be done. We did not mind at what date the translations were written, and were delighted to have a few pieces from the sixteenth century at the one end and some confessedly modern pieces at the other. Though a Greek poet revealed through a number of translators may present rather a motley personality, each reflects something in him, and from the combined effect a composite picture may emerge. Thomas had a talent for persuading young authors to write translations specially for us, and some of the best pieces are by them. Though on the whole most of the contributors, dead or alive, tended to write in a traditional style, there were moments when something more adventurous was required and brilliantly provided by Gilbert Highet, as in his version of some lines by Timotheus.

Thomas himself contributed some of the best bits. Just as his translations from English into Latin or Greek have a peculiar elegance, so have his translations from Greek into English. Though they read very easily, they are the result of many revisions. He would produce what seemed to me quite admirable pieces and then rewrite them several times, always adding something that was not there before, and yet none the less necessary. He was particularly successful with the lyrical songs of Aristophanes, whose airy, effortless flight he reproduced with extraordinary faithfulness in English, following the metres of the original and catching their sprightliness and speed. He also made admirable criticisms and suggestions to our new contributors, who usually welcomed them gladly and did not feel that their artistic honour had been insulted. We agreed that in a poetry like Greek, which depends for much of its shapeliness on a high degree of formality, this should be kept as far as possible in translation. This was why with rare exceptions we did not attempt the most modern methods of free verse. Today this would hardly be possible, since a cry would go up from all sides that if Greek is a living language, it must be translated into the free and easy shapes of contemporary verse. In 1938, when our book came out, this was much less the vogue than now, and I have few regrets that we acted as we did, especially when I see how easily the elegance of Greek verse can be destroyed by too enthusiastic a taste for the current vernacular. If some of our versions now seem dated, that is inevitable, for after all so do those of Chapman and Hobbes, Cowper and Shelley, Hobbes and Tennyson. But I regret that we did not more often try to reproduce Greek metres in English. This is never easy and sometimes extremely difficult, because the English use of accent is more uncertain and less powerful than the Greek use of quantity, but when we did include hexameters or elegiacs, they came out well and give to modern ears some small idea of what Greek rhythms are. The *Oxford Book of Greek Verse in Translation* was a diversion both for Thomas and myself. We did it in our spare time, in odd hours of leisure or holiday, and we did not ask that it should be treated as a work of serious scholarship. But we hoped that from it those who knew no Greek but wished to know some-thing about Greek poetry would at least learn something about its contents and the different ways in which it has affected English writers for some five centuries.

As a corrective to this diversion I spent the first half of the thirties in an attempt to write a serious work of scholarship on the early Greek lyric poets. They had long haunted me, and my visits to Greece had revealed the physical setting in which they worked and the artistic monuments which matched their poetry. I had examined the two fragments of poems by Sappho in Berlin, and thought that I had deciphered what was written in them. Here was a subject which both called for a full study of details and allowed for the free play of inquiry on many related matters, artistic, political and even philosophical. Greece of the seventh and sixth centuries, to which these poets belonged, appealed to me by its youthful strength and confidence and sense of style. There was no comprehensive book in English on the subject, and I felt that something was needed. While I was shaping the book in my mind, I lectured on its main points, and gained much from intelligent comments made by my hearers. I wrote the book in a state of high exaltation, often staying up late at night to finish a section or to correct a passage. I seemed continuously to be making discoveries or solving problems, and this made composition much easier and more enjoyable. But in fact though such a mood may inspire effort, and be in itself delightful, it has dangers for a work of learning. I was too often carried away by my imagination and did not pay a sufficiently critical attention to views which I put forward because they fascinated me. Nor was I careful enough with some small details. I knew that they mattered and I enjoyed discoursing about them, but with them too enthusiasm was not enough. In trying to find solutions for all problems I went further than the fragmentary evidence allowed, and too many of my hypotheses were flimsy and unsubstantiated. When the book came out, it received, as was to be expected, a sharp review in *The Times Literary Supplement*, which opened my eyes to some of its defects. It also came in for some deserved strictures in Oxford, where a clever young man, with a taste for eloquence and success, made play with it in remarks which were duly reported to me. I could not complain, since what he said was usually just. I came to dislike the book and was relieved when after a few years it went out of print. Much later, when I was able to look at it again with an open mind, I saw that if it were re-written, something quite good might emerge. This I attempted when I produced what was really a new book in 1961.

Yet from this miscalculated enterprise I derived one great benefit. When I was writing it, I discussed many points with a fascinating character who had come to Corpus as a tutor in ancient history in succession to the aged Grundy. Alan Blakeway had overlapped with me for a little as an undergraduate, and I had met him a few times and been much struck by him. He was a powerful, well-built man, whom nature intended to be an athlete, but as a schoolboy at Shrewsbury he had in a cross-country run poisoned his foot, and it never recovered. When I knew him first at Oxford, he had a bad limp and had to go away and postpone his finals because of it. It caused him suffering for the rest of his life, but he endured it with uncomplaining courage. It did not prevent him from taking long walks in Greece or at home, and, though it was obvious that he was in pain, he never spoke of it. After going down from Christ Church, where he had been a pupil of Dundas and learned a great deal from him, he went as a master to Winchester. There he not only inspired the clever boys with his passionate love of Greece but left his mark on others less gifted who could not fail to respond to his warmth and his candour. He came back to Oxford in the early thirties and much enlivened the classical scene.

Alan found in Greece an object for his passionate devotion. He was obsessed by almost everything in it, its history, its archaeology, its literature, its modern appearance. He set about its study with meticulous method and would, at the cost of much discomfort and even physical distress, examine the uncatalogued collections of Greek objects in the museums of southern Italy, Sicily, and Greece. He had an excellent eye for visible things and, well taught by Beazley and by his own contemporary Humphry Payne, knew what they were and to what period they belonged. But he knew much more than this. He was primarily concerned with Greece of the archaic period and of the fifth century. He loved the fine, youthful, adventurous work of the Greeks before sophistication took the edge off it. Anything from this time appealed strongly to him, and he would spare no trouble to find out all that he could about it. He kept numbers of photographs in paper bags, a device which he had learned from Beazley, and made endless notes in a small, neat hand. I found him wonderfully responsive to any matters which engaged my curiosity, and more than willing to set his large knowledge at my disposal. The time to see him was after lunch, when he would give me a glass of sherry and get down at once to discussion of the point at issue. He had a mind that was at once precise and capacious; he would put out a set of details and then bring them together in a revealing pattern. He opened my mind to many things which had never crossed it, notably the relevance of Greek vase-painting to Greek poetry, and the significance of Greek poetry as evidence for Greek history.

Alan notably lacked the faults commonly attributed to academic figures. He had excellent manners of rather an old-fashioned kind, but he always said what he believed and made no compromises with expediency. If he thought that a pupil was being unfairly treated by the college authorities, he would fight to the last for him, and did not mind what this cost him in the resentment of his colleagues, not all of whom equalled him in sanity or warmth of heart. He had no high opinion of his president, Sir Richard Livingstone, who, in Alan's view, did not deserve to be treated seriously as a Hellenist since he despised archaeology and interpreted Plato as if he were a Ruskinian moralist. Alan gave enormous care to his pupils, made them share his own standards and tastes, and inflamed them with his own enthusiasm. One of the best of them was Tom Dunbabin who became a fabulous figure in the Greek resistance to the Germans in Crete and survived only to die of cancer a few years later. Alan expected a high level of manners in others and always observed it himself. If at times he burst into ribald derision, that only added to his charm.

Yet Alan would also take rebuffs and defeats to heart as if important causes were at stake. This was partly due to the constant pain which he suffered and which undermined his resistance, but more to his complete integrity of character which would not allow even small concessions on a point of principle. In his attitude towards Greece there was something religious. He had no doubts about its paramount importance, and he was more than well disposed to anyone who shared his basic convictions. On colleagues who did not understand what he felt he could be sharp to the point of intolerance, as when he referred to a productive ancient historian as 'that rat'. Yet he never insisted on agreement and was more than willing to accept criticisms of his own views and to adapt them accordingly. What concerned him most deeply was that the Greek past should be studied with the keenest care and seriousness, and so long as these were present, he was happy. But attempts to dodge the main issues or to impose modern morality on the Greeks shocked and angered him. His fiery temperament responded immediately to every challenge and saw the best or the worst in it. His physical stamina was not strong enough to carry all that his indomitable will put on it, and when he was strained to the utmost, he had no reserves left. Yet even when he was cast down, he was more than ever himself, rather like some hero of Greek tragedy, who in his hour of trial feels that things are but phantoms and yet he must assert himself to the full. He needed friends to support him, and though he did not have a very wide circle of them, those whom he liked at all he liked very much and would put himself out to any length for them.

Alan knew a number of attractive young women, and among them was Alison Hope, who appealed to him not only by her spontaneous gaiety and her delight in the human scene, but by her generous warmth and ability to surmount any crisis without fuss or bother. In 1935 Alan married her, and for a few months they were rapturously happy in a pretty little house in Holywell. She was the perfect wife for him, since she shared his taste for enjoyment and, being herself beautifully courageous and imperturbable, was able to look after him with the care that he needed. Then in May 1936 the news arrived that Alan's great friend, Humphry Payne, had died of blood-poisoning in Greece while excavating Perachora in the Gulf of Corinth. Alan was not only bitterly distressed but worried about who was to carry on the work. There was no suitable successor on the spot, and he decided that he must himself take over. He and Alison went to Greece and for a few months enormously enjoyed themselves. I had gone to the United States in September, and just before Thanksgiving I got a cable from Wade-Gery to say that Alan was dead. He too died of blood-poisoning, but in his case it was the old trouble with his foot that was fatal. Later I was to know too often what the death of a dear friend means, but this was my first full experience of it. I was stunned and almost unable to believe that it was true. Alan had been so life-giving a figure in Oxford and especially in Greek studies that I could not see how we could get on without him. And even now I feel that his death was one of the worst disasters that have befallen us.

Alison moved to London, where she lodged with my old friends, Desmond and Molly MacCarthy. Molly and she took at once to each other, and she fitted admirably into their unpredictable household. While Desmond was in demand everywhere, Molly tended to stay at home. She had begun to suffer from deafness at quite an early age and was painfully conscious of it, feeling, quite wrongly, that she blighted other people's pleasure by forcing them to speak clearly. Yet this was perhaps a concealed blessing. She liked small, intimate parties of three or four and was entirely at her ease in them. She had little of Desmond's vivacity, and at times she seemed to find the ordinary struggles of a household rather too hard for her, but she was an enchanting companion, who never said a trite thing and kept her eyes open to everything around her. She was deeply attached to Desmond and her children, but content that they should go their own ways without being bothered by her. None the less she worried about them and related her troubles with a mild, humorous melancholy, which suggested that there was nothing to be done and yet she ought to do something. She was deeply attached to Philip Ritchie, who responded to her affectionate attentions by telling her the most intimate things about himself and even for a time preaching Communism at her. She did not treat this seriously and was conscious that her attempts at reform were rather ludicrous. So she laughed at herself and told me that she was getting a notice printed to send to her friends, 'Reverend M. MacCarthy. Services for men only'.

Her mother had been the famous Mrs Warre-Cornish, wife of the
Vice-Provost of Eton, whom Aldous Huxley put into *The
Farcical story of Richard Greenhow*, but though Molly liked to
tell stories of her mother and especially how, when some masters'
wives met to read a French play, she said to one of them, 'How
wise of you, dear, not to attempt the French accent', yet this was
a privilege reserved to herself. Molly had considerable authority.
She did not like being teased, and if anyone tried to do so, she
would put a neat pin into him. Nor was she unable to deal with
Desmond's more famous friends. She would accompany him on
visits to the Asquiths or the Morrells, with both of whom her
presence was a great comfort to me. Alison lived in the Mac-
Carthy's basement and was soon taken into the family. Molly told
her about her adventures in the past and her worries in the
present, and was entirely happy in her company, despite a considerable gap between their ages. Then in 1938 Alison married
Tony Andrewes, who had been Alan's favourite pupil and most
intimate friend.

Gilbert Murray, who had been Regius Professor since 1908, was
due to retire from his chair at the end of the summer of 1936. He
was still at the height of his powers, and Fisher tried to get the
tenure prolonged. But he had reached the age of seventy, and
there was no possible way of keeping him any longer. The
appointment lay with the Crown, which meant in effect the
Prime Minister, who was Baldwin. He was never a man to exert
himself very energetically about anything, though he took more
trouble about appointments of this kind than about many other,
more public matters. He knew and liked Murray, who appealed
to his literary tastes and provided him with conversation that
amused him. Murray liked him in return. Baldwin shelved or
solved the problem of a new professor by giving Murray *carte
blanche* to look round and make a recommendation. Murray did
not altogether relish this, since he felt that in principle the retiring
occupant of a post should have no say in the choice of his successor, but Baldwin pressed him, and Murray consented.

My own view was that the right man was Denniston. He was
not only a first-class scholar but had the complete confidence of

teachers in Greek at Oxford, many of whom owed something to him. He would certainly have liked the chair, since he would have had more time to get on with his own work. But for some reason Murray was against him. He gave no explanation, but said that he did not think him the right man. This encouraged some of my friends, notably Wade-Gery and Blakeway, to suggest that I should be appointed. In a way I should have liked it very much. I should have been better off financially and would not be tied to the regular round of teaching, which I was beginning to find burdensome and at which I felt that I was less good than I had been. On the other hand I had misgivings. I had no desire to leave Wadham, where I was very much at home, for Christ Church, to which the chair was attached. I felt that as a professor of Greek I should have to curb other literary interests which were beginning to occupy more of my mind. Above all, I knew at heart that I was not a good enough scholar for so central a post. I might have certain talents, but they were not of a professorial kind. However, I decided that, if I were to get the job, I might by hard effort improve my technical equipment and meet some at least of the needs. I was therefore quite happy that Wade-Gery should put forward my name to Murray, who was reported not to be hostile. During the summer term various rumours floated around, but Wade-Gery told me that Murray was seriously thinking of E.R. Dodds, then Professor of Greek at Birmingham. I hardly knew Dodds, and his only published book, a learned and impressive commentary on Proclus' *Elements of Theology*, was beyond my scope. The whole issue was discussed in Oxford with an embarrassing degree of frankness, and various conjectures and criticisms appeared in the Press, while local busy-bodies tried to pull strings. At the end of the summer term the Crown appointed Dodds. I soon saw that, so far as I myself was concerned, this was a good thing, though I disliked some of the publicity, which made it appear that I was an uppish young man who had been properly snubbed. But my real regret was for Denniston. He heard the news first from me, and was certainly disappointed. But it was a fine summer evening, and we spent it drinking wine with his wife in their garden. Dodds proved to be an excellent choice. He was very far from being a narrow specialist. He had a real knowledge of what matters most in Greek literature and applied to it not only a fine scholarship but an open and inquiring mind, which set old problems in new perspectives and brought them up to date.

When the news came out, I was surprised and touched by the number of letters which I received, not necessarily of condolence but at least of good will and regret. Roger Mynors, who was the best scholar of the younger generation, left a note on me, 'I take it very hard about the chair, seeing it is you who have taught me all I know about the classics.' Dundas, with his usual kindness and wisdom, wrote, 'This will need *all* your best qualities of philosophy and courage to bear and yet grin.' In Oxford people tend to keep their feelings in control, but several wrote to me in generous and outspoken terms. Perhaps the most prescient letter came from Cyril Bailey, who was a colleague on various ventures and had always been most encouraging to me. He pointed out that in his experience what might at the time seem to be a rebuff could easily turn into a blessing. He was quite right. I was saved from a post for which I was not naturally fitted, and before long my life took a new direction to which I was much more suited.

12

Germany Off
and On

Though I had passed through Germany in 1909 on my way to
China, my first visit there was in August 1922 after I had taken
Greats. I did not enjoy it. The country had not yet recovered from
the war, and Berlin in particular was depressingly down at heel.
Though the inflation had begun and a few pounds went a long
way, any advantages from this were counterbalanced by throngs
of English and Americans who crowded the restaurants and talked
incessantly of the bargains they had made. I felt no desire to return,
and much preferred spending my summer holidays in Italy,
Jugoslavia, and above all Greece, which I began to know quite
well. But in 1927 I found a new interest in Germanic countries
when I returned from Jugoslavia with Hugh Gaitskell and stopped
for a short time in Vienna and enjoyed its tranquil charm. When
in the later twenties Germany began to recover and even for a
while to look prosperous on borrowed money, I went there for
short visits in 1929 and 1930 and enjoyed the brief efflorescence of
the arts under the Weimar Republic. The cinema was adventurous
and inventive; the stage-craft at the theatres was far in advance of
our own; the highbrow revues had a sharp hectic humour which
shirked nothing and spared nobody. I did not realize how insecure
the whole structure was, nor how unrepresentative the arts were
of the German people, whose authentic temper could be better
seen in the military mechanism of public occasions. But I wrongly

regarded these more as a survival than as a presage. I met hardly any Germans, and those whom I did meet were too Anglophile to be informative on what was really happening. It was a good place for a holiday, since there was plenty to see and to do. I had not disliked the Germans in the war, and was relieved that they seemed to be recovering so successfully.

That I got to know Germany much better was due to my friendship with a remarkable man who reappeared in my life in 1931. His name was Herbert Frank Bishop, and he came from Dublin, where his father was maltster in John Jameson's distillery, and his mother, an O'Reilly, was a true daughter of the Protestant Ascendancy. Called Frank at home, he was called Adrian at Eton and Cambridge, and as such I shall refer to him. I had met him in 1921 when he came over to Oxford, and at first I was not sure that I liked him. He was tall and heavy and dark, with slightly curly hair, a receding forehead, and noticeably bad teeth. He was used to dominating any group in which he mixed, and in this, as in other ways, he resembled Oscar Wilde, who came from the same layer of Dublin society. He made rather fun of me, but I did not dare to reply in kind. I relished his overpowering vitality, his gift for juggling with words, and his quick, satirical wit. Soon afterwards I met him again at Cambridge and saw that he was more friendly and more subtle than I had thought. He was a good classical scholar in the tradition of Eton and King's, who treated literature seriously and made more mature judgements on it than most classical undergraduates at Oxford. He had taken the part of Aegisthus, with a spade-shaped Assyrian beard, in a famous production of Aeschylus' *Oresteia* by John Sheppard. His contemporaries were a little divided about him. On the one hand they were fascinated by his ebullient, infectious humour; on the other they were a little afraid of him, for at times he was disconcertingly censorious. But he more than compensated for it by his marvellous gift for transforming any gathering at which he was present. Everyone became more responsive and more agreeable when his genius turned their most casual remarks into fantastic and fanciful shapes. Talk was his supreme gift, and he applied it to enriching the life of those around him.

After taking his degree at Cambridge Adrian went to Vienna on the pretence of studying the classics, but wasted his time. He then disappeared to Persia, where he worked with an oil company, and I lost touch with him for nearly ten years. In the summer of 1931, when I was in Paris for the Byzantine Exhibition, I ran into him and for the next few days saw much of him. In Persia he had held a responsible post, learned the language, and developed a knowledge of Persian poetry, which he would quote with impressive resonance. Then a catastrophe fell on him. Something had gone wrong when he was on leave in Ireland, and he was told by the oil company that he must go there and see what it all meant. This he did not intend to do. It meant that he forfeited his post in Persia and did not know what to do next. A few weeks later I joined him at Porto Fino, where he showed his most amusing and charming side in playing with Italian children, and arranged outings in boats to keep me happy. He talked excellent Italian, though I could never find how he learned it, since he had been very little in Italy, and applied it to singing songs of his own invention to English hymn-tunes whenever an outboard motor broke down or sea-water soaked us. Yet though for a large part of the time he maintained this fine form, he would lapse into periods of black depression, when it was hard to cheer him or indeed to know what to say. He felt that his career was finished. He had saved very little money, and his parents could not give him much help. He talked of writing, and perhaps he had in him a novel crying to see the light. He must find somewhere to live and work. After some discussions he decided on Berlin, which was cheap and would provide him with the solitude in a crowd that he liked. He talked excellent German with a Viennese accent and up to a point liked the Germans, though he was keenly aware of their faults and made mocking fun of them. To Berlin he went, and after seeing him settled in some cheap and comfortable lodgings, I came home. Through the winter I heard nothing from him, but a friend of mine in the Embassy, to whom I had introduced him, saw him from time to time and reported that he was surviving.

In 1932 I had been at Wadham for nearly ten years and was due for sabbatical leave. I wished among other things to strengthen my inadequate knowledge of German, which I could read with a dictionary but hardly speak. I also hoped in the intervals to write a small book for the Home University Library on Greek literature. I was given leave of absence for the Trinity and Michaelmas terms, which meant that I could be away from Oxford without interruption from April to December. I decided to start in Berlin, where I could take lessons in German and rely upon Adrian to enliven my leisure. I wrote to him and got a welcoming answer, and went to Berlin. I had a good apartment in the Hohenzollern-strasse, which was just off the Tiergarten, and there I stayed for two months. I went daily for German lessons to Frau Meyer, who had been the Asquiths' German governess before 1914 and become almost an international figure in the propaganda against Asquith, who had given her away at her wedding. She was an excellent teacher and forced me to talk German, no matter how badly. In the afternoons I wrote my *Ancient Greek Literature*, which, being a small book, called for judicious omissions and rather hazardous generalities.

In the evenings I saw a lot of Adrian. We would dine together in some cheap restaurant, and spend the rest of the time either in talk or in going to the opera or the theatre or the cinema. Three opera-houses were running, and though they were half empty, they put on a fine variety of pieces, and I heard a lot of Verdi in German. At the theatre I developed a taste for Schiller's plays. Though I found them almost unreadable on the printed page, on the stage their resonant rhetoric and heroic gestures came over splendidly. On Sundays we usually made trips into the country round Berlin, and when the weather got warm, bathed in the innumerable lakes within easy reach. Adrian was much more at peace with himself than at Porto Fino and was an exhilarating companion, with a talent for finding unusual ways of passing the time, whether in sightseeing, or some small expedition, or a cinema in a suburb which put on excellent old films. He had given up the idea of writing a novel, but spent some time in translating Rilke's earlier poems into English verse. He did it freely and at times brilliantly, but he chose poems which I would not have chosen myself and which did not seem to me worthy of the

trouble which he took with them. He knew a great deal about
Berlin and had a few German friends, usually some sort of 'von',
who could not make him out and whom he both teased and encouraged with an easy confidence. They were usually as hard-up
as he was, and our ventures into conviviality were at a humble,
entirely enjoyable level.

Adrian had a very sharp and nimble mind, which was less
equipped for sustained discussion than for flashing strokes of insight and foresight. He was particularly quick at seeing others as
they saw themselves and absorbing their outlooks as his own. He
did this almost without knowing it, and if it sometimes meant
that he expressed views contrary to his wont, it was a tribute to
the warmth of his sympathy. Yet he tempered this with irony and
mockery. Though much of his prodigious fun was to be taken for
its own sake, there were times when it was intended to damage
and discredit established codes. He regarded most orthodox
opinion as a conspiracy against enjoyment conducted by Philistines
and Pharisees who did not know what it was and were therefore
determined to stop it. His own zest for pleasure was insatiable.
He liked almost everything that can be liked, and got the most out
of it. He was a good shot and a good golf player; he sang and
danced excellently; he could talk with natural ease to anyone of
any age or background; he picked up languages with an uncanny
speed; he read books rapidly and remembered what was in them.
Anything out of the ordinary had a special appeal for him, and he
much enjoyed bicycle races, non-stop dancing competitions,
circuses, and the more recondite kinds of drama. In the fantastic
night-life of Berlin he sought out the more esoteric places and,
while he laughed at their absurdity, he marked the melancholy
absorption of those who frequented them. Despite his belligerent
rejection of religion, he was obsessed by a belief in the fallen state
of man and insisted that he himself suffered from it more than
others. He was disgusted by the brutalities of the Nazis, but he
had no patience with anyone who was sorry for himself, and at
once released his blistering mockery. With money he was quite
hopeless. His parents sent him something, and at intervals he
'borrowed' from me, always in so candid a way that it was

impossible to refuse. Once he got it, he would insist on an evening out at which he himself was the host. He was not in the least ambitious, though sometimes he complained that he had not enough to do. He was content to squander his rare gifts, but that after all made him an ideal companion.

Before this I had hardly met any Germans and certainly not known any at all well, but now with Adrian's friends I began to learn something about them. They were not, as is often claimed, without humour, but their humour was of a sharp, even savage kind which found an outlet in wit. This was often amusing, sometimes laboured, and at intervals painful. Oddly enough they would take Adrian's mockery quite happily, but they were extremely touchy if anyone else tried to do the same thing. They thought it quite funny when he would point to a new lavatory and complain that it was built with 'good reparations money', but they were obsessed with the notion of national honour and deadly serious about it. I was distressingly surprised to see how large a part the war still played in their thoughts. They treated me politely as an 'alt Frontkampfer', ('old front-line soldier'), but it incited them to fight old battles again. A leading theme was the battle of the Skagerrak, as they called the battle of Jutland. At tedious length they would demonstrate that the Germans had won because they had sunk more of our ships than we had of theirs. This was true, and I admitted it. But that was not the point. They thought that they had been tricked because after these losses we had not admitted defeat and cleared off the high seas. I argued that after the battle the Germans had retired to harbour and hardly come out again, and that this was an admission of failure. At this they began to turn purple, and I would change the subject. Similar discussions took place about the war as a whole. Their thesis was that the Germans had never been defeated, but had been betrayed by traitors at home by the 'Dolchstoss', the stab in the back, which led to the Armistice, and that the Allies had taken advantage of this to impose the 'Diktat' of Versailles. It was useless for me to talk about the battle of 8 August 1918, which I had myself witnessed and which Ludendorff had called 'the black day of the German army'. They claimed that this had been a strategic with-

19. Wadham College

20. The Warden's garden and gardener's cottage at Wadham College

21 The author on the library staircase at Wadham College

drawal to a shorter line, which was hardly true, and as for the Armistice, it had been accepted by the German generals, whom they regarded as faultless. The arguments were interminable and inconclusive, and an alarming indication of how even quite civilized Germans falsified the past in their desire to prop their neurotic honour.

This obsession with the past was enforced by the disastrous and depressing state of Germany after the Wall Street crash of 1929. In 1932 the results of this were manifest everywhere. Unemployment was enormous and still growing. Prices in shops were cut to attract buyers. Places of amusement were half-empty. No building was being done, and there was an ubiquitous air of dirt and decay. All this found expression in political activities. Hindenburg had finished his first round as President and was, despite his eighty-five years, the only candidate upon whom the parties of the Right and Centre could agree. He was supported by the Chancellor, Heinrich Brüning, and had a large following in the country, which may have realized that he was almost imbecile, but could see no tolerable alternative. Against him Adolf Hitler, whose Nazis had already a powerful party in the Reichstag, was running. While Brüning campaigned for Hindenburg, Hitler campaigned for himself, and the difference between their methods was painfully enlightening. Adrian and I went to hear both of them more than once. Brüning, a bald, rather clerical-looking man, spoke in excellent, clear German and preached self-denial and deflation. If the Germans would only eat less and spend less and work harder and take lower wages, he thought that some improvement might follow. He expounded this dismal doctrine to patient, attentive crowds, who accepted it with patriotic resignation. He strengthened his appeal by promises, which were patently sincere, that he would do his best to right the wrongs of Versailles, and by assurances that so long as Hindenburg was President the worst could not happen. The whole performance was honest, but pathetic, and in the end hopeless. Brüning did not understand the national catastrophe, and what he offered was not a cure, nor even a palliative. It was a call to grin and bear it, if possible, but certainly to bear it.

Hitler's methods were not in the least like this. Berlin was infested by his Brown Shirts, who went about in uniform in small groups and, if the police were not looking and often if they were, attacked those whom they did not like, especially Jews and Communists. Frau Meyer's husband, who was an unsuccessful lawyer, had strong leanings towards them and aired his views to me. He insisted first that Hitler would restore the pre-1914 frontiers, next that he would put the Jews in their place, and on this he was rabid. He wanted a scapegoat for his own failure, and in the Jews, among whom were many lawyers, he found something made to his hand. Frau Meyer did not go nearly so far but wanted the restoration of the old eastern frontiers, which she treated as a matter of personal honour, and had a total contempt for the Poles, whom she regarded as sub-men. Herr Meyer, who wished his own country to be militantly powerful, paradoxically complained that the British had lost their old virility and become slack and peace-loving. I could not see why he should mind this, but it was a common complaint among men of his kind and reflected both their hate-love of Great Britain, which ought to be their little brother but somehow was not, and their respect for the more brutal virtues which they cultivated in the hope that these would redress the humiliations of defeat. It was useless to argue with him, as he merely repeated himself and was beyond any appeal to reason. Herr Meyer was not a full-blown Nazi, but he was a characteristic German of the kind which voted Hitler into power and found in him a voice for its own grievances.

Hitler's meetings were superbly staged and directed at exciting the audience to the highest degree of frenzy. Some 20,000 people attended. Seats had to be bought, and at intervals young Nazis with money-boxes came round and asked for more. It was prudent to give something, as otherwise one might be brutally handled and thrown out. The Führer did not arrive till about two hours after the start. The interval was filled partly by the singing of Nazi songs, which were of a shameless sentimentality, and by speeches from other prominent Nazis. On one occasion the first speaker was Wilhelm Kube, who was a Nazi member of the Reichstag and a prominent figure in the hierarchy. He was a gross, brutal-looking man, who shouted in a grating voice. He said almost nothing except in abuse of the Jews, and a typical sentence was, 'Wir haben Kant; wir brauchen nicht Einstein' ('We have Kant; we don't need Einstein'). Later he rose into foul notoriety as General Commissar for Belorussia, where from his palace at Minsk he sent out agents to fetch blonde girls for his pleasure. In the end one of them put a bomb, disguised as a hot-water bottle, in his bed, and blew him to pieces. On another occasion the first speaker was Dr Josef Goebbels. He at least spoke grammatical German. But his sentiments, though more elegantly clothed than Kube's, were equally narrow and violent. The worst thing about him was his face. He had a look of real evil, of loathing everyone and wishing to do nothing but destroy, and even when he spoke of Germany, he seemed to hate it. Nor did I mark any signs of that Latin logic with which he has since been credited. His appeal was to the nastiest emotions – envy, greed, resentment, vanity, and brutality. Both Kube and Goebbels were interrupted at intervals by deafening outbursts of applause, cheers, and cries of 'Sieg heil!', which, to judge from the men and women near me, were entirely spontaneous and needed no help from cheer-leaders.

In due course Hitler and his entourage arrived. To a fanfare of trumpets they came down the central passage but did not look like members of a master-race. They were in Nazi uniform, with brown shirts, military breeches, whips, and peaked army caps. As they were mostly middle-aged and inclined to plumpness, their large bottoms and bellies presented a grotesque, even obscene sight as they wobbled in. When they reached the stage, everyone sang the Horst Wessel Song, and this was followed by phrenetic cheers. Hitler looked just like all the pictures of him – the lock of hair dangling on his forehead, the preposterous tooth-brush moustache, the Iron Cross on his breast, the neat black tie and the tightly-fitting breeches. He had a very harsh, strident voice with an ugly Austrian accent, and barked rather than spoke his sentences. His gestures were few but formidable. He would throw both arms upwards, or shake a threatening fist, or fling out his hands sideways. He worked himself into a frenzy, which grew as he spoke, until he was quivering all over and sweating freely. The face revealed no ordinary human feeling. It was undeniably expressive, but of some violent emotion which I could not define. In his few attempts at jokes, which were savage and not funny, he had a spectre of a smirk or a sneer, but for most of the time he seemed to concentrate on imposing his will on the audience. The speech itself was extraordinary. The faulty syntax, the involved, clumsy, often unfinished sentences, the dreary recapitulation of German grievances and Nazi doctrine, the deafening, disturbing impact of that terrible voice were not what I expected from a great orator. Yet at times he would flash into an effect or a phrase which was more striking. In comparing himself with other parties in German politics Hitler ridiculed their aims – peace, happiness, money – and then burst out, 'Ich habe nur ein Ziel – Deutschland!' ('I have only one goal – Germany!'). More ambitiously he said of the Nazis, 'Wir haben ein Schwert von Stahl aus Eis mit Feuer gemacht' ('We have made a sword of steel out of ice with fire'), which though it does not bear analysis, has an obscure power and brought a deafening ovation. Hitler put such a spell on his audience that they interrupted only when they were so carried away that they could not restrain themselves, and then they burst into maniacal demonstrations, shouts and yells, umbrellas opened by women, hats thrown in the air by men, daggers slashed from sheaths by young Nazis. At the end the confusion was appalling. Everyone was in a state of wild exaltation, convinced that his sorrows were over and that he was master of the world. If an orator's task is to impose himself on his audience, Hitler was one of the greatest orators who ever lived. But neither Adrian nor I was in the least moved by him, and we slank away as unobtrusively as we could from the raving rabble.

In June I left for Vienna and found an agreeable contrast. Vienna had its own troubles but nobody seemed to worry about them. Instead of with patriotic Prussians I consorted with disillusioned Viennese, who were more interested in gossip than in politics, and did not seem to resent very deeply the vanishing of their imperial splendours. I stayed in a boarding-house near the Rathaus, kept by a Frau Keller, who was well educated and compensated for the absence of any Herr Keller by a devoted interest in children's welfare. The company was mostly feminine but varied by an occasional young Englishman. The big occasion of the day was lunch at 1.40 p.m., which was remarkably good and the time for the interchange of gossip and generalities. The gossip was mostly beyond me, since I did not know the persons involved, but I did my best in halting German to keep up with other topics. Unlike the Germans, the Austrians did not want to argue and did not lose their tempers, but they were not exciting. Their interest in the arts was genuine enough, but they seemed to judge them on the same level as a tea-party or a walk in the country. At times they could be painfully boring. Sitting next to a young woman, I asked her about a film which she had seen, and instead of passing a short judgement on it, she spent forty minutes in retailing the exact details of the plot, which were of course quite unintelligible. Austrians seemed to think that all facts are equal before the throne and that the more you can muster, the more the company will be pleased. They would discourse with deadly precision about various types of cottages to be found outside Vienna, or what kinds of roof-tile were manufactured in Austria. Yet Vienna had compensations. The innumerable cafés provided relaxation and comfort, and through the Dennistons I met the Professor of Greek, Ludwig Radermacher, and talked to him about common interests. Vienna had adapted itself to being the capital of a small, impoverished country and there was some truth in the current quip that 'the situation is hopeless but not serious'. There was no overt sign of a Nazi movement, and though I heard of its existence, nobody seemed to be troubled by the thought of it.

My routine was much enlivened when I met Berta Ruck. Herself a writer on many themes, she was the wife of the novelist whose *nom de plume* was Oliver Onions. For him she had a great affection and admiration, though it did not prevent her from visiting Austria by herself and having her own circle of friends in it. She spoke fluent German and extracted much comedy from its more pompous phrases. She was not in the least what I expected from her work. This I did not know very well, but Thomas Higham had put an article in a newspaper called 'How to hold him' into dashing Ovidian elegiacs, and I expected somebody much less stylish than she proved to be. She was tall and dark, well dressed and delightfully lively and quick in the uptake. Her good looks had a huge success in my boarding-house, where nobody expected anything so striking in an Englishwoman. She combined a deep tenderness with high spirits and much mockery of herself and of her Welsh antecedents. Her family had been for the most part army officers in India, and if the British rule in India came under attack, she put up a fine fight for it. She also surprised the Austrians by defending the English sense of guilt on the ground that it added enormously to forbidden pleasures. She had some Austrian friends who lived in a house in the country and took me to stay there for a week-end. The house had hardly seen any changes since the middle of the last century, and everything was tied to farming and shooting. Our host had in the war been on the staff of the Emperor Karl and accompanied him on a visit to Constantinople, when the Turks, in order to make a good impression, hung twelve men outside his window so that he saw them dangling when his curtains were drawn in the morning. Berta found Germans much too conscientious and greatly preferred Austrians, even liking their inefficiency and muddle. Yet her uncontrollable sense of humour found much to laugh at in what she liked most, and it was this which both flummoxed and captivated her Austrian friends, who found her Celtic mockery very English.

I left Vienna in July and met Adrian in Trieste. We did a slow tour of Dalmatia, Albania, and Greece. We travelled cheaply, slept on the decks of boats, and saw many unfamiliar and unfrequented places. None of these countries had become a tourists' pleasure-ground, and comforts were few, even if we could afford them. On the other hand very often we had places to ourselves without even the ubiquitous Germans, whose financial crisis was beginning to hamper their itch for travel and their illusion that they were the same as the ancient Greeks. At times indeed we found young Germans examining swastikas on Greek vases and explaining that the Greeks were Nazis, or old Germans handing out lists of measurements and technical terms as if they were sergeant-majors imparting instruction in the parts of a rifle.

Adrian was a splendid companion. He learned modern Greek with his usual fantastic speed and liked to talk to the peasants whom we met in the Peloponnese or on the islands. The chief troubles were the absence of plumbing and the presence of bed-bugs, especially in Crete, where the beds harboured all known kinds. We developed techniques against them by using our macintoshes as sheets, but even this did not ward off the nasty sort that falls from the ceiling. We much enjoyed travelling with a pair of mules and a man across country where there are now good roads, but then one walked along mountain-tracks. The only danger was sheep-dogs, who, in their heroic loyalty to their masters, viewed all strangers with hostility and rushed out with savage barks. Sometimes we kept them off with stones, sometimes by going down on our haunches and barking back at them. In Corfu we saw a shapely, small yacht in the bay. Adrian swam round it singing, with the result that we were asked on board for a drink. We were then asked to join them, and visited Actium and Ithaca, where I sprained my ankle in the Cave of the Nymphs. But I had to get to Athens, and left Adrian on the yacht. He stayed for a year and greatly endeared himself to the owners, the husband, who had been a regular soldier, and the wife, who was noticeably handsome and gifted and, having never met anyone at all like Adrian, became very fond of him.

In the autumn I moved back to Vienna, and thence again to Berlin, where I had some work to finish. The situation had got visibly worse since I was last there. Brüning had been treacherously thrown out by Hindenburg in May, and succeeded by the slippery von Papen. The Nazi newspaper, *Völkischer Beobachter*, was full of prognostications that Hitler would join the government any day, and the Nazis, who had quietened down when earlier in the year Groener took them out of uniform, were now back in it and behaved as if they were already in power. The bestial Streicher published his obscene attacks on the Jews in *Der Stuermer*, and the result was almost daily attacks by Nazis on small Jewish shops and their defenceless owners. In recent months anti-Semitism had become more bloodthirsty and the economic position worse. Von Papen had no popular hold, though he had some appeal for one or two of Adrian's old friends, who foolishly believed that he could manage and tame Hitler. One evening I found a battered body in a side-street near my lodging and called to a policeman to help. He was very unwilling to do anything, and when at last I got him to move, the man was dead.

At this time I had a mild adventure which was wrongly reported and did me more good than I deserved. With some admirable journalists I met a supporter of Hitler who talked appalling nonsense, and we did our best to withstand him. The next day we were summoned to Hitler's presence in his hotel. There were some six of us, and as we came into the room, Hitler raised his hand in the Nazi salute, and we did nothing in return. This was soon expanded by the English Press into a story that he had said 'Heil, Hitler!' and that I replied 'Heil, Bowra!' The story brought me nothing but credit, but it was not true. Hitler ranted at us in his usual way, and his theme was the unity of Germany. His peroration was that it was not a political unity, not an economic unity, not a geographical unity – 'Aber, verstehen Sie, es ist eine geistige Einheit!' ('But, understand, it is a spiritual unity'). After that we were dismissed. From a few yards off I watched those blue, glaucous eyes which looked not through but past you, and I marked the arrogant, brutal curl of his lips.

On 6 December 1932 von Schleicher succeeded von Papen as Chancellor, and soon afterwards I came back to England, appalled by what I had seen and deeply relieved to escape from it. I had little doubt that Hitler would soon gain power, and equally that a majority of Germans wished him to do so. I had read the un-expurgated text of *Mein Kampf* and was convinced that he meant what he said. I had no doubts of his savagery or of what a government directed by him and his party would mean, not only for Jews, but for anyone who opposed them. Though in December Nazis and Communists collaborated in a strike, this was not an omen that, when the time came, Hitler would let off the Communists lightly. When he was appointed Chancellor by Hindenburg on 30 January 1933, I knew that some of my worst fears would soon be realized and that atrocities would follow on a large scale. This view was not well received in England. Even the

Murrays were inclined to think that things could not be as bad as I said and that Hitler might be restrained by Conservative colleagues such as Hugenberg and von Neurath, while Alfred Zimmern, who was Professor of International Relations at Oxford and himself a Jew, welcomed Hitler's advent to power because it would reveal his incapacity to the world and finally discredit him. I had seen too much of Nazi organization to think that it would be incapable of keeping power once it gained it, and the first news of persecutions and barbarities in Berlin merely confirmed my belief that in Germany the reign of murderers had begun. In my dark prognostications I found warm and well informed support from Bob Boothby, who had access to sources of information beyond mine and, with his usual insight, saw how things were going and courageously said so. I went back to Berlin in 1933 to see how my friends were faring. I found that a pleasant young Prussian 'von' had joined the Nazi party and believed that Hitler had acquired a new dignity and begun to show signs of being a responsible statesman. More distressing was a young Jewish banker whom I found seated happily in his office, thinking that he at least would be left alone. He could not have made a more tragic mistake. My gloomiest forebodings were confirmed when I lunched at the British Embassy with Sir Horace and Lady Rumbold. The Ambassador was taciturn and discreet, but it was clear that he feared the worst both in internal and in external affairs. When the Nazis declared a boycott of all Jewish shops, Lady Rumbold, who was a woman of wonderful humanity and courage, insisted on walking past the pickets and making purchases.

After this gloomy experience I did not feel like going back to Berlin. That summer I went again to Greece, where I met Adrian and the yacht at the Piraeus and sailed on it among the Cyclades, suffering from the north-east wind, the Meltemi, which is the wind of Troy and blows savagely down the Aegean in the summer months. We were weather-bound for a week off Mykonos and were driven every day a little nearer to the rocks. In desperation Adrian and I deserted the yacht and took a ship to Samos, whence we did a tour of the northern islands on small steamers. Among other agreeable sights we particularly enjoyed seeing monks of

Mount Athos bathing with nothing on but their brimless top-hats. In September we came back to Vienna where Adrian settled down happily. He was horrified when Dollfuss suppressed the Socialists in 1934, and spent much time in collecting money for the victims and lurid information on what had happened. Here he met my beautiful friend Joan Eyres Monsell, who was captivated by his warmth and gaiety and gave to him that loving loyalty which she gives to all her friends. In 1935 he returned to England.

My desire not to return to Germany was soon countered by a new factor. Refugees were coming to England, and in an un-expectedly generous moment New College had invited Ernst Kantorowicz, author of a well-known and much debated book on Frederick II, to stay there and give some lectures. The invitation was ambiguous since some of his hosts confused him with the legal scholar, Hermann Kantorowicz, who was no relation and whom he did not much like. They made the point clear to Ernst, who was mildly embarrassed. Another trouble was that he was not paid anything, and since it was almost impossible to get money out of Germany, he did not know what to do. The New College people were much surprised that he should need money, but after some debate grudgingly agreed to pay him something. One day in April 1934 I met him at lunch in All Souls with Isaiah Berlin. He was not like any Germans I had met, and above all not pompous or dictatorial. He talked English fluently with many mistakes and bold improvisations on the principle that most French words can be used in English if they are pronounced suitably. Thus he would speak of 'my brother-in-law the medicine', or of physicists as 'physicians'. Though he was a professor at Frankfurt, he was not in the least professorial, had an excellent sense of humour, and picked up our atmosphere with extraordinary speed. I was much taken by him, and, when we went away together, he talked about poetry with real perception. When Tom Boase, of Hertford, took him and myself to Stratford to see *Julius Caesar*, Ernst was fascin-ated by it, and during the harangues in the forum muttered, 'Dr Goebbels, Dr Goebbels'.

Ernst was captivated by Oxford. He thought that Henderson was one of the stupidest men that he had ever met, and the conviction hardened when Henderson and his sister asked him to dinner. After dinner records of Wagner were played, and Ernst, who disliked music and particularly Wagner, must have found it impossible to hide his distaste. Henderson then, with a delicious touch of German tact, remembered that his guest was Jewish and said, 'Perhaps you would prefer Mendelssohn.' Henderson was already half enamoured of the Nazis. When I told him about Hitler, intending to illustrate how monstrous he was, and quoted some of his high-flown phrases, Henderson merely exclaimed, with a more than usually guttural *r*, 'Oh, but that's glorious.' On the other hand Ernst liked some of the other Fellows at New College very much. Alic Smith especially appealed to him, partly by his delightful detachment and good humour, partly because both liked swimming and used to meet on sunny afternoons at Parsons' Pleasure, where Smith did high dives. Ernst was absorbed by the concept of the diving philosopher and saw in it a nice variation on Plato's philosopher-king. One thing that struck him about the Fellows of New College was that they were so melancholy, but he saw my point when I explained that this was an English trait and accounted for the richness of English poetry.

Despite his very considerable learning, Ernst made no parade of it and preferred to discuss general ideas. He fell in love with Oxford and formed a real liking for England, which had hitherto been unknown to him except through an English governess whom he had hated. His exploration of it led to unexpected discoveries. He went for a week-end to Cambridge and came back very depressed. I asked him, why, and he said to my surprise, 'It is so behind the times.' I ventured that Oxford too was behind the times, but he dealt with it summarily, 'Cambridge is a week behind the times, and that's awful, but Oxford is a hundred years behind, and that's splendid.' He liked the insularity of England and was much pleased by a newspaper headline, 'Channel storms. Continent isolated', just as he liked the imagery in, 'Shepherd's Bush combed for dead girl's body.' He treated English politics as if they came straight out of Shakespeare and insisted that, so far from being histrionic, they formed an actual play in which everyone played a part without knowing that it was one. This idea, reached its climax with the abdication of Edward VIII in 1936, when Ernst saw everyone as playing to the full a truly Shakespearian part, from the proud archbishop and the cunning prime minister to the bewildered and deceived king and his unsuitable lady-love. Ernst thought the undergraduates at New College nicer and more stylish and better-looking than German students and much admired the liberty with which they were allowed to work or not as they pleased. He maintained that idleness is very good for the mind, and on this point Alic Smith agreed strongly with him, arguing that only in idleness do we find our best ideas and think them out. Ernst used to expound his theories to the Fellows of New College, who were not always quick to understand them.

Ernst had had a varied career. He was born of a well-to-do Jewish family at Posen when it was still German, and received an excellent education. At school he had been well trained in Latin and Greek; at the university he had combined geography and oriental languages. In the war he began as an interpreter in Turkish with the German troops in Istanbul and Smyrna, but this came to an abrupt end. He had an affair with a nurse, who was the mistress of the German general, Liman von Sanders. When this came out, Ernst was summarily transferred to Verdun, and his confidential record noted that he was not fit for employment in eastern Europe. After the war he took part for a time in the Freikorps and fought socialists in Munich. Then he came to know Stefan George and became a member of his circle. Under his influence he wrote his *Frederick II*, which reflects its origins in its romantic and poetical tone.

George was a remarkable poet whose work I had known for some years before I met Ernst. I had once seen but not met him in Heidelberg with some of his young followers. He was of middle height and had a fine head of white hair which he wore long *en brosse*. His profile, of which he was proud and which was much admired by his disciples, still kept its contours, but from the front he looked wrinkled and wizened like an old lady. In his earlier years he had been first and foremost a poet, and his friends, like

Ernst Gundolf and Karl Wolfskehl, were serious men of letters, but in the middle life he became a prophet and a teacher and gathered round him young men whom he wished to restore life to German literature and learning. For them he was 'der Meister', 'the Master', and their work was prompted and directed by him. He chose them largely from well-born families and claimed their undivided loyalty. Into them he inculcated a love of good literature and good living. Despite the seriousness with which he treated his own mission, he was not solemn and had a rather malicious humour. He saw himself as a kind of Socrates who did his work not through philosophy but through poetry, though his poetry became increasingly more dogmatic and instructive. He picked his disciples young, and the circle paid much attention to school-boys, chosen often but not always for their looks, and though it was in some sense homosexual, it was in a very high-minded way. Those in it who did not keep this standard were not ejected but regarded with tolerant amusement. After the war, which had brought bitter sorrow to George, he extended his influence over a younger generation which welcomed the reassurance that he gave them. He showed them how to make the best of their gifts, and in this displayed a canny insight. He insisted on knowing all about them, made them read their writings to him, and was a masterful critic. Some of his disciples failed him, and some were not at all agreeable, but he provided the attachment which Ernst needed. George built up his confidence, excited his imagination, and made him work. The circle provided excellent conversation and managed very well the material side of life. Subjects of all kinds were discussed freely and politics were kept at a decent distance. Some of the most gifted members were Jews, and Ernst was happily at home in it.

Ernst's family then lost most of their money, rather as my maternal grandmother had done, by entrusting a flourishing liquor-business to a crook, and Ernst had to make a living. This he did by becoming a professor of history at Frankfurt. When the Nazis came into power, he delivered an outspoken and courageous attack on them, but somehow escaped their vengeance. When Ernst came to Oxford in 1934, George was already dead, and the circle was split between those who hated the Nazis and those who tended to support them on nationalistic grounds. Ernst was emphatically of the first party, not merely because he was a Jew, but because he hated to see George's doctrines defiled and perverted by gangsters. At Oxford Ernst still reflected George's teaching. He was liable to talk about a thing called 'secret Germany', which, though meaningful enough in German, lacked substance in English. More importantly he had a real love for Greek poetry and Greek art, and for some parts of English poetry about which he wished to know more. Modern movements hardly touched him, and he saw nothing in Rilke, whose large vogue in England had already begun. George had also taught him something about France, but outside the Middle Ages and some poets of the nineteenth century, it did not appeal to him, perhaps because his knowledge of the language was faulty. He shared other of George's tastes, for good food and good drink, for everything Italian, for the cinema but not for the theatre, for bold ideas which made familiar facts less dull, and for pungent gossip. Like George, he liked male society, but, unlike him, was much attached to a few women friends, and on this point the Master had not been too pleased with him.

Ernst went back to Germany in July 1934, and asked me to join him at Heidelberg, where he was staying with an old friend, Baroness Lucy Wangenheim, the half-sister of Woldemar von Uxkull-Gyllenband, to whom he had dedicated *Frederick II*. She was strikingly handsome, intelligent, and well educated, and told fascinating stories about her earlier life. Her father had been the Kaiser's Ambassador at Istanbul, where amongst other things he had given asylum to Abdul Hamid, transferred the *Goeben* and the *Breslau* to the Turkish flag in 1914, and helped to bring Turkey into the war on the German side soon afterwards. Early in his career he had fought a duel with a man whom he suspected of being his wife's lover, and shot out a kidney. As a young girl the Baroness had stayed with the Kaiser on Corfu at the Achilleion, where she had seen the German generals doing Greek dances for their master. She did not at all like the Kaiser, who kept her in permanent doubt whether he was being the emperor or a mere country gentleman, and whichever decision she took, he blamed her for behaving wrongly. I fell at once for her when I arrived at Heidelberg on 2 August 1934, the day after the death of Hindenburg. She belonged to an aristocratic world and kept its independence and distinction. She was against the Nazis for many reasons, but largely because she hated violence and war. In 1918 her much loved half-brother, Bernhard, who was a poet of quite unusual promise, had with a friend deserted from the German Army and tried to cross into Holland. They were caught, and left to shoot themselves. George, who was very fond of the boys, wrote the poem 'Victor–Adalbert' in their memory. In 1934 the Baroness had been a widow for some years and lived with three daughters, not yet grown up. She drove Ernst and me round the beautiful countryside to such places as Speyer and Maulbronn and Heilbronn, and on these trips we had endless talks, in which she and I made mild fun of Ernst's more romantic notions. At last I had found a part of German life which not only appealed to me but offered some satisfactions that I could not find in England. Yet it was just this highly civilized existence which was rare enough at any time in Germany and was now in imminent danger of being destroyed by the Nazis.

From Heidelberg I went to Berlin, armed with an introduction from Ernst to the central surviving member of the George circle, Ernst Morwitz. He cherished the full tradition of the Master and gathered round him others of the faithful. He himself had a slightly sardonic manner and appearance and made apocalyptic remarks, for which there seemed to be no rational basis, but which turned out to be true, as if he had some private clairvoyance into the nature of things. At almost our first meeting he told me that Hitler wanted war, and he thought that four or five years would certainly see it. I met other members of the circle with him, including some of the younger generation, whom Morwitz treated with a mixture of humorous indulgence, in such matters as food, and intellectual stimulation. The tradition was that young men should be encouraged to talk, but must think for themselves and not talk nonsense. They were submitted to a mild grilling, which did them a lot of good in a country where far too much is taken for granted because a teacher says that it is so. Morwitz himself wrote poems and translated Greek lyrics into the metres of the original. He did some pieces from Sappho, which were published and to which I wrote an Introduction, almost my only attempt to write German. The first draft revealed not only my own shocking limitations, but the limitations of the English language, which, if translated direct into German, tends to be neither 'tief' (deep) nor 'dunkel' (dark), which are regarded as almost indispensable qualities. Fortunately Ernst rewrote it for me and made it presentable. Morwitz and his friends did not live in a fools' paradise but were fully alive to the appalling situation. They trained their young men, who might otherwise have been infected by the prevailing madness, to see what it really was and to become active opponents of it. This is what George himself would have wished, and later it was one of his disciples, Klaus von Stauffenberg, who was the leading spirit in the conspiracy against Hitler and came nearest to success. Though Morwitz's circle was almost exclusively male, I met with him a learned lady called Fraülein Renata von Scheliha. She was a close kinswoman of Dolf von Scheliha, who was one of the ablest plotters against the Nazis. He was a member of a spy-group called 'die rote Kapelle' and, being himself in the Foreign Office, sent information of the utmost value to a colleague in the Air Ministry, who passed it to the Russians.

Through Ernst I met in Berlin a remarkable couple, Kurt and Käte Riezler. Riezler, who came from a *bourgeois* Bavarian family, had almost by accident had a fabulous career. Before 1914 and for the first years of the war he was private secretary to Bethmann-Hollweg and was once sharply criticized by the Kaiser for wearing his hair too long, to which he replied that he was so hard-worked that he had no time to get it cut. He had once been tutor in a Russian family but had to leave for paying too marked attentions to one of the daughters, but his stay in Russia meant that he was regarded by the German Foreign Office as an expert on Russian affairs. As Minister in Stockholm he was involved in the complicated attempts to establish relations with the Bolsheviks, and when the Higher Command sent Lenin to Russia in a sealed railway-carriage, it was Riezler who supervised the sealing. When after Brest-Litovsk the Germans sent von Mirbach as their ambassador to Moscow, Riezler accompanied him and was in the room when the Bolsheviks shot him. Riezler hid under the table and lived to tell the tale. After a spell with President Ebert, he became Curator of Frankfurt University, where he was a great success. Though he had had so melodramatic a career, it did not mean much to him. What really interested him was Greek philosophy, especially Parmenides, and some general philosophical questions, which were more to the German taste than the English. Once when the Baroness and he were sun-bathing together in beautiful surroundings, she asked him what subject he was working at, and he said, 'Despair'.

His wife, Käte, was a beautiful and delightful woman. She was the daughter of Max Liebermann, who came from a Jewish family which had been established in Berlin for three hundred years, and was an excellent painter of the Impressionist School. She was an only child, and, since her parents were very well off, saved Riezler from any financial cares. They treated her severely, and even when she was fifty, she was not allowed a latch-key to the house in the Pariser Platz. She was still in love with her husband, who was strikingly handsome, and put up not too kindly with his various affairs. Her father had disciplined her extremely well in the arts. Himself the friend of Manet, Monet, and Renoir, he had a magnificent collection of pictures, and Käte had been taught to look at them properly. I met the old man in September 1934, when I lunched with him and his wife and the Riezlers at their beautiful house on the Potsdam side of the Wannsee. The garden went down to the water, and the pictures were ravishing. Liebermann was tall and formidable. He talked in the Berlin dialect and had a sharp and puncturing intelligence. He was an old man who did not care what he said, and spoke with authority, not only about painting. A year or two earlier he had been visited by some agents of Hindenburg, who wished him to do a portrait and asked if he could make a likeness in the very short time at his disposal. Liebermann flung the door open and, pointing to the snow that lay thick outside, said, 'If I were to piss on that now, I could do a very good likeness of Hindenburg.' When the Nazis came into power, they left him alone, and even said to him, 'If all the Jews were like you, there would be no Jewish problem', to which he answered, 'If all the Nazis were like me, there would be no Jewish problem.' He saw completely through them and said of them, 'I can't eat enough to vomit as much as I have to.' At home he was something of a tyrant, and if the food was not exactly to his liking, he would throw it round the room. To my grief he died soon after my visit, and I did not see him again.

I continued to pay short visits to Germany up to the summer of 1938. The situation appalled and horrified me, but I wished to see my friends and find out how they were faring. Ernst, who had been deprived of his professorship at Frankfurt, moved to Berlin on the principle that the best place in a maelstrom is at the centre, and established himself comfortably in a flat near the Zoo. Here he worked out a new pattern of life. He read a lot, but never allowed it to interfere with his friends or his pleasures. He was a first-class cook, who excelled at chrysanthemum soup, bouillabaisse, ducks done in brandy, and *crêpes Suzette*. We spent much time on preparing meals, and, though I was the merest tweeny, I greatly enjoyed it, since Ernst talked unceasingly with much fancy about the various ingredients and what must be done with them. The rest of the time was spent mostly in conversation, usually of a coherent kind, on single subjects. Politics could not be forgotten, but they were treated from unexpected angles, and Ernst would maintain that all the trouble began with Luther, or that Hitler was the only Nazi who did not believe in National Socialism, or that most important figures in history die at the age of fifty-six. He was beginning to move away from the doctrines which he had learned from Stefan George, and regarded his own ultra-patriotic activities in 1919 as an aberration. He was even capable of doubts about his old hero Frederick II, but decided that brutality based on metaphysics was better than brutality for its own sake. He suffered deeply from finding that as a Jew he was thought different from other Germans, and once or twice we had awkward scenes in restaurants when the waiters were offensive to him, and the only thing was to leave at once. He kept up with the relics of the George circle, and I was delighted to meet with him Karl Wolfskehl, who was one of George's first friends, and now, though very old and almost blind, was setting out to start a new life in New Zealand. Wolfskehl, who had met Rupert Brooke in Munich in 1911, belonged to a high age of European civilization and bore his troubles with a touching patience. He was less under the Master's influence than the younger disciples and looked at things from his own point of view. Ernst had women friends, who brought out all that was gayest and most original in him. The high-minded cult of youth, as practised and preached by the Master, was not really to his taste, and on the few occasions when he indulged in it, he was not at all paedagogic. He had been, and was to be again, a first-class teacher, but that was because he made his pupils share his own excitement and not be afraid of letting themselves go.

With Ernst and the Riezlers I met at least one German who contradicted by his behaviour the common notion that the Germans lacked moral courage. Some of them possessed it in a high degree, but what they lacked was means to make it effective. They could be little more than martyrs, and though in the long run martyrdom may yield a handsome dividend, its short-term rewards are not encouraging. Albrecht von Bernstorff, who had for many years greatly admired Käte Riezler, was a man of quite unusual courage who developed his own magnificent technique of combating the Nazis. He was a landowner from Holstein, whose family had gone not into the army but into diplomacy. Of this he was unashamedly proud, and he had himself been Brüning's *chargé d'affaires* in London. He was a very tall, heavy man, who enjoyed food and drink and had an enormous circle of friends. Before 1914 he had been a Rhodes scholar at Oxford, and he remained very friendly to the English. The Nazis appalled him, partly because their methods disgusted his humane spirit, partly because he thought that they would ruin Germany by desperate adventures. Ribbentrop hated him and pushed him out of the diplomatic service, but he was glad to leave it and to join a Jewish bank which had branches in foreign countries. His brother had been killed in the war, and the widow wanted to get Bernstorff's house at Stintenburg for her son. She persuaded the Nazis to send a gang to threaten Bernstorff. He gave them a proper dressing-down, and they were so humbled that they left without doing anything. His own estate people stood firmly behind him, and for a time he had no more trouble. Ernst and I stayed with him at Stintenburg, where we bathed in the lake, while he went out to shoot a buck. It was delightfully peaceful but not at all showy, and Bernstorff was an excellent but not an exacting host. At Stintenburg he lived the life of a country gentleman as it had survived in Germany from the eighteenth century, and it was all much less elaborate and less formal than its counterpart would be in England.

Bernstorff had unlimited courage. He expressed his views on the Nazis on any and every occasion, often in a loud voice in public places like restaurants. This he did on purpose, since he thought that by showing his own lack of fear he would encourage others to do the same. He was an assiduous collector of views and information and equally at home with the anti-appeasement party in England, represented by Vansittart, and with some German generals, notably von Hammerstein, who were for their own reasons frightened of Hitler's next move. He was in his humane way a patriotic German, but he belonged to the school of Strese-mann and Brüning and thought that far more could be done by diplomacy than by threats, and he was strongly opposed to any risk of war. His courage was enforced by his bubbling sense of humour which was not of the Prussian kind but more akin to what we like to think typically English. He spread extremely funny jokes and stories against the leading Nazis and, after hearing him, I had no illusions about the odious and contemptible character of Ribbentrop. Though a man in his position might perhaps have been anti-Semite, Bernstorff was the opposite. He liked Jews and cultivated their acquaintance. When they lost their jobs, he helped them to get others, and when Ernst was in Berlin, Bernstorff saw that he was paid from some private source to research into the history of Burgundy. His banking work made it easy for him to travel, and he often visited England, where he conducted much more than merely financial transactions. His total disregard of discretion made some English suspicious. They could not believe that the Gestapo would allow any one to go on talking as he did.

But it was his challenge to the Nazis, and for the moment they were not ready to take it up. He soon found that in England there were many who did not welcome what he told them and dismissed it as the exaggeration of a man who had lost his job. He left them alone and concentrated on those who thought otherwise.

Before the blood-bath of July 1934 Heinrich Brüning fled from Germany and came for a time to Oxford, where he stayed, more or less anonymously, at the Queen's College. Bernstorff brought him to lunch with me, and Wade-Gery also came. Brüning was in perfect command of himself, and though he must at times have feared that his life was in danger, he gave no sign of it. He talked freely in a quiet, precise voice about the situation, and gave no outward evidence of emotion. It is true that he never mentioned Hitler by name but called him 'he', but that seemed natural enough when he was the chief topic of talk, though for Brüning he was very much more. Nor did he complain overtly of Hindenburg, whom he had supported and put back into the Presidency, only to be betrayed by him. But he did emphasize that when he was sacked, he was on the edge of success and of getting the rectifications of the Versailles Treaty for which he had struggled. He disliked von Papen and von Schleicher, but the second of these was now dead, and the first had been side-tracked to a job at Vienna. Though Brüning talked openly about present politics, he did so in rather an academic way, discussing matters of principle and theory. He had charm and dignity and never boasted or stressed his own importance, but he gave the impression that he was fundamentally detached from common life and more at home in a private world. He was deeply religious and had some of the quiet assurance of a monk, but he was also a scholar who liked to translate brute facts into abstractions and so to feel more in touch with them. It was easy to understand that he was no match for the Nazis, or even for the slippery von Papen; it was less easy to see why Hindenburg's entourage turned against him, and the only answer was that they were frightened by his exposure of their corruption in getting public funds for their bankrupt estates in East Prussia. The Junkers, having used Brüning for their own ends and then betrayed him, hoped to do the same thing with Hitler, but this time they were less successful.

In 1934 I was convinced not only that the Nazis were a fearful menace to all civilized ways of life but that they wished to rule Europe and were preparing to do so by war. The concentration camps were already in existence, and it was easy to find out about them. Bernstorff was well informed on their hideous character, and denied that the Germans did not know about them. They were simply afraid to speak in case they themselves were thrown into them. Nor could the enormous expansion of the German Army and Air Force be directed to any goal except war or the threat of war. The signs were clear on all sides. Certain foods were almost unobtainable because they went to the army. There were endless stories of factories being turned over from perambulators and motor-cars to machine-guns and tanks. There were far more soldiers in the countryside than there had been two years before. Though I knew that Hitler intended to use his army to enforce his threats on other countries, I was also convinced that he intended to use it for its own sake, that the former corporal wished to rule Europe. This was in conformity with the doctrines of *Mein Kampf* and much more than a possibility. I was therefore horrified by the growth of appeasement, both for moral and for national reasons. In Oxford, especially at All Souls, there was a strong feeling for it, but there was an equally strong feeling against. Not only my immediate friends, like Isaiah Berlin, Leslie Rowse, and John Sparrow, but many others felt very much as I did, and we found ourselves in agreement with Churchill. When Simon visited Wadham, I avoided politics as far as possible, but at All Souls I found myself in company of the younger Fellows arguing against Geoffrey Dawson and his friends. What particularly embittered me was the cold-blooded indifference which the appeasers showed towards the barbarities of the Nazis. Themselves gentle and humane men, they refused to look facts in the face and invented disreputable sophistries to avoid them. Undergraduates for the most part saw the question differently. They felt that the emergence of the Nazis was but another testimony to the callous indifference and incompetence of their elders, and they clamoured for some larger cause which could set much more than Germany right. One incidental result for myself of this odious situation was that I found myself drawn to Lindemann. As a friend of Churchill he shared his views, and I reported to him what I heard from Bernstorff and others about the less publicized activities of the Nazis.

Meanwhile refugees had been coming out of Germany, and at Oxford we did our best to look after some of them. In classical studies we found posts of one kind or other for some eminent scholars. On the whole we found it wiser to create new posts specially for them, since their appointment to our own vacancies was liable to excite indignation. When A. C. Clark retired in the winter of 1934, the electors appointed Eduard Fraenkel, from Freiburg, to his chair. I was strongly in favour of this and did my best to help. Fraenkel was already known in Oxford and respected as an excellent scholar, but some people thought it hard that E. A. Barber, who had reasonably hoped to succeed Clark, should be kept out. Fortunately what might have developed into an unseemly squabble was settled when A. E. Housman, exerting all his authority, wrote a letter to *The Sunday Times* saying that Fraenkel was 'a Latinist of European reputation', but the other candidates were not, 'for no Englishman who could be so described was young enough to be eligible'. Fraenkel must have found our ways difficult at first; for as a regular professor he was deeply involved in our academic machinery. In Freiburg he had exercised considerable authority, but in Oxford he was a member of a faculty with no more and no less power than the other members. But he soon won respect by the devoted care which he took with his classes and the unusually wide range of his learning. He would study a classical author from every possible point of view and not rest content until he had examined him in all his depth and breadth. His insistence on thoroughness was at times a little daunting to undergraduates, but they saw how much trouble he took and were grateful. His teaching and example made classical scholarship in Oxford more meticulous and more professional, and if his pupils lost some of their freshness in the process, they made up for it by building on more solid foundations.

Other eminent scholars had posts created for them which were suited to their gifts and gave them time to pursue their own work. Paul Maas, who escaped from Germany at almost the last minute, was an expert on the texts of Greek poets and put his services to the use of the Clarendon Press, where his keen eye rescued many authors from slips and errors. He lived in extreme simplicity, had no relaxations except music and swimming, and never wore an overcoat even in the coldest weather. Felix Jacoby continued to edit on a monumental scale the fragments of the Greek historians, but, though he did not teach or lecture, he was always ready with help for English scholars who much enjoyed his relentlessly critical mind and his unwillingness to take 'Yes' for an answer. Rudolf Pfeiffer, who was somewhat younger, produced a majestic edition of Callimachus and from time to time lectured on the Humanists of the Renaissance, as well fitted a man who was attached to A. C. Clark's old college of Corpus. Perhaps the most lively and most fascinating was Paul Jacobsthal, who was a member of Christ Church and officially called Reader in Celtic Archaeology, but he knew quite as much about Greek archaeology as about Celtic and was an old friend and ally of Beazley. All these men produced large and learned books and set a high example of research. Our classical school throve through their help, and in the classics, as in other fields, German nationalism defeated its own ends. By expelling some of the best men it gravely impoverished studies which had for two centuries been built up with the highest devotion and integrity.

The lot of the refugees was not easy. They were after all Germans, who had been brought up in Germany and trained in the German way of life. For many years their Jewish blood had not mattered, but suddenly in middle age they found themselves pariahs. In England they found some measure of safety, but its ways were alien, and at first it was difficult for them to make the right allowances. Jacoby took it all with good-humoured detachment and went his way without complaining. Jacobsthal pursued a more active policy of amused and amusing criticism. His sense of humour kept him alive to many small anomalies, but like some other archaeologists, he was internationally minded, and tickled by English idiosyncrasies. But not all refugees were so adaptable, and some were liable to complain that in Germany things were done much better. The words 'bei uns' ('at home') passed into a catchword and suggested unfavourable comparisons. Even when refugees had fathomed the mysteries of English habits, they still had one another to deal with, and sometimes their German respect for hierarchy and propriety made things difficult. Jacobsthal used to travel every morning in a bus with a young man, who after a few days spoke to him and told him about himself. He was a research student, and it soon dawned on him that Jacobsthal was in a superior position. In a voice of amazement and envy, he asked, 'Essen Sie an der High Table?' ('Do you eat at the High Table?'), and abysses of social difference gaped between them. Once Mrs Jacobsthal was asked to tea by the wife of another refugee and in the German manner was made to sit on a high, stiff sofa, while the tea-table was jammed up against her. Having nowhere else to place her elbows, she put them on the table, but was told severely by her hostess, 'In Oxford we do not put our elbows on the table.' The poor things were eager to do what was right, to be as 'korrekt' as they would have been at home, but the transformation was not always easy, and they took it too seriously.

Nor were the English as sensitive to the feelings of refugees as they might have been. Once they had been fixed up with jobs and salaries, they were left to look after themselves in the immemorial Oxford tradition, which expects its members to live and let live. But the refugees had skins thinner than ours, and we did not always take into account that they were after all Germans with the common German suspicion that they were continually being insulted. I myself trod more than once on the corns of a scholar whom I respected, and suddenly found him spluttering in fury at me. It was partly because he did not understand what I said, but also because I was being jaunty about some topic which he thought should be treated with solemnity as part of his own intellectual life. I was deeply ashamed of my callousness and apologized as humbly as I could. Fortunately this was taken in a friendly spirit, but I realized what differences still remained between me and some Germans whom I thought I understood. Not all refugees lectured on subjects suited to our carefully defined curricula, and some felt affronted that their lectures were so sparsely attended. At home they could more or less compel students to listen to them; at Oxford they had to rely on good will, which was not always forthcoming, if only because undergraduates had enough to do already without going outside their own courses. Some of us hoped to ease the situation by attending such lectures ourselves, but it was not an unmixed success. At the lecture-desk German professors tend to assume the manner of a sergeant-major, and we were treated like recruits. Once I was put on to translate from Latin, and thought I did it rather well, but was told, 'That is quite correct, but it is not very good English.' Yet the refugees had their moments of triumph. My old tutor Joseph, who could be brusque in his dealings with others, was properly put in his place by a Frau Professor, whose husband was a learned historian of philosophy. There was at New College an undergraduate called Joseph, whose letters were sometimes delivered in error to the don. One from the Frau Professor went wrong in this way, and Joseph rather brusquely sent it back. The Frau Professor bearded him in his room and expostulated on his bad manners. Joseph lost his head and replied, 'The undergraduate Joseph is a Jew, and I'm not, not but what my grandfather was.' The Frau Professor was not standing for this and said with some finality, 'For Hitler and for me you are a Jew.' She dealt with Joseph with a skill which I could only envy, so far was it beyond my reach.

Meanwhile things in Germany were getting rapidly worse, and most of my friends began to see how dangerous it might be if they stayed there. After some hesitation the Riezlers decided to move to the United States. They had inherited old Liebermann's magnificent pictures, and if they could take these with them, they would be in no financial need. But the Nazis were strongly opposed to any wealth being taken out of the country, and this posed a problem. Fortunately at this point they started a propaganda campaign against 'ausgeartete Kunst' ('degenerate art'), and since this was directed by Hitler's own tastes in painting, which were on about the same level as Stalin's and would have found support in speeches at a Royal Academy banquet, it meant that the work of the French Impressionists was out of account, and Riezler adroitly took advantage of this to take the Liebermann collection with him. He settled with his wife in a flat in Riverside Drive in New York, and the walls were hung with masterpieces. This much perplexed their American neighbours, who would ask, 'But what are people like you doing with pictures like these?'

The crisis for two of my closest friends came in the autumn of 1938. The Baroness Wangenheim, whom I had visited several times in Frankfurt, seemed to be fairly safe. She had no Jewish blood, and her husband, dead for some years, had been an Italian. Though she was candidly anti-Nazi, her father's reputation meant that even the Nazis had some respect for her and left her alone. But a member of her family turned against her. She wished to do some job which did not appeal to the Baroness who spoke firmly against it. The young woman was extremely angry and threatened to go to the Nazis to tell them about the Baroness's long friendship with Ernst, upon which she put the worst interpretation, knowing that this might do untold damage and quite probably lead to a concentration camp. The Baroness found out just in time and saw that she must leave the country at once. This she succeeded in doing, but with almost no money or possessions. She came to England, where she settled first in London and then in Oxford. She bore it all with her usual courage and lack of complaints, and it was comforting to see how well the English immigration officers behaved. They saw the seriousness of her case and put no obstacles in the way of her staying here. In due course she was able to apply her fine intelligence on the BBC and to take British citizenship. England became a real home to her, and she never wavered in her loyalty to it.

Ernst meanwhile was still in Berlin and seemed to take little notice of the storms around him. In August 1938 I was in Paris on my way home from the south of France and on a bright inspiration of the moment sent him a telegram asking if a visit by me to Berlin would be welcome. The answer came at once, in Latin, saying that the Apostles had not waited with more eagerness for the second coming of Our Lord than he waited for mine. I found him well settled and seemingly not anxious. I also saw Morwitz and other survivors of the George circle, who talked about Runciman's mission to Prague and thought it an ingenious trick to gain time, but they were emphatic about Hitler's intentions. Among them was a young man in the *Luftwaffe*, who had just come back from fighting for Franco in Spain, and though I did not very much like him, he advised me to leave the country within the next week, if I did not wish to be caught by the declaration of war. I took him at his word, but asked Ernst whether he should not come with me. He said that he was all right, which I doubted, and that anyhow he had not got a passport and could not get one. I came away with dark forebodings and wondered what could be done for him. Then came Chamberlain's visit to Munich, and I saw how I might have been caught if things had gone otherwise, but Ernst continued to write quite cheerful letters until November when a sinister silence fell.

On the night of 9–10 November 1938 there was a 'spontaneous' outburst against the Jews in Berlin. It was highly organized by Heydrich, and Jewish shops were set on fire and many Jews murdered. I read the news in the paper with horror and fear, but a few days later I heard that Ernst had escaped. Bernstorff had, with his usual insight, known that something was in the offing, fetched Ernst to his house, and hidden him there for some days. It was an extremely brave thing to do, and it saved Ernst's life. Now the question arose what could be done for him. It was madness to stay in Berlin, and he himself at last admitted it. So an ingenious plot was contrived. One of Ernst's closest friends was a gentle, modest young man, who had been a member of the George circle and married a woman rather older than himself. Though her husband was entirely anti-Nazi, she herself not only was a friend of Frau Goering but was having an affair with one of Goering's adjutants. Here lay a hope. The husband went to the adjutant and said that hitherto he had never complained about his wife's relations with him, but now he asked for something in return. When the adjutant asked what this was, he was told that it was a passport for Professor Ernst Kantorowicz. He agreed at once, and a passport was produced within a few hours. Ernst left the country for England and came to stay with me at Oxford. His friend looked nobly after his possessions and kept his library safe until after the war, when he sent it to Ernst in the United States, whither he had gone early in 1939. He had some trouble in getting an entry visa, but eventually found a home and a job. He took it all with great gallantry and cheerfulness. His aged mother had to stay behind, and early in the war was led to believe that she could, by paying a large sum, cross into Switzerland. She was arrested at the frontier and sent to a concentration camp, where she died, in what agonies we shall never know. Old Frau Liebermann, left alone in Berlin, killed herself in 1939. Bernstorff, who had saved Ernst's life, was still more or less free and survived the first years of the war, but in July 1943 he was arrested and sent to prison in the Lehrter Strasse in Berlin. Two days before the Russians arrived he was let out and at once shot.

With another notable opponent of Hitler, who came to an even more terrible end, my relations were more tangled and have caused me much unhappy searching of heart. Adam von Trott zu Solz came as a Rhodes scholar to Balliol in the early thirties. He was a tall, handsome man, whose appeal to young women was irresistible. He was an excellent talker, but very often on a level where I was not at home. He was a fluent Hegelian, and in his metaphysical approach to reality the outlines of issues became blurred, and it was not easy to say what his actual position was. He made many friends at Oxford, and later I met him in Germany, where he was a friend of Bernstorff. He talked much about his own problems. He wished to do something against the Nazis, but was not sure what was best. He hovered between the army and the diplomatic service and produced excellent arguments for and against both. Like most Germans of his time and class, he attached much importance to making a good career, and he hoped to do this despite the unfavourable conditions which Germany offered. In the middle thirties I did not see him, but in May 1939, after Hitler had swallowed the rump of Czechoslovakia, he came to Oxford and paid me a visit. I was very glad to see him, since I had always thought that he was firmly against Hitler. Such he still claimed to be, and announced that, though he was in the German

Government service, he was working with the secret opposition. At this I felt uneasy. I could not believe that the Gestapo would allow so obvious an adversary to go about the world expressing his views in this free manner, and I became suspicious. My suspicions became worse when he went on to argue that we should let Hitler keep all his conquests, and so remain at peace with Germany. I then decided that von Trott was really on the side of the Nazis and asked him to leave the house. Knowing that he was going to the United States, I wrote to influential friends there and warned them against him, thinking that his plausibility might deceive friendly Americans. This was soon known to Trott's rich friends in England, who regarded me as having behaved in a criminal way. I still cannot see what else I could have done. As an Englishman I was strongly opposed to letting Hitler keep his gains, and I did not see why any possible successors to him should enjoy them. I decided that von Trott was playing a double game and trying to weaken our resistance just when at last it was beginning to grow stronger. I was wrong. What I overestimated was the competence of the Gestapo, who could be extraordinarily blind and seem actually not to have known about von Trott's efforts against Hitler. So my main reason for suspicion was quite unfounded. Von Trott was not only against Hitler, but after the failure of the plot of 20 July 1944, he was arrested and hung with a horrifying brutality on a wire cord. When I heard of this, I saw how mistaken I had been, and my rejection of him remains one of my bitterest regrets.

By the declaration of war most of my more intimate friends had left Germany, some only just in time. I had seen too much of the country to wish to see it again, and I have never returned. Yet I had formed friendships with Germans which were to last for a lifetime, and I had learned that, however helpless the mass of Germans might be, a few displayed heroic courage in defending a civilization which the Nazis wished to destroy. In contrast with them the English appeasers were a sorry lot. Nobody can blame them for wishing to avert war, but it is hard to understand their gross misreading of Hitler's character or of the true nature of his régime. They were totally wrong, and when they were forced by events to see the truth, they might have been forgiven if they had admitted that they had been deceived. Instead they preened themselves on their wisdom, and claimed that they had won time for rearmament. This had not been their intention, and was not entirely true. I am happy that I never supported them, and I still regard them as a set of complacent nincompoops.

13

American Interlude

Early in 1936 I received an invitation from Harvard asking me to lecture in the classical faculty during the following winter. I had not been in the United States since 1903, and I was fascinated by the prospect of visiting what was for me less another country than another planet. In September I crossed in a Dutch ship, which was slow and boring and far more American than Dutch. My fellow travellers were for the most part American families going home after holidays in Europe. They were affable and easy, but I was not ready for the assaults that they delivered with assiduous monotony on F. D. Roosevelt. I knew that he was disliked by the very rich, but I looked to him as a possible friend in our dire need and a man who had tried to get his country out of its appalling depression. This was not what I now heard. He was, it seemed, 'setting class against class', which meant that he made nasty gibes against the rich, and he was referred to as 'that man in the White House', or dismissed in the words 'We've got a president'. It was absurdly assumed that, if a Republican president had been elected, all troubles would have been brought to an end. Much worse than this was that, when the topic of Hitler came into the conversation, the Americans seemed positively to approve of him. For them he was a bulwark against Communism, and whatever they meant by Communism, they were very strongly against it. Most of them said the same thing in very much the same words, and I found this formulaic manner of conversation a little disheartening till I realized that it was not conversation but a substitute for it, and that there was no need to listen to what others said or to expect them to listen to me. This was of course an unfair and unrepresentative sample of American society, but it was a dispiriting start, and I wondered what Harvard would be like.

At Harvard I was allotted a set of rooms in Lowell House, a fine new red-brick building in a massive Banker's Georgian style, which aimed at carrying out some of the functions of an Oxford or Cambridge college. It was a good moment to arrive, since Harvard was about to celebrate its tercentenary. Though there are three universities on the American continent older than Harvard, three hundred years is by any standards a long time, and since Harvard had had a very distinguished history, there was really something to celebrate. Universities from all over the world had sent delegations, and that from Oxford consisted of A. D. Lindsay, who was now Vice-Chancellor, and F. M. Powicke, Regius Professor of History. Lindsay very kindly asked me to join them, so I was given a good place in all the celebrations. In the previous year I had attended a similar celebration for the University of Budapest, but it had been ruined by an embattled horde of Germans, who got up in the middle of banquets and bawled remarks in praise of their country. At Harvard they were much less to the fore, and there was no ugly scene like that at Budapest when they tried to march at the head of the procession but were firmly extruded by the representatives from Paris. J. B. Conant, who had recently been appointed President of Harvard, had made extensive plans. There was an open-air theatre between the chapel and the library with seats for several thousands of people. The proceedings began auspiciously when James Curley, Governor of Massachusetts, walked through the chapel wearing a hat and smoking a cigar. He was well known for his financial obliquities, and when he spoke of virtue shining like a candle in a wicked world, he was greeted with derisive hoots. A large number of honorary degrees was given, and each honorand was greeted by Conant with a neat and pointed citation. Unfortunately the skies darkened, and it began to pour with rain. We sat it out, and, as some wit said, this was Mr Conant's way of soaking the Harvard rich. I was protected by my gown from getting really wet, and some of the more provident had brought umbrellas, but salvation was not secure until I heard that there was whisky in the Widener Library. I made straight for it and saved not only myself but old Eduard Norden from Berlin, who was not built for such severe tests. Despite this I found the proceedings most heartening and saw how seriously universities were treated by the audience and what ties bound them together in an international society.

In the afternoon there was a meeting of the Harvard Alumni Association in the Memorial Hall, a Gothic revival building of the sixties which would have delighted John Betjeman. To this guests were invited, and since Oxford was fourth in seniority in the long list of universities, our party was in the front row. Lindsay made a moving speech about the appalling state of the world and the miracle that free universities survived in it. It was rather beyond some of his audience, and that evening I sat next at dinner to a young woman, who asked me, 'Is Professor Lindsay usually so cynical?' Much might be said, and much was said, against Lindsay, but not that he was cynical. However, I grasped that in American 'cynical' means 'pessimistic' and cleared the matter up. The chief excitement was the presence of President Roosevelt. It was an election year, and the Harvard Alumni were overwhelmingly against him, all the more because he was a Harvard man. There was a breathless moment when after three or four speeches A. L. Lowell, Conant's predecessor as President of Harvard, who was in the chair, said, 'The next speaker is Franklin Delano Roosevelt', then with a lowering of voice and the slightest hint of contempt, 'President of the United States.' Roosevelt was lifted up by two aides; his paralysed legs were held by steel contraptions, and he was placed against the lectern. His speech adroitly tempered sentiment with malice. Referring to the bicentenary of Harvard, he continued, 'At that time many of the Alumni of Harvard were sorely troubled concerning the state of the nation. Andrew Jackson was President. At the two hundred and fiftieth anniversary of the founding of Harvard College, alumni again were sorely troubled. Grover Cleveland was President. Now, on the three hundredth anniversary, I am President.' Since both Jackson and Cleveland had been Democrat and much disliked at Harvard, Roosevelt boldly declared his own position. It was a notable opening and it was greeted with loud laughter and applause by his overwhelmingly Republican audience.

After this titillating introduction I settled down to my Harvard routine. Life in Lowell House was agreeable. Meals were provided in a dining-hall on the cafeteria system, and the academic staff mingled, not very self-consciously, with the undergraduates. Unlike Oxford, Harvard did not insist that its inmates should be locked up at midnight, but it was strict about women guests, whose visits were confined to special hours and who had to enter their names and those of their hosts in a book at the lodge. When Lowell was designing the houses, he consulted the principal of a women's college on the visits of women. She was much less worried than he, but eventually agreed that entries should be made in a book, 'I have noticed that parents are not usually interested in whom their children go to bed with, nor when, but they do like to know where.' This no doubt influenced policy, and even instructors had to record the names of their lady visitors. The undergraduates were well behaved except in the week-end after the football match against Yale or Princeton, when a Saturnalia was held. Windows were broken, courtyards littered with smashed bottles and unconscious bodies, staircases slimed with vomit. The proceedings were too deliberate to be convincing, and inspired more by a desire to mark an outstanding occasion than by spontaneous gaiety. The undergraduates came from all parts of the United States and from a wider range of social backgrounds than I should have guessed. Nor were the very rich much in evidence. There were some clubs to which it was smart to belong, and there was a demand for suitable young men in the higher reaches of Boston, but the lines of demarcation were rather less obvious than in Oxford. The houses were more halls of residence than colleges in the English sense, and for this reason there was not too much 'house spirit', though from time to time efforts were made to inflate one.

The Master of Lowell House, Julian Coolidge, was an old

Balliol man. So indeed almost everyone at Harvard seemed to be, and they assumed either that I too must be, which was a compliment, or that I must have something wrong with me in not being. Coolidge was also an active moralist. He was Chairman of Watch and Ward, which looked officiously into people's behaviour, and a teetotaller. This was to some extent tempered by his Balliol background. Once a week there was a High Table in the dining-room. We put on dinner-jackets and dined, not very well, at 6 p.m. We then adjourned for coffee, and by 7.30 we were free, but 'all dressed up and nowhere to go'. The younger tutors were aware of this paradoxical situation and got round it by meeting at 5 p.m. and fortifying themselves against the bleak hour that lay ahead. With their help I was able to take my part and even to enjoy it. I was well cared for by them in many ways, notably by David Worcester, Elliott Perkins, and George Haskins, who were delightfully forthcoming and detached and hospitable.

I was looked after by Carl Newall Jackson, Professor of Greek. He was not much known outside Harvard, since he had written very little and in this respect flouted the American gospel that published work is a test of competence. Jackson was even more unusual in that he was a bachelor, but he made up for this by keeping a pretty little house on top of a hill in New Hampshire, where he was looked after by three generations of women, who were devoted to him and saw to all his needs. I stayed with him twice in the autumn, and he took me round the country to see the 'fall tints', which were all scarlet and yellow and almost too powerful to be comfortable. He showed me round Harvard and told me exactly what to do about meals and transport. At first I found him a little elusive, but I soon detected a pleasant eccentricity in him. He had an un-American irony and a quiet humour, which took the form of searching observations on his colleagues. He had no use for modernity, and when he bought a new car, insisted that the wireless-set should be removed from it. He was an excellent teacher, but did not like talking shop; so we tried more congenial topics such as P. G. Wodehouse and King Edward VIII. When the classical faculty met, he took the chair and managed the business with ruthless skill. At the mere suggestion of a change, his face would assume so forbidding a look of distaste that the proposal would at once be dropped. He seemed to have very few friends, but I found him excellent company, and much relished his wry comments. He had a neat way of exposing impostures in learned circles, and this may have been why he was not more liked.

The Professor of Latin, E. K. Rand, was a scholar of some renown both in classical Latin and in medieval and Renaissance studies. He was genial and jovial, a keen lover of France, a lifelong Republican but not intolerant of Democrats, a welcoming and amusing companion and an excellent host. Jackson was a little suspicious of him and thought that he overdid the propaganda for his subject, but it helped to keep Latin in good repute and was probably worth the effort. He asked me to dine with him and some of his cronies in Boston. It was a large and rather splendid affair. I sat on his right and saw no danger ahead until after dinner Rand got up and began to speak in Latin about everyone present, starting with the man on his left. I saw that I should have to do something, and in the next few minutes, which were all the time available, I put together in my mind a few sentences in Greek. He stopped, and I got up and delivered these and found that I could continue for a bit in not too halting a manner. My bold effort was a nine hours' wonder, and Rand was delighted.

Outside the teachers of classics I had an old friend in John Livingston Lowes, whom I had known in Oxford in 1931, and much respected and liked for his gentle charm and immense learning. He had come to his present eminence by a long journey, which began when at some southern college he had been Joseph K. and Sophronia Y. McKee Professor of Ethics and Christian Evidence. This he boldly interpreted to mean English Literature, in which he came to win world-wide renown, especially for his work on Coleridge and Chaucer. Unfortunately in 1936 his memory was beginning to fail. He had overloaded it for years, and now he would give the same lecture twice in two consecutive hours and could not be relied on to turn up when he had asked someone to lunch or dinner. But apart from this he was still his old self, with graceful, old-fashioned manners and a passion for good talk. His wife, alas, was no longer visible. She must have broken before he did, and he never spoke of her to me. He could still enchant his listeners at the Society of Fellows, which was composed of clever young men engaged in research and seeking to catch the atmosphere of an Oxford common room over the port, and he came to my rescue at the Saturday Luncheon Club in Boston, when a member suddenly asked me to get up and talk about the date of Homer. Lowes was indignant at what he thought a breach of hospitality and would not permit it.

Another noble elder was Alfred North Whitehead, who was now seventy-five and in full command of his faculties. After one career at Cambridge and another at London, he had begun a third at Harvard in 1924, and soon established himself as a philosopher and a sage. He wore clerical broadcloth and looked and spoke as if he were descended from a long line of archdeacons. He was not only delightfully modest but sharp and original and quite unpredictable. He made no attempt to come to terms with the American language or American place-names, and put the accent of Potomac on the first syllable and of Idaho on the second. When Conant was appointed president of Harvard, he was known to be a very good chemist, and it was argued that he would be a good president because Eliot in the nineteenth century, who had done a lot for Harvard, had also been a chemist. Whitehead punctured this piece of nonsense by saying, 'Oh, but Eliot was a *bad* chemist.' In comparing English and American universities he said of their respective undergraduates, 'In Cambridge, England, one felt here you are knowing so much and caring so little, but in Cambridge, Massachusetts, one feels here you are knowing so little and caring so much.' The Americans do not come badly out of it, and it is delightfully just. He had a genius for inspiring young scholars and though his creative days were past, he liked the play of ideas and kept it going in a society where facts tended to have priority.

Below these giants was a younger generation of men who had still their way to make and were not yet professors or even sure of their tenure at Harvard. Among these I made friends especially with John Finley, who had a passion for Greek and Greece and was ready to talk about it at any time for hours. He had in him

something of a poet and approached Greek with a special understanding of its strength and beauty, and this made him an excellent
teacher, whom his pupils admired and loved. He knew the
literature quite as well as anyone at Oxford and was far more
forthcoming about it. He would talk with a fluent eloquence,
using imaginative images and enlightening parallels, and find in
his exposition of a Greek author a field for his own creative insight. He had friends whom I met with him and who were in due
course to become well-known figures at Harvard. Harry Levin
was already an expert in European literature and a remorseless
champion of high standards in learning. Ted Spencer was a gentle,
fanciful student of Elizabethan drama, who had been at Cambridge, England, and caught some of the liberal atmosphere of
King's. F. O. Matthiessen was already working on Henry James
and proving himself a careful and scrupulous scholar with ideas of
his own. These men were later to become familiar figures in the
world of learning, but even at this date it was refreshing to meet
them and see how serious and happy they were in their work.
Their terms were longer than ours, and they had more papers to
correct, but so far as their research was concerned, they had an
enormous advantage in the Widener Library. In 1936 the Bodleian
at Oxford had not yet been modernized and presented many
obstacles to sustained reading, but in Widener Jackson lent me his
own room, which was on the book-stack, and I could in a few
minutes get almost any book I wanted. If the library did not
possess it, it would be acquired as quickly as possible. This was an
inspiriting incentive, and I managed to make up a lot of reading
which I had missed.

Through the Finleys I met William James and his wife Alice.
Bill was the son of the philosopher of the same name and the
nephew of Henry James. He lived at 95 Irving Street, which had
for many years been the house of the James family. He was very
tall and slim and quite a good painter. He did not have to work
for a living and was free to apply his finest gifts to life. In this his
large and energetic wife gave him full support. She was warm-
hearted and courageous and infinitely welcoming. With them
talk was not only lively but life-giving. All kinds of topic were

discussed in every kind of spirit, always with candour and profit. Both Bill and Alice were Democrats, outspoken admirers of Roosevelt and implacably against Hitler, and both belonged to a large liberal tradition which was both American and European. After dinner we would sit in the fine library, which was crowded with books and had on the mantelpiece an excellent photograph of William and Henry James, 'my old dad' and 'Uncle Henry'. Bill, like his uncle, insisted on producing the scrupulously right word and would pause while he hunted for it. It was useless, it was even offensive, to try to supply it for him, for when it came, it was far better than anyone else could have found. There was at Harvard an English immigrant, A. D. Nock, from Cambridge, who excelled in displaying recondite knowledge in footnotes and was now Frothingham Professor of the History of Religion. He liked to emphasize *in partibus infidelium* what he thought to be the traditional qualities of an English scholar and would lay down with authority the virtues of different vintages of port, or relate the oddities of Cambridge dons whom he had known in his youth. Bill James met him and reported to me, 'I met a colleague of yours last night, called Nock. He was a . . . a . . . a circus.' The last word came out triumphantly and was, with its American associations, inexorably right. Bill tempered his fine observations of life with an airy, quite unpredictable fancy. Speaking of some man he had known and being asked what he looked like, he said, 'Like Jesus Christ, but thicker set.' He combined the broad tolerance of his father with something of his uncle's passion for words, and he stood out as an entirely original and fascinating character.

The couple that I knew best at Harvard was Felix and Marion Frankfurter. They were old friends of Sylvester Gates, but I got to know them when they were in Oxford in 1934, and I liked them enormously. Felix was a slight, short, dapper little man, very neatly dressed and bursting with vitality. He had come from Vienna as a boy of twelve and made his way upward by extreme ability. He was now a Professor at the Harvard Law School, but regarded with suspicion by a number of people outside it. Jackson was amazed when he heard that I knew and liked him, and dismissed it as an inexplicable English eccentricity. The reasons went far back. Felix had battled for a proper trial of Sacco and Vanzetti after the war, and though in the end he failed and they were executed, he spared no effort to get justice done, and this, at a time when many Americans sniffed Communists under every bed, was counted very much for unrighteousness. Now things were no better because he was known to be a close friend of Roosevelt and thought to give him advice on appointments and even on policies. Felix was very much in with the White House, from which telephone calls came frequently by day and night, and with some of the leading figures in the New Deal, but he was not really a man of the left any more than he was a man of the right. His guiding principles, to which he adhered with rigid constancy, were not political but legal, and his judgement of causes meant much less to him than his judgement of personalities.

Felix believed in the paramount importance of the law, and it was partly because he admired its administration in England that he was notably Anglophile. For him the law was the main safeguard of liberty, and he insisted that it should be treated with the utmost respect. This was why he took up the cause of Sacco and Vanzetti. Though they appealed to him as human beings, what drove him to fight so long and courageously for them was his conviction that injustice was being done. Conversely, when he became a Justice of the Supreme Court in 1938, he was accused of abandoning his liberal views and joining in reactionary judgements. This may superficially have been true, but what guided Felix was his respect for the law and his determination that new judgements must be in accordance with precedent. Yet he tempered this somewhat abstract loyalty by strong personal attachments. He insisted that men must be judged not by their opinions but by their individual worth, and this he found in many different spheres. It made him a friend alike of Harold Laski and Lord Eustace Percy, of F. D. Roosevelt and Henry L. Stimson, of Justice Holmes and Justice Brandeis. He had a boundless curiosity about human beings and liked almost anyone who had something to say for himself and was not stuffy or cagey. Some Americans regarded him as a snob and attributed it to his humble beginnings, but he was certainly not a snob in the usual sense of seeking out his social superiors. He liked human qualities wherever he found them, and this was why he was an excellent teacher and guide to the young. He was impossible to shock so long as you said what you meant, and, though he was naturally loyal to his fellow Jews and to Zionism, it was largely because he felt, with good reason, that their situation in the world was deteriorating at an alarming rate.

Felix was not in the least troubled by the abuse which Republicans heaped on him. He did not even make any show of suffering for a good cause; he did not suffer, and he was very far from being self-righteous. If he spoke at all of it, it was on the principle that 'to cause pain to the brethren' was often both salutary and enjoyable. What carried him through was his invincible courage. Once he made up his mind on a course of action, nothing would deter him, and he would stick to it with high spirits and unshaken equanimity. Even with his most rabid opponents he was seldom annoyed, let alone angry, and saw them as rather grotesque figures. His courage made him an invincible optimist. Though he was inflexible in his adherence to certain principles, he did not flaunt them, but let them govern his conduct in the most natural way. In his enjoyment of the human scene he found a justification for his strong belief in personal liberty. He liked any display of originality or liveliness. At Oxford he had been much taken by the bursar of Balliol, Colonel Cecil Duke, who talked army slang, wore a hat indoors, and arranged for Felix to take a party to see the Derby. He was also attracted by Guy Burgess, who occasionally came to Oxford, was still a sparkling talker and had not yet been turned into a bore by the squalid habits which brought him to a dismal end in Moscow. Though Felix and his wife, Marion, were entirely happy together and shared everything, she was in most ways very unlike him. She was a New Englander from Connecticut and still unusually beautiful. She was highly fastidious and critical, and though she was courteous to all Felix's friends, she did not always like them and shrank from too wide a social life. She much preferred small intimate parties where she could say what she thought and distil an occasional drop of acidity when she thought that someone was too highly praised. Felix had a great respect for her judgement, but was not discouraged by it.

With Felix I met some of the first New-Dealers and was not attracted by them nor sorry when in due course Roosevelt threw them over. Being largely of Irish origin, and aggressively conscious of it, they disliked England and liked to air their grievances against us. They worked themselves up about our behaviour in India and refused to believe that we were at last trying to do something about it. Knowing that we were in a tight place with Hitler, they crudely said that they were not going 'to pull England's chestnuts out of the fire' and reiterated the old slogan that England was prepared 'to fight to the last American'. They blamed us in the same breath for not having conscription and for having a navy, which they regarded as designed solely for imperialist aggression. Fortunately they formed only a small part of Felix's vast acquaintance, and I do not think that even he liked them very much, though he strongly supported the New Deal. I was much more at home with his other friends. Felix had a real respect for learning, and his admiration for men like Whitehead and Rand was not tempered or hampered by political considerations. His closest friends at Harvard were in the Law School, where his humanity and scholarship were properly appreciated. He was a keen observer of human nature, and one of the things that he liked in Roosevelt was his ability to take knocks and brush them aside. When just after his appointment to the Supreme Court Justice Black was found to have been in his youth a member of the Ku Klux Klan, there was a fearful hullaballoo, but when Felix rang up the President, the answer was, 'Yes, it's tough luck', and that was all. Conversation at the Frankfurters' took unexpected turns, and particularly lively was a long discussion with Judge Learned Hand about which Presidents, if any, had conducted love-affairs at the White House. Harding, it was claimed, confined them to a yacht, but there were legitimate suspicions about Wilson and even about Cleveland. All agreed that 10 Downing Street had a richer record. The Frankfurters were a haven of enjoyment at Harvard, largely because with them there was no need to make concessions to American susceptibilities.

With the Frankfurters I met a far bigger cross-section of American society than anywhere else. Social life at Harvard was, however, much more rewarding than I anticipated and offered many surprises. Most of the younger instructors were poorly paid and had to support wives and families. I was particularly impressed by the wives, who were often more attractive and more enterprising than their counterparts in England. They had all been to college, and I saw liberally displayed how much education can do to increase women's worth and charm in the home. They turned themselves out very nicely, and when they invited me to meals, they not only cooked well but made themselves unusually agreeable. All this was at the end of a crowded day in which they had taken children to school and fetched them from it, and done the shopping and probably the cleaning, since any domestic aid was very difficult to find. More than this, they were interested in interesting things, talked freely about fruitful subjects, and assisted their husbands in typing their books or making indexes. They were not in the least unsophisticated, but lacked the hard-boiled scepticism which I encountered in New York, where everyone seemed to know more than he should and to be a little gloomy about it. Academic circles at Harvard had a quality different from their parallels at Oxford. They had many connections with the big world, but these were not so much a concession to it as a sign that it cultivated intellectual interests and was glad to know scholars and to help learning. Moreover, Harvard changed its population more rapidly than Oxford. A man with a job there was by no means set for life but tended to look round for something better at another university. A good offer from outside might mean that Harvard raised his salary in order to keep him, and this sometimes led to chicanery in the form of extracting letters from friends which hinted at fine offers but were not entirely genuine about them. In the United States the academic profession had ties all over the country and was not divided as in England into Oxford and Cambridge on the one side and 'provincial' universities on the other.

Another pleasurable surprise was the quality of the Harvard students. They were remarkably approachable, lively, keen, and not at all eager to show off. They lacked the inhibitions and the self-deprecatory airs which seemed to be ingrained at Oxford, and they were not shy of talking on the topics which interested them. The paradox was that American children, who were often un-attractive and noisy and assertive, could be turned into such pleasant young men, and clearly there was something right in the educational system somewhere. In classes and lectures their worst defect was their faulty control of the written word. Their hand-writing was usually as bad as my own, and what was worse, they did not have any sure command of language and were much clumsier at expressing their ideas on paper than in talk. This was largely because they were not drilled into writing essays as Oxford undergraduates are, and so lacked the criticism which a tutor can give on structure and expression. Nor did I very much like the readiness with which they handed back to me what I had said to them. This was due to the system by which a lecturer examines his own class, but in this respect I found it faulty and told them that they would get better marks if they expressed their own ideas instead of mine. They were surprised but took it well and did what I asked, with encouraging results. Their curiosity ranged well out-side the actual subjects which I taught, and when once or twice I illustrated Homer from the heroic epics of other peoples, I evoked a delightfully warm response and found that in their more general education my Harvard pupils usually knew more than my Oxford ones.

A particular line of inquiry which was to occupy much of my time in later years was very well suited to Harvard. For a few years previously a man of genius, Milman Parry, had been on the staff at Harvard. He was concerned to find out why there are so many formulaic phrases in the Homeric poems, and, when he was working for a doctorate in Paris, he proved schematically that the formulas were worked out with utmost economy to meet almost any need of narrative, and he suggested that they provided the material with which poets, who recited their poems more or less extemporaneously, composed them during recitation. He then set out to prove this theory by visiting Yugoslavia, where he recorded the songs of living bards after plying them freely with drink, at the expense of the American Council of Learned Societies, and found that their use of formulas was even more extensive than Homer's, and that his explanation was correct. This was an epoch-making discovery in Homeric studies and had endless repercussions. On coming back from Europe to California Parry died in a horrible and grotesque way. He kept in his suitcase a loaded revolver, and of course this was a mad thing to do. On his return home, he put the suitcase down, and the revolver went off and killed him. He was only thirty-three, and his death was an irreparable disaster. Fortunately the records which he had taken of Yugoslav songs are safely housed in an attic of Widener Library and affectionately guarded by his assistant, Albert Lord. Lord would take me there, give me a written text in a notebook, and then play the records, which were easy to hear and to follow, though I cannot pretend that any of the songs approached Homer's in any distinction whatsoever. This gave a great fillip to my own studies, and I like to think that I was one of the first Englishmen to grasp the importance of Parry's work. Of course if he had lived, he would have made many additions to his theories, but what he did revolutionized the subject, and that is why at first many scholars found it hard to believe that the Homeric poems consisted largely of formulaic phrases. To them it was a blasphemy against Homer, but in fact it proved that a great poet makes the best of whatever material is at his disposal, and since in Homer's case this was not so much single words as short phrases, his command of them is a testimony to his genius.

Cambridge, Massachusetts, is a suburb of Boston, and Boston loomed rather large in our eyes. I was often asked there and quite enjoyed going, but found it rather stuffier than Cambridge and much more occupied with social distinctions. As an Englishman I was more or less exempt from them, but not free from hearing genealogies of Boston families. I had to give talks to more than one society concerned with this kind of thing and got away with a balanced comparison between Oxford, England and Cambridge, Mass., but found that everyone was far more interested in the peculiarities of Oxford than in any resemblance or contrasts between it and Harvard. This fitted the general atmosphere of friendship for England which prevailed among the well-to-do in Boston. They liked to recall their ancient ties with us and were proud of them. I was once asked to a large dinner of colonial families, and when the chairman asked me if any member of my family had had any connection with the United States, I answered with truth, 'None since my great-great-grandfather surrendered at York-town.' The poor man felt that he had touched an open wound, not indeed because my connection was in some sense disreputable but because this recalled a defeat of the English by the Americans. This showed a nice regard for national pride and was very unlike the self-righteous tirades of the New-Dealers.

1936 was the year of a presidential election, and it was notice-able that while the Republicans at Harvard flaunted a sunflower for their candidate, Alfred Landon, who came from Kansas, the Democrats showed no visible sign of their allegiance. Moreover the Republicans talked freely against Roosevelt, while the Demo-crats said very little for him. I assumed that they must be in a minority and unwilling to engage in controversy against superior numbers, but I doubt if this was the case. It was rather that they were quietly confident that they would win, as they handsomely did when Roosevelt carried every state except Maine and Vermont. I had to maintain a tactful neutrality except with my own friends, but I was naturally curious about what the future foreign policy of the United States would be. Though I surmised that Roosevelt would like to do something to discourage Hitler, it was clear that isolation was still a dominating force. The younger generation said all too often, 'I just don't believe in war', which might not mean very much but did not suggest a desire for an active policy. Much worse was the occasional rich Jew who said, 'I agree with Hitler's policy, except of course with regard to the Jews.' This was not only disreputable and disgusting but showed a complete misunderstanding of Hitler, whose anti-Semitism was the central and most constant feature in his monstrous career and one of the very few matters to which the adjective 'sincere', so favoured by the appeasers, could be justly applied. Most Americans still wished to keep clear of foreign entanglements, and though they were greatly interested in what was happening in Europe, decided that it did not concern them. This was perhaps inevitable at a time when the American entry into the war in 1917 had come in for much disingenuous and disillusioning criticism, and most people were determined not to be caught a second time. They could hardly be blamed, but so far as England was concerned, it was deeply depressing.

My light duties at Harvard made it possible for me to see something of the United States during long week-ends, and I was fascinated by relics of the past. It was agreeable to examine the really remote past, whether dead, like the fossilized foot-prints of dinosaurs near Newhaven, or alive, like the giant trees in California, but I was more interested in what might by our own standards not be very remote but in the United States recalled a very distant age. Such is Bishop Berkeley's church at Newport, Rhode Island, which remains unspoiled from the eighteenth century with box-pews, a wineglass pulpit, and the Lord's Prayer and the Ten Commandments inscribed behind the altar. Yet even this seemed near in comparison with the desolate mansions not far from it where the millionaires of the nineties had lived in grotesque extravagance, but now the windows were broken and the gardens had become wildernesses. At Gloucester, on the coast north of Boston, is a quiet Baroque church, painted blue and gold, with models of ships presented as thank-offerings by Portuguese fishermen. In a Negro quarter of Baltimore, among what were once elegant red-brick Regency houses, from which brilliantly coloured washing now hangs in reckless display, is a small stucco church in the Perpendicular revival style, and in the graveyard is the tomb of Edgar Allan Poe. It is not his original grave, but was put up in 1871 and celebrated by a noble poem specially composed by Stéphane Mallarmé, but its marble top had cracked. In death, as in life, nothing went right with Poe. At Brattleboro in Vermont was Kipling's house, 'Naulakha', which he built in his first years of success and where he lived from 1892 to 1896, when he had to leave owing to a ridiculous and undignified row with his brother-in-law. Kipling's room could be reached only through his wife's. She sat there protecting him from all intrusion, while she managed his affairs and insisted that her maids should wear mob-caps and her groom a top-hat with a cockade. In her husband's room his father had inscribed over the mantelpiece, 'The night cometh when no man shall work', and there the stories of *The Day's Work* were written. In those days Kipling was still writing from the resources which he had accumulated in India, but the secluded room was the symbol of what was to hamper him for the rest of his life, when Mrs Kipling cut him off from the human supplies on which his genius had lived so abundantly.

The happy tenor of my life at Harvard was broken by two very different blows from England. The first was the death of Alan Blakeway, of which I have already spoken. The second was a letter from Adrian Bishop saying that he had been brought to God. In the previous summer he had been very ill indeed with sleepy sickness, and when I visited him was much reduced in health and spirits. He had, however, recovered and gone to live near the Betjemans at Uffington. His hostility to religion and his derisive jokes about it indicated that it played a larger part in his mind than if he had been merely indifferent. His letter was in his usual comical vein and did not state anything clearly, but there was no doubt that something transcendent had happened. He had had a vision, and it had changed his life. He took his tale to Penelope's friend, F.P. Harton, who was extremely reassuring and urged him to think of entering the religious life. Adrian decided to do so and before long entered as a novice the Anglican monastery at Nashdom Abbey and treated it with the utmost seriousness. He accepted with delight all its obligations and much enjoyed the niceties of theological and ecclesiological discussion. At times his ebullience was a little too much for his fellows. When Penelope visited him on Corpus Christi Day, she was delighted to hear him using his fine baritone voice to some effect as he walked in procession. She made complimentary remarks on him to one of the monks, who answered, 'Yes, it would be all right if he did not drown all the rest of us.' All this took place a little later. In the meanwhile I had to accustom myself to Adrian's conversion. In the end I saw that so far from being indifferent to religion he had been drawn to it but fought against it. Now some obstacle had been removed, and he was happy that it had been. It made no difference to our relations. He seemed to be free of his black moods and acerbities, and yet to enjoy things just as much as ever.

In late November I began to realize that I was at Harvard 'on approval'. Naturally nothing of this had been said in the invitation, but one day Jackson told me that I must let him know if any other university offered me a job. I had not thought of such a possibility and dismissed Jackson's request from my mind. Then President Conant asked me to see him. He got down to business at once and asked me if I would accept a professorship in Greek at Harvard, where a vacancy would soon occur with the retirement of a senior professor. Conant's offer was quite a shock. I had never dreamed of emigrating to the United States, and now I had to face the possibility. Conant very generously gave me as much time as I wished to think about it. The terms were good, the pay several times what I got in Oxford and the hours of work fewer. I could teach more or less what I wished, and of course the Widener Library was an enormous attraction. I could live in one of the houses, not so well as in Oxford, but not uncomfortably. Also I had begun to think that after fourteen years as a college tutor at Wadham I was ready for a change. I was tired of the routine duties and especially of repeating myself hour after hour to individual pupils. It was therefore a matter to be treated seriously. Before I had time to think I got a telegram from Nicholas Murray Butler summoning me to New York where he was still President of Columbia University. After telling me what a failure Matthew Arnold had been in the United States, he made me an offer on the same terms as Conant's, and when I turned this down, he at once raised it by 2,000 dollars. This too I rejected, since I knew that I should never be able to work in New York and the standard of Greek was not so high as at Harvard. A little later I gave a lecture at Princeton and was offered a job there at a rate higher than Butler's final bid. This I left open. On returning to Harvard I told Jackson what had happened, and he assured me that Harvard could do quite as well as that, and better.

I greatly enjoyed these negotiations in which I was put up to auction. I had honestly not made up my mind and was more flattered than I realized by the offers. I told the Frankfurters, who at once assumed that I could not possibly accept, since I should be bored to tears and anyhow Oxford was much more agreeable than Harvard. More than this, Felix sent a telegram to Isaiah warning him of the temptations to which I was being subjected. Isaiah passed the news round, and while I was still in two minds what to say, a cable arrived from him,

Panic stop Dundas Wade-Gery Mynors profoundly upset stop entreat defer final decision until spate of letters reaches you nobody able face up to the real facts surely highest disinterestedness on your part demanded in this crisis.

This was followed by a long letter from him and other letters from Fraenkel, Mynors, Denniston, and Higham. The best was a card from Dundas, which contained some wise words, 'Though you make friends easily, you don't make old ones easily, and are in that respect a domestic man. And I think you'll feel a bit exiled and tire after a bit of *such* nice people.' Roy Harrod wrote more firmly, 'Now, Maurice, don't be naughty. We can't have the whole world tumbling about us like this.' All this was a little shaking, but I realized that I was in a strong position and wrote back stating frankly the advantages of the Harvard offer and saying that I would refuse it if there was any hope of a job at Oxford with a smaller burden of teaching than I now had. For instance, I might be made a Reader, which is a kind of sub-professor. It soon became clear that there was no chance of this. I put off my answer to Conant, but in the meanwhile I began to see things in a new perspective. I was sure that war was coming – and what would I do if it came? Would not any advantage of salary be outweighed by the cost of coming to England every summer? Would I be happy cut off from the friends of a lifetime? Would the Americans, after wooing me with such ardour, treat me equally well when they got me? I made up my mind to refuse, and, after I got home, I wrote to Conant saying so. Oddly enough my decision was not shaped by a new and highly relevant consideration which Wade-Gery put to me. He wrote that Stenning would be retiring from the Wardenship in 1938 and that there was a good chance that I would be elected to succeed him. I had never thought of becoming Warden, and even now I did not treat the idea very seriously. My refusal had been based on other reasons, but when I got back to Oxford I turned my thoughts to Wade-Gery's suggestion and decided that I should like it very much – more in the long run than being a professor even in England. My friends were relieved, and my only serious critic was Lady Mary Murray, who, in explaining that it was my duty to teach Greek to the Americans, somehow conveyed the impression that she wished to get me out of England. The vacant post at Harvard was given to Werner Jaeger, who had been Professor of Greek in Berlin and secured very good terms for himself.

While this crisis was still in progress, I went from Cambridge to San Francisco to spend Christmas with a cousin. She belonged to my father's generation, but was about my age. Her father, George Bowra, had gone to Australia in the eighties and done very well in horse-dealing, and she had come as a young woman to the United States. Her first marriage, into United States Steel, had broken down, and she was now married to a charming man, Frank Griffin, who was some years older than herself and had something to do with gold-mining in New Guinea. I had met her in England, where my father had taken very strongly to her, and I liked her vitality and determination. My idea was to fly out rather than to endure the horrors of an American train, but I was grounded by fog at Salt Lake City, where I failed to get into the Mormon tabernacle but much enjoyed Brigham Young's hut and the photographs of his wives, all very unglamorous and looking like old-fashioned Oxford landladies. At the bedside in my hotel was a copy of the Book of Mormon, which I tried to read but found even duller than the Koran. I was, however, delighted to hear a local legend that the Wandering Jew had been in Salt Lake City in 1868, and this was his last recorded appearance. I also met a Mormon Modernist, who explained that in one important respect science had proved the Book of Mormon right against the attacks of historical criticism. The Book said that the horse was brought to America soon after creation, but historians said that it was brought by Cortés, which was some 5,500 years later. But all was now well, since eohippus, which is about the size of a fox-terrier, had been found fossilized in Arizona. It is true that this created new chronological difficulties, since eohippus is said to be very much earlier than the date of creation as settled by the Book of Mormon, but at any rate the historians were routed. In much of this I was accompanied by a fluent and friendly man with long hair and a strong German accent, whom I had met on the aeroplane and identified as Ernst Toller. He had been involved on the revolutionary side in the troubles in Munich after the war, and had instituted a currency made from fallen leaves. He had fought against Ernst Kantorowicz and was delighted that all should know it. By this time neither of them thought that he had been right.

My cousin was very well off and lived in an irreproachable street in San Francisco. Her staff was by American standards large but eccentric, since it consisted of a Philippino chauffeur, a Scottish nanny, and a coloured cook. Everything else was done by daily women who blocked up the entrance with their cars. Her gentle and humorous husband had the greatest affection and admiration for her. Though she had had rather a sketchy education, she had plenty of shrewdness and always knew what she thought or wanted. Their friends were rich business people who lacked the cultural ambitions of Boston and were more deeply involved in the financial struggle for survival. While the men talked of business, the women talked of 'beaux' and 'débuts' and graded people by their incomes, on which they were fully informed. When my cousin gave a large dinner for me, it was all done by a firm which came in, occupied the house, and cooked and served the meal, which looked splendid but had no very distinctive taste. At each place at table was a photograph of my head fixed on to some alien body like a horse or a fish, and this was thought very *chic*. My cousin and Frank took me for a long motor-drive which ended up at Los Angeles, which I thought shapeless and inhuman. I was not impressed by what I saw of the Californian rich. They had a discouraging habit of drinking themselves silly before dinner and remaining either sour or incoherent during it. The only ideas which interested them were those which they had in common and repeated like incantations to one another in the hope that this would make them feel good. They were perfectly polite to me, but had no notion who or what I was, though they knew that I was not one of them. My cousin saw their absurdity and made fun of them, but did not find anything very wrong. She accepted their world because she had moved into it as a young woman and never been properly acquainted with anything different.

I left Harvard for home at the beginning of February 1937. I had enjoyed some of my time very much indeed and made some very good friends with whom I kept up for many years. I saw how impossible it was to generalize about the United States, since the different sectors which I had touched were very unlike one another. On the one hand I noted how stupefying and tyrannous a god Mammon is and into what a conformity he can drill his votaries, until they die of stomach ulcers or alcoholism. On the other hand academic Americans were more forthcoming and more adventurously minded than many of their opposite numbers in England. Their profession was not regarded as very distinguished in a country keenly alive to social distinctions, and they had to maintain an unceasing vigilance to see that their liberties were not violated, but they were not in the least discouraged. I felt that in the United States, especially in a university, if you wanted something strongly enough, you could usually get it. This enabled me to look on Oxford with fresh eyes and to consider how much could be learned from American example.

14

The End of an Era

From 1919 to 1939, between the end of one war and the start of another, Oxford remained comparatively stable, and in this it reflected the country. In the first years, when Fisher was still Minister of Education, it looked as if some serious reforms might be carried out, and in two matters they were, on the University's own initiative. The first was that women, who had for many years had their own colleges and been admitted to lectures and examinations, were now allowed to become full members of the University and to take degrees. The second was the abolition of Greek as a compulsory subject for anyone who wished to matriculate. This had often been debated, but it took a world war to get anything done. It meant that Oxford no longer rejected applicants who might be more than admirable, but lacked this technical qualification. Among such was Winston Churchill, who told me in 1949, 'After Omdurman I wanted to go to Oxford, to read history, to be told what books to read. But there was a fatal obstacle. Compulsory Greek lifted a forbidding finger and said, "Thou shalt not."' Greek gained by the change and instead of being a nuisance to the uninterested became a challenge to the interested who studied it because they wished to. The number of classical students did not drop, and Greek studies became livelier than before. In 1919, while reform was still in the air and finance had not yet raised its ugly objections, the government appointed a Royal Commission on the Universities of Oxford and Cambridge, with Asquith as chairman. It deliberated for four years and then produced a report, which recommended some reforms in administration, to which nobody could object, and demanded that entry to the University should be controlled by an examination. As this was at the lowest possible level, it too was accepted, though not without misgivings. More important was the institution of a retiring age for all holders of university and college posts. In the old system heads of colleges saw no reason why they should ever retire. If Providence had called them to a post, it was their duty to stay there until death released them, and many of them did. A prominent case was that of J. R. McGrath, who was Provost of Queen's for some fifty years, and for the last twenty or so retired to bed, while under an Elizabethan statute he appointed a pro-provost to do his work for him at £50 a year.

Otherwise the Royal Commission did not recommend very much of importance, and some of its recommendations were not carried out. Asquith, whose knowledge of Oxford was based on his time at Balliol in the early seventies, saw no large need for reform and was content with a little tidying up, while Sir John Simon, who was a member of the commission and a Fellow of All Souls, proclaimed his belief that, whatever else was changed, All Souls should not be. Nor was it in any essential respect, and this happy survival from a less urgent age went on as before. By 1922 the country wished for nothing more than to restore the conditions of 1914, and Oxford agreed with it. The Royal Commission, which might have anticipated reforms that had to wait for many years, failed to do so and was content to patch some damaged parts and to coat the rest with whitewash.

This nostalgic spirit was to the taste of a majority in the University. Most older members wanted to get back to the old times and run things as they were used to running them, and some of the younger members were so pleased to be alive that they did not trouble themselves with thoughts of change. This was abundantly clear in the middle twenties when, having admitted women to the University, the local panjandrums began to have qualms. They could not reverse the decision, but they could apply it in an unpleasant and humiliating way, and this they proposed to do by limiting the number of women in residence. This was unjust and offensive, because there was no limitation to the number of men and no suggestion that there should be. Nor was there any likelihood that the numbers of women would increase at all substantially. The proportion of them to men was about one to seven, and this figure was likely to be maintained, since the women's colleges had not enough money either to build the necessary accommodation or to pay additional staff. There was no possibility that women would come near to equalling men in numbers. But morbid fears were at work, and a motion was brought before Congregation that the number of women should be rigorously restricted. Why this was done was not clear. The arguments put forward by the proponents were of a technical kind based on the difficulty of providing teaching and so forth, but these were patently false and known by their advocates to be so. What counted was a neurotic fear that the presence of women, even on the existing scale, would somehow ruin the morale, if not the morals, of the men. This was absurd, but for that reason all the more difficult to counter. In the debate Margery Fry, Principal of Somerville, demolished with ease the arguments for restriction, but her charming voice and appearance and her dignified restraint in the face of an insulting attack failed to sway the multitude, and the motion was carried. I had recently taken my MA and voted with Miss Fry and some liberal-minded elders like Gilbert Murray and Cyril Bailey. But it was a crushing defeat, and a nasty blow to my ideal of the University.

The only other serious controversy in these years concerned the Bodleian Library. Nearly everyone agreed that it was too small and too crowded and that something ought to be done, but the question was what. The conservatives, who rightly appreciated the Bodleian's beauty and antiquity, were in favour of a book-dump outside Oxford, from which books could be fetched by vans when wanted. Since the book-service was already quite slow enough, this did not meet with favour among those who wished it to be quicker. The reformers wanted an up-to-date library on the American model, where scholars could have access to the shelves and small pens to work in. This party was led by Alic Smith, with Roy Harrod as a staunch supporter, and had the backing of Joseph Wells, who had just retired from being Warden and was to die before the year was out. The strength of this case was that the Rockefeller Foundation was prepared to put up a large sum of money for it, but it suffered from grave defects. First, it left the old Library almost out of action, and it was useless to argue that it could be kept for old books and manuscripts, since it was too big for this and anyhow they ought to be in the same building as new books related to them. Second, it was not clear where the new library should go. Some of its advocates were prepared to put it in the University Parks, but this was extremely unpopular with a large majority, and other sites, though possible, could not be mentioned since their owners were not known to be ready to part with them. After much private discussion in which Smith was invincibly energetic and optimistic, the University rejected both plans, and after a long interval produced a third by which a large annexe to the Bodleian was built at the north-east corner of Broad Street. It met some needs, but did not provide shelf-access, and unfortunately the architect was Sir Giles Scott, who with bland complacency refused to listen to criticisms and produced a building which pleased nobody but himself.

If University policy remained static, so did the conduct of life in the colleges. Compulsory chapel, from which I had been delivered by Alic Smith, was almost universal, and even at Wadham was not abolished until the early thirties. Women were still regarded with grave suspicion and allowed into colleges on rather the same terms as dogs and perambulators. The rules were often evaded, but undergraduates found it hard to understand why, if it was quite all right to mix with women at home, it was wrong at Oxford. Nor, if their elders were asked for the reason, could they easily supply one. It was the old case of 'because not'. Once indeed the situation nearly got out of hand. A number of young Swedish women came to Oxford to study English and overwhelmed the men's colleges. They were not only handsome and forthcoming but generous in their affections and insistent in their wish to be entertained. They ran their hosts into debt, and college officers, unaccustomed to Nordic enterprise, suspected darker menaces. In the end the Swedes left, and rumour told that a pantechnicon had been sent by the Swedish ambassador to fetch them. Not long afterwards I met one in Vienna, and asked her why they had descended upon Oxford in such numbers, and she replied innocently, 'Oh, all those young men.'

Prejudice was strong, not only in disciplinary matters, but in the spirit in which academic appointments were made. In 1925 the chair of Military History was vacant, and an obvious candidate for it was Sir Frederick Maurice, who was a learned and acute historian with a special appeal for classical scholars because he had worked out the probable size of Xerxes' Army by calculating how much water it needed on its advance into Greece. Denniston had served under him in the War Office and spoke warmly of his charm and integrity. But Maurice had been involved in a famous episode in 1918 when he provided Asquith with evidence that Lloyd George had lied about the number of troops in France. It lost him his job, and it began the break-up of the Liberal Party. But he acted on the highest motives, and everyone knew it. However, it was enough to keep him out of the chair, which was given to Sir Ernest Swinton, an amusing and friendly man, who had taken a leading part in the invention of the tank, but was intellectually much inferior to Maurice. How strongly some of the older generation still felt on such matters emerged when in the same year G. D. H. Cole was appointed Reader in Economics. There was no doubt of his high claims, but he was a Socialist and had been against the war. The electors showed courage, but they were reproved for it, when Wells, making his inaugural speech at the beginning of the third year of his Vice-Chancellorship, announced that the appointment brought the whole University into disrepute. Fortunately he spoke in Latin, and his words did not have a wide circulation. Politics are close to morals, and these too affected or frustrated appointments. In 1927 the Slade Professorship of Fine Arts was vacant. It was a visiting post for a limited tenure. An obvious candidate was Roger Fry, who was an inspiring lecturer and had done more than anyone in the country to make known French painting of the Impressionist and

Post-Impressionist periods. But he was rejected by the electors, not, as some of them pretended, because his views on art were unsound, but because he was said to be living with a woman not his wife. In his place we got an art master from a well-known school, who took no special trouble with his lectures. Once indeed the opposition to a suitable appointment was more open. It was suggested that Bertrand Russell should be asked to give a lecture, and on the General Board, of which I was a member, this was violently opposed by the Principal of Jesus, A. E. W. Hazel, who had been a Liberal member of parliament and had a large share of the Nonconformist conscience. Hazel said that if we asked Russell, we should 'turn the place into a stock-yard'. Knowing Russell's pacific views, I thought that Hazel had made a mistake, and flippantly suggested that he meant a stud-farm. He was so angry that I never found out whether he did or not.

One of the University's leading characteristics in these years was the restricted field from which it drew undergraduates. This was not deliberate, nor even very conscious, but a result of social conditions. In the past Oxford had always admitted a number of students from poor homes by giving them scholarships. In the nineteenth century a scholar by frugal living might find that his emoluments were enough to carry him through his three or four years, but after 1919, while scholarships remained at the figure of £80 or £100 a year, costs had doubled, and only those could come to Oxford who had private resources. There was indeed a minimum test of intellectual qualifications for entry, but the real and often insuperable test was financial. Occasionally a broad-minded Local Education Authority would supplement a scholarship with a grant, but this was very rare and Oxford remained a preserve for the well-to-do. In consequence it lost students who were better than many accepted and might have brought it lasting credit. Another result was that, socially speaking, the undergraduate population was more or less homogeneous. But English snobbery was not wholly exorcized, and since real members of the working class were extremely few, public school boys might instead look down on the products of grammar schools. This was more obvious in some colleges than in others. At Wadham it caused no trouble, since we had a sprinkling from schools of every kind, but very few of them were at all rich. In these years we had only two members of the smart Bullingdon Club, and they were both Americans. But at two or three wealthier colleges a poor undergraduate might feel himself out of things, though he was more likely to be neglected than to be despised. The financial demands of Oxford restricted its numbers to those who could pay for themselves, and the result was that the academic standard of undergraduates was not always high. The best, who were usually scholars, were very good indeed, but the lower reaches made no claims to distinction and would certainly not be admitted nowadays.

More controversial was the admission of coloured undergraduates from the Commonwealth. Before 1914 there had been a certain number of these, and many of them rose later to high authority in their own countries. The same policy persisted after 1919, largely because the Colonial and India Offices demanded it. One college at least resisted them altogether. Trinity, under the presidency of the Reverend H. E. D. Blakiston, prided itself on being an 'all white college', and on rowdy occasions its inmates used to shout abuse over the wall at Balliol, where the policy was more liberal. At Wadham we took a handsome young man of Armenian origin, called Noel Agazarian, who had fair hair and blue eyes and won a 'blue' both for boxing and for Rugby football, and was later killed in the war. He had applied to Trinity, but been rejected by Blakiston, who wrote, 'The last man of your colour we had here was not at all happy.' Blakiston, who was a shy, twisted character, had known my paternal grandfather, and, unaware of the full weight of his words, once said to me, 'Your grandfather was a very intelligent man. He once gave me five shillings.' He had a clear sense of priorities, but a tolerance of Asians and Africans was very low on it.

Though the years between the wars were cursed with depression and unemployment, and to a large part of the population life offered no prospects and was hard even by very low standards, this scarcely affected Oxford. The colleges, whose money was invested either in land or in gilt-edge securities, did not suffer financial loss and continued to draw their members from the well-to-do classes. There were no reductions of stipend for dons, and though the scales were never very high, they were quite good for all, and particularly good for unmarried Fellows living in college, where they got many advantages for nothing. I myself was not troubled about money. My salary rose from £600 to about £1000, and if I was hard up, I could always make something by examining. I cannot remember that I went without anything that I really wanted. Since the pound was stronger than most continental currencies, travel was cheap, and I went abroad for at least a month every summer, while I often visited Paris at Christmas or Easter. I combined some of these trips with work, especially when I was editing a text of Pindar.

Pindar is a good author to edit because his more important manuscripts are in such places as Rome, Paris, Venice, and Florence. I examined them on the spot, largely because it was a good excuse for foreign travel, though I could have procured adequate photographs, which might have been more reliable than what I could see with my own eyes on a limited visit. My only regret is that I did not know about a manuscript on Mount Athos, which I could easily have inspected when I went there with Adrian Bishop. I did not go on Hellenic cruises. They were too expensive and too formal. Everyone dressed for dinner, and the lecturers, were said to be chosen on the principle that they 'provided daily contact with first-class minds'. I much preferred my own methods of mules and caiques, of sleeping on decks or beaches, and of eating Greek food and drinking Greek drink. By such means I managed to see many parts of mainland Greece and a number of islands. In Italy I got to know the north and Sicily quite well, but left the south for later exploration. I tried Portugal but found the language and the food equally indigestible. What can one do in a country where, as Sacheverell Sitwell said, 'Tottenham Court Road is pronounced as a single syllable'? My only visit to Switzerland was when I spent a few hours at Basle, where I had a bath at the railway station and looked at the Holbeins in the museum. I vaguely felt that it was under British occupation and insufficiently European for my tastes.

In 1924 my father, mother, and sisters came back from China for good and settled at Ightham, where I spent part of every vacation with them. For a few years my father went up on four days a week to the Chinese Customs office in London, but in 1929 he gave this up and passed the rest of his life at home. He was just sixty and physically in very good shape. Though he worried about his health, there was nothing wrong with him, and he was hardly ever ill. His routine was regular and tranquil. He gardened in the morning, rested after lunch and went for a short walk, and after tea read a book while he listened, or did not listen, to the wireless. By 10 p.m. he was ready for bed. At first he enjoyed himself digging up records of the Bowra family and writing accounts, which he did not publish, of his own and his father's careers. He renewed ties with a few old friends, but he had not very much to say to them or they to him. When my elder sister got married, he was delighted by her children, but saw very little of them since she spent most of her time with her husband in Shanghai. He never looked again at a Chinese book and ceased to have any interest in the language, if not in the country, whose chaotic politics convinced him that much of his life-work had been wasted. He remained calm and good-tempered and seemed to be satisfied. A home in England was what he had dreamed of and worked for during nearly forty years in China, and now he had it. He cherished no regrets and no resentments. Yet there was a certain pathos in a man of his gifts and energy acquiescing in so monotonous a lot. It was as if his time in China had taken something out of him and left him with no spare impetus. Though he tried to interest himself in village life, it did not really appeal to him. He was interested in the English past and enjoyed sightseeing and archaeological outings, but contemporary England did not mean much to him. What he most enjoyed was making improvements to the house and converting an almost derelict cottage across the road. In this quiet way he continued until his death in 1947.

My mother was perfectly content to live in England, where she liked the countryside and the quiet routine of domestic duties. She often spoke of China and its splendours, but also of its miseries. She found housekeeping at Ightham much easier than in Peking, where the many servants presented incessant problems, whether in taking too much 'squeeze' in marketing, or in quarrelling with each other when gambling, or in having bouts of opium-smoking. For a short time she had a Chinese manservant, who was brilliantly efficient, but wilted in the English climate and his separation from his family and had to be sent back. My mother had a talent for finding good servants and keeping them, largely because she was unusually considerate of their comforts and their feelings and really won their affection. But what really pleased her was that at last she could, from time to time, have her whole family round her. This she had hardly ever enjoyed except on short periods of home leave, but now she got much happiness from it. Edward had done well in the war and after it went to Jesus College, Cambridge, where he read engineering. After that he resumed work with the Royal Engineers, and though this meant that he often did tours of duty abroad, he was often at home and took a full part in family life. He had a fine capacity for working out plans in meticulous detail and seeing that they were carried out without fuss. It was some years before he got married, and soon after doing so, after the end of the Second World War, he retired with the rank of Brigadier and bought a house in Ightham near ours. My elder sister married a Dane in 1925 and went with him to Shanghai, but when she came home with two small daughters, my mother was enchanted by them and found a new and lasting scope for her active affection. My younger sister, Francesca, was sent to school, which she much enjoyed, and in due course got married and had two daughters. I fancy that my father regretted the lack of any male descendants in the second generation, but my mother liked little girls and had many happy ways of amusing them. Later, when war came and the Japanese occupied Shanghai, she was deeply worried because Norah and her daughters were there, while her husband had gone to Australia with tuberculosis. After long months in which we heard nothing, messages began to come through saying that all was well, as indeed they were. Norah was left in her own house, with a Norwegian seaman to look after her. The money we sent reached her, and she survived when others died in the appalling conditions of prison-camps. The Japanese Governor of Shanghai knew my father, and saw that his friend's daughter was well treated. My mother was very active into old age. She did much in the house, continued to do admirable and useful work with her needle, and kept up with her old friends by having them to stay. Her relations with my father remained as happy as ever. They understood each other perfectly, and she looked after him without his noticing it.

At this period the city of Oxford began to change its character. It had for centuries been a mixture of university town and market town, and though since about 1860 it had been growing, not always with elegance, it was still more or less homogeneous. But now it was transformed through the activities of William Morris, who had kept a bicycle shop in Holywell and then in the early twenties become a leading manufacturer of motor-cars. His friends said that by putting a cheap car on the market he conferred an inestimable benefit on the people of this country; his enemies, that he made so much money, either because he underpaid his workmen, or because he charged too much for his cars. Both agreed that for Oxford the results were lamentable. A large new manufacturing town grew at Cowley, and since almost nothing was done to provide it with amenities or even to satisfy its elementary needs, it became a parasite of Oxford, which was ill equipped to sustain it and lost much of its spacious tranquility in catering for a large daily invasion. Morris, translated into Lord Nuffield, was reputed to have given money to a Fascist organization and was loved neither by his workmen nor by most members of the University. Yet he proved to be one of its most generous benefactors. The first of his large benefactions was to medicine, and the result was that the Oxford hospital provides some of the best services in the country, though the excellent pre-clinical school has gained very little. Nuffield was much interested in his own health and boasted of his fitness, and this may have been his reason for endowing medicine. Yet he made his gift at an unfortunate moment, and not entirely with happy results.

In 1936 the University, of which A. D. Lindsay had recently

become Vice-Chancellor, issued an appeal for funds. These were greatly needed for many purposes, especially for the expansion of scientific research, of which people were becoming rapidly more conscious. The appeal began well, but soon after its start, Nuffield rose in Congregation, which he was not technically entitled to do, and said that he had decided to give £1,000,000 for medical work; he then doubled the figure, and sat down. This was a magnificent gesture, but it meant that old Oxford men at large thought that there was now no need to do anything, since Nuffield had done it for them. This he certainly had not. His benefaction was for an object which had almost no place in the appeal. His attempt, however unconscious, to make amends for all the harm that he had done hit the University when it was trying to put its house in order. Medicine, however, was not his only interest. Though his cars had been designed for him by others, he liked to think that he was an engineer and admitted his debt to engineering. He proposed to found a new college mainly concerned with it. From the Oxford point of view this was not too desirable. The idea of a college devoted to a single subject was novel and unwelcome, since one of the chief claims of the college system is that it mixes students of all disciplines. Lindsay saw this and set out to persuade Nuffield to found a college with quite different objects. Instead of being devoted to engineering, it was to encourage research in social studies and to make easier the co-operation of academic and non-academic persons. This was purely Lindsay's idea, and Nuffield would never have thought of it. He agreed to give the money for this purpose, but probably did not know what he was doing. Very soon he felt that he had been cheated by Lindsay, and no doubt Lindsay's skilful arguments were beyond his understanding. The first years of Nuffield College were overshadowed by the resentment of the founder, who showed animosity even towards the architect. He had built some notable buildings in Jerusalem and seemed likely to offer a welcome change from the Gothic Scott and the Germanic Worthington. He produced a graceful plan, but when he went to see Nuffield about it, Nuffield kicked the model under the table and rejected it rudely because it was not 'collegiate Gothic'. Much discouraged, the architect produced another plan which was not in the manner which he had made his own. Uneasy relations between the founder and his foundation lasted for years, and Nuffield was even more troubled when he found that economists and political scientists tended to have liberal views. Then the college became for him 'that Kremlin'. Nor was he fully appeased until after the war when after much patient handling by the Warden and Fellows he began to see that it might be good for something to be known in Oxford about industry.

Though he was outwitted by Lindsay, Nuffield had a considerable personality. He was proud of being born and bred in Oxford and believed that his enterprises had brought untold benefits to it. His gospel was of the survival of the fittest, and in this he saw himself at the top of the class. He had done little to educate himself, but this did not diminish his self-assurance. He knew his own mind, and when some of his first colleagues disagreed with him, he got rid of them. He was not hampered by either a religious or a social conscience, but he had some engaging qualities. He was agreeably outspoken, especially when he spoke about his grievances. He had a fine repertory of Edwardian music-hall songs, which he would sing at the slightest encouragement after dinner, with a particular relish for those of Albert Chevalier such as 'My old Dutch' and 'Last week down our alley came a toff'. He had none of the ostentation of the self-made rich and lived without pretension. He was physically indefatigable and liked to talk into the middle of the night. In the nineteenth century there must have been many like him, but in his own time he was rather a rare specimen. He did not move much in University circles, though some colleges cultivated him in the hope of benefactions. Once at least he helped a college out of a nasty hole. St Peter's Hall had been founded with inadequate funds to give a place at Oxford to young men with evangelical leanings. Its foundation was opposed in Congregation on the grounds that, despite protestations to the contrary, it was imposing something very like a religious test. But the desire to get something for nothing won the day, and St Peter's Hall came into existence. Its finances were largely in the control of an anomalous and shifty character, the Reverend

Percy Warrington, known as 'the financier in the surplice', who represented a trust which aimed ruthlessly at the spread of evangelical Christianity. The accounts of St Peter's were inextricably confused with those of other institutions, and through Warrington's incompetence or chicanery most of its capital vanished. Nuffield stepped in and saved it from ruin. Thus given a new start, St Peter's was much better fitted to take a full part in Oxford.

Nuffield's antagonist, Lindsay, was equally tough but more agile and more resourceful. He had been a pupil of Gilbert Murray when Murray was Professor of Greek at Glasgow, and his wife had been at school with my mother, who did not share her childlike simplicity or her desire to go back to nature, 'Why can't we be like the birds?' Lindsay was a philosopher but not a very good one, and when about 1930 the subject took new shapes, he was out of touch and therefore hostile. For him philosophy was the theoretical part of morality, especially of his own Scottish kind. As an undergraduate at University College he had fallen in love with the young wife of a don. There was a fearful row, and his letters to her were read by the Master and Fellows, one of whom, A. S. L. Farquharson, commented to me, 'Pretty hot they were.' The college, however, after discussing whether to send him down, decided not to because his work was too good. This chastening experience did not make Lindsay tolerant of human frailties. He remained a remorseless Puritan and suspected the worst of undergraduates who wore bright clothes, calling one whom I knew 'a gilded popinjay'. He was vain and sure of himself and hated opposition. If you gave in to him, he thought nothing of you, but if you opposed him, he would say 'Shut up' or 'Close your trap.' I was under him when as Vice-Chancellor he was chairman of the General Board and more than once received these genial slaps. I took no notice of them and found that this was what he liked, for he told a friend that I was 'the only man with any bite in him'. He was in complete command of University business and not shy of disingenuous tactics. Once when a vote was taken and he found himself in a minority of one, he did not accept the decision but said, 'We seem to have reached an impasse' and moved on to the next item. He had a clear notion of what a university ought to be, and though he did not believe in learning and thought that most research was twaddle, he believed in teaching and in keeping Oxford in touch with contemporary needs. Old Balliol men thought that he was ruining their ancient traditions and appointed a small delegation to talk to him. He was to meet them at 7 p.m., and at 6 they gathered to discuss their line of action, but Lindsay was already there and, having won the first round, won every other.

Lindsay's redeeming virtue, which could not be praised too highly, was that he could rise to big occasions as almost nobody else in Oxford could. In the General Strike he had taken a lead for sanity and reconciliation; when the Nazis came into power, he was deceived by none of their promises and saw how evil they were; when the public thought that nothing could be done about unemployment, he thought that something could and should, and encouraged practical schemes for providing work; he was aware that Oxford, like Cambridge, was too exclusive a preserve of the moneyed classes and not loved by other universities, and he set out to counter both tendencies. On the platform he was a commanding figure, a little too fleshy perhaps, but with candid blue eyes and a thoughtful manner of speech which suggested his earnest commitment. He claimed, and perhaps at times believed, that he was continuing the work of Jowett and providing the world with trained men able to face its problems, but he did not share Jowett's belief in success for its own sake, or emulate his cult of the famous. He was a man of frugal habits, who did not notice what he ate or drank and left the High Table at Balliol very much the same at the end of his mastership as it had been at the beginning. Though he despised those who made up to him, he needed yes-men around him if only to be sure of their votes, and some of his appointments were poor imitations of himself. At other times he would be led astray by some vague ideal. When the chair of Chinese was vacant, he strained all his efforts for the appointment of an ex-missionary who was interested in Chinese religion but unfortunately knew very little Chinese. In this he failed, but he regarded it as a triumph of pedantry and irreligion. When I had dealings with him, I found them quite enjoyable. He was quite ready to 'talk turkey' and, in the best Balliol tradition, was not above a deal. Though his judgements on people were usually as far as possible from my own, he had an occasional eye for quality and if he liked someone, would press relentlessly for him. Above all, when it came to a showdown on a matter of principle, he was on the right side and ready to give a lead to it. At such times I turned to him with confidence and forgot his foibles.

Though Lindsay's deep engagement in politics went back to his radical past and was fortified by his Scottish Christianity, it accorded with a widespread mood of the thirties, when after a long lull it was no longer possible to ignore what was happening in the world. In the newest generation of undergraduates many were very much concerned and liable to denounce anyone who did anything for its own sake as an 'escapist'. Their enemy was Fascism, wherever it existed and whatever form it took. Under the leadership of Oswald Mosley it was already making itself unpleasantly felt in England. I had met him in the twenties, when I was in Venice and John Strachey took me to dine with him in his *palazzo* on the Grand Canal, where his gondolas were steered by Venetians in white uniforms with blue sashes. His first wife, Lady Cynthia, was there and enchanted me by her charm and humour. She must have inherited them from her mother, Curzon's first wife, who had a genius for healing the wounds which her husband inflicted on all kinds of people. Mosley, ably encouraged by Strachey, expounded the right policy for the Labour Party, of which he was a promising member, and put forward bold and constructive ideas. He was a forcible talker, who set out to be magnetic and tried to win my support by saying that he wished Britain to resemble ancient Athens, but this did not convince me, and I found his manner a little disturbing. I did not see him after he left the Labour Party, but heard something of him from a beautiful and silly woman who was infatuated with him and gulped down all his ideas with rapture. Brian Howard made the right comment, 'Hatpins, my dear . . . that's what she wants . . . to put in your eyes.' I hardly met any of Mosley's followers, but in 1937, when I was staying with the Kenneth Clarks at Lympne,

Bob Boothby, of all people, brought over a guest who was an avowed and uncompromising Fascist. I got engaged in argument with him and at the end of it found myself saying, 'I look forward to using your skull as an inkpot.'

It was hard to tell how far the ordinary British public thought that Fascism offered a cure for its troubles, but though it seemed unlikely that it could, it was too disagreeable a symptom to be left alone. In Oxford anti-Fascist meetings were held, and the speakers usually discredited it by appealing to the English taste for moderation and dislike of violence. In Oxford its supporters seemed to be mainly industrialists, like Nuffield, or local officials who saw in it a means to increase their authority, or disgruntled members of the middle class who felt that they did not have their deserts, or clergymen of uncertain tastes. The Fascists made themselves felt in Oxford in June 1936, when they held a public meeting. The police, some of whom were not unsympathetic, let them supervise their own arrangements and order was kept by stewards, who walked in sinister silence up and down the passageways looking for any signs of opposition. Gilbert Murray's son, Basil, who had certain personal faults but was politically courageous and incorruptible, had taken a newspaper with him and read it ostentatiously, presumably to show his contempt for what was being said. The stewards set on him and threw him out, and next day he was charged before the magistrates for a breach of the peace. The police supported the Fascist witnesses, and the magistrates accepted their word, and fined Murray. But the behaviour of the stewards made a nasty impression on many Oxford people and turned them against Fascism. Many undergraduates saw in this yet another portent of the growing bloodthirstiness of the world, and when very soon afterward the Spanish Civil War broke out, they treated the resistance to Franco as their own cause, the defence of everything on which their lives and liberties depended. For me the chief enemy was still Germany, which, I feared, would make Spain an appendage and offer a new menace to France from the south.

Mr C. R. Fox, C.B.E. who was Chief Constable of Oxford City in 1936, has kindly sent me his own account of what happened in the affair of Basil Murray and the Fascist meeting:

He (Murray) was the ringleader of from 50 to 100 men, many of whom were bus employees, who were having labour trouble in which Murray was interested. Mosley had hardly commenced his speech when the whole of them opened wide their newspapers with a flourish, followed by stamping their feet in concert. Then they shut their papers altogether. This was repeated at frequent intervals and I marvelled at Mosley's tolerance and the inactivity of his stewards. After about half an hour of this he shouted 'Put that man out'. Immediately there was pandemonium. The iron chairs were hurled into the milling crowd and fighting was general. You will perhaps remember that Pakenham was injured in this and I thought he asked for all he got, as he went into it as into a rugby scrum.

The offence for which Murray was charged occurred outside the Hall, in Cornmarket Street. He was arrested by Constables who saw the incident and acted quite independently. There was no question of their afterwards supporting the Fascist witnesses – they merely gave evidence of what they saw. I prosecuted.

In these years my routine went on much as before, and when I came back from the United States in 1937, I settled down again happily. The Warden, J. F. Stenning, was due to retire on 30 September 1938, and though the statutes did not allow a pre-election, there was nothing to prevent the Fellows from agreeing among themselves whom they wished to elect. Wade-Gery pressed my claims and was loyally supported by Lindemann, with whom our complete agreement about Germany had brought me into closer contact and far happier relations than ten years earlier. I was kept out of the consultations and had very little notion of what was happening, though I gathered that my path was not without obstructions. It was argued that I was not married, that I would not know how to keep up the Warden's garden, that I was not a good man of business, that I would not entertain enough. In return I might have said that wives of heads of colleges are not always an unmixed blessing; that I was willing to keep a good gardener; that though I was not a businessman, I was quite adept at University business; that I rather fancied myself at entertaining. But the criticisms, such as they were, seemed to make little impact.

Nor in those days did colleges scour the wide world for suitable heads and choose retired ambassadors, or headmasters, or civil servants, rather than one of their own body. There was indeed an elderly judge in the offing who would have liked the post, but he lacked support. At the end of the summer term Wade-Gery and Lindemann came to my room and asked me whether I was willing to be Warden. I assured them that I was and that I would do my best to make a success of it. Stenning, very considerately, moved out of the Lodgings in August and left me free to move in, though I could not be formally elected until October.

After a holiday with Cyril Connolly and his wife on Cap Ferrat, which I enjoyed to the utmost in sun and sea and excellent company, and a few days in Berlin, I came back to Oxford to supervise my move, but was almost at once caught in the crisis which ended in Munich. In Germany I had heard that Hitler was eager to move against the Czechs, but Bernstorff had told me that the generals were not ready and that the Czechs had a formidable army and fortifications. I hoped that Chamberlain might still withstand Hitler, but did not believe that he would, and all through these days I was deeply depressed by his obstinate and dishonourable role. Most of my Oxford friends agreed with me, but a curious exception was Alic Smith, who was a shrewd realist in University affairs, but too rational to understand how anyone could go to war, and cherished a belief that by showing a will for peace Chamberlain would carry millions with him and avert a European catastrophe. Then came Munich. Like everyone else I admired Léon Blum's honesty when he spoke of 'shameful relief', but was certain that the relief would not last for long. My German friends wrote in the utmost distress, and Ernst telegraphed the last lines of Wordsworth's sonnet *On the Extinction of the Venetian Republic*. His sentiments coincided with my own.

To the anxieties and the shame of these days I found an antidote in moving into the Warden's Lodgings. They are part of the original buildings at Wadham built by Dorothy Wadham's master-builder, William Arnold, in 1611-13 and occupy the north-west corner of the main quadrangle. Their main structure remains intact from this date, though the staircase was shifted in 1810, and in 1831 Edward Blore fitted the dining-room and the drawing-room above it with Gothic windows reaching to the ground. They do not belong to the style of the building, but they are not too discordant and give spacious views of the garden. By Oxford standards the house is not very large, but with five sitting-rooms it was more than large enough for me. The main rooms were panelled in the eighteenth century and painted white. The Stennings had put in central heating, but there were only two bathrooms; so I installed two more. The garden had some fine trees brought at the beginning of the nineteenth century from the West Indies by an admiral who was a brother of Warden Wills. Though it lies in the centre of Oxford, it has the look of being in the country, since it has a high stone wall and, apart from the actual college, the only visible man-made objects are the gardener's cottage on Parks Road, which is older than the college, and the Gothic tower of the Science Museum, which emerges above the tops of the trees like a fanciful folly. The house carries with it a stock of silver from the seventeenth and eighteenth centuries, a few good pictures including the only authentic portraits of Nicholas and Dorothy Wadham, and some pieces of furniture, few of which are both useful and beautiful. I had to do most of the furnishing myself, but in those days there were good second-hand furniture-shops in Oxford, and I bought a number of things to my liking. One incidental advantage in the general anxiety at this period was that shopkeepers were so nervous that they reduced their prices at the smallest pressure. I had ample space for my books, which were already too many for my old rooms, and in due course established myself in a library on the first floor, where I have done most of my work ever since. Though I enjoyed all this, I had a carking fear that in a year or two the college might be destroyed from the air and that I myself might be, as Ernst gloomily prognosticated, the last Warden of Wadham.

The actual election to the Wardenship took place in the College Hall on the afternoon of 3 October 1938. Wade-Gery, as Sub-Warden, presided and conducted the proceedings, which lasted for only a few minutes. My name was proposed and seconded and carried without debate. I then gave my solemn pledge that I would keep the statutes and was handed a bundle of large but not obviously useful keys. Whatever disagreements may have existed were tactfully concealed, and I did not make inquiries about them. It was a very black day, and almost at the actual moment of election there was an unusually loud clap of thunder, which could be taken as an omen either for good or for ill. But almost at the same time not far away something horrible happened. I had a colleague, E. A. Milne, who was a friend of Einstein and well known for his work in astrophysics. He had once had sleepy sickness, and it made him look pale and ill, though his prodigious industry belied it. His wife at this time was suffering from mental trouble in the Warneford Hospital just outside Oxford, and almost at the moment of the thunderclap she killed herself by cutting her throat with a saw in an outhouse. Poor Milne heard the news just after our proceedings closed, and came to tell me about it. There was almost nothing that I could say to comfort him, especially as he had two girls of school age and a small boy. What made it more painful was his determination to be rational and calm about it. He was very deeply distressed, and it would have helped him if he could have burst into tears. But of that he was incapable.

At forty I was on the youngish side to be a head of a college, but there were good precedents for youthful heads, and on the whole they were more encouraging than for those elected in riper years in recognition of services done but not likely to be continued. I should, with an ordinary expectation of life, stay in office for thirty years, but it did not seem to trouble my colleagues, and it did not trouble me, since there was nothing I wanted more. My father was delighted. This was something which appealed to his sense of a career and proved that I was not a mere book-worm but head of an august institution with a full share of responsibilities. Among letters of congratulation was one from Miss Hale, who must have been nearly ninety, but showed no trace of it in her clear, elegant handwriting. I was much touched by another from Humbert Wolfe, an old Wadham man, who, despite all his wit and gaiety, was agonized by the state of Europe and wrote, 'Your election has been the only faint point of light for me in these abominable days.' F. W. Hirst also wrote charmingly, but did not strike quite the right note when he suggested that my reign would coincide with many years of peace after Chamberlain's action at Munich, and that we ought to produce Aristophanes' *Peace* in Wadham Garden. Sir John Simon had reservations. After congratulating me with neat felicity, he dined at All Souls and announced that Wadham had elected 'a mere child', which came oddly from a man who was a cabinet minister at the same age. Nor did my election cause much pain in Oxford. At least I heard of very few hostile comments and was cheered rather than discouraged when W. T. S. Stallybrass, Principal of Brasenose, genially told me at dinner in his college that I was not his candidate.

Even in 1938 the post of head of a college, with its lack of regular hours and prescribed duties, was an anomaly and might soon be thought an abuse and even a scandal. However, I appreciated my good fortune and knew that my colleagues and I might manage to do something for the college. I was particularly lucky in them, and we began to hatch plans for the future. But my first year of office was troubled by political menaces. I knew that after the surrender of Munich Hitler would ask for more next time, and that this would almost certainly mean war, which we might have avoided if we had taken action earlier. I welcomed the introduction of conscription, but was at first rather taken aback that some of the brightest undergraduates had genuinely conscientious objections to it. To me the Nazis were so flagrantly more evil than the Kaiser that at first I found this attitude surprising, but, knowing how cruelly conscientious objectors had been treated in the First World War, I was determined to see that their cases were put intelligibly before the tribunals which were to decide about them. What impressed me was that their motives were usually not Christian but humane, and that, while they hated the idea of killing, they were quite willing to risk their lives in such non-combatant work as looking after the wounded in bombing raids. Nor were the tribunals in the least unfair. Lindsay was chairman of one, and, having in the First World War been very close to objection, knew why young men felt like that and dealt generously and wisely with them.

In the winter of 1938 the Member of Parliament for Oxford died, and there was a by-election for his successor. The Conservative candidate was a young man who had been at Christ Church, Quintin Hogg. I had spotted him in 1924 when I was examining at Eton, and he was quite a small boy who showed unusual promise. I had met him once or twice at Oxford and even debated against him at the Union on the only occasion when I spoke there. I had liked him for his vitality, his quick mind, and his obvious truthfulness. He was unreservedly, even passionately on the side of Chamberlain and appeasement and fought the election on this issue. After some poorly concealed manœuvres the Labour Party agreed that their candidate should stand down and that Lindsay should take his place as an Independent on an avowedly anti-Munich programme. I was in full agreement with this and signed Lindsay's nomination-paper. I also joined other heads of colleges in writing to *The Times* explaining why we supported him and why his recent experience in the Vice-Chancellorship entitled him to be considered seriously as a member of parliament. I had no doubt that Lindsay was just the man for a grave crisis like this. He had the courage and the ability to make a notable mark, and he was not hampered by too close a connection with either of the two main political parties. Slightly to my surprise I was reproved by a distinguished old member of the college on the ground that I was too junior a head to take such action, but I did not see why, just because I had become Warden, I should abandon a policy which I had advocated for years, and I was not troubled by the complaint that my action was improper. The times were too serious for considerations at that level. The election was conducted with much spirit on both sides. Hogg stood on the simple position that he was for peace and we were for war, which would have been foolproof if it had been true, while we argued that his policy would lead us into war but without the means of fighting it. Lindsay rose finely to the occasion. He believed that Europe was being betrayed to murderers, and said so. He argued that by a proper handling of alliances and armaments we might still deter or even discredit Hitler, and even if we failed in that, we should be less unprepared to meet him. In the end Hogg got in, but not by an overwhelming majority. When a little later Chamberlain was disillusioned about the Germans, Hogg was much too intelligent not to see how real the danger was, and when war came, joined the army as a fighting soldier.

In the long vacation of 1939 I decided to take a holiday before the next crisis came. I was certain that in September after the harvest Hitler would start a new aggression and that, because of our pledge to Poland, this would lead to war. I motored through France with two friends. At Chartres we saw the great stained-glass windows being taken out of the cathedral to be stored in safety, but occasional Frenchmen seemed to like Hitler, 'Il est fort. Il est notre homme.' I ended up at Monte Carlo, where I met the Baroness. We took things easily, and everything looked tranquil, but the news was obscure and frustrating. For weeks the government had been negotiating with the Russians, but it did not look as if it was treating the matter seriously, and I suspected that the whole thing was a spoof to keep critics quiet. We tried to put the matter out of our minds and intermittently succeeded, though it always recurred with its nagging menace. Then out of the blue came the news of the Molotov–Ribbentrop pact. I decided that this meant war, and that we must leave for England at once. We fought our way into a very crowded train, where it was almost impossible to get anything to eat or drink or even to walk down the corridor. We arrived at Paris that night and found an excellent hotel where we were able to talk things over. The next day we had a memorable lunch at 'Lapérouse', knowing that it would be the last in Paris for many years, and took the afternoon train to London. Since the Baroness had a German passport, it might be difficult for her to enter England, but the risk had to be taken, and on the boat she went to the immigration officer, while I waited anxiously outside. She showed all her usual courage, and to our delighted relief, when the man had looked at her papers and asked her a few questions, he allowed her to enter.

I got back to Oxford before the end of August and proceeded to make preparations for war. There was much to be done, and we were all kept busy, devising air-raid shelters, preparing to receive medical students from London, taking the stained glass out of the chapel and sending it away for safety, fixing up blackout, and trying to find out what the government's policy for universities was. My Austrian housekeeper, Mrs Grafe, who had a refugee's distrust of the British Government, assured me that we would again give in to Hitler, but I did not think that this was possible, for I knew nothing of the tergiversations of Halifax and others which suggested that they might be planning, with highminded excuses, to betray their pledge to Poland. When war was declared, I felt something like relief. The long years of shame and frustration had come to an end, and though undeciphered evils might lie in the future, they could be faced with a good conscience and a clear mind. Joseph Wells, who was elected Warden in 1913, had a year of peace before the First World War broke out, and lived to survive its end for nine years and to revive the college. I was in much the same position. I had had my year of peace, and now war lay ahead, for how long I could not guess, but I knew it could not possibly be short. It was certain to be quite different from the First World War, and seemed likely to be even more horrible and inflict more deadly damage. Last time Oxford had survived, not merely physically but in its institutions. This time it was possible that its buildings, erected with pious and loving care over seven centuries, might be destroyed, but even if they were not, its institutions could hardly survive another challenge on so enormous a scale.

Index

Index

Index

Index

Index

Index

Index